Cybersecurity and Privacy in the Era of Smart Technologies

Mohammed Amin
University of Jordan, Jordan

IGI Global
Scientific Publishing
Publishing Tomorrow's Research Today

Vice President of Editorial	Melissa Wagner
Director of Acquisitions	Mikaela Felty
Director of Book Development	Jocelynn Hessler
Production Manager	Mike Brehm
Cover Design	Jose Rosado

Published in the United States of America by
IGI Global Scientific Publishing
701 East Chocolate Avenue
Hershey, PA, 17033, USA
Tel: 717-533-8845 | Fax: 717-533-7115
Website: https://www.igi-global.com E-mail: cust@igi-global.com

Library of Congress Cataloging-in-Publication Data

LCCN: 2025007579 (CIP Data Pending)
ISBN13: 979-8-3373-2282-7
Isbn13Softcover: 979-8-3373-2283-4
EISBN13: 979-8-3373-2284-1

British Cataloguing in Publication Data
A Cataloguing in Publication record for this book is available from the British Library.

Table of Contents

Detailed Table of Contents

to analyse vast datasets, detect anomalies in real-time, and predict future threats is revolutionizing cybersecurity practices. While AI presents numerous benefits, including automation of time-consuming tasks and proactive defense, ethical and privacy considerations must be addressed to ensure fairness and transparency in its deployment. This chapter explores AI's critical role in modern cybersecurity, its techniques and applications, and the challenges that need to be navigated as AI continues to evolve in the field.

Blockchain enables decentralization, transparency, and security and faces threats from cybersecurity and legal. The cryptographic algorithms and consensus protocols add a layer of security, while the associated risks of possible 51% attack, inappropriate private key management, and smart contract vulnerabilities still persist. Legal issues arise with the clashes with data protection laws like the GDPR and with the challenge of finding who is liable due to this decentralization. The uncertain legal context around smart contracts is preventing their enforcement. Also emerging threats like quantum computing will require quantum-resistant cryptographic standards. A proposed solution includes better security, adaptive regulations, and collaboration of governments, industry, and academia. An equilibrium will allow for a secure, legally complaint, and sustainable blockchain fit for applications into the future.

Cyberbullying is the use of technology to harass, threaten, embarrass, or target another person. Cyberbullying is a growing problem in our digital age, and it can have severe consequences for victims. Online bullying can be particularly damaging and upsetting because it's usually anonymous or hard to trace. It's also hard to control, and the person being victimized has no idea how many people have seen the messages or posts. They can be easier to commit than other acts of bullying because the bully doesn't have to confront their target in person. Detecting cyberbullying and preventing it is crucial in creating a safe online environment for all. The work involves the use of natural language processing and sentiment analysis to find abusive

in SIEM implementation. The discussion extends to the impact of external factors like political, economic, technological, and legal on SIEM evolution.

Preface

The rapid evolution of smart technologies has transformed the way individuals, organizations, and societies interact with digital systems. From intelligent transportation networks and smart healthcare to Industry 4.0 and connected cities, the integration of the Internet of Things (IoT), artificial intelligence (AI), cloud computing, and edge systems has redefined efficiency, connectivity, and innovation. However, this unprecedented digital growth has also introduced new complexities, vulnerabilities, and risks to security and privacy.

This book, *Cybersecurity and Privacy in the Era of Smart Technologies*, has been developed to address these challenges by bringing together a diverse collection of perspectives, frameworks, methodologies, and case studies. It examines how cybersecurity and privacy concerns evolve in environments driven by automation, data exchange, and ubiquitous connectivity. The volume is designed to provide both theoretical foundations and practical insights that can assist researchers, practitioners, policymakers, and students in understanding and mitigating the risks of emerging technologies.

The chapters included in this book cover a broad spectrum of topics, ranging from secure communication protocols and intrusion detection in IoT, to blockchain-based authentication, privacy-preserving AI, risk management frameworks, and regulatory perspectives. Each contribution reflects the latest advancements in cybersecurity research while highlighting open challenges and future directions. Collectively, they emphasize the importance of proactive strategies and cross-disciplinary approaches to safeguard critical infrastructures, sensitive data, and personal privacy.

We envision this book as more than just a compilation of research; it is intended to be a comprehensive resource that inspires dialogue and fosters collaboration among academics, industry professionals, and decision-makers. By examining both the technical and human dimensions of cybersecurity and privacy, we aim to contribute to building a secure and trustworthy digital ecosystem that can sustain the promises of smart technologies.

We extend our gratitude to the authors for their valuable contributions, the reviewers for their constructive feedback, and the editorial team for their dedication in shaping this work. We also thank the research communities and institutions whose continued efforts in advancing cybersecurity and privacy inspired this project.

ORGANIZATION OF THE BOOK

"AI and IIoT Enabling Smart Connectivity and Automation in Healthcare" by Dankan Gowda V, emphasizes IIoT, in particular discusses how machine learning and edge computing and data analytics contribute to IIoT. In this context, the chapter presents selected cases of AI application in IIoT, including predictive and prescriptive maintenance, optimization of production processes, and intelligent manufacturing.

"Cybersecurity in Smart Devices Challenges, Threats, and AI-Driven Protection Mechanisms" by Tarun Kumar Vashishth, Vikas Sharma, Sharad Kumar, Puneet Chauhan, Mukesh Kumar Sharma, Rajeev Sharma explores the security vulnerabilities in smart ecosystems, highlighting threats such as unauthorized access, data breaches, and malware attacks. It examines AI-driven security mechanisms, including machine learning-based anomaly detection, behavioural analytics, and automated threat response. Additionally, the role of blockchain in ensuring data integrity and secure communication in smart devices is discussed. The chapter also covers privacy concerns, user-centric security approaches, and the need for regulatory frameworks to protect connected environments. By leveraging AI and blockchain technologies, organizations can enhance the resilience of smart devices against emerging cyber threats.

"Automatizing Crypto Asset Tracking in Cyber Crimes" by Mehmet Kaya, Gurkan Tuna aims to automate the manual tracking of crypto-related criminal transactions by implementing an algorithm based on the FIFO principle. Blockchain technology has created a major transformation in the digital world with features such as decentralization, security, transparency, and traceability. Emerged with Nakamoto's introduction of Bitcoin in 2009, this technology finds applications in various sectors, primarily finance, supply chain, healthcare, and public services. The fundamental principles of blockchain are based on elements such as hashing, distributed ledger technology (DLT), and consensus mechanisms. Innovative technologies such as smart contracts and side chains increase the potential of this system. Cryptocurrencies are an application area of blockchain technology and come across different types such as Bitcoin, altcoins, and NFTs. APIs facilitate software development processes and enable integrating systems with blockchain. In the investigative phases, blockchain traceability provides a significant advantage in solving crimes like crypto fraud.

"Fortifying Digital Frontiers Cybersecurity and Privacy Strategies in Smart Ecosystems" by Puppala Naga Sravanthi explores key security risks in smart environments, including AI-driven threats, IoT vulnerabilities, and privacy concerns in smart cities. It examines the evolving cyber threat landscape with case studies and ethical dilemmas in technology adoption. Strategies for mitigating risks are discussed, such as encryption, blockchain applications, AI-based threat detection, and compliance frameworks. The chapter also highlights privacy-preserving methods like differential privacy, homomorphic encryption, and secure identity management. Future directions include quantum-safe cryptography and policy recommendations for global cybersecurity governance. Balancing innovation with security, this chapter aims to guide researchers and policymakers toward building resilient and privacy-aware smart ecosystems.

"Decentralized Applications and Distributed Ledger Framework" by Amit Kumar Tyagi, Hemamalini V, Jeyaselvi M, Shabnam Kumari explores the principles, frameworks, and applications of dApps and DLFs. It begins by examining the foundational concepts of decentralization, followed by an analysis of how distributed ledger technologies enable secure and transparent transactions. Subsequently, it discusses key frameworks—such as Ethereum, Hyperledger, and Corda—that provide diverse solutions for both public and private ecosystems. Finally, the chapter highlights real-world applications, challenges, and future directions, emphasizing the critical role these technologies play in advancing trust, resilience, and innovation in the era of smart digital transformation.

"Artificial Intelligence and Cybersecurity" by Rupam Hazra, Parag Chatterjee, Yash Singh, Gopal Podder, Titli Das explores AI's critical role in modern cybersecurity, its techniques and applications, and the challenges that need to be navigated as AI continues to evolve in the field.

"Enhancing Cybersecurity in Blockchain Legal Challenges and Solutions" by Sudipta Dhar, Shivangi Kashyap, Pravin Kumar explores how blockchain enables decentralization, transparency, and security and faces threats from cybersecurity and legal. The cryptographic algorithms and consensus protocols add a layer of security, while the associated risks of possible 51% attack, inappropriate private key management, and smart contract vulnerabilities still persist. Legal issues arise with the clashes with data protection laws like the GDPR and with the challenge of finding who is liable due to this decentralization. The uncertain legal context around smart contracts is preventing their enforcement. Also emerging threats like quantum computing will require quantum-resistant cryptographic standards. A proposed solution includes better security, adaptive regulations, and collaboration of governments, industry, and academia. An equilibrium will allow for a secure, legally complaint, and sustainable blockchain fit for applications into the future.

"Enhancing Online Security a Cyberbullying Detection and Prevention System for Monitoring Abusive Language" by J Jesy Janet Kumari, Thangam S. involves the use of natural language processing and sentiment analysis to find abusive language and negative sentiment in online conversations. Before the comment is posted the detected instances of cyberbullying can be warned to the sender and prevented from being sent in a conversation.

"Advancing Ransomware Resilience in Critical Infrastructure" by Soumya Roy, Kaushik Chanda, Subhadip Nandi, Anudeepa Gon examines the evolution of ransomware attacks on critical infrastructure by synthesizing research findings from 2018 to 2025. The study systematically reviewed literature and industry reports from databases including Google Scholar, Scopus, IEEE Xplore, and Web of Science using keywords such as "ransomware," "critical infrastructure," "cybersecurity," and "machine learning." Comparative analysis was conducted through tables that illustrate rising incident frequencies, extended downtime, and significant economic impacts—up to a 500% increase in some sectors. Advanced technologies, including AI and ML, are shown to reduce detection and response times by up to 50%. The chapter also identifies emerging tactics such as double extortion and backup encryption, proposes an enhanced risk assessment model integrating dynamic threat intelligence, and outlines recommendations for policy and future research to bridge gaps in legacy system security and adaptive defense measures.

"The Role of SIEM in Modern Cybersecurity: A Comprehensive Analysis" by Shilpa Mahajan gives a detailed overview of existing SIEM technologies by comparing commercial and open-source solutions based on their features, benefits, and limitations. It also examines classification frameworks like Gartner's Magic Quadrant that emphasis on the importance of SIEM systems and their role in protecting key sectors such as energy, healthcare, and finance. Additionally, the chapter highlights major challenges in SIEM implementation. The discussion extends to the impact of external factors like political, economic, technological, and legal on SIEM evolution.

CONCLUSION

The evolution of smart technologies has undeniably reshaped the digital world, driving innovation, efficiency, and connectivity across every sector of society. Yet, as highlighted throughout this book, the same forces that power intelligent healthcare, smart transportation, Industry 4.0, and connected cities also create new vulnerabilities and unprecedented risks. Security and privacy are no longer optional considerations; they are foundational to sustaining trust and ensuring the safe adoption of these transformative systems.

This volume, Cybersecurity and Privacy in the Era of Smart Technologies, has brought together diverse perspectives, frameworks, and case studies to illuminate both the challenges and opportunities of securing emerging technologies. By examining issues such as secure communication protocols, IoT intrusion detection, blockchain-based authentication, privacy-preserving AI, and risk management frameworks, the book underscores the critical need for comprehensive, interdisciplinary approaches.

A recurring theme across the chapters is the necessity of proactive strategies—embedding security and privacy into the very design of systems rather than treating them as afterthoughts. Equally important is the call for collaboration across domains: researchers, practitioners, regulators, and policymakers must work hand in hand to anticipate threats, develop adaptive solutions, and implement effective governance structures.

Looking ahead, the path forward requires balancing the benefits of digital innovation with the responsibility to protect individuals, organizations, and societies from evolving cyber risks. By fostering resilience, strengthening ethical frameworks, and advancing cutting-edge solutions, we can ensure that smart technologies not only enhance our quality of life but also safeguard the values of security, trust, and privacy in the digital age.

Mohammed Amin
University of Jordan, Jordan

Chapter 1
AI and IIoT Enabling Smart Connectivity and Automation in Healthcare

Dankan Gowda V.
https://orcid.org/0000-0003-0724-0333
BMS Institute of Technology and Management, India

Arudra Annepu
https://orcid.org/0000-0001-5535-6045
Department of Computer Science and Engineering, Rajiv Gandhi Institute of Technology, Bangalore, India

Sheetal Vijay Kulkarni
https://orcid.org/0000-0002-3045-8202
Department of Instrumentation Engineering, AISSMS Institute of Information Technology, Pune, India

Shanmukha Sreenivas Madras
https://orcid.org/0009-0003-7983-0882
Independent Researcher, USA

B. Kameswara Rao
Department of Computer Science and Engineering, Gandhi Institute of Technology and Management, GITAM University, Visakhapatnam, India

ABSTRACT

IIoT is revolutionizing industries through connectivity of things, devices, and even the machines in an industrial setting. AI, when integrated with IIoT, enhances the existing automation to sophisticated levels, real-time analysis, and allows the specu-

DOI: 10.4018/979-8-3373-2282-7.ch001

lation methodologies to be implemented. This chapter emphasis on IIoT, in particular discussing how machine learning and edge computing and data analytics contribute to IIoT. In this context, the chapter presents selected cases of AI application in IIoT, including predictive and prescriptive maintenance, optimization of production processes, and intelligent manufacturing. The report systematically outlines how artificial intelligence can enhance the automation of various production processes, industrial operations, and decision making. In addition, other issues like security of data, the system's ability to grow with an organization, and integration of the system into an organization environment are discussed.

INTRODUCTION

Technological advancement in the 21st century can be described as revolution brought by the technology mainly the Industrial Internet of Things (IIoT) and Artificial Intelligence (AI). These technologies are going to define industries by optimizing them, automating and providing detailed information about the various processes and systems in the industries. In a nutshell, IIoT is defined as a system of interconnected machines, devices, instruments, sensors that are integrated with software, hardware, connectivity, and the capability to communicate and collect data (Bader et al., 2016; Alkattan et al., 2024; Dutta et al., 2023; Mensah et al., 2025). Unlike, for instance, Business Intelligence that is composed of analytical tools and methods allowing business leaders to uncover insights from data, and then make decisions and automate these insights, AI refers to a range of technologies including data analytics, cognitive systems, as well as machine learning that allows systems and machines to learn from data and optimise processes.

AI in collaboration with IIoT has the possibility to directly affect industries by increasing productivity by providing better data through the improved decision-making system, achieving better results in maintenance prediction, automating the existing processes, creating smart factories (Raza et al., 2020). The integration of AI in IIoT systems is crucial given that a holistic approach is required in the organization and analysis of the large data sets which originate from the IIoT systems (Gummadi & Damacharla, 2024; Al-Attar, 2023; Almaiah et al., 2025; Omotunde et al., 2023). Real-time data and decision making is a major area with the help of which many machine learning algorithms, particularly, are useful. They apply to enhancing production, recognizing equipment failure before they happen, enhancing supply chain, and decreasing energy use in operations.

Cyber physical systems have paved its way and become popular aspects of the modern industries since they make it possible for the machines, devices, and people to work together in an intelligent way. Thus, the systems of IIoT become no more just such systems of automation, but intelligent systems which are capable of making decisions on their own. Smart connectivity makes it possible for several devices in IoT to communicate in a continuous manner through the implementation of IoT protocols (Kedari et al., 2023). These devices do not only communicate but they are able to process collected data and use it to control process, thus producing high increase in productivity and operations' efficiency (Ingole et al., 2024). For instance, in the manufacturing industry AI can perform various tasks such as assembly, examination, and distribution of products without calling for the services of humans.

It is fundamental to understand that AI is critical in IIoT since it is the tool that enables the analysis of the big data produced by the IIoT devices. These can be applied in decision making, demand modeling, real time observation of situations, and frequent maintenance. Predictive maintenance is one of the areas that AI and IIoT can complement to bring the maximum value (Kaumudhi et al., 2024). Real-time data makes it possible for the AI models to forecast the time when equipment's are most probably to fail hence reducing the overhaul frequency to when is necessary from the traditional calendar basis maintenance! This lessens the time that the machinery is out of use, increases the time the machinery lasts before it requires maintenance and lower maintenance expenses (Minoli et al., 2017). Also, the integration smart technology in both sections leads to efficiency improvement in the quality control process. The use of such algorithms will also enable it to track the production lines, determine areas with defects for immediate attention, and guarantee consumer satisfaction and quality production without compromise of resources and time (Alshuaibi et al., 2025; Mousa & Shehab, 2025; Albahri et al., 2023; Kavitha et al., 2024).

The IIoT can be dominated as one of the major ways of enhancing industries with artificial intelligence and smart connectivity (Almuqren, 2025; Otoom, 2025; Almanasir et al., 2025). But for these technologies to be practical, such uses are needed at the definite level, with real-life data available. The main criteria to assess the effectiveness of IIoT in the use cases of PdM and process optimization should be based on factors such as accuracy, latency, and success rate of prediction. For instance, case studies that focus on implementation of real time predictive maintenance for manufacturing industry can provide an understanding on how IIoT solutions backed by AI can lower the machine downtimes by a fifth while improving the efficiency in changing parts (Addula et al., 2025; Alshinwan et al., 2025; Albinhamad et al., 2025).

In conclusion, AI and IIoT are significantly revolutionizing the contemporary industries as the operations are becoming smarter, more efficient, and more autonomous. The chapter has the primary objective of explaining the commonplace between these two technologies in detail which includes the benefits, uses and how they can revolutionize industries around the world. Using applied AI and integrated IIoT, new business advantages and opportunities of increasing productivity, enhancing sustainability while increasing profitability can be reached which leads to the formation of the further development of industrial conditions

LITERATURE SURVEY

The historical development of AI in industrial applications can be traced back to several decades ago as one of the developments that originated with early computing and automation (Ali, 2024; Al-Shareeda et al., 2024; Almaayah & Sulaiman, 2024; Alsahaim & Maayah, 2023; Burhanuddin, 2023; Safour, 2024). First of all, AI was implemented in the framework of the so-called expert systems, aiming to mimic expert's decisions in conditions of manufacturing, diagnostics, and others (Chaudhary et al., 2024). The first AI systems were developed in the 1970 and 1980 and were based on the rule of decision making which was extremely useful in industries. Nevertheless, these limitations such as the weakness of the model in learning from new data resulted in some of the challenges associated with scalability and flexibility. In the later years, artificial intelligence and machine learning (ML) and and neural networks commenced to emerge as promising approaches to conceive self-learning, efficient and self-improving artificial systems through the means of experience and number data. These brought way for the more complex AI advancement to come into industries for uses such as; Maintenance prediction, supply chain management, and quality assurance.

This growth and development of the Industrial Internet of Things (IIoT) initiative is a result of improvement in the networking technologies and sensors that started around the last quarter of the twentieth century (Breivold, 2017). The availability of cheap sensors, low-power machinery and fast communication technologies made it possible for physical objects to gather and send great amount of data in real-time. When these systems became connected they then paved way for IIoT, that is, systems as well as the machines, and even the structures in the industrial field could communicate without the outside interference (Sharma & Sharma, 2024). In the initial IIoT implementation, most of the concentration was on using the technology to enhance the operation productivity of manufacturing (Srinivasan et al., 2022). But soon, due to large amount and density of the data accumulating, came a requirement of more sophisticated analysis and smart decision making control systems. This resulted in Small programs being embedded into IIoT platforms over time to enable aspects such as predictive analytics, improving processes, and even better automation.

One of the crucial issues when it comes to IIoT applications is safety in terms of data protection. IIoT networks are becoming more common in the world, however, in most cases, the networks are exposed to cyber threats. Cyber threats are classified in the following: the denial of service (DoS) attack, the man-in-the-middle attack, and unauthorized accessing to system. In order to lower the threats that accompany them, security models like blockchain technology, as well as edge AI encryption have been considered. However, to follow IIoT security standards, Industrial systems need to follow norms like IEC 62443 and NIST 800-82.

The combination of AI with IIoT has created the following technological development that has improved industrial processes (Barron, 2021). Two of the strongest features of this integration are the integration of real-time data from connected devices and analysis of this huge amplitude data flow. For instance, machine learning can be used to extract data from sensors, production and various systems and make conclusions whether a failure will occur or a process should be improved without involving a human (Jion & Ahmad, 2024). In this regard, the expansion of edge computing fulfills this need and helps the processing to take place at or near the device or on closer servers rather than in the cloud. This not only decreases latency but also guarantees that decisions in Real-time can be made quickly, which is especially important for such areas as autonomous robotic systems, real-time control of quality and conditions of equipment.

Additional progress made in tying IIoT with AI includes methods for creating more enhanced algorithms within datasets so that machines can obtain deeper knowledge. Big Data analytics involve computation and analysis of data collected from industrial sensor, machines and other instruments (Khir et al., 2019). The increased ML capability makes it effective in enhancing data processing, demand analysis, scheduling of the products to be manufactured, and inventory control. On the same note, the incorporation of deep learning and neural networks in IIoT systems has led to the enhancement of analysis of the real-time information for automation of decision-making processes (Billady & Rajlakshmi, 2024), for instance, visual checks or detection of defects in production lines, or assessment of suboptimal utilization of energy in industries.

Some of the examples in the industries like manufacturing, logistics, and energy sector exhibit how AI and IIoT works in parallel to increase efficiency, cut down the expenses in several organizations while providing safety (Kodali et al., 2016). In the manufacturing sector, there is application of AI in IIoT in that, machines and equipment are fitted with sensors that track the amount of utilization and issue notifications that a certain part is at risk of failure in production (Roy et al., 2024). The predictive maintenance system uses certain algorithms to indicate when a piece of machinery requires maintenance and this helps to avoid breakdowns that would otherwise lead to time wastage and tool depreciation (Guja et al., 2024). This is particularly so in organizations where there are costly equipment and high production capacity, as such interruptions can be costly. Moreover, there is growing use of the AI-powered quality control systems to monitor defective streaks on production lines in an efficient manner through reducing defect rates on products.

In logistics, aspects of IIoT and AI are being used in the supply chain, for analyzing the delivery of goods, total inventory, and environmental tracking. Some of the advantages may include use of smart sensors and GPS tracking in renowned supply chain so as to get end-point point visibility, optimization of routes, fuel consumption, and such other things as timely deliveries. The forth one is about the ability of the algorithm to predict the demand variation to allow the business excess or lack of stock by applying appropriate business strategies (Illakya et al., 2024). Self-driving cars and drones resulting from AI and IIoT technologies are gradually entering into warehouses and delivery services to save costs and increase productivity.

There is another area that has recently observed thrilling progress in adopting AI and IIoT, and that is the energy sector. Modern IIoT systems are widely implemented in industrial plants, buildings, and factories for energy management with the help of efficient data obtained from smart meters, sensors, and other devices (Kumar et al., 2022). These systems can detect wastage in energy consumption or even determine the periods when energy demand is highest so that management could make the appropriate readjustments. Likewise, in renewable energy, AI has responsibilities in the enhancement of efficiency of photovoltaic panels and wind generators based on weather conditions (Shankar et al., 2020). Further, AI and IIoT are applied for intelligent power grid that can independently control voltage, frequency and other aspects to stabilize the power grid that is bound to become more unreliable as more organizations adopt solar power.

Technologies Enabling AI and IIoT

Artificial intelligence (AI) with the Industrial Internet of things (IIoT) employs some of the following trends which are a combination of technologies offering smart and connected IIoT devices. Such deliverable technologies are IoT infrastructure, ML algorithms, edge computing, cloud computing, and big data analytics to ensure streamlined processing of data, analysis, and decision-making in IIoT applications.

Internet of Things (IoT) Infrastructure

The similar meaning and definition base of IIoT is IoT that refers to the connection of several devices, Sensors, and machines that deliver data in the industrial environments. These IoT devices are provided with the basic sensors necessary for the optimal determination of different operation parameters including temperature, pressure, humidity, motion, and vibration (Mane et al., 2021). These devices are connected with central systems with the help of wireless or wired communications like Wi-Fi, Bluetooth, Zigbee or cellular communication etc. IoT layout delivers the data on which IIoT systems are built and sustained in monitoring their machinery, equipments, and environment. It also means that it is possible to monitor the performance of the assets in real time for troubleshooting or analysis, and determine the efficiency of the business operations.

Artificial intelligence and machine intelligence rely on machine learning for the functionality of IIoT systems. SVM and other machine learning is used for the detection of anomalies, ANN for the modeling of the data and CNN for the images data. At the same time, it is somehow important to consider the criteria of measuring the performance of these algorithms, the latency, power, and bandwidth., and as such, under certain conditions, SVM may be the best to use while other condition may recommend using ANN or CNN for large volume and real time data.

The IoT does not only encompass devices and sensors meant for gathering data but it also encompasses network technologies and interfaces that regulate the communication between IoT entities and the cloud or edge systems (V. Tsankov, B. Evstatiev, 2024). This kind of structure of infrastructure is important in making sure that such data collected are accurate and easily available for analysis at the right time. Lastly, security and connectivity of IoT networks should be improved, as IIoT systems involve handling a vast amount of data which comes from a great number of connected devices. The security of data and the integration of such devices into an Industry asset remains a challenge and is a critical sector in the establishment of IoT system.

Figure 1. Technologies Enabling AI and IIoT

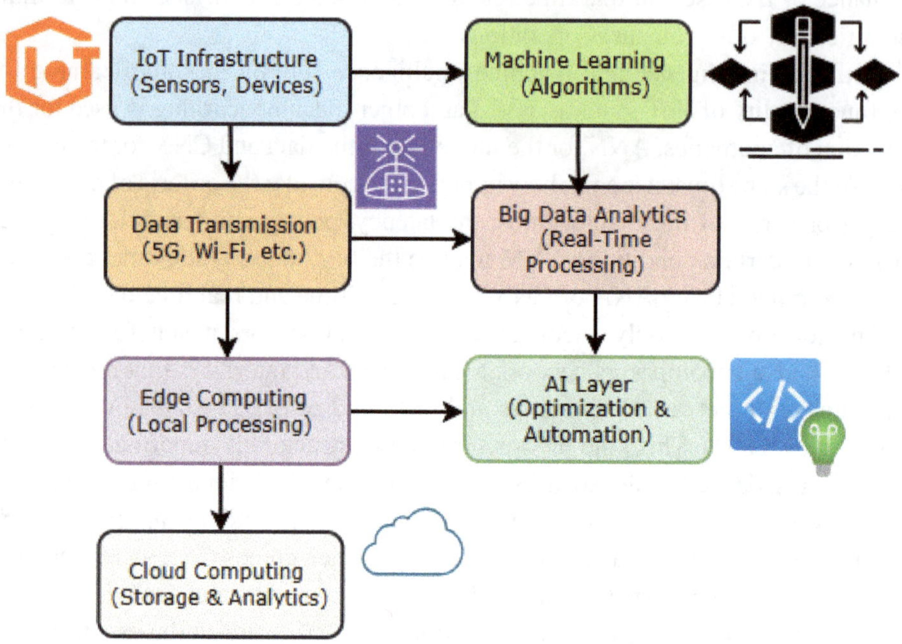

It is vital to explain that the four technologies identified in figure 1 are central to combining AI with IIoT. Understanding relationship between the layers of Technology: This diagram diagram explains how the layers of technology help in optimizing the operational efficiency of IIoT systems (Chowdhary & Singh, 2024). The lowest layer of the diagram is the IoT Infrastructure which can be the sensors or devices that gather data from different physical system as machines or equipment. These devices make up the core of the IIoT ecosystem since they facilitate communication as well as the sharing of other data types in real-time. The third layer, Data Transmission is the medium through which data collected by IoT devices is communicated through various 5G, Wi-Fi, and other networking protocols etc.

Proceeding further, the data collected is processed at a point closer to the source in Edge Computing this makes decisions at device level more efficient and real. This is especially important in matters that require quick response that depends on the availability of information. On the other hand, Cloud Computing describe the ability of storing huge files, processing larger data sets, data analysis, and supporting machine learning algorithms. Machine Learning is the fundamental capability in the AI layer since it involves applying them to datasets to identify and understand relationships for better outcomes on industrial procedures and judgments. Big Data Analytics supplements this by using large amounts of data to make decisions in real-life time, such as making tactical changes in the production schedules or discovering of inefficiencies. Last but not least, the AI Layer is also formed by the integration of all these components to facilitate automation, optimization, and decision-making for IIoT systems to make smarter and more efficient the industrial processes.

Real-time requirements denote that IIoT systems should perform their functionalities within millisecond time based on the efficiency requirements of a system. For such business environments as manufacturing or log in terms of data processing, it is crucial to analyze high-frequency data coming from sensors, robots, and equipment with the help of real-time data processing. To meet these demands, the use of edge computing offers the possibility of doing some data processing at the edge as opposed to the cloud computing paradigm.

Machine Learning (ML) Algorithms in IIoT

Its integration into the IIoT context is significant in increasing capabilities of more advanced Machine learning (ML). Using ML, it is possible to provide devices with big amounts of information produced by IoT devices and get recommendations, patterns discovered, and processes improved automatically. These use statistical and probabilistic models to scour data that is past and/ or present, to try and predict the possible eventualities and make decisions on their own. In IIoT systems, some applications of the Advanced ML include Predictive maintenance, anomaly detection as well as process optimization.

Machine learning also has an essential function in the processes optimization, based on constant analysis of the sensor data for workflows mutations and better performance. They can know areas that require changes, suggest changes, or even make changes autonomously due to prevailing circumstances. As the IIoT systems grow smarter through the use of ML, there is always an ability for organizations to make sound decisions on the productivity, and overall minimization of wastage.

In the application of IIoT, the scalability of the system determines the efficiency of the used ML algorithms. This is in line with the fact that as the IIoT systems evolve, there is a rapid expansion in the use of the model. For instance, it is evident that ANNs can handle big data algorithms excellently although they may subject to higher irregularities if the model was not well trained or if the data are heterogeneous. Therefore, the procedure of model retraining and adaptive learning is required to keep the system optimum as the size of the data keeps growing.

Edge Computing and Cloud Computing in IIoT

Both edge computing and cloud computing are two substantial technologies that support real-time processing and data storage in IIoT platforms. As both paradigms complement each other, one of them is to ensure that the IIoT systems have data processing capability in the shortest time possible.

Edge computing is the practice of processing data near to the source, which means near to where the IoT devices and various sensors are deployed. Hence, through data analysis in a smaller network, edge computing mitigates the problem of massive data transmission to centralized cloud servers, which causes latency. This is especially important for applications in which the results need to be produced at the earliest, for example, in the case of robots or industrial automation. Edge computing enables devices to work on data and make the corresponding decision simpler and quicker by reducing response time to the action.

On the other hand, cloud computing offers a centralized storage and computation to support IIoT systems, including a data aggregation as well as data analysis for different devices in the organization as well as its supply chain. Due to the inherent benefits, the multi-cloud can collect and organize the data from various end devices to analyze it, train machine learning models, and store the data for further long-term analysis. The scalability of IIoT is also made easier by cloud computing since more information can be stored when needed without the need for expensive equipment upgrades.

The two models of computing distributions, the edge computing and cloud computing, are two general elements of the IIoT structure that offer different benefits and drawbacks. Edge computing allows numerous calculations to be done in parallel at the edge of the network which leads to reduced latency thus being highly useful in upcoming applications such as predictive maintenance in the chemical plant. On the other hand, cloud computing refers to sharing of computing resources such as storage space and computing power over the internet but, it can cause delays. There is an opportunity to achieve the best of both worlds through the use of edge and cloud computing both in processing capacity.

With the integration of edge and cloud computing, the performance of IIoT systems is improved as well as the process of data to be analyzed is effective. Edge computing solves the problem of analysis in real-time, whereas cloud computing helps to make deeper analysis, archival, and decision-making in large workplaces.

Big Data Analytics and Real-Time Data Processing

Big data analytics and real time data processing are some of the core components in AI-integrated IIoT system. As the number of IoT devices increases, organizations required sophisticated methods to process, analyze and utilize data from these devices. Big data analytics can be defined as the methods and tools to analyze the large volumes of off-conventional data types and structures that cannot be handled by conventional data processing tools. These analytics assist the organizations in establishing trends, out of normal range deviations, as well as other information that can be latent.

Real-time data processing is of significant importance in IIoT as decision making is usually done based on real-time data. Real-time data obtained from connected sensors and equipment are ingested into IIoT systems to help in the monitoring of the health of equipment, process optimizations, and ensuring business operations. This way organizations can be able to capture changes in the operation conditions in real time and be in a position to counteract these changes in real time so that their system is not compromised with lots of time wasted or not being efficient.

That is why, when integrated with AI and machine learning algorithms, big data analytics makes IIoT system capable of not only analyzing data, but also, accumulating new knowledge about them. This integration of analytics and real-time leads to organization's ability to make the right decisions that will make the difference in the organization productivity, cuts expenses and overall system return.

Real time processing is fundamental to IIoT systems to enhance operations but when analyzing for such characteristics as latency, bandwidth utilization, and power consumption must be given adequate consideration. They affect the utilization of the IIoT and the possibility of extending the solutions to a wide range of clients. For instance, applying large data analytics with cloud AI provides valuable information but it thwarts due to the network bandwidth and power constraints. It should be noted that the best practice of performing analytics partially at the edge and partially in the cloud combines the possibilities of optimization for large-scale IIoT.

The use of big data analytics in IIoT encompasses the fact that it offers extensive endogenous data analysis from enormous data sources including sensors, machines, and operational data. Some of the key applications of big data include predictive modeling, pattern recognition that pinpoints the potential areas of process enhancement, prediction of equipment failure and demand forecasting.

AI IN IIOT APPLICATIONS

AI is vital to the applications of the IIoT as it anchors itself in the components of automation, productivity, and decision making across several industrial fields. Integrating AI and IIoT leads to the ability of industries to harness the power of data and to make better decisions, detect faults and ultimately bring about better change into their processes and systems. AI-driven IIoT solutions are already been used in various applications such as predictive maintenance, process optimization, supply chain, quality control and smart factories to enhance operation efficiency and cut costs.

Predictive Maintenance

Predictive maintenance is one of the most publicized use of AI in IIoT systems to provide an indication of one's level of understanding. In traditional maintenance techniques, maintenance tends to be either time-based or based on a detection of an actual failure in the facility's equipment. However, predictive maintenance takes advantage of AI and IIoT to make use of historical and real time data on the machinery and equipment with an aim of anticipating failure before it actually occurs. This is where sensors, which allow an AI system to colleting data like acoustic or vibration signals, temperature or pressure, comes in handy as it can identify patterns of how machinery or structures is wearing out and when it is likely to fail.

This data is fed to the machine learning algorithms that make suggestions on when it is most suitable for a particular component to undergo maintenance so as to avoid cases of breakdown and yet at the same time not pay a lot of money for frequent maintenance checks. It also has a useful impact in the sense that it conserves the durability of machines that are used and at the same time reduces the frequency of operational intermissions. For instance, in the line of manufacturing, predictive maintenance comes in handy assists to determine which of the parts are likely to fail towards the production line, and they can be sorted out for replacement or repair. AI applied in predictive maintenance enables industries to use resources wisely and increase the efficiency of the existing tools to boost the OEE in industries, resulting in lower costs and better production.

One of the most useful application's IIoT is the predictive maintenance through the use of Artificial Intelligence. Maintenance schedules for equipment are based on the AI models and equipment failures are estimated before they happen which helps in reducing the time during which the equipment is not in use. For instance, through machine learning, AI can detect specific vibrations from motors to intricate levels, predict that it will fail while its accuracy rate is over 90%. These models depend on sensors wherein the data fed to the models has to be timely and accurate, and there must be the provision to accommodate an enormous amount of data from remote devices.

Process Optimization

AI integrated IIoT solutions are adopted for enhancing productivity in different sectors of industries. This can be achieved by always analyzing data from production lines, the machinery and the various systems in use in the factory. This can be realized as the adjustment of production processes in order to increase its output, reduce excess or increase productivity and efficiency and thereby decrease resource consumption and operational cost.

One of the primary benefits of IIoT involves utilizing the big amounts of data collected by linked devices in making and improving processes through machine learning models. They can then give an operator specifics in real time ranging from changing the speed of production, or which resources to channel towards which resource, or which setting of the equipment would charge performance. For instance, in the chemical production, AI can keep an eye on the temperature, pressure and flow rates of chemical reactors and on the basis of certain parameters make changes so that to achieve the highest quality of outcome with the least power use. Likewise, in automobile manufacturing industry, AI can study the production data to see that there is some hindrance in the manufacturing line and make sure correction as needed.

Another area of business where they use AI is controlling energy expenses. An example of applying AI systems includes the ability to process data on energy consumption and find out that the energy consumption could be optimized, for instance by scheduling the usage of equipment during periods of high consumption rates or by correctly setting up HVAC systems. Such optimization in the industries where cost of energy is a major factor of production can therefore make a big difference in the cost cutting and use of resources in a more sustainable manner.

Figure 2. AI in IIoT Applications

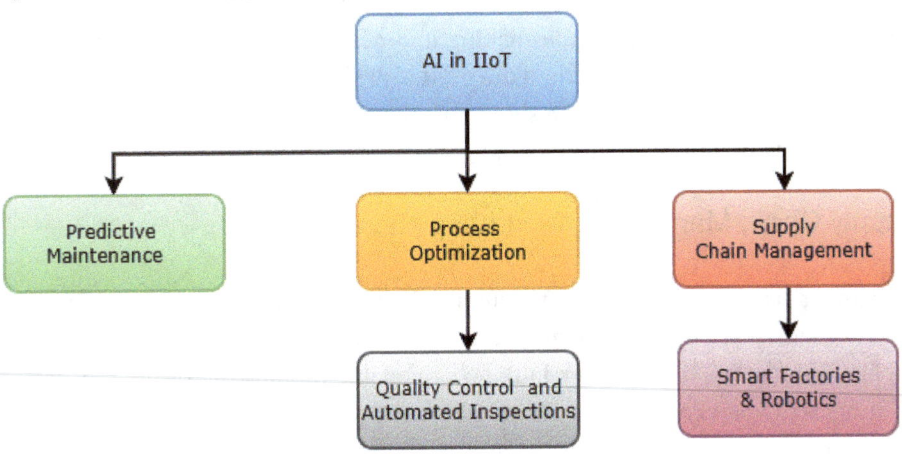

The various specific areas of Artificial Intelligence (AI) application within the Industrial Internet of Things (IIoT) are explained with reference to figure.2. below. The applications of IIoT are placed around the central block known as AI in IIoT, where it acts as the leading factor of the applications. Five branches spread out radially from this central box namely Predictive Maintenance, Process Optimization, Supply Chain Management, Quality Control and Smart Factories & Robotics.

Predictive Maintenance is an application of AI that involves the utilization of algorithms to monitor data from sensors implanted in the machines or equipment to predict the failure of the machines or the equipment beforehand. It helps to avoid frequent breakdowns of equipment and, therefore, cuts on costs of having to repair such parts, which all makes the operation more effective. A Paper on Process Optimization – Applying AI to the Enhancement of production by constant checking of parameters and tend to have all processes as efficient as possible. It will increase the work speed, cut costs, including expenditure on energy, and reduce wastage of resources.

AI is most useful to Supply Chain Management and Logistics as it can help maintain appropriate inventory, forecast demand, as well as plan the delivery route. Artificial intelligence in IIoT can give a practical solution to represent real-time data of sensors so that companies can take intelligent decisions that lead to cost-effective, efficient, and improved customer satisfaction. For example, in Quality Control, AI models use data from sensors and cameras in order to find defects in a manufactured product so as to conform to the set standards. It also helps in creating better quality, less rate of erroneous and helps in maintaining the quality of the product in between the manufacturing process.

Last but not the least is Smart factories and Robotics which refers to AI combined with Robotics 3.0 and IIoT. It empowers machines as well as robots to function independently and provide decision-making in order to enhance production line and adapt towards change. The overlaid diagram also shows how all these applications are related, are all based on AI to show how the technologies blend to make better smart systems in industrial processes.

Supply Chain Management and Logistics

Business is experiencing a shift in supply chain and logistic management because now, decision making is done using accurate data collected through artificial intelligence. Connected IIoT devices in the chain enable monitoring of the movement, location, status, and quantity of the retail products, inventory, as well as the status and performance of tools and equipment as the complex AI systems endeavour to make forecasts on the demands of consumers, inventory control, and vehicle routing, among other issues.

The analysis of historical data sales activity other external factors like market trend, weather and the general economic conditions gives the ability predict the likely demand. Thus, improved demand forecasts enable consumers to provide better synchronization between production and inventory control, and manage stockouts and overstocks, hence, a reduction in costs of holding inventory while at the same time increasing value for customers. Another benefit of integrating AI for demand forecasting is efficient and effective just-in-time inventory methods that deliveries materials and products only when they are needed and not allowing for storage to take up much space.

In the area of logistics, AI-embedded IIoT helps in the manipulation of several operations like routing and management of the fleet, conditions, and schedules of vehicles are determined with the help of real-time information provided by IIoT. AI can also provide the best routes to take, how much fuel to use and delivery time to employer to use in delivering goods. In addition, AI is capable of tracking vehicle conditions so as to bring to the notice of the fleet managers any developing problem which if not prevented can cause a vehicle to break down thus putting down the recurring costs of maintenance and increasing on the overall vehicle availability. They also improve logistics by including robots and also robotic systems in operations such as storage, picking as well as packaging.

Quality Control and Automated Inspections

Inspection is an important operation in quality assurance since it aids in avoiding the delivery of substandard products to the market. AI and IIoT facilitate constant supervision and control of the quality of a product in the making which increases the quality of the end product and reduces on the issue of products which were not up to standard. Self-initiated and time-consuming manual inspection some of the drawbacks which prove costly and error-prone, while on the other hand AI inspection offers thorough inspection and within a very small fraction of time.

Machine vision using algorithms is a common way of carrying out inspections automated in the manufacturing processes. AI can examine photos or videos in real time from cameras mounted on the manufacturing lines and define specific flaws, for instance the existence of scratch, dent, or variations in shape or size of the product. These algorithms demonstrate the ability to learn patterns from the data set and identify deficiencies that would cause deficiencies with high accuracy, which means that the products that are shipped would be free from defects. In manufacturing industries such as electronics or automotive industries where accuracy is paramount, there is no way that the firms can be able to operate without implementing AI technologies for quality assurance.

Besides visual inspection, other specifications can also be examined through other checking features connected to the IIoT like weight, temperature or chemical content. However, the author failed to address likely improvements AI systems achieve by continuously analysing data from these sensors whereby products can be made to conform to a certain quality to eliminate defects hence enhancing reliability of most products.

Smart Factories and Robotics

A smart factory is the evolution of intelligent manufacturing where AI, IIoT and robotics come together to from fully automated production line. These components encapsulate the concept of a smart factory where machines and robots connected through IIoT devices are in a constant data exchange process as well as performing responsive activities. AI algorithms allow machines to reason on this data so as to optimize those production process, work flow and self running.

Great emphasis is placed on the concept of smart factories which requires an extensive use of robots to perform operations such as assembly and packaging, as well as handling of goods, and inspection. Human and Artificial co Robotic systems can be able to work in a rather integrated system since robots are flexible in responding to change of production processes, have capabilities of remembering past experiences, and are capable of displaying efficiency over time. For instance, in car manufacturing, robotic arms that have AI integrated into them can be used in the assembly of complicated components, advance through knowledge in the previous tasks performed in order to enhance the rate of cycles done.

Smart factories also allow the control of the entire production line since relevant parameters can be changed in real-time by artificial intelligence. For example, if a specific machine in the production line is taking a long time to work, then AI can work the schedules of other machines so as to ensure the production process is not affected. Furthermore, it has flexibility when it comes to raw materials variations or change in the production line, which will reduce on quality issues and time wastage.

Smart factories utilize AI, IIoT, and robotization, that would help manufacturers to create flexible and extensible shop floors capable of quickly adapting to the change in demand, reduce the cost of production, and rise efficiency. These factories are designed to learn from data the way to optimisation and constantly improving the quality of the product and its production rate.

RESULTS AND DISCUSSION

This research investigates on potential application of IIoT integrating with AI that has inclusive of significances of three industrial segments. AI is now emerging as one of the key components of the IIoT landscape with a virtually unlimited number of applications that have demonstrated quite remarkable results in terms of productivity, safety, and cost optimisation. In this section, the author presents the current applications of AI and IIoT, the advantages of this synergy, the current issues and limitations, as well as future prospects for AI and IIoT.

Overview of Current Use Cases and Implementations

The IIoT applications powered by AI in the current world have showcased their benefits in several industries such as manufacturing, energy, logistics, as well as healthcare. For instance, in the concept of predictive maintenance, the artificial intelligence algorithms are used to audit data from sensors that have been installed on machines and equipment in order to identify potential problems and prevent equipment failure. Figure 3, AI-Driven Predictive Maintenance Performance, captures the probable range of using AI to identify any signs of failure in the equipment based on data feed in real-time. It entails anticipating when a given machine will be requiring maintenance services so as to prevent its breakdown hence reducing on the overall costs incurred in repairing the machines as well as increasing the lifespan of machines that are in a company's possession.

In its theoretical framework of application, the IIoT systems for process optimization utilize AI algorithms to monitor and control the production processes based on real-time data analytics. As described in Figure 4 – Process Optimization in IIoT using AI, the parameters as well as the machine learning models can change the process variables like temperature, pressure and flow rates so that the production process runs optimally. Such changes may bring about increased output in terms of product rates, necessity in use of energy, and cutting on expenses on resources.

Another area that is experiencing the impact of IIoT is the supply chain management and logistics by the use of Artificial intelligence. Applications of IoT will include demand forecast, inventory management, and even traffic and fleet control. Figure 5:Real Time Data Analysis In IoT Systems demonstrates how an IIoT system incorporates AI models to analyze real time data collected from IoT devices such that proper adjustments can be made in the logistics flow. Such specific application can also be used to determine the best routes for delivery on the basis of traffic situation, weather conditions and delivery schedules in order to decrease fuel consumption and delivery time.

There is also improvement in quality control & automated inspections with the help of integration of machine learning & IIoT. In areas such as automobile and electronics, trained models are able to recognize people or objects on cameras or sensors that should not be present or missing features for the product. Figure 6: Quality Control in IIoT using Machine Learning Models illustrates how by using visual inspection machines even micro-defects on the products will be noticed to avoid any substandard products to be shipped to customers. It contributes to product standardization, cuts down on production of the subpar products and minimize the chances of defective products getting into the market.

Benefits of AI Integration in IIoT: Efficiency, Cost Reduction, Safety, Etc.

The combination of AI with IIoT gives rise thereto, attainable values which greatly improve industrial processes as per the following ways. This is due to the fact that it offers one of the highest advantages of capacity utilization and is efficient in terms of space utilization. Using AI algorithms in analyzing the data collected from the IoT devices, industries can design the production schedules, control the bottleneck time and enhance the throughput. For instance, artificial intelligence in the types such as AI-based prediction maintenance guarantees timely servicing of machinery while increasing efficiency. This system minimizes the number of interventions that require manual intervention and ensures proper flow in the production line.

Another major advantage is the issue to do with establishment of costs is solved since the information acquired can be used to cut costs of operations and improve efficiency. III IIoT based systems can help companies select the most efficient way of energy use and avoid or improve productivity of the unused resources. Thus, in the process of analyzing the collected information in real-time, AI can point out that the range of activities in the production lines requires specific improvements that would help to minimize operating expenses. For instance, in manufacturing, with the use of artificial intelligence, the frequency of material wastage can be cut, energy consumption can be minimized, and human resource can be well utilized. This is because through PDCA, it will be possible to predict when the machines will be requiring service and thus give services to the machinery before it develop a problem and hence offering expensive repairs and lost time to replace it.

Integration of AI and IIoT also has other advantages: Safety is one of the greatest advantage. It hence becomes possible to check on the health of the equipment, detect early signs of malfunction or emerging risky conditions and produce alerts to alert the relevant parties to take required precautions. AI can help in tracked performance of the machinery and sensors for given hazardous environments like oil refinery or chemical plants to prevent any safety hazards and standard safety procedure of a plant can be followed to minimum the number of risks. Also, with the use of robots that are enhanced with the artificial intelligence it is possible to offload risky operations such as material handling in risky zones thus minimizing risks on the workers.

In order to substantiate the argument in this chapter, case studies of IIoT systems will be incorporated a first-hand evidence of quantitative outcomes such accuracy, latency and predictive success rate. For instance, a predictive maintenance system that is implemented in a steel manufacturing plant realized 20% reduction in its maintenance expenses and 15% decrease in its equipment downtime since it is useful in predicting the faults of equipment that may occur in the next six months. This section will also explain the problems that this method posed during implementation; such as the problem of data integration and constant retraining.

Challenges and Limitations in Adopting AI and IIoT

However, there are quite a number of drawbacks and limitations that an organization needs to overcome when opting for AI and IIoT integration. The first key issue is about the possibility to incorporate AI into the existing industrial systems. Currently, most organizations still employ typically phased systems that may not thrive in the modern IIoT environments. For these systems to be upgraded to accommodate AI and IIoT, there is needed a substantial investment, or to acquire such expertise.

Figure 3. AI-Driven Predictive Maintenance Performance

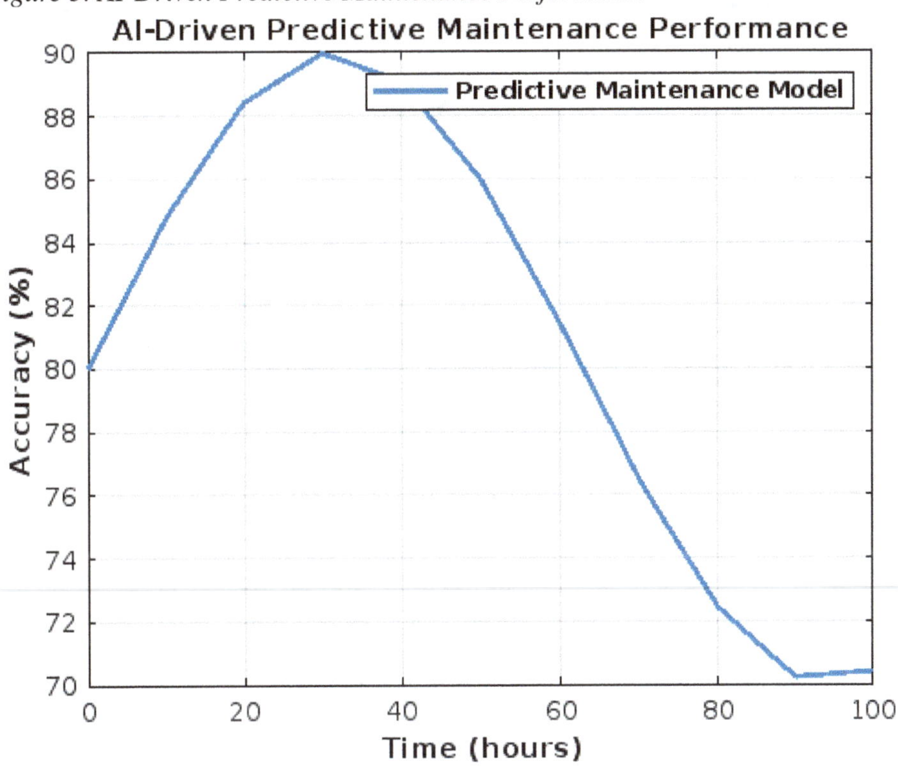

Figure 4. Process Optimization in IIoT using AI

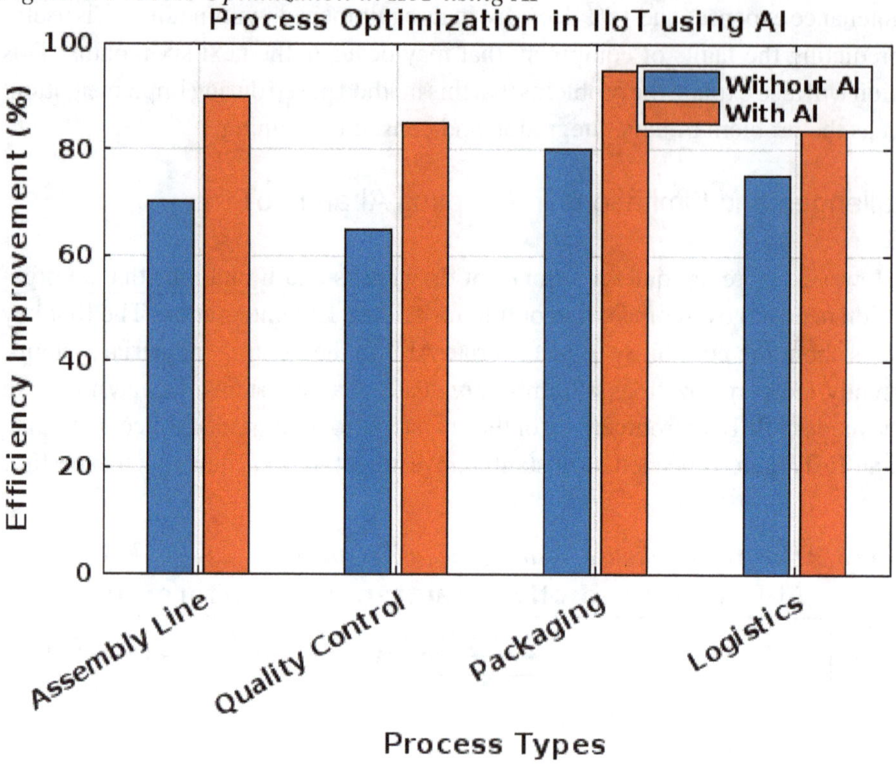

Figure 5. Real-time Data Analysis in IIoT Systems

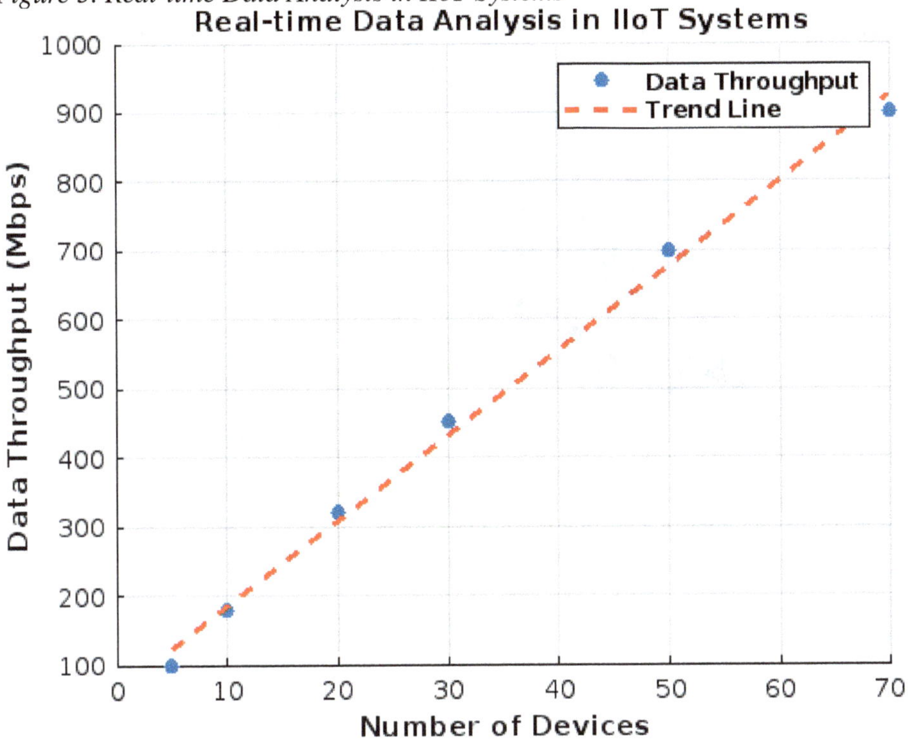

Figure 6. Quality Control in IIoT using Machine Learning Models

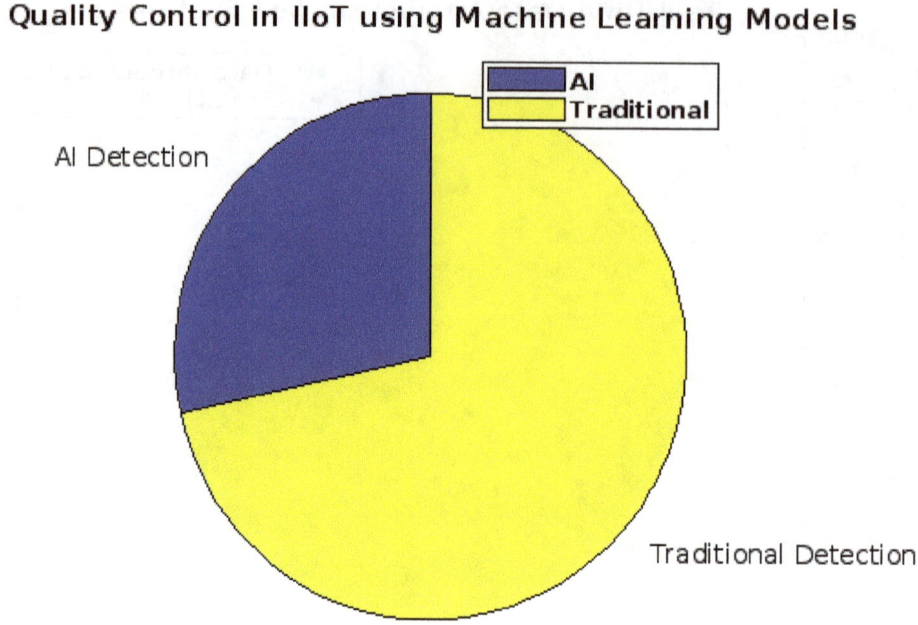

The fourth important issue is a protection of the IIoT data that is practically impossible to secure for such enormous amounts of information generated through the systems. The proliferation of millions of devices for collecting operational data also means that chances of being compromised are rife. It is therefore crucial when implementing AI-driven IIoT systems to have protection measures that will ensure the IIoT networks do not undergo unauthorized access or tampering.

The last problem of greed is related to the scalability of AI models. Neural structures of AI depend on large databases to learn; therefore, it can be challenging to scale up in scenarios with for limited historical information or scenarios where data acquisition is decentralized across the different devices. Furthermore, it was found that if AI models are not retrained from time to time depending on the intensity and frequency of new inputs then the performance of the model deteriorates, therefore effective process for updating model needs to be implemented.

The final factor is the cost factor; the system comes with its cost factors that may make it unattainable by a number of users. Currently, the establishment of integrated manufacturing and smart IIoT systems powered by artificial intelligence pose certain costs, which may be quite challenging for SMEs. Sensors, investments in infrastructures, and human capital to man the technology can be very expensive, and, therefore, place systems out of reach of many organizations.

Future Trends and Potential Advancements in AI and IIoT

The future of AI and IIoT has been seen as full of potential with trends such as the consistent evolution of the use of machine learning and data analytics as well as rising automation. One of the visible trends is the growing use of the edge computing in the IIoT systems. This is one of the most significant challenges of IoT as the amount of processed data is increasing; therefore, handling it at the edge of the network will be more effective. Edge computing minimize the latency from the cloud-based systems and supports the real-time decision making criteria such as robotic control, predict & control, process optimizing.

So another future trend of innovative design can be described as the emergence of artificial intelligence self-governing systems. This is because, as the sophistication of the models that are incorporated in the IIoT increases, the systems will be in a position to make their decisions and take the required actions without the assistance of humans. This will for sure be of advantage where there is need to have constant overseeing and readjusting, for instance in the smart factories where robots and other machines will understand from data and readjust itself or itself's without consulting a human being.

Same as in other areas considerable role will play 5G networks, thanks to which it will be possible to provide a necessary data transfer speed and minimal response time needed for AI and IIoT between millions of devices. The dependable implementation of 5G will help satisfy the need for a faster and more coherent connection between connected devices in the IoT environment to support the synergy of AI and IIoT technologies for business and industries including manufacturing, managing, and health care among others.

Thus, the integration of AI with IIoT has promising impacts across every industry, based on potentiality of improvement in performance, cost effectiveness and safety advantages. However, there are certain barriers like integration, security, scalability and cost which needs to be overcome in order to have successful implementation and integration of these technologies. Such technological developments as artificial intelligence, edge computing, five generations of network connections as well as autonomy will lead to further enhancement of industrial processes and improvement of industries.

CONCLUSION

The combination of AI with the Industrial Internet of Things (IIoT) in different industries has been revolutionary. There are many ways that AI contributes towards IIoT technology through real-time data analysis for maintenance, improving services and products as well as decision making. Several applications of artificial intelligence include data-driven predictions, increased production, supply chain, improving product quality, and Industries 4.0 can be regarded to be valuable additions. Hence, industries through artificial intelligence have been able to minimize on time wastage, enhance organization and production standards, enhance production standards and efficiency among others. Besides, the application of AI-controlled IIoT systems has also impacted favorably on reduced costs, safety, and sustainability in industries involving manufacturing, logistics, and energy. In other words, the future potential of AI and IIoT will be held in the establishment of smart and self-optimizing industries. These include machine learning, edge computing, deeper integration of 5G, and IIIoT, which will provide solutions to make real-time and near real-time decisions, and opportunities for end-to-end optimization at an even higher level. In the coming years, the IA & IIoT will open new horizons in industries, better factories, efficient supply network and optimal utilization of energy and many more.

It is an important task to retain the quality of the data and the effectiveness of the AI model in every IIoT application. In the long run, there is an issue of model drift whereby the model deviates its accuracy as the patterns of figures change. For example, IIoT systems should have the ability to handle the issue of data versioning and re-training of models to counter these problems. Moreover, with the development of the models, it is essential to create correct data governance guidelines to orient the models in a proper way and make them compliant with standards.

REFERENCES

Addula, S. R., Norozpour, S., & Amin, M. (2025). Risk Assessment for Identifying Threats, vulnerabilities and countermeasures in Cloud Computing. *Jordanian Journal of Informatics and Computing, 2025*(1), 37–48. DOI: 10.63180/jjic.thestap.2025.1.5

Al-Attar, B. (2023). Network Security in AI-based healthcare systems. *Babylonian Journal of Networking, 2023*, 112–124. DOI: 10.58496/BJN/2023/015

Al-Shareeda, M. A., Najm, L. B., Hassan, A. A., Mushtaq, S., & Ali, H. A. (2024). Secure IoT-Based Smart Agriculture System Using Wireless Sensor Networks for Remote Environmental Monitoring. *STAP Journal of Security Risk Management, 2024*(1), 56–66. DOI: 10.63180/jsrm.thestap.2024.1.4

Albahri, O. S., Alamleh, A., Al-Quraishi, T., & Thakkar, R. (2023). Smart Real-Time IoT mHealth-based Conceptual Framework for Healthcare Services Provision during Network Failures. *Applied Data Science and Analysis, 2023*, 110–117. DOI: 10.58496/ADSA/2023/010

Albinhamad, H., Alotibi, A., Alagnam, A., Almaiah, M., & Salloum, S. (2025). Vehicular Ad-hoc Networks (VANETs): A Key Enabler for Smart Transportation Systems and Challenges. *Jordanian Journal of Informatics and Computing, 2025*(1), 4–15. DOI: 10.63180/jjic.thestap.2025.1.2

Ali, A. (2024). Adaptive and Context-Aware Authentication Framework Using Edge AI and Blockchain in Future Vehicular Networks. *STAP Journal of Security Risk Management, 2024*(1), 45–56. DOI: 10.63180/jsrm.thestap.2024.1.3

Alkattan, H., Al-Nuaimi, B. T., & Subhi, A. A. (2024). Machine Learning techniques to Predictive in Healthcare: Hepatitis C Diagnosis. *Mesopotamian Journal of Artificial Intelligence in Healthcare, 2024*, 128–134. DOI: 10.58496/MJAIH/2024/015

Almaayah, M., & Sulaiman, R. B. (2024). Cyber Risk Management in the Internet of Things: Frameworks, Models, and Best Practices. *STAP Journal of Security Risk Management, 2024*(1), 3–23. DOI: 10.63180/jsrm.thestap.2024.1.1

Almaiah, M. A., Sulaiman, R., Islam, U., Badr, Y., & El-Qirem, F. A. (2025). Federated Learning in Healthcare: A Bibliometric Analysis of Privacy, Security, and Adversarial Threats (2021-2024). *SHIFRA, 2025*, 46–61.

Almanasir, R., Al-solomon, D., Indrawes, S., Almaiah, M., Islam, U., & Alshar'e, M. (2025). Classification of threats and countermeasures of cloud computing. *Journal of Cyber Security and Risk Auditing, 2025*(2), 27–42. DOI: 10.63180/jcsra.thestap.2025.2.3

Almuqren, A. A. (2025). Cybersecurity threats, countermeasures and mitigation techniques on the IoT: Future research directions. *Journal of Cyber Security and Risk Auditing*, *1*(1), 1–11. DOI: 10.63180/jcsra.thestap.2025.1.1

Alsahaim, S., & Maayah, M. (2023). Analyzing Cybersecurity Threats on Mobile Phones. *STAP Journal of Security Risk Management*, *2023*(1), 3–19. DOI: 10.63180/jsrm.thestap.2023.1.2

Alshinwan, M., Memon, A. G., Ghanem, M. C., & Almaayah, M. (2025). Unsupervised text feature selection approach based on improved Prairie dog algorithm for the text clustering. *Jordanian Journal of Informatics and Computing*, *2025*(1), 27–36. DOI: 10.63180/jjic.thestap.2025.1.4

Alshuaibi, A., Almaayah, M., & Ali, A. (2025). Machine Learning for Cybersecurity Issues: A systematic Review. *Journal of Cyber Security and Risk Auditing*, *2025*(1), 36–46. DOI: 10.63180/jcsra.thestap.2025.1.4

Bader, A., Ghazzai, H., Kadri, A., & Alouini, M.-S. (2016). Front-end intelligence for large-scale application-oriented internet-of-things. *IEEE Access : Practical Innovations, Open Solutions*, *4*, 3257–3272. DOI: 10.1109/ACCESS.2016.2580623

Barron, L. (2021). The Road to a Smarter Future: The Smart City, Connected Cars and Autonomous Mobility, 2021 26th International Conference on Automation and Computing (ICAC), 1-6. DOI: 10.23919/ICAC50006.2021.9594125

Billady, R. K., & Rajlakshmi, P. V. (2024). A Novel Framework for AI-Driven, Cloud-Integrated Energy-Efficient IoT Solutions in Smart Homes. 2024 8th International Conference on Electronics, Communication and Aerospace Technology (ICECA), 327-332.

Breivold, H. P. (2017). Internet-of-Things and Cloud Computing for Smart Industry: A Systematic Mapping Study. 2017 5th International Conference on Enterprise Systems (ES), 299-304. DOI: 10.1109/ES.2017.56

Burhanuddin, M. A. (2023). Secure and Scalable Quantum Cryptographic Algorithms for Next-Generation Computer Networks. *KHWARIZMIA*, *2023*, 95–102. DOI: 10.70470/KHWARIZMIA/2023/009

Chaudhary, G., Pathak, S., Choudhary, V., Chauhan, L., & Tripathi, A. N. (2024). Smart Surveillance Object Detection System. 2024 3rd International Conference on Artificial Intelligence For Internet of Things (AIIoT), 1-6. DOI: 10.1109/AIIoT58432.2024.10574574

Chowdhary, Y. S., & Singh, G. (2024). The Convergence of IoT and 5G: Transforming Connectivity in Smart City Applications. *2024 Second International Conference on Intelligent Cyber Physical Systems and Internet of Things (ICoICI)*, 311-318. DOI: 10.1109/ICoICI62503.2024.10696019

Dutta, P. K., Singh, B., Lal, S., Arora, M. K., Raghav, A., Mensah, G. B., & Alkattan, H. (2023). Encoding IoT for patient monitoring and smart healthcare: Connected healthcare system fostering health 6.0. *Babylonian Journal of Internet of Things, 2023*, 48–58. DOI: 10.58496/BJIoT/2023/007

Gujar, S. S., Shaikh, S. F., Shandilya, S., & Reddy, N. S. (2024). AI-Enhanced Cloud Security Framework for IoT Networks Using a Predictive Analytics Approach. 2024 3rd International Conference for Advancement in Technology (ICONAT), 1-8.

Gummadi, A. K., & Damacharla, P. (2024). An Intelligent Framework for Energy Management in IoT Networks Using Machine Learning. 2024 5th International Conference on Smart Electronics and Communication (ICOSEC), 765-771.

Illakya, T., Keerthana, B., Murugan, K., Venkatesh, P., Manikandan, M., & Maran, K. (2024). The Role of the Internet of Things in the Telecom Sector. 2024 International Conference on Communication, Computing and Internet of Things (IC3IoT), 1-5. DOI: 10.1109/IC3IoT60841.2024.10550390

Ingole, B. S., Pandey, S., & Chandra, S. H. (2024). AI-Driven IoT Framework for Vehicle Accident Avoidance and Detection with Cloud Integrated Energy Efficient Solutions. *2024 First International Conference on Innovations in Communications, Electrical and Computer Engineering (ICICEC)*, 1-8.

Jion, M. S. A., & Ahmad, M. (2024). A Smart and Secured Office System Using IoT. 2024 International Conference on Advances in Computing, Communication, Electrical, and Smart Systems (iCACCESS), 1-6. DOI: 10.1109/iCACCESS61735.2024.10499529

Kaumudhi, B. M., Sita Kumari, K., Sai, A. D., & Tejaswini, T. (2024). Smart Door Lock System using Facial Recognition with Home Automation. 2024 5th International Conference on Data Intelligence and Cognitive Informatics (ICDICI), 24-29. DOI: 10.1109/ICDICI62993.2024.10810778

Kavitha, T., Amirthayogam, G., Hephzipah, J. J., Suganthi, R., & Chelladurai, T. (2024). Healthcare analysis based on diabetes prediction using a cuckoo-based deep convolutional long-term memory algorithm. *Babylonian Journal of Artificial Intelligence, 2024*, 64–72. DOI: 10.58496/BJAI/2024/009

Kedari, A., Singh, A., Kharche, G., & Mapari, R. (2023). Augmented Reality Enabled Internet of Things for Smart Visualisation in Applications. 2023 7th International Conference on Computing, Communication, Control and Automation (ICCUBEA), 1-7. DOI: 10.1109/ICCUBEA58933.2023.10392215

Khir, N. A. M., Malik, N. N. N. A., Latiff, N. M. A., Said, D. M., & Hamzah, S. A. (2019). Smart Micro-Grid Delivery Response System via Internet of Things. 2019 IEEE 14th Malaysia International Conference on Communication (MICC), 75-80. DOI: 10.1109/MICC48337.2019.9037590

Kodali, R. K., Soratkal, S., & Boppana, L. (2016). IOT based control of appliances. *2016 International Conference on Computing, Communication and Automation (ICCCA)*, 1293-1297. DOI: 10.1109/CCAA.2016.7813918

Kumar, V. A., Renaldo Maximus, A., Vishnupriyan, S., Sheikdavood, K., & Gomathi, P. (2022). IoT and Artificial Intelligence-based Low-Cost Smart Modules for Smart Irrigation Systems. *2022 International Conference on Automation, Computing and Renewable Systems (ICACRS)*, 254-260. DOI: 10.1109/ICACRS55517.2022.10029299

Mane, V. S., Pandharipande, M. M., Joshi, H. J., & Kotalwar, S. S. (2021). Manual, Internet and Bluetooth all-in-one Smart Home (MIB-AIO). *2021 International Conference on Computational Intelligence and Knowledge Economy (ICCIKE)*, 187-191. DOI: 10.1109/ICCIKE51210.2021.9410775

Mensah, G. B., Mijwil, M. M., Abotaleb, M., Ali, G., Dutta, P. K., Mzili, T., & Eid, M. M. (2025). Explainable AI for Healthcare: Training Healthcare Workers to Use Artificial Intelligence Techniques to Reduce Medical Negligence in Ghana's Public Health Act, 2012 (Act 851). *EDRAAK, 2025*, 1–6. DOI: 10.70470/EDRAAK/2025/001

Minoli, D., Sohraby, K., & Occhiogrosso, B. (2017, February). IoT Considerations, Requirements, and Architectures for Smart Buildings—Energy Optimization and Next-Generation Building Management Systems. *IEEE Internet of Things Journal, 4*(1), 269–283. DOI: 10.1109/JIOT.2017.2647881

Mousa, R. S., & Shehab, R. (2025). Applying risk analysis for determining threats and countermeasures in workstation domain. *Journal of Cyber Security and Risk Auditing, 2025*(1), 12–21. DOI: 10.63180/jcsra.thestap.2025.1.2

Omotunde, H., & Mouhamed, M. R. (2023). The modern impact of artificial intelligence systems in healthcare: A concise analysis. *Mesopotamian Journal of Artificial Intelligence in Healthcare, 2023*, 66–70. DOI: 10.58496/MJAIH/2023/013

Otoom, S. (2025). Risk auditing for Digital Twins in cyber physical systems: A systematic review. *Journal of Cyber Security and Risk Auditing*, *2025*(1), 22–35. DOI: 10.63180/jcsra.thestap.2025.1.3

Raza, A., Qadeer, M. A., Tariq, Z., Ahmed, Z., Yousaf, S., & Shah, A. (2020). Smart Assistance for Disables using Bluetooth and Arduino. 2020 IEEE 7th International Conference on Engineering Technologies and Applied Sciences (ICETAS), 1-4. DOI: 10.1109/ICETAS51660.2020.9484245

Roy, R., Sen, H., Roy, I., Paul, R., Akthar, F., & Barman, U. (2024). Cloud-Enabled Voice Control for Home Appliances: A Secure and Accessible IoT Approach. 2024 IEEE 4th International Conference on Applied Electromagnetics, Signal Processing, & Communication (AESPC), 1-5. DOI: 10.1109/AESPC63931.2024.10872037

Safour, R. A. (2024). Electrochemical nitrogen reduction: Towards efficient ammonia production. *Khwarizmia, 2024*, 1–3. DOI: 10.70470/KHWARIZMIA/2024/001

Shankar, V. R., Suchitra, S., Pavithra, B., Rajendran, P. S., Sophia, S. G. G., & Leo, M. J. (2020). Energy Optimization for Smart Home Automation in Multi-Cloud Environment. *2020 International Conference on Inventive Computation Technologies (ICICT)*, 534-539. DOI: 10.1109/ICICT48043.2020.9112537

Sharma, J., & Sharma, S. (2024). Sustainable Solar Powered Bluetooth Enabled Smart Home Automation System Using Internet-of-Things. 2024 IEEE International Conference on Communication, Computing and Signal Processing (IICCCS), 1-6. DOI: 10.1109/IICCCS61609.2024.10763780

Srinivasan, K. R., Mallikarjuna, B., Kavitha, M., Kavitha, R., & Naib, B. B. (2022). A Comparative Study: Wireless Technologies in Internet of Things. 2022 2nd International Conference on Advance Computing and Innovative Technologies in Engineering (ICACITE), 675-679. DOI: 10.1109/ICACITE53722.2022.9823664

Tsankov, V., Evstatiev, B., & Valova, I. (2024). Concept for an IoT-based Electronic System for Smart Home Automation. 2024 9th International Conference on Energy Efficiency and Agricultural Engineering (EE&AE), 1-5. DOI: 10.1109/EEAE60309.2024.10600500

Chapter 2
Cybersecurity in Smart Devices

Amrutha Kolhar
https://orcid.org/0009-0001-4940-3172
Karnatak University, Dharwad, India

Sridevi
https://orcid.org/0000-0002-9768-1599
Karnatak University, Dharwad, India

ABSTRACT

The widespread adoption of smart devices in homes, businesses, and critical infrastructure has revolutionized efficiency and connectivity. However, this rapid growth introduces significant cybersecurity risks, including weak authentication, data breaches, malware attacks, and unauthorized access, threatening user privacy and system integrity. This chapter examines key cybersecurity challenges in smart devices, analyzing common attack vectors and their consequences. It explores real-world case studies of IoT security breaches, highlighting lessons learned. Additionally, the study discusses mitigation strategies such as encryption, network security measures, and regulatory frameworks to enhance protection. Addressing these vulnerabilities is crucial for ensuring the resilience and security of smart ecosystems. The findings provide actionable insights for stakeholders to strengthen IoT security amid evolving threats.

1. INTRODUCTION

Smart devices have become an important aspect in our lives today and they have helped to streamline our lives through communication, work and the running of our

DOI: 10.4018/979-8-3373-2282-7.ch002

homes. Everything with the internet connection is a basic thing: smartphone, smart watch, home and industrial appliance, in other words, the matter is in simplifying our life and making it more efficient. With the increased number of people operating smart technology, the risks of cybersecurity also increase. The issue is that smart devices are highly vulnerable, which poses the risk of fraud and abuse of information and major cyberattacks. Lack of many computing and security options is making the smart devices fall under the scope of hackers. Unless there is robust encryption and passwords are not updated or software patches ignored there is a threat of malware, ransomware and spying on the user without authorization. The consequences of having an unsecure cybersecurity in the smart devices can be enormous. The attackers will avail any weakness in the system to steal the sensitive data of users, utilize end devices in bot net attacks, or even gain control of the critical infrastructure. Such incidents as the use of Mirai botnet that has attacked insecure IoT devices and caused large Internet services disruptions show the real dangers. The growth of smart technology both in healthcare, transportation and smart cities brings about security and reliability concerns because once cyberattacked, this can cause death. The most effective means of curtailing these problems is by making security the top priority to manufacturers, policy teams and all day-to-day users. This implies the strict authentication, update to the latest on a router and the encryption of the entire traffic. Companies and governments are writing into existence stricter cybersecurity guides to help devices be more secure. The thing is that many security violations can be blamed on people as they use default passwords or delay updating their software. Smart devices are getting better every day, and that is why we need to be more cautious about our cybersecurity. Managing security in addition to the development of new intelligent functions prevents the leakage of confidentiality and social faith of users. This confrontation with these challenges will contribute to establishing a cyberspace that will enable smart gadgets to bring usefulness in our lives and at the same time ensuring that we are secure (Lee, 2020; Raimundo & Rosário, 2022; Sun et al., 2021; Gundoor, 2022).

1.1 Evolution of Smart Devices

Consumers are connected to technology through the vast and thoughtful smart devices that are closely connected to one another. The emergence of smart, connected devices was in the late 20 th century, when personal computers and cellular phones were first put into use. The release of the iPhone by Apple in 2007 integrated computing, internet and touch screens into one single smart handheld device and transformed the concept of smart device a lot. With the internet being distributed at high speed and to more individuals, IoT has come into existence and now refrigerators, thermostat, wearables and security cameras, among other objects, can access the internet and automatically interact with each other. They added the technology to devices, like the use of sensors, AI and ML to provide the users with the experiences that best fit their needs like voice-enabled assistants (such as Amazon Alexa and Google Assistant) and proactive maintenance of smart homes. Then, there was the stage of edge computing that allows individuals to analyze data near the source of information gathering. Thanks to this, the smart devices are now more responsive, and they consume less energy. The development of 5G networks accelerated the growth of IoT even more and made it even more robust because smart cities, driverless cars, and most of the industrial processes became connected much faster and more reliably. Nowadays, clever gadgets develop beyond automation to smart AI that learns what the user desires and changes to address it. Nonetheless, it is not only positive news because along with this fast development, a connection problem was presented in the form of cybersecurity challenges because the more devices are connected, the more attack points there are. The trend they are pursuing involves making smart devices safer, more private, and such that they can be accessed on any platform, starting with simple connections to the internet, up to powerful independently operating systems. The rise of smart devices is defining the digital world as it motivates the innovative solutions and their implementation by prioritizing cybersecurity (Avancini et al., 2019; Lee, 2020; Raimundo & Rosário, 2022; Sun & Li, 2021; Usman & Shami, 2013; Sridevi & Gundoor, 2025)

1.2 Importance of Cybersecurity in IoT

The Internet of Things (IoT) has brought a lot of benefits in the contemporary life in that now people can communicate in a much easier way with hundreds of billions of devices such as the smart device at home, sensors on factory floors and medical equipment via the net itself. However, the cyber has now been a major hacking target as a result of the sharp growth of the networked devices and secure cyberspace should, therefore, be a top priority. Devices associated with IoT also handle and transfer sensitive information about people and enterprises, e.g., health data, money transactions, and in-real-time location. Lack of proper security may mean that the information can be stolen by other persons and lead to corporate, email or financial problems. Besides, the vast majority of IoT tools are not designed in an effective way in terms of security and therefore, they can be easily hacked. Broken devices can be exploited to facilitate large scale cyberattacks such as DDos attacks that may bring down many of the web connections. The risks of IoT are not limited to data leakage and the safety issues should also be considered as a matter of the physical safety. As compared to losses that might have happened because of IT systems that were constructed in the past, the associated losses would be terribly disastrous with potential loss of lives in case of cyberattacks on IoT devices. An example is that hacked industrial systems, implants, or smart cars may lead to disasters that endanger people with the prospects of losing their lives. Just in the same way, power, water and the transportation systems are the key power systems that will face interruption of basic services in the country as well as posing threats of the security issues of the country. Another serious issue that unsafe IoT devices like cameras and voice assistants can result in is people having their privacy violated because they can spy on private information, thus resulting in a lack of confidence and not complying with the GDPR and HIPAA regulations. Companies that are victimized by IoT cyberattacks lose much since they suffer interference in the running of the business, ransom payments, penalties and loss of reputation. The most effective way of dealing with these risks is to use multiple tools and technologies. If you want to build quality products, it is necessary that when you design things that you encrypt, you release regularly, and binary has security built into it. Consumers must take control of their IoT networks through change of default credentials and segmenting them with the other networks. In the meantime, government and regulatory bodies have to set high security requirements to ensure all industries stay in line. With AI and edge computing now in use in IoT, it is going to be more important to guard systems actively. By addressing these issues now, we will be able to take full advantage of IoT and ensure that privacy, safety and trust will never be compromised (Angyalos et al., 2022; Bonaventura et al., 2025; Cvitić et al., 2023; Kolluru et al., 2019; Rahayu & Aprillia, 2025; Raimundo & Rosário, 2022; Gundoor & Sridevi, 2022)

2. CYBERSECURITY THREATS IN SMART DEVICES

The smartphone, wearable, IoT outfitted home appliances are being considered as great targets of hackers due to the lack of good security features. One of the major issues is malware attack where hackers infect the computers or phones to steal the information or monitor people or their operations. Another common threat present in emails or applications is phishing, whereby the attacker will use this target people to give away sensitive information. Passwords of plenty of smart devices are not safe in any way, and the devices become targets of the brute-force attacks. There are systems that are not fixed to any kind of known vulnerability that cybercriminals can exploit. Others include man-in-the-middle otherwise known as (MITM) which is when hackers in that process occupy the middle part of two communicating networks and steal or inserted your software to the computer without your knowledge. There are ransomware threats to some devices used at home and office and these are capable of locking users out until they provide money. Also, when there are vulnerable devices, they form zombie networks with other botnets and are capable of undertaking significant operations in the cyberspace such as

DDoS attacks. Things that run on voice control and cameras can even be hacked and used to monitor someone or invade privacy. Due to the increased usage of smart gadgets, the security priority should be placed on it most of the time by vendors and those operating them via encryptions, frequently updating the systems, multi-step authentication of identity and isolation of the network against the emergence of new risks. Unless precautionary mats are taken, adoption of smart technology in some circumstances may lead to a loss of security by individuals and firms (Aldahmani et al., 2023; Alshboul et al., 2021; Lee, 2020; Rahayu & Aprillia, 2025; Raimundo & Rosário, 2022; Sridevi & Gundoor, 2024).

2.1 Malware and Ransomware Attacks

Malware is a term used to refer to any ill intent programming designed to inflict damage or exploit or access computer systems, networks or machines. It encompasses numerous types of malicious programs among which there are such as viruses, worms, Trojans, spyware, adware and ransomware. With malware, a person would misappropriate information that he/she was not supposed to use, disrupt the work of the company, damage vital documents or even use machines to perpetrate crime. The most common way is that it ends up on your computer through phishing email, corrupted download, infected web sites or under protected software. Once gaining an entrance into a system malware is capable of behaving furtively by following whatever somebody is typing, encrypting information and setting up backdoors to be infiltrated again. The primary purpose of cyber attackers utilizing malware is the economic gain, spying, and/or sabotage or simply making things messy. Otherwise, malware chooses to disguise itself as innocuous files or in sound software on your computer. The advice in this aspect that one should use antivirus software, a firewall, keep it up to date and should be careful not to run anything that appears dangerous to them. In event of malware being particularly serious, it can cost a user his/her data, his/her money or destruction to his/her system, which is often difficult to repair. That is why all people should remain conscious of the cybersecurity risks (Kara & Aydos, 2022; Reshmi, 2021; Gundoor & Sridevi, 2024).

2.1.1 Types of Malware

Virus: Viruses are the malware that use healthy files and send the virus each time the files are executed. This kind of software could corrupt, delete or modify your files and you will need to respond to it like opening an infected email attachment to enable it to do what it is set out to do. The way through which viruses can enter your computer system is by becoming loaded onto a shared drive, software or memory devices. Some viruses do not cause harm to cells before invading them, but others cause harm to them immediately they have made a contact. They tend to slow our work down; this can cause the programs to freeze up and steal data without us even being aware. There should be an antivirus software to ensure that viruses do not cause any major damage.

Worm: The user does not need to take any action to transmit worm on networks. They take advantage of loopholes in computer systems to transmit and proliferate not through the attachment in files. Worms consume so much of your network resources; they have the ability to overload previous servers and even introduce other malware into the network. The invasion of WannaCry and Stuxnet impacted the vast number of people around the world by violating the vast quantity of devices in the short term. Spread of threats The most common means of spread of threats are emails, messaging software and network sharing. Worms have the ability to infect whole networks very fast since they can do this operationally without requiring any type of help. The chances of worms infecting your computer are low when you use the latest software in your computer and it is frequently visited by your network admin.

Trojan horse: The Trojan leads the users to the impression that it is good software, however, its internal contents have got malicious instructions. A Trojan does not propagate itself in any way; unlike some other forms of malicious code, a Trojan is tricked upon the installation by users. Once they have been executed, the actions will enable the hackers to get into your system, steal your valuable information and insert additional malicious software. Some of the Trojans include RATs and banking Trojans. In the majority of the cases, the malware can be spread by using false downloads, pirated applications or some email attempts to steal your data. Trojans operate through deceiving individuals hence it is good to learn safety in downloads.

Spyware: It is a software that tracks what you do and can acquire your passwords, what you view on the internet and your money details without you noticing it. Most of the time, it lands on your computer with the help of hazardous downloads or installers. Spyware (key loggers) is software that captures the login credentials of a user, by recording what you type in on your keyboard. It is common to find spyware capabilities being present in adware. Most of the time, spyware will be missed out as it is programmed to work in the shadows. Indicators of a virus are a computer that becomes slow and has pop-up messages that are not related to each other. Not downloading any unknown files and the use of a anti-spyware is going to minimize risk.

Ransomware: The ransomware is a program in which you pay cryptocurrencies that your systems or documents are decrypted. It can be transferred in form of deceiving emails, special kits which are programmed in websites or downloads that come packed with viruses that are malicious. WannaCry and REvil are only two examples of attacks that companies and governments fell on their knees. One of the threats of ransomware is that the stolen data is threatened to be published publicly in case the ransom is not paid. Preventative measures include backups, updates, and training of the employees. They should not charge you since there are no assurances that your information can be retrieved.

Adware: Adware is always full of excessive advertisements in the browser and can redirect a user to a malicious site. In some cases, the adware is merely a bother but in other instances, it may backup your browsing history or send malware. Most of the time, you get it together with the software free of charge. It may cause your computer to run slower and result in a loss of your personal privacy that is created by running aggressive adware. The solution to this is not to keep clicking unrecognized sites and getting ads to download in order to be safe.

Rootkit: Rootkits grant those who instil them privileges as administrators and keep their existence unrecognised. They slow down the detection process by deactivating essential security programs. Most of the times the rootkits simply creep in as a result of a person falling for a phishing scam or used a security hole. Even a reboot will not help to clarify some of these issues. They can only be removed with special rootkit-removal tools and updated firmware.

Botnet Malware: Attackers use networks of malicious machines called bots to conduct massive actions such as DDoS attacks, spam sending or cryptocurrency mining. Once computers are infected with malware, they turn into bots. Many Internet Things devices have been infected by the Mirai botnet. You must also make sure you keep your passwords strong and update the firmware of your router to prevent infections.

Fileless Malware: Unlike the common types of malwares that infect your disk, all the interference process of fileless malware runs in Memory. These threats also find a way of avoiding the virus checks of the antivirus by running scripts or common tools. Companies rely on user action-based security to identify the attacks (Dean & Avenue, 2011; Reshmi, 2021; Suarez-Tangil et al., 2014; Kolhar & Sridevi, 2025).

2.1.2 Ransomware Attacks

A ransomware attack occurs when some strong software turns the files or an entire system of an individual into something that cannot be read till a ransom is paid in a cryptocurrency. In the vast majority of cases, the attack is initiated through the process of sending phishing emails, attachments to which are malicious or gaining access to the places where the weak points in the software or network can be identified and then exploited. Predominantly, as soon as they unleash the ransomware, it spreads across the system, locking the data and presenting a note that asks to pay a ransom within a specific timeframe. Criminals can say your files will be deleted or your confidential information will be forwarded to other individuals until you pay. Examples of these targets which are known to be popular targets are hospitals, government services and individuals, firms and businesses, which cause problems in daily functioning, losses and damage to the reputation of the firm. Owing to the existence of strains of ransomware like the WannaCry, Ryuk and REvil cash, they are popularly sold through RaaS where attackers pay the manufacturers to hire the malware. Occasionally, the attackers will do this by stealing your information, and then encrypting it to hold you at ransom so that you will pay. You can pay someone to help you but even then, you cannot be sure that your files will be recovered and ransomware complicates things even further to other people on the internet. Some of the ways to prevent the incidents are to regularly backup data, train employees, implement robust cybersecurity (such as firewalls and endpoint protection) and ensuring that updates are installed at all times. They are recommending that companies should not pay ransoms and that they should only report any incidences to the police. Since ransomware is growing at a high rate, it is evident that countries across the globe need to collaborate when it comes to cybersecurity efforts (Brewer, 2016; Kara & Aydos, 2022; Reshmi, 2021; Silva et al., 2019; Tailor & Patel, 2017; Sridevi & Gundoor, 2024)

2.2 Unauthorized Access and Data Breaches

When a person or group obtains unauthorized access, this is when what they do is not sanctioned by a person or group to a computer system, network or database. Humans can undergo it by getting hacked, having their credentials stolen/superseded or exploited security vulnerabilities. A data breach occurs when a person is able to access, copy, transfer or steal valuable information on a system without the permission of the owner. Unauthorized access refers to sharing information with other people without making them aware of such shared information unlike when dealing with a data breach where there is direct access to or theft of data that attracts financial impacts and legal and reputational damages to individuals and businesses alike.

Common Causes of Unauthorized Access and Data Breaches

There is a variety of other causes that may result in unauthorized penetrations and data loss. Simple and regular passwords is a call to a cyber-attack because they are easy to crack and thus your accounts. Phishing refers to those attacks that deceive users to satisfy them through phony mails or sites. Provided a software vulnerability remains unaddressed, hackers would exploit the loopholes. Information is subject to theft or leakage since some of their staff members or contractors have distorted the access to their systems. Some of the Hacker intrusion techniques and tools are the Malware, brute force and SQL injection.

Impacts of Unauthorized Access and Data Breaches

The outcome of unwanted access and breach of information can be very exigent. Companies Risk of loss of business funds can arise through theft of property, litigation by citizens and shareholders, as well as via fines imposed by regulation agencies due to non-conformance with the regulations. When the reputation of a firm is spoilt, the firm will not be able to get new customers and the chances of getting business will be on the low scale. Organizations are fined because of a data breach due to laws like GDPR, HIPAA and CCPA. Once your personal data is lost, a thief may blackmail you and buy an identity, conduct fraud and jeopardize your privacy in the future. In such critical areas as healthcare and finance, cyberattacks can disrupt significant processes and endanger the safety of all people.

Prevention Measures Against Unauthorized Access and Data Breaches

Providing the organizational protection should be strong due to measures like MFA and biometric verification. Updates and patches to your software ensure that security issues are solved. An adequate education of employees would save the company against mining through phishing and social engineering. When the data is encrypted they cannot be accessed or read by any third party who gets a hold of it. The principle of the least privilege is one such measure where users get to do only what is necessary, and not more. Solutions software like SIEM (Security Information and Event Management) can both discover and fire upon any suspicious activities in real time.

Response to a Data Breach:

In case a violation occurs, you must act with speed. Containment or isolation, of infected systems so as not to jeopardize the environment is the main priority. Then analysts investigate the incident in order to determine the cause behind breaking it, the extent of the accessed and the number of affected. According to the legislation, the people involved and the authorities should be informed about the event within 72 hours (as the GDPR states). After the recovery of the data is complete, the next thing put under consideration must be how to enhance the defense such that fewer incidences would occur. Through the post-breach analysis, companies can revise their safety policies, conduct more effective trainings of the employees and anticipate future misfortune (Posey Garrison & Ncube, 2011; Raghupathi et al., 2023; Seh et al., 2020; Kolhar & Sridevi, 2025).

2.3 Weak Authentication and Password Exploits

Weak authentication occurs where organizations are employing access codes that are easily compromised like easy passwords or regular log in information. The criminals exploit such mistakes to access your accounts, your network or personal information they have no right to. Many users put themselves in a vulnerable position by reusing passwords, by failing to make use of MFA, and by not altering default log in credentials. Hackers can steal information, plant malware or attack other systems when they can do so. In the same way, organizations should ensure the passwords are more demanding and use MFA to prevent unauthorized access. When there is insufficient protection, weak authentication remains one of the major causes of cyber breaches and cyber-attacks across the globe.

Brute-Force Attacks: These attacks are achieved when the hackers use software to run through numerous numbers of passwords one at a time. These passwords will be cracked easily as they are short and uncomplicated. These methods are able to crack into moderately difficult passwords very fast because of computing power available. Firms can fight these assaults by having strong password policies, disabling systems after a certain amount of failed attempts, as well as rate-limiting. In the event that protection does not exist, it is possible that non-authorized users can log in and steal data and breach the system via brute-force hacks.

Credential Stuffing: Credential stuffing refers to an attempt to use stolen logins and passwords during a previous breach on other accounts that the victim has used the same login and password. Some individuals share the password to various websites and this is why this form of attack is so efficient. Hackers keep logging in through computer programs to various systems whereby they can view other people emails, banks account, employee account among others without authorization. As opposed to usernames and passwords, fingerprint lasts longer, and monitors any accidental log in activity. Firms can erect platforms that detect bots in order to combat bot attacks. Failing to handle this risk exposes the accounts to a risk of being compromised by another person who can fraudulently use it.

Dictionary Attacks: Sometimes when dictionary attack occurs; the computers utilize the available lists of guesses, in order to attempt the login credentials faster than the brute force. This is in contrast to blind guessing, as the attacks exploit what users tend to use as their passwords. Attackers are more successful with the use of leaked lists dictionaries. To protect you against dictionary attack, you are always advised to use passwords that incorporate the use of numbers, symbols and capital and small letters. Also, such attacks are preventable with the locking of accounts and the use of MFA. Not having the appropriate security can lead to such that weak passwords can be used to find sensitive information or access a system in situations where there are dictionary attacks.

Phishing and Keylogging: Keylogging and phishing are two ways through which a thief can get hold of a password. In phishing, the scammers may send letters that mimic legitimate mail or display phony account sign-in pages, expecting copies of the information to be disclosed. Keylogging software has the ability to act secretively and records all the passwords that are entered using the keyboard. The two methods of attacks exploit human errors to bypass defences. To avoid phishers, people should be taught about phishing, emails should pass through filters and malware-detecting endpoint security measures. The introduction of MFA entails confirming that you are who you say you are or better still using multiple authentication factors and plays an important role in averting cyber-attacks. No one knows phishing and keylogging very well and has no security blocks to use to protect his/her log-in details being stolen and used anywhere; in other words, all people fall under this.

Low-and-Slow: Low-and-slow attacks include a particular type of attack not previously widely known or reported, known as password spraying, where hackers use the same password on numerous accounts, as opposed to attempting numerous passwords on a single account. This leads to accounts not getting locked or detected by the security systems. The simplest kind of guesses often used by attackers against default or frequently used passwords to get access should be filtered out, or at least enhanced MFA enabled and anomalous logins monitored, which these are all considered a part of mitigation. Organizations require to educate users on the way to create unique passwords. Neglect of such items also enables the attacker to crack into various accounts using mere several attempts on passwords.

Take Advantage of Users with default Credentials: Most individuals do not change the default passwords of various devices, and in fact, most forget to change the passwords. Attackers can find anyone who utilizes these weak passwords, and this gives them access to routers, cameras and IoT devices within a short period. Once they are in, they can install a malware, steal your data or send the device to benefit a botnet. Once you make all the set up, make sure you employ alternative credentials and withdraw the use of any accounts that you are not utilizing. Segmentation of the network and firmware update are often of assistance to bring down the risks. When such critical activities are not taken, necessities can expose critical systems to easy and malicious attacks.

Prevention and Mitigation: To combat weak authentication, some of the policies that organizations should employ include establishment of minimum and secure password policies. Having multi-factor authentication ensures that it is easier and safer to log in because it requires your identity to be proved in a number of ways more than one. Password managers remember different passwords on behalf of the users. The other thing you will be required to monitor is malicious logins and have account lockouts in place in the case a user continues to produce inaccurate logins. Individuals need to be educated on good password hygiene and how to prevent phishing. The application of proactive techniques has the great impact of decreasing the possibility of your data being accessed by unauthorised individuals due to poor authentication (Joshi & Singh, 2017; Reshmi, 2021; Usman & Shami, 2013; Sridevi & Kolhar, 2025).

2.4 Denial-of-Service (DoS) and Botnet Attacks

Figure 1.

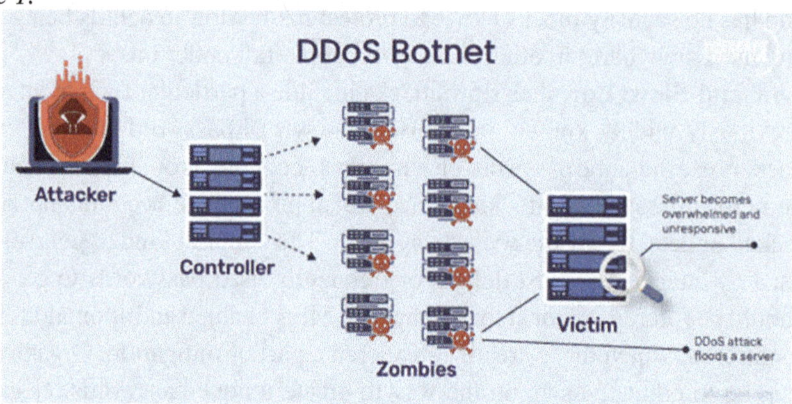

The illustration depicts how a DDoS botnet attack will work in terms that an intended network or site will remain inaccessible to its consumers since they are suffocated by bulk traffic of various sources. An attack is a combination of four key components working in unison that is the Attacker, Controller, zombie devices and the Victim server. It all begins when the Attacker also referred to as a bad actor sets up the attack. Having infected many computers and IoT devices or servers, this malware person or group of persons transform them into Zombies otherwise known as bots. In most cases, the gadgets are assaulted by the phishing attacks, fixed bug holes or inexpert logon data. Our purpose using Humanizer is to make your writing sound natural and bring more of it like a regular writing. Using our technology, you can get on with your ideas instead of being mired in wordiness, be it when writing an essay or a report, or just emailing. You are able to transform complex phrases into interesting readable material with just clicking some keys. Not only does this enhance your ability to write and make your work very smooth, it also saves you a lot of time. Just give it a go and the experience of writing will be much simpler by pressing the Humanize button and letting our tools do the heavy lifting, unlike the DoS attack which is easily mitigated, DDoS attack is more difficult to stop because it uses thousands of devices to become more powerful. Typical DDoS attacks would involve volumetric forms of denial-of-service attack, protocol attackers, protocol abusers, which exploit network layers, and application attackers, which exploit some specific services. To overcome such attacks, organizations employ strategies such as filtering traffic, rate limitation, cloud-based DDoS protection, network monitoring to detect something out of the usual. What is more, the devices should be secured using anti-malware, strong passwords, and regular updates to avoid the involvement in botnets. The diagram focuses on the effectiveness of DDoS botnets in causing damages as well as the importance of proactive cybersecurity to safeguard cyber infrastructure on the internet spaces (Alomari et al., 2012; Kalinin et al., 2021; Kuzlu et al., 2021; Salim et al., 2020; Sridevi & Kolhar, 2025).

3. CASE STUDIES OF SMART DEVICE SECURITY BREACHES

Table 1.

Case Study	Year	Target Devices	Attack Method	Impact	Lessons Learned
Mirai Botnet	2016	IoT cameras, routers	Exploited default credentials to create botnet for DDoS attacks	Disrupted major platforms (Twitter, Netflix) via Dyn DNS outage	Enforce unique passwords, regular firmware updates, and disable default logins
Ring Doorbell Hacks	2019-2020	Amazon Ring doorbells	Credential stuffing to access cameras/microphones	Privacy violations, harassment, lawsuits	Mandate 2FA, educate users on password security
Stuxnet Worm	2010	Industrial IoT (nuclear centrifuges)	Zero-day exploits to physically sabotage equipment	Destroyed uranium enrichment infrastructure	Air-gap critical systems, implement network segmentation

continued on following page

Table 1. Continued

Case Study	Year	Target Devices	Attack Method	Impact	Lessons Learned
Verkada Camera Breach	2021	Enterprise security cameras	Exploited shared admin credentials to access 150K live feeds	Exposed sensitive footage (Tesla, prisons)	Adopt role-based access controls and zero-trust policies
Smart Thermostat Ransomware	2022	Nest thermostats	Ransomware locked users out during extreme weather	Life-threatening disruptions, forced ransom payments	Ensure offline backup modes and regular patch updates

4. MITIGATION STRATEGIES AND SECURITY FRAMEWORKS

Safe Device Onboarding and authentication: Insecure credentials and unauthorized access to devices remain the largest threats to IoT. Multi-Factor Authentication (MFA) mitigates the chance of a breach by adding such layers as biometrics or one-time passwords. Due to the certificate-based authentication, only validated devices are permitted to attach to networks through a PKI. To eliminate lateral attacks, Zero-Trust principles involve constant revalidation even with internal requests. These security measures avoid credential stuffing and brute force attacks which occur often in attack cases such as Mirai. Companies can minimize the threats posed by the use of default passwords and credentials stolen credentials by carrying out strict identity authentication and assuring them that only trusted devices will be running in networks.

Bulletist Secure Communication: Over the air IoT Data Can be Captured. End-to-End Encryption (E2EE) prevents eavesdropping on data that is in transit as well as when it is stored. As opposed to HTTP that is a susceptible protocol, TLS/ HTTPS encrypts the communications. Misuse or unauthorized access is blocked by the secure APIs using the rate-limiting and OAuth 2.0. With the illustration of the Verkada hack, such measures are protective against leaks of data and man-in-the-middle attacks. Encryption ensures data privacy and even when the devices are compromised, the information cannot be used by the attackers.

Routine Firmware Updates & Patch Management: Firmware is another area that is commonly exploited by IoT hackers in the case of Mirai botnet and Stuxnet worm attacks. OTA updates should be automated to make maintenance of patches across devices possible without intervention because it is imperative that devices are updated with the most important security patches. Malicious tampering is avoided during firmware updates because they are cryptographically signed and secure boots are used. It should also be a commitment on the part of the manufacturers to release patches throughout the lifecycle of the device as part of the long-term support. With Vulnerability Disclosure Programs (VDPs), ethical hackers will be encouraged to report vulnerabilities before then get exploited by hackers. The management of patches is vital in maintaining security in interconnected ecosystems because IoT products are prone to known attacks when exposed to patches once in a long time.

Network Segmentation & Monitoring: Since the Mirai botnet has utilized the flat network architecture as a launching point to the subsequent lateral attacks, segmenting the network and monitoring activities proves to be an effective measure. Using network segmentation, one can minimize this risk by isolating IoT devices in various VLANs or micro-segments and not permitting an unauthorized flow. The traffic is, at the same time, monitored by Intrusion Detection/Prevention Systems (IDS/IPS) in order to detect any suspicious activity or botnet traffic. Using AI, behavioral analytics is practiced with the implementation of more advanced techniques to recognize abnormal threads, such as unauthorized data exfiltration with no warning. With demanding firewall policies and access controls combined with segmentation and monitoring, adversaries cannot move to other critical systems even in the case one of the devices was compromised since it serves as a layer of defense. This strategy plays a very important role in the security of large scale IoT applications.

Supply Chain and Vendor Risk Management: The Solar Winds and Colonial Pipeline attacks are just two of many examples proving that third-party components that are often used will create a security vulnerability, and IoT security is as weak as its weakest link. The initial steps in a robust vendor risk management strategy are software bill of materials (SBOM) tracking to identify exploitable dependencies, security audits to assess development practices of vendors. Devices are kept clean and trusted through the installment of a Hardware Root of Trust (like TPM or HSMs) all the way up to the deployment. Organizations should also promote contractual security necessities and continuous third-party risk surveillance. By securing the supply chain, a company can ensure end-to-end reliability of connected devices components and prevent compromised components affecting IoT systems.

Privacy by Design & Reg T Compliance: Privacy breaches are a critical issue as we see with incidents as with the Ring camera hacks because IoT devices are often capable of sensitive data collection on users. Privacy by Design incorporates data protection in Internet of Things systems in its early stages by incorporating concepts of data minimization, by enabling end to end encryption, and by implementing procedures to obtain user consent. It can be made sure by legal compliance with such laws as the CCPA or GDPR that presuppose transparency in data gathering and breach reporting practices. Separate administration of anonymization tools also reduces the risk to privacy to even greater levels By implementing such procedures, the businesses can demonstrate their commitment to safeguarding personal information in the world that is increasingly interconnected as well as avoiding the fines that can be quite substantial and garnering customer trust (Rahayu & Aprillia, 2025; Lokare, n.d.; Rahayu & Aprillia, 2025).

4.1 NIST IoT Cybersecurity Framework

These three cores for 71 conversion standard concepts in the NIST IoT Cybersecurity Framework are device identification, authentication, and data protection offering an organized method of tackling IoT related menace. It gives a significant focus to the planning of incident response with the aim of reducing the breaches and securing the update processes in order to correct the vulnerabilities. Its flexible architecture helps the business to support risk assessment, implementation of security and sustainability in continuity of IoT-based ecosystems. The compliance with the NIST standards helps the businesses to deal with the traditionally widespread threats like unauthorized access and leak data and regulatory changes. This framework is a critical framework used both in the consumer and business context to secure network gadgets

ISO/IEC 27001 on IoT: The standard of ISO/IEC 27001 employs their robust information security management system (ISMS) to the IoT environment to ascertains the effective systematic methods of managing risks. It needs cryptographic protection of data integrity, access control, that limits the unwanted use, and asset management of IoT devices. Through the adoption of risk analysis process and continuous improvement process as outlined in ISO 27001, organizations will be in a position to be compliant and prevent breach on IoT implementation. It is a generally accepted framework that provides a systematic approach in securing interconnected gadgets, data traffic and infrastructure against the evolving cyberattacks and is compatible with IoT particularities.

OWASP IoT Top 10: The OWASP IoT Top 10 enumerates several serious security threats with which connected devices have to grapple, such as weak credentials, and unreliable network services and lack of secure update mechanisms. Instead, it exhibits weaknesses like the insufficient physical security, unsecure storage devices, and the absence of the protection of privacy. By fixing such weakness such as clearing the default password and securing the communication with encryption algorithm, regular attack types such as botnets and data exposures can be prevented. This handy guide can assist designers and institutions to set priorities when it comes to optimizing security of their products against IoT executions, so as to make them less vulnerable to hacks that destroy the use of their products, their own network connections, and their privacy.

Industrial IoT Frameworks (ISA/IEC 62443): ISA/IEC 62443 is a framework that provides robust security of the operation technology (OT) and industrial internet of things (IIoT) system. It deters such risks as supply chain attacks, malware, and unauthorized access as it features the ability of zonal segmentation, secure remote access, and active monitoring. The model lays a lot of emphasis on vulnerability management, asset inventory, and secure development process of industrial devices. Through adoption of ISA/IEC 62443, organizations will be able to achieve resistance to threats like Stuxnet attack or other threats that would disorient an organization like the Colonial Pipeline. This will protect important infrastructure like plant and power grid against cyber-physical assaults.

Regulatory Mandates (EU CRA, U.S. IoT Act): The new policies such as the U.S. IoT Cybersecurity Improvement Act or the EU Cyber Resilience Act (CRA) are requesting that IoT devices should be compliant with security standards to improve the overall situation of raising cybersecurity threats. These policies are vulnerability disclosure policies, default passwords, and security updates with minimum five years life cycle. The U.S. legislation defines minimum requirements of the federal procurement of IoT, and the CRA provides compliance with the cybersecurity marking requirements (CE). There are bans to the market and penalties in case of noncompliance. To have safer connected devices and to minimize such threats like botnets (Mirai) or privacy loss (Verkada) these regulations are forcing the manufacturers to utilize security-by-design (Alshar'e, 2023; Davis et al., 2020; Lee, 2020; Rahayu & Aprillia, 2025; Taherdoost, 2022; Sridevi & Kolhar, 2026).

5. FUTURE TRENDS AND CHALLENGES IN SMART DEVICE SECURITY

Future security of smart devices will witness innovations in the sphere of threat detection using AI, block chain technology securing transactions with data and diminishing the level of vulnerability by the means of zero-trust design. Nevertheless, there are still problems, such as more complicated cyberattacks, no single security guidelines, and higher attack surface with increased IoT. Moreover, security strategies will be defined by privacy related issues and regulation. There will need to be just the right amount of innovation vs. robust security, as smart gadgets are more than ever being deployed in critical infrastructure and as part of our day-to-day life.

5.1 Emerging Threats in IoT Ecosystems

AI powered Cyberattack: Artificial intelligence is used by cybercriminals to enhance and automate the attacks on internet of things devices. Machine learning provides hackers with the possibility to find security vulnerabilities, to evade traditional defense systems, and perform complex, multi-tier and sophisticated attacks. It is also made hard by the fact that the malware propagated by AI on the machines makes use of real-time adaptation. In any case, hackers might even use AI to replicate the regular traffic in the network to beat the anomaly-based security systems. Due to this dynamic threat, AI-enhanced tools in cybersecurity are required to preempt, detect and prevent attacks before they can achieve maliciousness on the smart device.

Botnet-based DDoS Attacks: Botnet constitutes the network of compromised devices ironically controlled by the hackers in order to launch a DDoS Attack using an insecure camera or router as an exemplar of that. It is these botnets that perform Massive Distributed Denial of Service (DDoS) attacks, and the traffic on the target server overwhelms it, causing server outages. The 2016 botnet attack on Mirai revealed the vulnerability of IoT ecosystems in compromising the working of the major online services. The measures that can prevent such attacks include the regular update of firmware, deactivation of default passwords, and enhanced device authentication.

Supply Chain Vulnerabilities: Many IoT gadgets rely on other exterior equipment and software to be operational and these could be tampered with during manufacturing or distribution. Backdoors can be constructed by the hackers by taking advantage of the vendor security flaws or implanting malicious code on a firmware. These tampered machines pose a threat in the long run after they have been implemented. To ensure integrity prior to the delivery of devices to the customers or the businesses, strict supply chain audits, safe boot procedures and tamper proof hardware designs would need to be put in place as part of mitigation.

Edge Computing Hazard: Incurs edge computing hazards since by inclusion of processing at or near the sites that the IoT equipment reside at, the latency is lowered rather than centrally processing all initiations. Nonetheless, on the one hand, this decentralization opens more attack surfaces. The security on local edge nodes may not be very good and this subjects them to manipulation or data interceptions. The attackers can use the vulnerability of the edge weak auth or unencrypted communications. Such solutions include zero-trust architecture, end-to-end encryption, continuous monitoring that can protect edge-enabled IoT ecosystems against new threats.

Physical Tampering: The majority of the IoT devices such as industrial sensors and streetlights are exposed to the physical environment as opposed to typical IT systems. They can also be physically compromised by the attackers who want to install malware, delete information or disrupt services. In the case of smart thermostat, for instance, one can end up manipulating it and access a building unauthorizedly. Among countermeasures in identifying and eliminating physical breaches, one should mention the remoteness of intactness of the equipment, geofencing and tamperproof devices.

Invading Privacy: Smart home devices, such as security cameras, voice assistants, collect such a lot of personal data that it is super easy to access them and spy on the owner illegally. A sensitive user data might be revealed as a result of inefficient encryption or improperly set cloud storage. More imperative regulations about data protection (like the GDPR) as well as user privacy setting controls are essential to prevent any abuse and ensure laws are followed (Aldahmani et al., 2023; Cvitić et al., 2023; Kolluru et al., 2019; Lone et al., 2023; Shafique et al., 2020).

5.2 Advancements in Smart Device Security Technologies

Cybersecurity technologies are developing to combat new threats as smart devices become more commonplace. Real-time threat detection is now possible thanks to AI and machine learning, which examine behavioural patterns and spot irregularities in device activity. By generating tamper-proof logs for Internet of Things transactions and preventing unwanted changes, blockchain technology improves data integrity. Insider threats are reduced by Zero Trust Architecture (ZTA), which guarantees rigorous identity verification for each device and user. By embedding encryption keys directly into chips, hardware-based security measures like Secure Elements and Trusted Platform Modules (TPMs) guard against physical tampering. Vulnerabilities are decreased by automated patch management systems, which guarantee timely firmware updates. Sensitive information is protected even in the event of interception thanks to homomorphic encryption, which enables data processing without decryption. Access controls are further strengthened by multi-factor authentication (MFA) and behavioral biometrics (such as keystroke dynamics). Federated learning improves privacy by facilitating collaborative threat intelligence without disclosing raw data. To guarantee baseline protections, governments and businesses are also promoting standardized security certifications (such as the UL IoT Security Rating). Together, these developments increase the resilience of smart devices, striking a balance between strong security and innovation in a world growing more interconnected by the day (Rahayu & Aprillia, 2025).

6. CONCLUSION

Unquestionably, the quick spread of smart devices has changed modern life, but it has also brought with it difficult cybersecurity issues. Risks from ransomware and AI-powered cyberattacks to supply chain weaknesses and privacy violations increase with the size of IoT ecosystems. Although security is being improved by innovations like block chains, AI-driven threat detection, and zero-trust architectures, proactive steps must be taken to guarantee strong defence. Stakeholders must use a multi-layered strategy to improve IoT security. By incorporating hardware-based safeguards like TPMs and guaranteeing end-to-end encryption, manufacturers should give security-by-design top priority. Strong authentication methods must be required in place of default passwords. To quickly fix vulnerabilities, regular firmware updates and automated patch management ought to be the norm. In order to hold manufacturers responsible, governments and regulatory agencies are essential in implementing universal security standards, such as the requirement to adhere to frameworks like NIST or GDPR. Vigilance is required of both consumers and businesses, who should segment IoT networks, disable unused features, and keep an eye out for unusual device activity. Collaboration is also essential. Sharing threat intelligence across the industry can aid in anticipating new attack avenues. Putting money into employee education and public awareness initiatives will guarantee that users are aware of dangers like phishing and physical manipulation. Redundancy and air-gapped backups can lessen the effects of ransomware on vital infrastructure. In the end, protecting IoT necessitates a team effort that strikes a balance between resilience and innovation. We may protect smart devices from changing threats and realize their full potential in a connected world by combining cutting-edge technologies, enforcing strict regulations, and encouraging a culture of cybersecurity awareness. Now is the moment to take action because inaction puts global infrastructure, privacy, and safety at risk in addition to data breaches.

Publisher's Note

A correction to this manuscript has been published:

Correction Notice: Cybersecurity in Smart Devices

Correction Date: November 12, 2025

It was recently brought to our attention that the chapter originally submitted by *Amrutha Kolhar* and *Sridevi* was mistakenly replaced with the text of a different chapter authored by *Tarun Vashishth, Vikas Sharma, Sharad Kumar, Puneet Chauhan, Mukesh Sharma,* and *Rajeev Sharma.*

This error has now been corrected. The proper chapter by *Amrutha Kolhar* and *Sridevi* has been reinstated in place of the incorrect version.

REFERENCES

Aldahmani, A., Ouni, B., Lestable, T., & Debbah, M. (2023). Cyber-Security of Embedded IoTs in Smart Homes: Challenges, Requirements, Countermeasures, and Trends. *IEEE Open Journal of Vehicular Technology*, *4*(January), 281–292. DOI: 10.1109/OJVT.2023.3234069

Alomari, E., Manickam, S. B., Gupta, B., Karuppayah, S., & Alfaris, R. (2012). Botnet-based Distributed Denial of Service (DDoS) Attacks on Web Servers: Classification and Art. *International Journal of Computer Applications*, *49*(7), 24–32. DOI: 10.5120/7640-0724

Alshar'e, M. (2023). Cyber Security Framework Selection: Comparision of Nist and Iso27001. *Applied Computing Journal*, *3*(1), 245–255. https://doi.org/10.52098/acj.202364

Alshboul, Y., Bsoul, A. A. R., & Zamil, AL, M., & Samarah, S. (2021). Cybersecurity of Smart Home Systems: Sensor Identity Protection. *Journal of Network and Systems Management*, *29*(3), 1–27. DOI: 10.1007/s10922-021-09586-9

Angyalos, Z., Botos, S., & Szilagyi, R. (2022). The importance of cybersecurity in modern agriculture. *Agrárinformatika Folyóirat*, *12*(2). Advance online publication. DOI: 10.17700/jai.2021.12.2.604

Avancini, D. B., Rodrigues, J. J. P. C., Martins, S. G. B., Rabêlo, R. A. L., Al-Muhtadi, J., & Solic, P. (2019). Energy meters evolution in smart grids: A review. *Journal of Cleaner Production*, *217*, 702–715. DOI: 10.1016/j.jclepro.2019.01.229

Bonaventura, D., Esposito, S., & Bella, G. (2025). A case of smart devices that compromise home cybersecurity. *Computers and Security, 151* (July 2024), 104286. DOI: 10.1016/j.cose.2024.104286

Brewer, R. (2016). Ransomware attacks: Detection, prevention and cure. *Network Security, 2016*(9), 5–9. DOI: 10.1016/S1353-4858(16)30086-1

Cvitić, I., Peraković, D., Periša, M., Jevremović, A., & Shalaginov, A. (2023). An Overview of Smart Home IoT Trends and related Cybersecurity Challenges. *Mobile Networks and Applications, 28*(4), 1334–1348. DOI: 10.1007/s11036-022-02055-w

Davis, B. D., Mason, J. C., & Anwar, M. (2020). Vulnerability Studies and Security Postures of IoT Devices: A Smart Home Case Study. *IEEE Internet of Things Journal, 7*(10), 10102–10110. https://doi.org/10.1109/JIOT.2020.2983983

Dean, , E. AAvenue, , M. (2011). *Ransomware: a research and personal case study of dealing with this nasty malware. 14*, 43–46.

Gundoor, T.K. & Sridevi. (2024). Optimized Feature Selection and classification for Non-Portable Executable Malware. *International Journal of Communication Networks and Information Security (IJCNIS), 16*(4), 546–552. Retrieved from https://ijcnis.org/index.php/ijcnis/article/view/7107

Gundoor, T. K. (2022). IoT-Enabled 5G Networks for Secure Communication. In *Information Security Practices for the Internet of Things, 5G, and Next-Generation Wireless Networks* (pp. 1-29). IGI Global.

Gundoor, T. K., & Sridevi, (2022) Identification of Dominant Features in Non-Portable Executable Malicious File. *Second International Conference on Computer Science, Engineering and Applications (ICCSEA)*, Gunupur, India, pp. 1-6, doi: DOI: 10.1109/ICCSEA54677.2022.9936451

Gundoor, T. K., Sridevi, & Mulimani, R. (2025). AI-Based Solutions for Malware Detection and Prevention. In M. Almaiah & Y. Maleh (Eds.), *Machine Intelligence Applications in Cyber-Risk Management* (pp. 107-134). IGI Global Scientific Publishing. https://doi.org/10.4018/979-8-3693-7540-2.ch006

Joshi, C., & Singh, U. K. (2017). Information security risks management framework – A step towards mitigating security risks in university network. *Journal of Information Security and Applications, 35*, 128–137. DOI: 10.1016/j.jisa.2017.06.006

Kalinin, M., Krundyshev, V., & Zegzhda, P. (2021). Cybersecurity risk assessment in smart city infrastructures. *Machines (Basel), 9*(4). Advance online publication. DOI: 10.3390/machines9040078

Kara, I., & Aydos, M. (2022). The rise of ransomware: Forensic analysis for windows based ransomware attacks. *Expert Systems with Applications, 190*(December 2020), 116198. DOI: 10.1016/j.eswa.2021.116198

Kolhar, A. & Sridevi. (2025). Future Trends and Innovation in Machine Intelligence for Cyber Risk Management. In M. Almaiah & Y. Maleh (Eds.), *Machine Intelligence Applications in Cyber-Risk Management* (pp. 415-438). IGI Global Scientific Publishing. https://doi.org/10.4018/979-8-3693-7540-2.ch018.

Kolhar, A. & Sridevi (March, 2025) Optimizing IoT for secure authentication and interoperability: API frameworks using rolling code pattern" vol. 14, issue 03 03/23. DOI: 10.48047/IJIEMR/V14/ISSUE

Kolluru, V., Mungara, S., & Chintakunta, A. N. (2019). Securing the Iot Ecosystem: Challenges and Innovations in Smart Device Cybersecurity. *International Journal on Cryptography and Information Security, 9*(2), 37–51. DOI: 10.5121/ijcis.2019.9203

Kuzlu, M., Fair, C., & Guler, O. (2021). Role of Artificial Intelligence in the Internet of Things (IoT) cybersecurity. *Discover Internet of Things, 1*(1). Advance online publication. DOI: 10.1007/s43926-020-00001-4

Lee, I. (2020). Internet of Things (IoT) cybersecurity: Literature review and iot cyber risk management. *Future Internet, 12*(9). Advance online publication. DOI: 10.3390/FI12090157

Lokare, A. (n.d.). *Integrating Cybersecurity Frameworks into IT Security : A Comprehensive Analysis of Threat Mitigation Strategies and Adaptive Technologies.*

Lone, A. N., Mustajab, S., & Alam, M. (2023). A comprehensive study on cybersecurity challenges and opportunities in the IoT world. *Security and Privacy, 6*(6). Advance online publication. DOI: 10.1002/spy2.318

Posey Garrison, C., & Ncube, M. (2011). A longitudinal analysis of data breaches. *Information Management & Computer Security, 19*(4), 216–230. DOI: 10.1108/09685221111173049

Raghupathi, W., Raghupathi, V., & Saharia, A. (2023). Analyzing Health Data Breaches: A Visual Analytics Approach. *AppliedMath, 3*(1), 175–199. DOI: 10.3390/appliedmath3010011

Rahayu, E. R., & Aprillia, A. (2025). *Cybersecurity in the Age of IoT and Developing Frameworks for Securing Smart Devices and Networks.*, 2(1), 46–54.

Raimundo, R. J., & Rosário, A. T. (2022). Cybersecurity in the Internet of Things in Industrial Management. *Applied Sciences (Switzerland)*, *12*(3). Advance online publication. DOI: 10.3390/app12031598

Reshmi, T. R. (2021). Information security breaches due to ransomware attacks - a systematic literature review. *International Journal of Information Management Data Insights*, *1*(2), 100013. DOI: 10.1016/j.jjimei.2021.100013

Salim, M. M., Rathore, S., & Park, J. H. (2020). Distributed denial of service attacks and its defenses in IoT: A survey. *The Journal of Supercomputing*, *76*(7), 5320–5363. DOI: 10.1007/s11227-019-02945-z

Seh, A. H., Zarour, M., Alenezi, M., Sarkar, A. K., Agrawal, A., Kumar, R., & Khan, R. A. (2020). Healthcare data breaches: Insights and implications. *Healthcare (Switzerland)*, *8*(2). Advance online publication. DOI: 10.3390/healthcare8020133

Shafique, K., Khawaja, B. A., Sabir, F., Qazi, S., & Mustaqim, M. (2020). Internet of things (IoT) for next-generation smart systems: A review of current challenges, future trends and prospects for emerging 5G-IoT Scenarios. *IEEE Access : Practical Innovations, Open Solutions*, *8*, 23022–23040. DOI: 10.1109/ACCESS.2020.2970118

Silva, J. A. H., López, L. I. B., Caraguay, Á. L. V., & Hernández-álvarez, M. (2019). A survey on situational awareness of ransomware attacks-detection and prevention parameters. *Remote Sensing*, *11*(10). Advance online publication. DOI: 10.3390/rs11101168

Sridevi & Gundoor. T.K. (2024). Artificial Intelligence on Knowledge Management and Industry Revolution 4.0. In R. Kumar, V. Jain, V.C. Ibarra, C.A. Talib and V. Kukreja (eds) Knowledge Management and Industry Revolution 4.0. https://doi.org/10.1002/9781394242641.ch6

Sridevi, , & Gundoor, , T.K. (2025). Identifying Nobel Features in Non-Portable Executable Malware Files. *IAENG International Journal of Computer Science*, *52*(1), 121–129.

Sridevi, , & Gundoor, , T.K. (2025). ResNet50MalClassifier: Deep Convolutional Neural Networks. *IAENG International Journal of Computer Science*, *52*(2), 287–297.

Sridevi, Gundoor, T. K., & Mulimani, R. (2025). Integrating Machine Learning Techniques for Comprehensive Malware Classification. In Minakshi, A. Bijalwan, & T. Kumar (Eds.), *Exploiting Machine Learning for Robust Security* (pp. 165-182). IGI Global Scientific Publishing. https://doi.org/10.4018/979-8-3693-7758-1.ch008

Sridevi & Kolhar. A. (2025). Machine Learning Algorithms and IoT Sensors for Securing the Networks. In Minakshi, A. Bijalwan, & T. Kumar (Eds.), *Exploiting Machine Learning for Robust Security* (pp. 183-210). IGI Global Scientific Publishing. https://doi.org/10.4018/979-8-3693-7758-1.ch009

Sridevi & Kolhar. A. (2025). Energy-Efficiency Strategies for Wireless Sensor Networks in IoT. In A. Sathio, M. Rind, S. Awan, & A. Junejo (Eds.), *Energy-Efficient Deep Learning Approaches in IoT, Fog, and Green Blockchain Revolution* (pp. 167-192). IGI Global Scientific Publishing. https://doi.org/10.4018/979-8-3373-0300-0.ch006

Sridevi & Kolhar. A. (2026). Fundamentals of 6G Networks. In R. Shaikh (Ed.), *6G Networks and AI-Driven Cybersecurity* (pp. 1-32). IGI Global Scientific Publishing. DOI: 10.4018/979-8-3373-0568-4.ch001

Suarez-Tangil, G., Tapiador, J. E., Peris-Lopez, P., & Ribagorda, A. (2014). Evolution, detection and analysis of malware for smart devices. *IEEE Communications Surveys and Tutorials*, *16*(2), 961–987. DOI: 10.1109/SURV.2013.101613.00077

Sun, C. C., Sebastian Cardenas, D. J., Hahn, A., & Liu, C. C. (2021). Intrusion Detection for Cybersecurity of Smart Meters. *IEEE Transactions on Smart Grid*, *12*(1), 612–622. DOI: 10.1109/TSG.2020.3010230

Sun, Y., & Li, S. (2021). A systematic review of the research framework and evolution of smart homes based on the internet of things. *Telecommunication Systems*, *77*(3), 597–623. DOI: 10.1007/s11235-021-00787-w

Taherdoost, H. (2022). Understanding Cybersecurity Frameworks and Information Security Standards—A Review and Comprehensive Overview. *Electronics (Switzerland)*, *11*(14). Advance online publication. DOI: 10.3390/electronics11142181

Tailor, J. P., & Patel, A. D. (2017). A comprehensive survey: Ransomware attacks prevention. *Monitoring and Damage Control*, *IV*(June), 116–121.

Usman, A., & Shami, S. H. (2013). Evolution of communication technologies for smart grid applications. *Renewable & Sustainable Energy Reviews*, *19*, 191–199. DOI: 10.1016/j.rser.2012.11.002

Chapter 3
Automatizing Crypto Asset Tracking in Cyber Crimes

Mehmet Kaya
Ahmet Yesevi University, Turkey

Gurkan Tuna
https://orcid.org/0000-0002-6466-4696
Trakya University, Turkey

ABSTRACT

Blockchain technology has created a major transformation in the digital world with features such as decentralization, security, transparency, and traceability. Emerging with Nakamoto's introduction of Bitcoin in 2009, this technology finds applications in various sectors, primarily finance, supply chain, healthcare, and public services. The fundamental principles of blockchain are based on elements such as hashing, distributed ledger technology (DLT), and consensus mechanisms. Innovative technologies such as smart contracts and side chains increase the potential of this system. Cryptocurrencies are an application area of blockchain technology and come across different types such as bitcoin, altcoins, and NFTs. APIs facilitate software development processes and enable integrating systems with blockchain. In the investigative phases, blockchain traceability provides a significant advantage in solving crimes like crypto fraud. This study aims to automate the manual tracking of crypto-related criminal transactions by implementing an algorithm based on the FIFO principle.

DOI: 10.4018/979-8-3373-2282-7.ch003

INTRODUCTION

Blockchain technology has provided a revolutionary transformation in the digital world with features such as security, transparency, decentralization, and traceability. Introduced by Nakamoto with Bitcoin in 2009, this technology has quickly expanded its impact and found application in a variety of fields, including public services, healthcare, and supply chains, particularly in the finance industry (Frizzo-Barker, Chow-White, Adams, Mentanko, Ha, & Green, 2020). Building blocks like distributed ledger technology, hashing, smart contracts, and consensus mechanisms form the foundation of blockchain's fundamental operations (Tripathi, Ahad, & Casalino, 2023; A. K. Abed, 2025; Khalaf & Steiti, 2024; Zaman & Mazinani, 2023).

By guaranteeing the safe storage of data and the traceability of transactions, these building blocks offer high security, cost savings, and operational efficiency across a range of industries (Ang et al., 2025; AlShuaibi et al., 2025; Almelehy et al., 2025. Innovative digital assets like cryptocurrencies and their related altcoins, or non-fungible tokens, are a significant application area for blockchain technology. But these digital assets' anonymity also makes it easier for crimes like money laundering, fraud, and illicit transactions to occur. Tracking crypto asset transfers by hand is a laborious and error-prone procedure, even though the blockchain network's traceability feature is a crucial tool in the detection and resolution of these crimes (Aldossary et al., 2024; Ali and Shehab, 2023; Davarasan et al., 2024; Burhanuddin, 2023; Jishkariani, 2024; Saleh et al., 2023).

The aim of this chapter is to explain how cryptocurrrency transfers are realized and develop an application using an algorithm that adheres to the First-In-First-Out (FIFO) principle to automatically analyze cryptocurrency transfers. WinForms technology and C# programming language have been used to create a software application. In order to track cryptocurrency transactions more quickly and effectively, the application intends to automate manual processes and offer better defenses against blockchain-based fraud. It is desired to make a substantial contribution from a technical and legal perspective by showcasing the security and transparency capabilities of blockchain technology.

WHAT IS BLOCKCHAIN?

Using distributed ledger technology, Nakamoto's Bitcoin-based electronic cryptocurrency payment system, created in 2009, allows for safe and transparent network transaction verification (Tripathi, Ahad, & Casalino, 2023). Blockchain creates a structure that is resistant to fraud by sharing transactions that are encrypted using the hashing method among network members. This system ensures that transactions are verified without the need for any intermediaries, reducing intermediary-related errors and costs (Nakamoto, 2009). The advantages of blockchain, including trust, transparency, traceability, security, auditability, control, anonymity, cost savings, and scalability, are highlighted in the literature. Research shows that blockchain reduces transaction costs, increases supply chain performance, supports human rights protection, improves patient privacy in healthcare, and contributes to the circular economy by reducing the carbon footprint (Upadhyay, Mukhuty, Kumar, & Kazançoğlu, 2021; S. A. Abed & Gök, 2023; Al Barazanchi & Hashim, 2023; Ali et al., 2025; Gopalakrishnan et al., 2024; Kareem, 2024; Salih & Mahmood, 2024; Vaigandla, 2025).

By enabling safe execution, recording, and tracking of transactions, blockchain offers security and transparency. This structure is particularly ideal for increasing the security of digital assets and eliminating intermediaries (Yaga, Mell, Roby, & Scarfone, 2018). Every blockchain block includes a distinct hash code of the previous block as well as transactions that took place over time. Since the blocks are interconnected, any change to the content of one block will affect the entire chain. The blockchain's security is primarily due to its structure, which makes it extremely difficult to alter or manipulate data (Addula et al., 2025; Alshinwan et al., 2025; Albinhamad et al., 2025).

The fundamental idea behind blockchain technology is that, as a distributed ledger technology, every node maintains a copy of the ledger, and consensus processes are used to validate transactions (Ali, 2024; Al-Shareeda et al., 2024; Almaayah and Sulaiman, 2024; Alsahaim and Maayah, 2023. Proof of Work, one of the most popular consensus algorithms, requires nodes to solve challenging mathematical puzzles in order to validate transactions. Although this system's structure guarantees transaction security, it also uses more energy. In addition to Proof of Work, other consensus methods that use less energy include Proof of Stake (Bonneau, Miller, & Clark, 2015). The most important feature of blockchain technology is decentralization. Transactions on the blockchain take place without the need for a central authority or middleman, in contrast to traditional databases. This enables users to add transactions to the blockchain and independently verify them. Therefore, blockchain is a technology that has a lot of potential for application, particularly in fields where privacy and security are necessary (Tapscott & Tapscott, 2016; Mohammed & Aljanabi, 2023; Saleh, 2024).

The areas of use of blockchain extend beyond financial services and are also evident in different sectors. For example, blockchain technology in supply chain management provides the ability to track where products are in the supply process. This provides information about the source and originality of products and contributes to the prevention of counterfeiting (Saberi, Kouhizadeh, Sarkis, & Shen, 2019). Blockchain technology can be used to securely store and share patient data in the healthcare sector. More efficient data sharing between healthcare service providers is made possible while maintaining the privacy of patient information (Agbo, Mahmoud, & Eklund, 2019),

Blockchain Facts

Blockchain is a decentralized digital ledger system where data is stored transparently and reliably. This structure is based on the sequential storage of transactions in a chained sequence. Each new transaction is recorded as a block, and these blocks become irreversible and unchangeable with the chain they form over time (Yaga et al., 2018). In the fields of public services, healthcare, supply chain management, and finance, this technology is especially useful for guaranteeing data security and transparency. The working mechanism of the blockchain is secured by a specific algorithm or protocol. The dependability and integrity of transactions are guaranteed by these protocols, which are validated by nodes throughout the network.

The Proof of Work or Proof of Stake algorithm is the standard consensus algorithm used in the majority of blockchain networks to guarantee the accuracy of transactions. Miners in the Proof of Work algorithm use a specific amount of processing power to solve intricate mathematical problems in order to validate transactions. Verification in the Proof of Stake algorithm is based on user asset counts rather than mining (Bonneau et al., 2015). When a block is added to the blockchain, it is encrypted with a distinct digital signature, or "hash." This hash is linked to the previous block, ensuring that the blocks remain in the chain. Since altering one block will alter the hashes of every subsequent block, it is exceedingly challenging to make any changes to the blockchain. This feature makes it harder to alter the data and guarantees the blockchain's security.

In a Bitcoin transaction, the transfer process between users takes place on the blockchain as follows:

- **Creating the Transaction:** For instance, when Ali wants to send Bitcoin to his friend Aisha, he initiates this transaction in Ali's wallet. Ali's wallet creates the transaction and specifies the amount of Bitcoin he wants to send to Aisha's wallet address.
- **Transaction Broadcasting and Verification:** Ali's transaction is broadcasted to the blockchain network. Miners or nodes in the network use a consensus mechanism to verify this transaction. Working according to the Proof of Work algorithm, miners solve a mathematical problem to verify the transaction.
- **Creating a Block and Adding it to the Chain:** Once the transaction is verified, it is collected into a block with other transactions. This new block is add-

ed to the chain by linking with previous blocks. Alice receives the transaction verified by the blockchain network and her Bitcoin balance is updated.

This process demonstrates the security and transparency advantages of blockchain. Everyone can see the transactions that occur on the blockchain, but no user can change the transaction data. This example is illustrative in understanding the decentralized and immutable nature of blockchain (Tapscott & Tapscott, 2016).

Blockchain Technologies

Blockchain is supported by various technologies based on digital data security, transaction verification and decentralization. It is based on distributed ledger technology, a digital record system. This technology makes it possible for the database to be spread across numerous nodes in a decentralized structure. The main benefit of distributed ledger technology is that it eliminates the need for a central authority while offering a secure record system. Every modification made to one node is updated concurrently with all other nodes since every node has a copy of all the data. This guarantees the data's dependability and immutability (Yaga et al., 2018). In essence, a distributed ledger is a single database that is decentralized and overseen by several people. This is a database where several identical copies are shared among several users and updated simultaneously. A distributed ledger and a "traditional" distributed database differ primarily in how they are updated: To maintain data consistency in a traditional distributed database, participants collaborate and have mutual trust. However, in a distributed ledger, the parties may have conflicting interests or lack complete trust in one another, so a method must be put in place to collectively check the ledgers before sharing them.

Smart Contracts

Blockchain-based digital agreements known as "smart contracts" carry out transactions automatically in response to specific triggers (Ante, 2021). These contracts are created with logical conditions and coded programs, and other blockchain network users validate them. Smart contracts eliminate intermediaries, allowing for more secure, transparent, and condition-based transactions. Data integrity and security are improved because transactions are initiated automatically when specified criteria are satisfied.

Smart contracts and blockchain technology operate together. Smart contracts can be made on a blockchain platform like Ethereum and authorized by network nodes. These contracts can have certain functions and conditions; when these conditions are met, the contract is automatically activated and performs the desired transaction.

For instance, a smart contract can guarantee the delivery of a product or the payment on a specific date. The parties develop trust in this way, and when the requirements are fulfilled, the transaction is finished automatically.

Consensus Mechanisms

Consensus mechanisms are algorithms used to ensure the authenticity and reliability of transactions made on the blockchain. The most commonly used consensus mechanisms include Proof of Work and Proof of Stake.

- **Proof of Work:** It is the consensus mechanism that Bitcoin uses and is carried out by miners who are responsible for adding new blocks to the network (Schinckus, 2021). Miners receive incentives in the form of fixed amounts of block rewards and transaction fees paid by users. To earn these rewards, miners compete by adding computational power to the network; the more computational power provided, the greater the chance of winning the reward. However, this mechanism causes a large amount of energy waste.
- **Proof of Stake:** It was developed to reduce the energy consumption of Proof of Work. In this mechanism, the verification process is done according to the amount of assets that users have. Major blockchain platforms such as Ethereum aim to increase energy efficiency by switching from Proof of Work to Proof of Stake. Proof of Stake encourages more decentralized blockchain applications than proof of work and requires chains to be governed by specific stakes (Spasovski & Eklund, 2017). A stake in a blockchain is the money that the blockchain tracks. It consists of balances in the unit and what is the share in each chain. The more it is, the more block production is required.

Cryptography and Encryption Methods

The security infrastructure of Blockchain is built on cryptography and encryption methods. Each transaction on the Blockchain is protected by encryption algorithms. In particular, asymmetric encryption allows users to perform transactions securely using a unique private key and public key. In addition, hash algorithms such as SHA-256 are used to ensure the integrity of data.

Decentralized Applications

Decentralized applications (DApps) are applications that use blockchain infrastructure and are not connected to a central server. These applications are usually developed on blockchain platforms that support smart contracts, such as Ethereum.

DApps offer users a decentralized, secure, and uncensored environment in various areas such as social media, finance, and gaming. Since they run on blockchain, DApps are much more difficult to manipulate or hack than traditional applications (Xu et al., 2021).

A DApp is a software application that runs on a blockchain network and has the following key features:

- **Open Source:** The source code is publicly available, allowing anyone to examine, use, copy, and modify the code.
- **Decentralized and Cryptographically Secured:** All information in dApps is cryptographically secured and stored on a decentralized blockchain maintained by many users (or nodes).
- **Tokenization System:** dApps are accessed via a cryptographic token. These tokens can accept cryptocurrencies or generate their own tokens using a consensus algorithm such as Proof of Work or Proof of Stake.

The emergence and proliferation of DApps is associated with the development of Web3 technologies. The term Web3 was defined by Gavin Wood and refers to the next generation of the Internet based on decentralized digital technologies such as cryptocurrencies, non-fungible tokens, decentralized autonomous organizations, decentralized finance (Gasser, 2023). In addition, innovations such as artificial intelligence, machine learning, and big data as supporting technologies strengthen the Web3 ecosystem. The evolution of DApps is directly linked to the introduction of blockchain technology and smart contracts. Smart Contracts are a critical component for DApps to fulfill their decentralized functionality (Moharrer & Nogoorani, 2020).

Side Chains

Sidechains are alternative chains that operate independently of the main blockchain and are connected to it. Sidechains are used to lighten the transaction load on the blockchain, reducing speed and transaction costs. Different rules or consensus mechanisms may be implemented than the main blockchain. Sidechains allow developers to try out new applications without affecting the main chain (Back et al., 2014).

Sidechains are secondary blockchains that are connected to the main blockchain via a two-way peg. A two-way peg is a mechanism that allows assets to be transferred bidirectionally between the main chain and the sidechain at a fixed or predetermined rate. Sidechains can have a completely different protocol and implementation than the main blockchain. This flexibility allows users to access various functionalities and features offered by sidechains using their assets on the main chain. Additionally, sidechains are isolated from the main blockchain. This ensures that in the event of a cryptographic vulnerability or a maliciously designed sidechain, the damage is limited to the sidechain only and protects the main blockchain. This feature enables innovative solutions to be developed without compromising the security of the main blockchain while providing additional functionality for users (Singh, Click, Parizi, Zhang, Dehghantanha, & Choo, 2020).

Blockchain Oracles

Blockchain oracles provide the connection between data sources outside the blockchain and the blockchain. Oracles enable smart contracts on the blockchain to access and interact with data from the outside world. For example, using a weather oracle, a smart contract can be set to pay out below a certain temperature level. In this way, real-world events outside the blockchain can be integrated into the blockchain system (Ellis et al., 2017).

Blockchain oracles are third-party services that provide information to smart contracts from the outside world, and they act as a bridge between blockchains and the outside world. Blockchains and smart contracts cannot directly access data outside the network (off-chain). However, many contract agreements require relevant information from the outside world to be fulfilled. This is where blockchain oracles come into play and provide a link between on-chain and off-chain data. Oracles play a vital role in the blockchain ecosystem as they expand the range of use of smart contracts. Without oracles, smart contracts would only be able to access data within the network, so their range of use would be quite limited (Beniiche, 2020).

CRYPTOCURRENCIES

The concept of digital money was first brought to the agenda by David Chaum in 1982 and it was argued that it should be managed by a central structure (R. Porras & Daugherty, 2021). Later, it became possible to make transactions with a peer-to-peer (P2P) system without the need for a central structure, and with this innovation, Bitcoin emerged. Following Bitcoin, other cryptocurrencies using the same infrastructure also developed as altcoins (alternative cryptocurrencies).

Cryptocurrencies are digital currencies that have no tangible or physical equivalent. As a decentralized network technology, it allows transfers from A to B without the need for a third party. Written in open source code, this system offers equal access to its users and does not contain any usage restrictions. Cryptocurrencies are produced by "miners" and the total production is limited to 21 million units. They can be converted to other currencies and their transactions are recorded at a high level of security by miners who work independently to ensure security.

Bitcoin

Bitcoin is often referred to by the abbreviations "BTC" or "XBT" and has the ability to be divided to eight decimal places. The smallest unit of Bitcoin is called "Satoshi"; this name was inspired by Satoshi Nakamoto, known as the creator of Bitcoin (Bertucci, 2024). One Bitcoin is equal to 100 million Satoshi. Bitcoin is limited to a maximum of 21 million units, and this total is expected to enter circulation by 2140. No central authority has the authority to create a money supply on Bitcoin.

Altcoins

With the success of Bitcoin, different types of Altcoins have emerged. Altcoins are traded as an alternative version of Bitcoin and often claim to offer superior projects. Altcoins, which can be converted to other cryptocurrencies at any time, are similar to Bitcoin in their purchase and usage processes. Ethereum, the Altcoin with the highest trading volume, offers advantages such as fast transaction times, low costs, more suitable mining equipment and reliable encryption. However, sudden news flows in the market can trigger investor reactions and lead to sharp price fluctuations. Altcoins, especially those that lose value, can bring various problems. While projects such as NFT and decentralized finance have different goals and features, some cryptocurrencies can be used in illegal activities. On the other hand, cryptocurrencies that adopt environmentally friendly approaches focus on alternative energy sources. This reveals that the purposes and strategies of cryptocurrencies vary greatly.

Non-Fungible Token

Non-Fungible Tokens (NFTs) are tokens that represent a unique digital asset on the blockchain. Unlike cryptocurrencies, each NFT is unique and cannot be changed. Thanks to these features, they find use in various areas such as digital art, collectibles, or in-game assets. NFTs are typically created and verified via smart contracts on the Ethereum blockchain (Wang et al., 2021).

NFTs are unique and cryptographic digital assets created using blockchain technology. NFTs, which provide proof of ownership thanks to the code they contain, also provide copyright protection to the author. The purchase and sale of these digital assets are carried out through special NFT platforms. These platforms offer artists the opportunity to bring their works together with a global audience in a digital environment. In the first half of 2021, the NFT trading volume, the majority of which consists of digital artworks, collections, music and in-game items, exceeded $800 million. In particular, the development of technology and the digitalization of social life play an important role in the increase in interest in NFT assets.

Cryptocurrency Wallets

Wallets used to store cryptocurrencies are classified as "hot" and "cold" wallets based on their connection status. Hot wallets are usually software-based wallets that are connected to the internet. These wallets allow users to access their crypto assets quickly and easily. They can be in the form of mobile applications, desktop software, or web-based platforms. However, they are more vulnerable to cyber attacks because they are constantly online. Therefore, hot wallets are generally preferred for daily transactions and storing small amounts of crypto assets.

Cold wallets are usually hardware-based wallets that are not connected to the Internet. These wallets offer a higher level of security against cyber attacks by storing private keys offline. They can be in the form of physical devices such as USB sticks or paper wallets. Cold wallets are ideal for long-term storage and safekeeping of large amounts of crypto assets. However, they may be less practical for daily transactions due to their offline nature. Cold wallets are among the more preferred cryptocurrency storage methods, especially in terms of security. In an environment where the virtual world is rapidly developing and transforming, securing transactions and ensuring that users can easily make transactions has become an important necessity. However, one of the biggest disadvantages of cold wallets is that they are a physical device (e.g. USB) and therefore cannot be returned in case of theft. On the other hand, hot wallets also carry a risk of data loss that may occur in the virtual environment. Although there are certain risks in both types, hardware wallets stand out as a safer alternative compared to other methods. The biggest advantage of hardware wallets is that they ensure that no monetary loss occurs in the event of theft. This feature makes them a safer option for cryptocurrency users.

TRONSCAN

Tronscan is a blockchain browser and analysis tool used to track transactions on the TRON blockchain network, manage users' accounts and balances, and analyze activities in the TRON ecosystem. TRON is a blockchain protocol that offers high transaction capacity and ease of decentralized application (DApp) development (TRON DAO, 2018). Therefore, Tronscan plays an important role by ensuring that data in the TRON ecosystem is transparent and easily accessible to users. Since blockchain networks are public, all transactions can be tracked through block browsers; this facilitates analysis processes in high-volume networks like TRON and meets users' demand for transparency.

Tronscan's remarkable features include its ability to detail transactions made on the TRON network and its user-friendly interface. Users can view their account balances, transaction history, and the status of tokens connected to the TRON network on Tronscan. They can also examine the transactions of smart contracts on the TRON blockchain, detail token transfers, and observe the mining processes of blocks. Block crawlers are an indispensable tool for blockchain networks, and Tronscan can be considered a successful example of such crawlers for TRON.

The ease of use and transparency of a blockchain browser is important not only for individual users, but also for developers and investors contributing to the TRON network. In addition to analyzing transactions on the TRON network, Tronscan also facilitates users' access to DApps. Many DApps running on the TRON network can be tracked via Tronscan, allowing users to view transaction details for these applications. This increases the transparency of decentralized applications, supporting user trust. This integration of Tronscan into DApps expands the use of the TRON network by meeting the demand for transparency in blockchain-based applications.

Transactions made on the TRON network constitute a significant source for big data analysis, and Tronscan plays a critical role in making this data analyzable. The data obtained through Tronscan allows detailed analysis of many metrics such as the network's growth rate, transaction volume, and user activity. These analyses can be used to evaluate the network's transaction capacity and efficiency, as well as provide information about the overall health of the TRON ecosystem. Such data analyses can support the expansion of the blockchain and its adoption by more users.

INVESTIGATION AND LEGAL REGULATIONS

Blockchain is a system where transactions are recorded permanently and unchangeably, allowing you to track fraudulent activities. In this process, tools such as Chainalysis and Crystal Intelligence can be used to track criminals' transaction history, detect suspicious movements, and uncover money laundering activities. However, in order to benefit from these tools, teams specialized in the logic and working principles of blockchain technology must be present. The correct use of technological tools is critical, especially in terms of detailed examination of transactions taking place on cryptocurrency exchanges and the identification of suspicious transaction addresses. Another important point to consider in investigations is the supervision of cryptocurrency exchanges. Exchanges are important platforms that store users' identity information and record transaction history. It is easier to track fraudulent activities through exchanges that implement Know Your Customer

(KYC) and Anti-Money Laundering (AML) policies. However, many criminals prefer unregulated or unregulated exchanges to maintain anonymity. Therefore, law enforcement agencies need to develop effective cooperation with these exchanges. It is important to use the right legal mechanisms to request data from exchanges, especially when it comes to international transactions.

International cooperation also plays a vital role in combating crypto fraud. Since crypto transactions are often cross-border in nature, solving the crime requires coordination with international organizations. Organizations such as INTERPOL (INTERPOL, 2025), Europol (EUROPOL, 2025), and the Financial Action Task Force (FATF) (FATF, 2025) can play an active role in this process. The risk-based approaches and standards set by FATF for virtual asset service providers serve as a guide for investigations (FATF, 2025). It is important to comply with international regulations and share information with authorities in other countries when investigating fraudulent activities.

Digital forensics is another important element in cryptocurrency fraud investigations. Examining devices linked to fraud is crucial for identifying digital wallets and private keys found on these devices. Examining physically seized cold wallets or hot wallets on computers in particular can be a critical step in uncovering criminal evidence. In this process, it is necessary to assign expert forensic teams and have detailed information about how crypto assets are stored. In addition, attention should be paid to the legal aspect of the investigation. The legal framework regarding cryptocurrency fraud crimes varies from country to country.

The most important feature of Blockchain is that the transactions made are transparent and traceable. Each transaction can be viewed by everyone on open source blockchain platforms because it is recorded with details such as timestamp, sender address, recipient address and transferred amount. When a transaction is performed on the blockchain network, the details of this transaction can be monitored with the blockchain explorer tools where the transaction was made. While this transparency facilitates legal auditing processes, it also causes criminals to turn to services such as mixers to hide their transactions.

While cryptocurrencies have the potential to make financial transactions faster and more secure, they can also be used for illegal activities. Crimes such as fraud, money laundering, and illegal trading take advantage of the anonymity in the cryptocurrency ecosystem. In addition, due to the inadequacy of regulations regarding the cryptocurrency ecosystem in most countries, combating cryptocurrency crimes has become a serious challenge for law enforcement and legal systems. Investigating these crimes is a process intertwined with technology, and such investigations require technical, legal and international cooperation.

There are legal and technical issues that need to be considered in crypto asset tracking. First of all, transactions that do not have a criminal element should be separated from suspicious transactions. In addition, the information obtained should be protected and used within legal frameworks. Data security and ethical principles should be taken as a priority in such investigations.

Various data is needed to conduct a crypto asset investigation. This data consists of elements such as account addresses, transaction IDs, block details, and suspicious transaction data. The accuracy and reliability of the data obtained is critical to the effectiveness of the investigation. The increasing number of crypto asset service providers offers new opportunities to fraudsters with phishing traps. Exchange companies, cryptocurrency exchanges and platforms, or organizations that only provide wallet services operate as service providers. Especially in online wallets, when the private key is managed by a service provider rather than the user himself, malicious crypto asset service providers can cause victimization.

APPLICATION DEVELOPMENT

The FIFO method relies on a mechanism in which the first asset or good that enters is considered the first asset or good that is sold (Andarsyah, 2022). The application of the FIFO method in blockchain networks provides an effective method for understanding the distribution logic of transactions. For example, while the inputs in a transaction are transferred to the outputs in order, the asset contained in which output can be clearly tracked. This method can be used as a reliable tool in the detection of illegal activities such as money laundering and in the analysis of cryptocurrency theft cases. The FIFO allows users to evaluate their transaction history more transparently, as it clearly shows the contribution of each input to the outputs (Tironsakkul, Maarek, Eross, & Just, 2019).

The application developed in this study is based on the FIFO method and analyzes blockchain transactions in a sequential manner. It distributes inputs to outputs according to the FIFO principle, while also providing transparency and accuracy by monitoring which outputs the inputs are transferred to. Therefore, transactions are analyzed according to the FIFO method by taking them from blockchain data and the results are reported.

Windows Forms (WinForms) technology was preferred in the user interface development process. WinForms is a graphical user interface library based on .NET Framework provided by Microsoft. C# was chosen as the software development language.

The use of Tronscan APIs in blockchain analysis optimizes the data access process, allowing transactions to be processed more quickly and reliably. In this context, the software development process is divided into certain stages based on the Tronscan API integration and the features it provides.

TronScan API

TronScan API provides a powerful tool for accessing transaction and transfer data on the Tron blockchain. This API provides comprehensive query parameters (start, limit, start_timestamp, end_timestamp, fromAddress, toAddress, tokens, block, and type) that allow users to easily filter and retrieve data according to their different needs. The method parameter, which is used specifically for smart contract transactions, enables the analysis of specific contract calls. The data obtained from the API is transformed into classes, each representing a specific data structure, and the aim is to provide this data with a more understandable, reusable and manageable structure. This approach makes it easier for developers to process blockchain data, while also providing high efficiency in analysis and application development processes. This adaptation of the TronScan API provides an important reference point, especially for developers and researchers working on data modeling and system integration.

TronScan API offers a query mechanism based on transaction hash to access detailed information about a specific transaction. This feature allows users to access all details about the transaction using the hash value that uniquely identifies a transaction. Endpoint works by providing the transaction hash as a parameter and provides comprehensive information about the transaction. This information includes elements such as the sender and recipient addresses in the transaction, transaction amount, token information used, transaction timestamp, block number, and whether the transaction was successful or unsuccessful. This API, which is of critical importance especially in blockchain-based financial analysis, debugging processes, and application development, is a powerful tool for providing fast and reliable access to transaction details. The ability to query data via transaction hash makes a significant contribution to the transparency and verifiability principles of blockchain technology.

The modeling of the transaction data in json format received from the request made to the sample API URL address with the Transaction class allows the blockchain data to be transformed into an understandable and manageable structure. This class provides flexibility and efficiency in data analysis and software development processes by covering elements such as transaction details, contract information, party addresses and meta-data.

TronScan API provides a special query engine to list TRC20 token transfers belonging to a wallet. This API offers detailed filtering of transactions made from a specific wallet with parameters such as address, trc20Id, direction, start_timestamp, end_timestamp and reverse. In particular, querying both types of transfers as well as inbound and outbound transfers made from a wallet allows for comprehensive analysis of transactions. Adapting the transfer information coming from this API to the WalletTransaction class makes transactions more manageable in software development processes. This class can be configured to include details such as wallet address, transfer direction, transaction time, transferred token information and block confirmation status. Such modeling allows developers to query, analyze and present wallet transactions more easily.

The API URL is used to list TRC20 token transfers for a specific wallet in JSON format. The data returned from the API contains details of incoming and outgoing transfers from a wallet. This data should be modeled under the WalletTransaction class so that it can be used more effectively in software development processes. In order to model the JSON format data in C# language, a Token class can be created corresponding to each token information in the data. This class can be configured to include features such as token_price_in_usd, token_value, token_id, balance, token_name, token_url. In addition, a WalletTransaction class is defined to represent the main structure in JSON and the modeling done in accordance with the data list and count value.

TronScan API provides an endpoint developed to access detailed information about a specific account address. This API allows accessing detailed information about a specific account using only the address parameter. This information may include an account's balance, transaction history, token transfers, and other relevant metrics. In this context, an AccountDetail class was created to represent account details such as wallet address, balance, number of transactions, token details, and verification status. Then, an AccountResponse class representing the key-data structure was created. This class contains basic properties such as account_number, last_24h_account_change, total and a TronAccount subclass representing the data list. In addition, complex objects such as contractMap and contractInfo were modeled with appropriate dictionaries and subclasses to obtain a complete structure.

Analysis and Visualization of TronScan API Data

Data received from the TronScan API was converted into an object-based structure in C# language and made it processable. As a result, analyzing this data and obtaining more meaningful information by visualizing the transfer information became possible. The MainForm class represents the main user interface window of the application shown in Figure 1 and provides a central control for multiple operations.

Figure 1. MainForm of the application

As shown in Figure 2, when btn_Start button is clicked, the form processes the transaction details by getting a transaction ID (TXID) from the user. First, it is checked whether a TXID has been entered in textBox1; if it is left blank, the user is informed with a message box that the TXID must be entered and the transaction is stopped. If the TXID entered is valid, the text of the button is changed to "Transaction in Progress" and the button is disabled (btn_Start.Enabled = false) to prevent it from being clicked again during the transaction. Then, an asynchronous method called GetTransaction is called to get the transaction details. When the transaction is completed, the text of the button is updated to "SAVE PNG" and the previous click event (btn_Start_Click) is removed and replaced by the SaveAsPng method. In this way, the button allows the user to save the transaction results after getting the transaction details. Finally, the button is enabled again (btn_Start.Enabled = true) so that the user can start a new transaction. This function provides a mechanism to manage user interaction and dynamically change the transaction flow.

Figure 2. Running the program

```
private async void btn_Baslat_Click(object sender, EventArgs e)
{
    if (string.IsNullOrEmpty(textBox1.Text))
    {
        MessageBox.Show("Lütfen TXID girin!");
        return;
    }

    btn_Baslat.Text = "İşlem Yapılıyor";
    btn_Baslat.Enabled = false;

    await GetTransaction();

    btn_Baslat.Text = "PNG KAYDET";
    btn_Baslat.Click -= btn_Baslat_Click;
    btn_Baslat.Click += SaveAsPng;
    btn_Baslat.Enabled = true;
}
```

As shown in Figure 3, SaveAsPng method allows the user to save the current panel content as a PNG file. First, a SaveFileDialog object is created to allow the user to select a file name and save location. The type of the file to be saved is filtered as PNG and the necessary settings are made to automatically add the extension.

Figure 3. Saving the panel image in PNG format

```
private void SaveAsPng(object? sender, EventArgs e)
{
    using SaveFileDialog saveFileDialog = new SaveFileDialog
    {
        Filter = "PNG Files (*.png)|*.png",
        DefaultExt = "png",
        AddExtension = true,
        Title = "PNG Olarak Kaydet"
    };

    if (saveFileDialog.ShowDialog() != DialogResult.OK) return;

    Bitmap bitmap = new Bitmap(panelMain.Width, panelMain.Height);
    panelMain.DrawToBitmap(bitmap, new Rectangle(0, 0, panelMain.Width, panelMain.Height));
    bitmap.Save(saveFileDialog.FileName, System.Drawing.Imaging.ImageFormat.Png);

    MessageBox.Show("PNG dosyası başarıyla kaydedildi: " + saveFileDialog.FileName);
}
```

Details of the Process to Be Followed

GetTransaction shown in Figure 4 was designed to retrieve and process transaction details based on a user-entered transaction ID (TXID). The function notifies the user that the process is ongoing by making a progress bar visible during the transaction. First, the HashValidator.IsValidHash method is used to check whether the entered TXID is valid; if the TXID is not valid, the user is shown an error message and the transaction is terminated. In case of a valid TXID, an asynchronous call is made to the TronScan API via a TransactionApiClient object and the transaction information is retrieved. If the transaction is not found, the user is shown a message indicating that the transaction ID needs to be checked. When the transaction is successfully received, the main transaction details are extracted with the Figure 4.

Figure 4. Details of the transaction to be followed - 1

```
private async Task GetTransaction()
{
    try
    {
        progressBar1.Visible = true;
        string hash = textBox1.Text;

        if (!HashValidator.IsValidHash(hash))
        {
            MessageBox.Show("TXID değeri yanlış!");
            return;
        }

        var client = new TransactionApiClient();
        Transaction transaction = await client.GetTransactionInfoAsync(hash);

        if (transaction.Hash == null)
        {
            MessageBox.Show("İşlem bulunamadı! TXID kontrolü gerekiyor!");
            return;
        }

        string toAddress = GetMainTransaction(transaction);
        Color color = ContrastingColor.GenerateRandomColor();
        AccountTransactions accountTransactions = new AccountTransactions();
        await accountTransactions.GetWalletTransactions(hash, toAddress, panelMain, color, "down", 10, 10);
    }
    finally
    {
        progressBar1.Visible = false;
    }
}
```

GetMainTransaction shown in Figure 5 extracts the main transfer details within a transaction object (Transaction) and displays them visually to the user. First, the initial TRC20 token transfer information in the transaction is retrieved (Trc-20TransferInfo[0]) and the transferred amount is converted to a readable form using the AmountConverter.ConvertToDecimal method. Then, the transaction details (transaction hash, date, sender address, recipient address, transferred amount, and token name) are structured using a StringBuilder and displayed in the lblResult tag. The tag is stylized with a border, padding, and background color to make it visually apparent. Finally, the recipient address of the transfer (To_Address) is returned. This function serves both the purpose of data processing and presenting the transaction details in a meaningful way to the user, so that critical information about the transaction can be quickly seen.

Figure 5. Details of the transaction to be followed - 2

```
private string GetMainTransaction(Transaction transaction)
{
    var info = transaction.Trc20TransferInfo[0];
    decimal convertedAmount =
AmountConverter.ConvertToDecimal(info.Amount_Str, info.Decimals);

    lblResult.Text = new StringBuilder()
        .AppendLine("TAKİP EDİLECEK İŞLEMİN DETAYLARI")
        .AppendLine($"Hash: {transaction.Hash}")
        .AppendLine($"Tarih:
{Functions.OtherFuncs.ConvertUnixTimestampToDateTime(transaction.Timesta
mp)} UTC")
        .AppendLine($"Gönderen: {info.From_Address}")
        .AppendLine($"Alıcı: {info.To_Address}")
        .AppendLine($"Tutar: {convertedAmount} {info.Name}")
        .ToString();

    lblResult.BorderStyle = BorderStyle.FixedSingle;
    lblResult.Padding = Padding.Add(new Padding(8), new Padding(8));
    lblResult.BackColor = Color.WhiteSmoke;

    return info.To_Address;
}
```

Wallet Transactions

AccountTransactions.GetWalletTransactions method shown in Figure 6 retrieves and visualizes a wallet's transaction history based on a given transaction hash and destination address. First, the WalletTransaction.GetDataAsync method is called asynchronously to retrieve the relevant transaction data and load it into a List<TransactionData> object. The transaction hash and recipient address (To) information are extracted from the first element of this data set. If only one transaction data is returned (transactionData.Count == 1), a loop is started and the related transactions are retrieved in a chained manner again with the WalletTransaction.GetDataAsync method. This process continues until no more transactions are found. If more than one transaction data is returned or if no data is found while chaining the transactions, the progress bar is hidden and the process is completed. This function is capable of visualizing related transactions by retrieving the transaction history of a wallet in a chained manner. The related data is dynamically rendered with parameters such as color and layout in the panel (panelMain) visualized on the UI.

Figure 6. Wallet transactions-1

```
public class AccountTransactions
{
    public async Task GetWalletTransactions(string hash, string toaddress, Panel panelMain, Color color, string direction, int locX = 10, int locY = 10)
    {
        List<TransactionData> transactionData = await WalletTransaction.GetDataAsync(hash, toaddress, panelMain, color, direction, locX, locY);

        string transactionDataHash = transactionData[0].Hash;
        string transactionDataTo = transactionData[0].To;

        if (transactionData.Count == 1)
        {
            for (; ; )
            {
                transactionData = await WalletTransaction.GetDataAsync(transactionDataHash, transactionDataTo, panelMain, color, direction, locX, locY);

                if (transactionData.Count > 1)
                {
                    MainForm.Instance.ProgressBarPublic.Visible = false;
                    break;
                }
                else
                {
                    transactionDataHash = transactionData[0].Hash;
                    transactionDataTo = transactionData[0].To;
                }
            }
        }
        else
        {
            MainForm.Instance.ProgressBarPublic.Visible = false;
        }
    }
}
```

WalletTransaction.GetDataAsync method shown in Figure 7 retrieves, analyzes, and visualizes a wallet transaction. The GetDataAsync method asynchronously retrieves and analyzes transaction data based on a transaction hash and destination address. First, a client is created to retrieve data via WalletApiClient. The DataAnalyze method is called to analyze the transaction data in detail and the results are added to a walletDataListData list. The list is reversed and the wallet balances are calculated with the CalculateBalance method. The target transaction is found from the list according to the hash and the relevant transaction amount, balance and total amount are calculated. The target wallets are defined by calling the DefinitionTargetWallets method and this transaction is processed in a chained manner into a list called TransactionDataList. This data is created as a visual label with a DynamicLabel object and displayed on the panel. If there is more than one transaction, additional labels and redirect indicators (AddLabel) are created to visualize the transaction connections. Otherwise, the current transaction is visually presented to the user by indicating that it is being followed.

Figure 7. Wallet transactions-2

```
public class WalletTransaction
{
    public static async Task<List<TransactionData>> GetDataAsync(string hash, string toaddress, Panel panelMain, Color color, string direction, int locX = 10, int locY = 10)
    {
        var client2 = new WalletApiClient();

        List<TransactionData> walletDataListData = new List<TransactionData>();
        TransactionData outtransaction = new TransactionData();
        bool hasDuplicateBlockTimestamp = false;

        hasDuplicateBlockTimestamp = await DataAnalyze(toaddress, panelMain, locX, client2, walletDataListData, outtransaction, hasDuplicateBlockTimestamp);

        walletDataListData.Reverse();
        CalculateBalance(walletDataListData);

        TransactionData targetdata = walletDataListData.First(x => x.Hash == hash);
        int targetindex = walletDataListData.IndexOf(targetdata);
        decimal targetamount = AmountConverter.ConvertToDecimal(targetdata.Amount, targetdata.Decimals);
        decimal targetbalance = targetindex == 0 ? 0 : walletDataListData[targetindex - 1].Balance;
        decimal sumAmount = 0;

        List<TransactionData> TransactionDataList = new List<TransactionData>();
        DefinitionTargetWallets(walletDataListData, targetindex, targetamount, ref targetbalance, ref sumAmount, TransactionDataList);

        int transactionDataListCount = TransactionDataList.Count;
        outtransaction = TransactionDataList.First();
        DynamicLabel dynamicLabel = new DynamicLabel();
        Label newlabel = dynamicLabel.Create(walletDataListData, outtransaction, panelMain, locX, locY, false, transactionDataListCount, color, direction);
        bool isRight = TransactionDataList.Count > 1;
        direction = "down";


        if (isRight)
        {
            AddLabel(panelMain, color, direction, walletDataListData, TransactionDataList, ref transactionDataListCount, ref newlabel, isRight);
        }
        else
        {
            newlabel.Text = $"Takip edildi\n{newlabel.Text}";
            Panel arrow = OtherFuncs.CreateArrowPanel(newlabel.Right - (newlabel.Width / 2), newlabel.Bottom, 30, 40, color, "down");
            panelMain.Controls.Add(arrow);
        }
        return TransactionDataList;
    }
}
```

The function shown in Figure 8 is designed to analyze transaction data for a specific wallet address (toaddress) and detect potentially problematic situations. The DataAnalyze method works asynchronously and retrieves transaction information associated with the given address in chunks (limit: 50). The loop continues to retrieve a new data group with each request. The transaction data received via the client2. GetWalletInfoAsync method is added to the walletDataListData list.

Figure 8. Analysis of transactions

```
private static async Task<bool> DataAnalyze(string toaddress, Panel panelMain, int locX, WalletApiClient client2, List<TransactionData> walletDataListData, TransactionData outtransaction, bool hasDuplicateBlockTimestamp)
{
    for (int i = 0; ; i++)
    {
        try
        {
            await Task.Delay(300);
            List<TransactionData> walletDatas = await client2.GetWalletInfoAsync(address: toaddress, start: i * 50, limit: 50, direction: 0);
            walletDataListData.AddRange(walletDatas);
            hasDuplicateBlockTimestamp = walletDatas
                                          .GroupBy(w => w.Block_Timestamp)
                                          .Any(g => g.Count() > 2);

            if (walletDatas.Count < 50)
            {
                break;
            }

            if (hasDuplicateBlockTimestamp)
            {
                await ExchangeControl(toaddress, panelMain, outtransaction, locX);
                MainForm.Instance.ProgressBarPublic.Visible = false;
                break;
            }

            if (walletDatas.Count > 10000)
            {
                await ExchangeControl(toaddress, panelMain, outtransaction, locX);
                MainForm.Instance.ProgressBarPublic.Visible = false;
                break;
            }
        }
        catch (Exception ex)
        {
            throw;
        }
    }

    return hasDuplicateBlockTimestamp;
}
```

During this process, the hasDuplicateBlockTimestamp variable is updated by checking whether the received data contains more than one transaction with the same block timestamp (Block_Timestamp).

The loop ends when:

- When the number of transactions received is less than 50 (i.e. there is no more data).
- When multiple transactions with the same block timestamp are detected.
- When the total number of transactions received exceeds 10,000.

When such a state is reached, a transaction check is performed by calling the ExchangeControl method and using panelMain for visual feedback. Also, the progress bar is made invisible. This function efficiently ingests large amounts of transaction data while also analyzing data quality and potential issues (such as duplicate timestamps). This provides critical functionality for reliable review and reporting of wallet transactions.

The function shown in Figure 9 was designed to identify target wallets and the transaction amounts sent to these wallets in relation to a particular transaction. The DefinitionTargetWallets method examines the given transaction list (walletDataListData), determines the wallets to which the target transaction amount (targetamount) was sent, and adds them to the transaction list (TransactionDataList). The function iteratively checks the transactions after the target transaction (targetindex) in the transaction list with a loop. If the transaction direction is 1, i.e. the transaction is a sending transaction, the sent amount (Amount) is calculated and the current balance (targetbalance) is updated. This update is done by subtracting the sent amount from the current balance. If the balance drops to zero or less as a result of this transaction, this transaction is identified as being related to the target transaction. In such a case, the transaction amount is added to the total transaction amount (sumAmount) and if the transaction amount is greater than zero, this transaction is included in the TransactionDataList. The cycle is terminated when the total amount sent (sumAmount) reaches a value equal to or greater than the target transaction amount (targetamount). This mechanism helps identify the transaction flow and associated wallets by tracking transactions sent to target wallets in a given transaction chain. The function plays a critical role in analyzing transaction movements and visualizing the transaction chain.

Figure 9. Detection of target wallets

```
private static void DefinitionTargetWallets(List<TransactionData> walletDataListData, int targetindex, decimal targetamount, ref decimal targetbalance, ref decimal sumAmount, List<TransactionData> TransactionDataList)
{
    for (int i = targetindex + 1; i < walletDataListData.Count; i++) //hedef paranın gönderildiği cüzdanlar tespit ediliyor
    {
        if (walletDataListData[i].Direction == 1)
        {
            if ((i + 1) == walletDataListData.Count)
            {
                break;
            }
            else
            {
                decimal amnt = AmountConverter.ConvertToDecimal(walletDataListData[i].Amount, walletDataListData[i].Decimals);
                targetbalance = targetbalance - amnt;

                if (targetbalance <= 0)
                {
                    sumAmount += amnt;
                    if (amnt > 0)
                    {
                        TransactionDataList.Add(walletDataListData[i]);
                    }
                    if (sumAmount >= targetamount)
                    {
                        break;
                    }
                }
            }
        }
    }
}
```

The function shown in Figure 10 calculates the balance values of each transaction for a list of transactions (walletDataListData). The CalculateBalance method processes each transaction in the list in order and updates the balance according to the direction of the transaction. If the direction of the transaction is 2 (incoming transfer), the current transaction amount (Amount) is added to the previous balance. If the direction of the transaction is 1 (outgoing transfer), the transaction amount is subtracted from the previous balance. During the loop, the initial balance for the first transaction is assumed to be zero ($k = 0$). For subsequent transactions, the balance of the previous transaction (walletDataListData[k].Balance) is used as the basis and the calculation is made accordingly. Transaction amounts are converted with the AmountConverter.ConvertToDecimal method to work with the correct units. This function dynamically calculates the balance for each transaction in a transaction list and provides the data needed to correctly analyze the financial flow of transactions. It plays a critical role, especially in visualizing and analyzing transaction chains.

Figure 10. Balance calculation

```
private static void CalculateBalance(List<TransactionData> walletDataListData)
{
    for (int i = 0; i < walletDataListData.Count; i++) //balance hesaplaması yapılıyor
    {
        int k = i == 0 ? 0 : i - 1;
        decimal amountt = AmountConverter.ConvertToDecimal(walletDataListData[i].Amount, walletDataListData[i].Decimals);
        walletDataListData[i].Balance = walletDataListData[i].Direction == 2 ? walletDataListData[k].Balance + amountt : walletDataListData[k].Balance - amountt;
    }
}
```

The function shown in Figure 11 checks whether a specific wallet address (toaddress) belongs to an exchange company address and creates a warning tag based on this information. The ExchangeControl method retrieves the wallet information for the given address via the GetAccountInfoAsync method and based on this information, notifies the user that the transaction has reached an exchange company. If the address can be associated with an exchange, the outtransaction object is updated and the relevant exchange information (AddressTag) is added to the transaction details. A Label object is dynamically created to provide a visual alert to the user. This label contains a message explaining that the transaction is associated with the stock exchange firm and is highlighted with a red background. This function detects whether a transaction is associated with a stock exchange firm and provides the user with a clear visual warning of this information. In particular, it highlights that in cases where the transaction chain is interrupted on an exchange, the user should contact the relevant exchange for more information.

Figure 11. Exchange account control

```
private static async Task ExchangeControl(string toaddress, Panel panel, TransactionData outtransaction, int locX)
{
    AccountTransactions accountTransactions = new AccountTransactions();
    TronAccount account = await accountTransactions.GetAccountInfoAsync<TronAccount>(toaddress);
    outtransaction.Hash = "Exchange";
    outtransaction.To = toaddress;
    outtransaction.Token_Name = account.AddressTag;
    string text = $"Para {account.AddressTag + " isimli" ?? "KİMLİĞİ BELİRSİZ bir"} Exchange Firmasına Ulaştı!\nBir önceki işlemin bilgilerini {account.AddressTag} firmasından talep ediniz. \nAdres: {toaddress}";

    int yOffset = 10;
    int spacing = 10;

    Label dynamicLabel = new Label
    {
        Text = text,
        AutoSize = true,
        BorderStyle = BorderStyle.FixedSingle,
        Padding = new Padding(8),
        BackColor = Color.DarkRed,
        ForeColor = Color.White,
        Name = toaddress
    };

    int currentY = yOffset;
    foreach (Control control in panel.Controls)
    {
        currentY = Math.Max(currentY, control.Bottom + spacing);
    }

    dynamicLabel.Location = new Point(locX, currentY);
    panel.Controls.Add(dynamicLabel);
}
```

API Management for Transactions, Wallets and Accounts

The class, shown in Figure 12, is a base class designed to be used as an API client and provides the GetAsync method to perform HTTP GET requests. This method sends an HTTP GET request to a given URL, checks the response, and returns the JSON data converted to an object of the specified type. First, the method sends the HTTP request and verifies that the response was successful. If the response is successful, the content is read and the JSON data is converted to the target object type (T) using JsonConvert.DeserializeObject<T>. If the response contains an internal server error or some other error occurs, a certain number of retries (10 by default) are made. A certain amount of time is waited (5000 ms by default) before each retry. If the retries fail, an exception is thrown with the final error message.

Figure 12. Main API request object

```
using Newtonsoft.Json;

public abstract class BaseApiClient
{
    protected readonly HttpClient _client;

    public BaseApiClient()
    {
        _client = new HttpClient();
    }

    public async Task<T> GetAsync<T>(string url, int maxRetryAttempts = 10, int delayMilliseconds = 5000)
    {
        int retryAttempts = 0;

        while (true)
        {
            try
            {
                HttpResponseMessage response = await _client.GetAsync(url);
                response.EnsureSuccessStatusCode();
                string responseData = await response.Content.ReadAsStringAsync();

                if (responseData.Contains("internal server error"))
                {
                    throw new Exception("Internal server error detected in response data.");
                }

                T result = JsonConvert.DeserializeObject<T>(responseData);
                return result;
            }
            catch (Exception ex)
            {
                retryAttempts++;

                if (retryAttempts >= maxRetryAttempts)
                {
                    throw new Exception($"Failed after {maxRetryAttempts} attempts. Last error: {ex.Message}");
                }

                await Task.Delay(delayMilliseconds);
            }
        }
    }
}
```

The class, TransactionApiClient, shown in Figure 13, provides a specialized client for retrieving transaction information via the TronScan API. The GetTransaction-InfoAsync method retrieves transaction details based on a given transaction hash. The base URL for the API request is defined as the BaseUrl constant, and the hash parameter is added to this URL to create the full URL for the API request. This full URL is passed to the GetAsync<T> method of the BaseApiClient class, and the response from the API is converted into an object of the specified type (Transaction) and returned. This class provides a specially designed tool for retrieving details about blockchain transactions and supports asynchronous operation, making interactions with the API more efficient.

Figure 13. Operations API request object

```
using ScamTracker.Model.Transactions;

namespace ScamTracker.Functions.Apis
{
    public class TransactionApiClient : BaseApiClient
    {
        private const string BaseUrl =
"https://apilist.tronscanapi.com/api/transaction-info";

        public async Task<Transaction> GetTransactionInfoAsync(string hash)
        {
            string url = $"{BaseUrl}?hash={hash}";
            return await GetAsync<Transaction>(url);
        }
    }
}
```

The WalletApiClient object shown in Figure 14 was designed to retrieve TRC20 token transfer information of a wallet via the TronScan API. The GetWalletInfoAsync method retrieves transaction information based on a wallet address. The method uses a base URL (BaseUrl) to make a request to the API, and the full request URL is generated with user-supplied parameters (start, limit, direction). Also, using the trc20Id constant, only transactions related to a specific TRC20 token type (e.g. USDT) are retrieved. This full URL is sent to the API via the GetAsync<T> method, and the response from the API is converted into a WalletTransaction object. The transaction data (Data) in the response is returned as a list. This class provides a powerful tool to easily query a wallet's TRC20 transactions and retrieve the relevant data.

Figure 14. Wallet API request object

```
using ScamTracker.Model.Wallets;

namespace ScamTracker.Functions.Apis
{
    public class WalletApiClient : BaseApiClient
    {
        private const string BaseUrl =
 "https://apilist.tronscanapi.com/api/transfer/trc20";

        public async Task<List<TransactionData>> GetWalletInfoAsync(
            string address,
            int start = 0,
            int limit = 50,
            int direction = 0)
        {
            string trc20Id = "TR7NHqjeKQxGTCi8q8ZY4pL8otSzgjLj6t";
            string url = $"{BaseUrl}?address={address}&trc20Id={trc20Id}&start=
 {start}&limit={limit}&direction=
 {direction}&reverse=true&db_version=1&start_timestamp=&end_timestamp=";

            var data = await GetAsync<model.Wallets.WalletTransaction>(url);
            return data.Data;
        }
    }
}
```

The AccountService class shown in Figure 15 was designed to retrieve account information for a wallet address via the TronScan API. The GetAccountDataAsync<T> method sends an HTTP GET request to the API to retrieve account data for a specified wallet address. The request is made using the https://apilist.tronscanapi.com/api/accountv2 API endpoint, and the wallet address is appended to the URL. The response returned from the API is checked against the HTTP status code (EnsureSuccessStatusCode), then the content in JSON format is read and converted to an object (T) of the specified type with the JsonConvert.DeserializeObject<T> method. This object is then returned. This method provides a flexible and type-safe way of retrieving information for a wallet address, and improves performance by working asynchronously.

Figure 15. Accounts API request object

```
using Newtonsoft.Json;

namespace ScamTracker.Functions.Apis
{
    public class AccountService
    {
        private static readonly HttpClient _httpClient = new HttpClient();

        public async Task<T> GetAccountDataAsync<T>(string address)
        {
            string url = $"https://apilist.tronscanapi.com/api/accountv2?address={address}";
            HttpResponseMessage response = await _httpClient.GetAsync(url);
            response.EnsureSuccessStatusCode();

            string jsonResponse = await response.Content.ReadAsStringAsync();

            T account = JsonConvert.DeserializeObject<T>(jsonResponse);
            return account;

        }
    }
}
```

The functions shown in Figure 16 include a set of helper functions to validate, generate, and hash the hash values associated with blockchain transactions. The IsValidHash method validates that a given hash value is a valid SHA-256 hash; this validation checks that the hash must be only 64 characters long and in hexadecimal (af, 0-9) format. The ComputeSha256Hash method converts a given text into a hash value using the SHA-256 algorithm and returns the result in string format. The VerifyHash method checks that the hash is valid by comparing an input data with its hashed form. Finally, the GetShortenedHash method takes the first 8 and last 8 characters of a long hash value and adds "..." between them to make it more readable. These methods perform the functions of generating, validating, and presenting hash values for blockchain transactions in an easily readable form to the user.

Figure 16. Hash functions

```
public static class HashValidator
{
    public static bool IsValidHash(string hash)
    {
        return Regex.IsMatch(hash, "^[a-fA-F0-9]{64}$");
    }

    public static string ComputeSha256Hash(string rawData)
    {
        using (SHA256 sha256Hash = SHA256.Create())
        {
            byte[] bytes =
sha256Hash.ComputeHash(Encoding.UTF8.GetBytes(rawData));
            StringBuilder builder = new StringBuilder();
            foreach (byte b in bytes)
            {
                builder.Append(b.ToString("x2"));
            }
            return builder.ToString();
        }
    }

    public static bool VerifyHash(string input, string hash)
    {
        string computedHash = ComputeSha256Hash(input);
        return computedHash.Equals(hash, StringComparison.OrdinalIgnoreCase);
    }

    public static string GetShortenedHash(string hash)
    {
        if (hash.Length <= 16)
        {
            return hash;
        }

        string start = hash.Substring(0, 8);
        string end = hash.Substring(hash.Length - 8, 8);

        return $"{start}...{end}";
    }
}
```

The function shown in Figure 17 converts blockchain transaction data into a DataTable format and presents it to the user on a visual table control, the DataGridView. The BindDataToGrid method first creates a DataTable object and adds columns representing transaction details to this table (Hash, Date, Sender, Receiver, Amount, Balance). Then, the given transaction data list (data) is looped through and the information from each transaction is added to the table as rows. While the transaction dates are converted from a Unix timestamp to a readable date format, the transaction amounts (Amount) are converted to a negative or positive value according to the direction of the transaction (sending or receiving). Finally, the table data (DataTable) is bound to the DataGridView (DataSource), so that the transaction data is visualized in an orderly and understandable way.

Figure 17. Showing the transactions in the table

```
private void BindDataToGrid(List<TransactionData> data)
{
    dataTable = new DataTable();
    dataTable.Columns.Add("Hash", typeof(string));
    dataTable.Columns.Add("Tarih (UTC +0)", typeof(string));
    dataTable.Columns.Add("Gönderen", typeof(string));
    dataTable.Columns.Add("Alıcı", typeof(string));
    dataTable.Columns.Add("Tutar", typeof(decimal));
    dataTable.Columns.Add("Bakiye", typeof(string));

    foreach (var item in data)
    {
        dataTable.Rows.Add(item.Hash.ToString(),
Functions.OtherFuncs.ConvertUnixTimestampToDateTime(item.Block_Timestamp).ToString(),
item.From.ToString(), item.To.ToString(), item.Direction == 1 ? -1 *
AmountConverter.ConvertToDecimal(item.Amount, item.Decimals) :
AmountConverter.ConvertToDecimal(item.Amount, item.Decimals),
item.Balance.ToString());
    }

    dataGridView.DataSource = dataTable;
}
```

The function shown in Figure 18 allows users to save the data in the DataGridView to an Excel file. The btnToExcel_Click method uses a SaveFileDialog to prompt the user to select a location and file name to save the Excel file. When the save window opens, only Excel files with the .xlsx extension are allowed to be selected (Filter = "Excel File (*.xlsx)|*.xlsx"). When the user selects a file name and location and confirms the operation (DialogResult.OK), the ExportDataTableToExcel method is called to print the current DataTable data (the transaction data in the table) to the selected file path.

Figure 18. Transferring the table to Excel

```
private void btnToExcel_Click(object sender, EventArgs e)
{
    using (SaveFileDialog saveFileDialog = new SaveFileDialog())
    {
        saveFileDialog.Filter = "Excel Dosyası (*.xlsx)|*.xlsx";
        saveFileDialog.Title = "Excel Dosyasını Kaydet";

        if (saveFileDialog.ShowDialog() == DialogResult.OK)
        {
            Functions.OtherFuncs.ExportDataTableToExcel(dataTable,
saveFileDialog.FileName);
        }
    }
}
```

RUNNING THE APPLICATION

Figure 19 shows the user interface showm when the application is run. At the top, there is a special title bar and the name of the window "SCAM TRACKER". In the upper right corner, there is a red close button. In the center of the user interface is a text box that asks the user to enter a transaction ID (TXID). Directly below or next to this text box is a button called "START". The button is designed to start a transaction based on the entered TXID. The rest of the screen is left blank, designed as an area that is planned to be filled dynamically after the transaction is made.

Figure 19. The applicaton's user interface

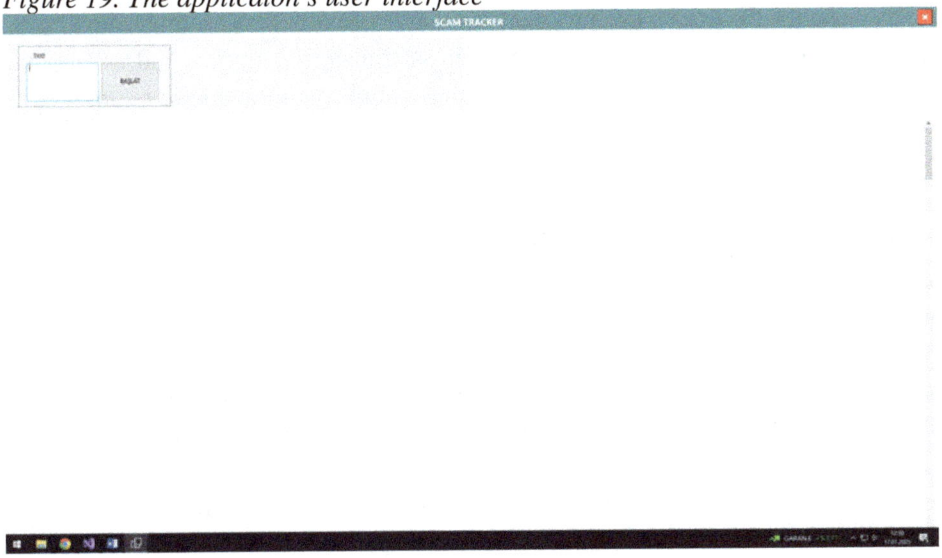

Figure 20 shows the interface that the application presents to the user during a transaction query. The details of the transaction (TXID) being queried and the transaction flow are visualized on the screen.

Figure 20. Running a query

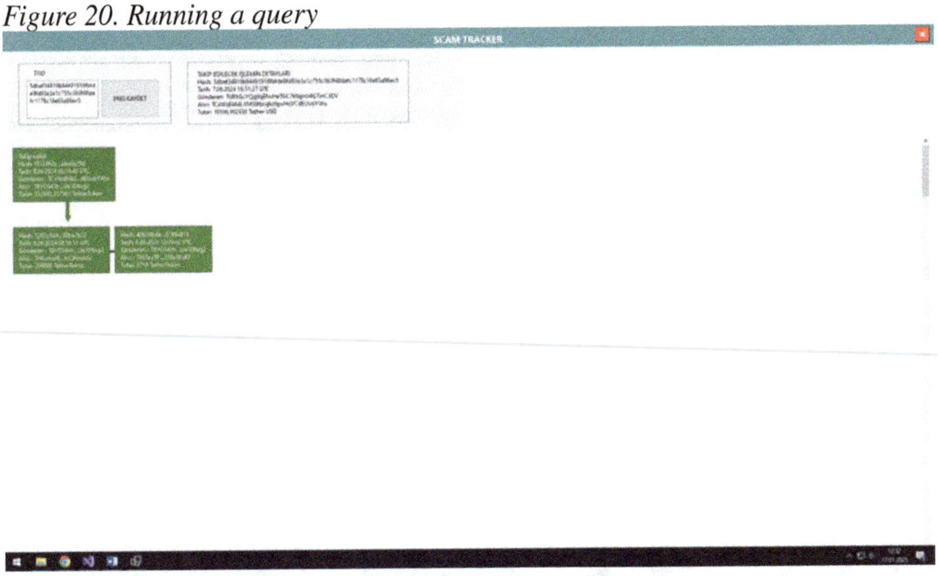

In the upper right section of the user interface, the details of the queried transaction are displayed to the user. This information includes details such as transaction hash, date and time, sender address, recipient address, transferred amount and token type. This information box provides the user with a summary of the queried transaction. The image visually represents the chain of links of the queried transaction. The first transaction is marked with the label "Followed" and connected to subsequent transactions by a line.

Each transaction is detailed in a box with information such as hash, date, sender, recipient, and amount transferred. This form allows the user to visually and textually analyze transactions associated with the queried TXID.

Figure 21 shows an information window that opens when a label showing a transaction detail. This window allows the selected transaction to be examined in more detail. The window contains details such as the hash value of the selected transaction, date and time (in UTC format), sender address, recipient address and amount transferred. This information provides the user with the full content of the transaction, allowing them to understand which parties the transaction took place between and how much was transferred. This information window provides the user with comprehensive and organized information about a particular transaction. Accessible by right-clicking, this detailed view allows users to perform more in-depth analysis on a single transaction. This ensures that critical details are quickly available when querying or tracking transactions, helping the user to make the right decisions.

Figure 21. Transaction details

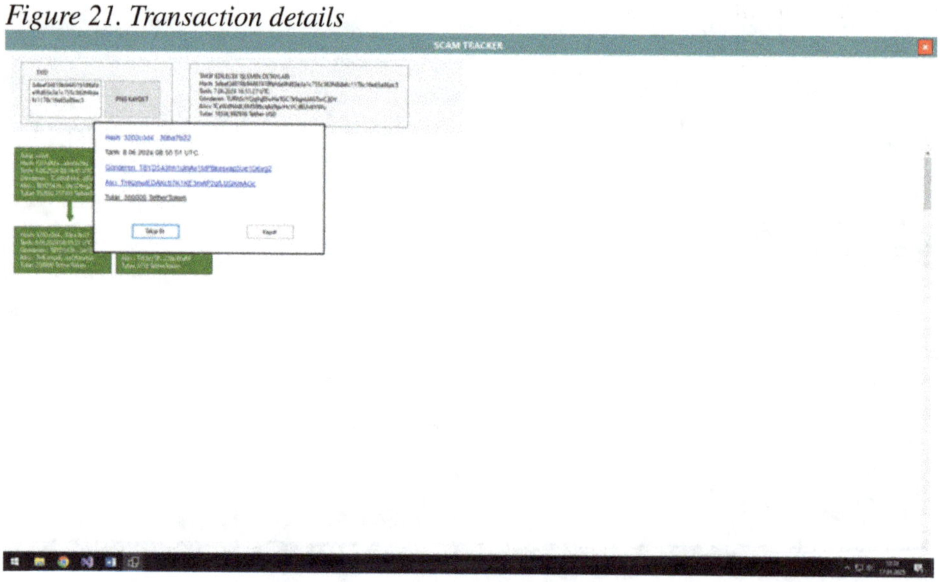

Figure 22 shows a window that opens when a label is left-clicked in the application, showing a detailed table of all wallet transactions belonging to the sender address of the selected transaction. This window allows the user to analyze all transactions belonging to the selected wallet in detail. Transactions are displayed in a tabular format, providing the user with a complete view of the financial flow of transactions and associated addresses. By examining this information, the user can establish connections between specific transactions or detect suspicious situations. In addition, the ability to export data to Excel makes it easier to perform these analyses later or use them in reporting processes. There is a ProgressBar at the bottom and this bar shows that the process is in progress. When the ProgressBar is active, it indicates that the process is not yet completed and no further action is required from the user. This means that the system is currently processing data, analyzing the process chain or receiving new data. The ProgressBar visually indicates to the user that they should wait until it is completed.

Figure 22. List of transfer operations

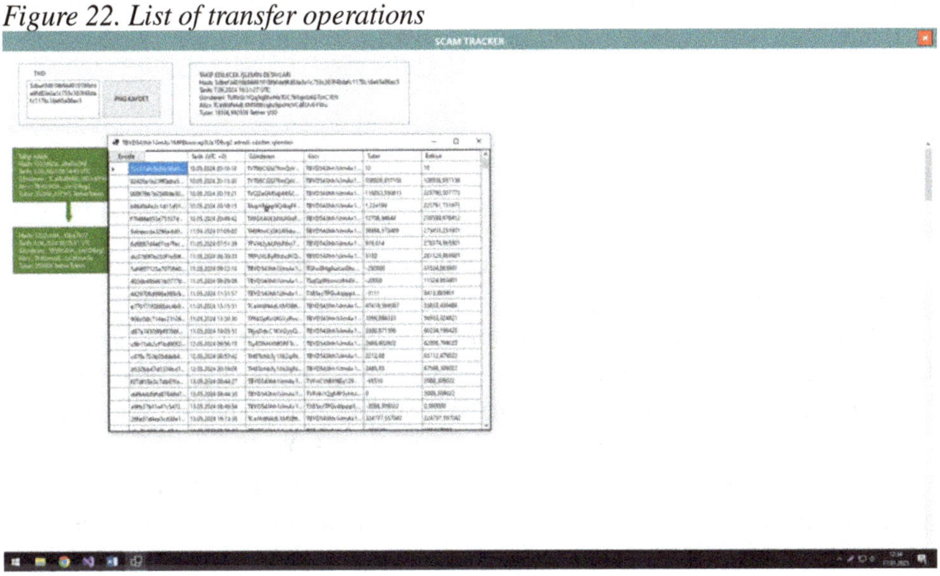

FINDINGS AND DISCUSSION

While the anonymity and decentralization of crypto assets provide numerous advantages for financial transactions, they also facilitate the activities of various criminal elements. Currently, there is a noticeable increase in blockchain-based fraud and money laundering cases, both domestically and internationally. Traditional investigation methods often fall short in the blockchain ecosystem, where record manipulation is challenging, and tracing becomes complex due to the vast number of addresses and transactions involved.

In this study, a software application was developed to reduce the time lost and the risk of human error associated with manual tracking processes. The application retrieves transaction data from the TRC20 network using the TronScan API and analyzes it based on the FIFO principle. One of the key benefits of this application is its ability to visualize complex flows that involve multiple wallets and transactions through a user-friendly interface. This enables investigators to quickly identify addresses linked to criminal activity without becoming overwhelmed by data-intensive analyses. As a result, they can smoothly transition to the next steps, such as requesting information from crypto exchanges or obtaining wallet movement records. By clearly indicating the destination wallet of the digital asset being tracked according to the FIFO principle, the application enhances transparency and traceability in the process of tracking criminal proceeds. Additionally, its intuitive design allows personnel with varying levels of technical expertise in law enforcement to quickly adapt to the system.

CONCLUSION

One of the biggest limitations encountered in practice is when exchanges or "mixer" services come into play. If the relevant exchange does not implement strict identity verification policies or mixers making it difficult to track the crypto asset, the tracking continuity becomes extra difficult. As a result, legal requirements, technological solutions, and international cooperation also stand out as essential.

In this study, a software application based on the FIFO principle was developed to offer a quick and accurate tracking process that speeds up the work of forensic specialists and law enforcement in particular. The application could open the door for the creation of more sophisticated and adaptable automation tools in this area. However, it must stay current and guarantee its network adaptability given the rapidly evolving blockchain technologies and new crypto asset types.

ACKNOWLEDGMENT

Some parts of this chapter were produced from the first author's master's project. This research received no specific grant from any funding agency in the public, commercial, or not-for-profit sectors.

REFERENCES

Abed, A. K. (2025). Utilizing artificial intelligence in cybersecurity: A study of neural networks and support vector machines. *Babylonian Journal of Networking, 2025*, 14–24. DOI: 10.58496/BJN/2025/002

Abed, S. A., & Gök, M. (2023). Big data and artificial intelligence on the blockchain: A review. *Babylonian Journal of Artificial Intelligence, 2023*, 1–4. DOI: 10.58496/BJAI/2023/001

Addula, S. R., Norozpour, S., & Amin, M. (2025). Risk Assessment for Identifying Threats, vulnerabilities and countermeasures in Cloud Computing. *Jordanian Journal of Informatics and Computing, 2025*(1), 37–48. DOI: 10.63180/jjic.thestap.2025.1.5

Agbo, C. C., Mahmoud, Q. H., & Eklund, J. M. (2019). Blockchain Technology in Healthcare: A Systematic Review. *Healthcare (Basel), 7*(2), 56. DOI: 10.3390/healthcare7020056

Al Barazanchi, I. I., & Hashim, W. (2023). Enhancing IoT device security through blockchain technology: A decentralized approach. *SHIFRA, 2023*, 10–16. DOI: 10.70470/SHIFRA/2023/002

Al-Shareeda, M. A., Najm, L. B., Hassan, A. A., Mushtaq, S., & Ali, H. A. (2024). Secure IoT-Based Smart Agriculture System Using Wireless Sensor Networks for Remote Environmental Monitoring. *STAP Journal of Security Risk Management, 2024*(1), 56–66. DOI: 10.63180/jsrm.thestap.2024.1.4

Albinhamad, H., Alotibi, A., Alagnam, A., Almaiah, M., & Salloum, S. (2025). Vehicular Ad-hoc Networks (VANETs): A Key Enabler for Smart Transportation Systems and Challenges. *Jordanian Journal of Informatics and Computing, 2025*(1), 4–15. DOI: 10.63180/jjic.thestap.2025.1.2

Aldossary, A., Algirim, T., Almubarak, I., & Almuhish, K. (2024). Cyber Security in Data Breaches. *Journal of Cyber Security and Risk Auditing, 2024*(1), 14–22. DOI: 10.63180/jcsra.thestap.2024.1.3

Ali, A. (2024). Adaptive and Context-Aware Authentication Framework Using Edge AI and Blockchain in Future Vehicular Networks. *STAP Journal of Security Risk Management, 2024*(1), 45–56. DOI: 10.63180/jsrm.thestap.2024.1.3

Ali, A., & Shehab, R. (2023). A Systematic Review of Security Risk Management for Banking Systems. *Journal of Cyber Security and Risk Auditing, 2023*(1), 49–72. DOI: 10.63180/jcsra.thestap.2023.1.4

Ali, G., Samuel, A., Kabiito, S. P., Morish, Z., Thomas, A., Robert, W., Denis, A., Sallam, M., Mijwil, M. M., Ayad, J., Salau, A. O., & Dhoska, K. (2025). Integration of artificial intelligence, blockchain, and quantum cryptography for securing the Industrial Internet of Things (IIoT): Recent advancements and future trends. *Applied Data Science and Analysis, 2025*, 19–82. DOI: 10.58496/ADSA/2025/004

Almaayah, M., & Sulaiman, R. B. (2024). Cyber Risk Management in the Internet of Things: Frameworks, Models, and Best Practices. *STAP Journal of Security Risk Management, 2024*(1), 3–23. DOI: 10.63180/jsrm.thestap.2024.1.1

Almelehy, B., Ahmad, M., Nassreddine, G., Maayah, M., & Achanta, A. (2025). Analytical analysis of cyber threats and defense mechanisms for web application security. *Journal of Cyber Security and Risk Auditing, 2025*(3), 57–76. DOI: 10.63180/jcsra.thestap.2025.3.4

Alsahaim, S., & Maayah, M. (2023). Analyzing Cybersecurity Threats on Mobile Phones. *STAP Journal of Security Risk Management, 2023*(1), 3–19. DOI: 10.63180/jsrm.thestap.2023.1.2

Alshinwan, M., Memon, A. G., Ghanem, M. C., & Almaayah, M. (2025). Unsupervised text feature selection approach based on improved Prairie dog algorithm for the text clustering. *Jordanian Journal of Informatics and Computing, 2025*(1), 27–36. DOI: 10.63180/jjic.thestap.2025.1.4

AlShuaibi, A., Arshad, M. W., & Maayah, M. (2025). A hybrid genetic algorithm and hidden Markov model-based hashing technique for robust data security. *Journal of Cyber Security and Risk Auditing, 2025*(3), 42–56. DOI: 10.63180/jcsra.thestap.2025.3.6

Ang, S., Ho, M., Huy, S., & Janarthanan, M. (2025). Utilizing IDS and IPS to improve cybersecurity monitoring process. *Journal of Cyber Security and Risk Auditing, 2025*(3), 77–88. DOI: 10.63180/jcsra.thestap.2025.3.10

Ante, L. (2021). Smart contracts on the blockchain – A bibliometric analysis and review. *Telematics and Informatics, 57*, 101519. DOI: 10.1016/j.tele.2020.101519

Back, A., Corallo, M., Dashjr, L., Friedenbach, M., Maxwell, G., Miller, A., & Poelstra, A. (2014). Enabling Blockchain Innovations with Pegged Sidechains.

Beniiche, A. (2020). A study of blockchain oracles. arXiv preprint arXiv:2004.07140.

Bertucci, L. (2024). Bitcoin Ordinals: Determinants and impact on total transaction fees. Research in International Business and Finance, 70(A), 102338. DOI: 10.1016/j.ribaf.2024.102338

Bonneau, J., Miller, A., & Clark, J. (2015). Sok: Research Perspectives and Challenges for Bitcoin and Cryptocurrencies. *IEEE Symposium on Security and Privacy*. DOI: 10.1109/SP.2015.14

Burhanuddin, M. A. (2023). Assessing the vulnerability of quantum cryptography systems to emerging cyber threats. *SHIFRA*, *2023*, 26–33. DOI: 10.70470/SHIFRA/2023/004

Buterin, V. (2014). Ethereum: A Next-Generation Smart Contract and Decentralized Application Platform.

Davarasan, A., Samual, J., Palansundram, K., & Ali, A. (2024). A Comprehensive Review of Machine Learning Approaches for Android Malware Detection. *Journal of Cyber Security and Risk Auditing*, *2024*(1), 38–60. DOI: 10.63180/jcsra.thestap.2024.1.5

Ellis, S., Juels, A., & Nazarov, S. (2017). ChainLink: A Decentralized Oracle Network.

EUROPOL. (2025). EUROPOL. https://www.europol.europa.eu/crime-areas/cybercrime

FATF. (2025). The Financial Action Task Force (FATF). https://www.fatf-gafi.org/en/home.html

Fielding, R. T. (2000). *Architectural Styles and the Design of Network-based Software Architectures*. University of California.

Frizzo-Barker, J., Chow-White, P. A., Adams, P. R., Mentanko, J., Ha, D., & Green, S. E. (2020). Blockchain as a disruptive technology for business: A systematic review. *International Journal of Information Management*, *51*, 102029. DOI: 10.1016/j.ijinfomgt.2019.10.014

Gasser, L. (2023). WEB3. In Mulder, V., Mermoud, A., Lenders, V., & Tellenbach, B. (Eds.), *Trends in Data Protection and Encryption Technologies*. Springer. DOI: 10.1007/978-3-031-33386-6_34

Gopalakrishnan, S., Ruby, E. D. K., Hemanand, D., Anitha, R., Suresh, D., & Choubey, S. B. (2024). Leveraging AI and Blockchain in MANETs to enhance Smart City Infrastructure and Autonomous Vehicular Networks. *Babylonian Journal of Machine Learning*, *2024*, 112–120. DOI: 10.58496/BJML/2024/011

INTERPOL. (2025). INTERPOL. https://www.interpol.int/Crimes/Cybercrime

Jacobson, D., Brail, G., & Woods, D. (2011). *APIs: A Strategy Guide*. O'Reilly Media.

Jishkariani, M. (2024). Assessment of Cyber Security Risks in Electrical Engineering System of Georgia. *Mesopotamian Journal of Civil Engineering*, *2024*, 54–59. DOI: 10.58496/MJCE/2024/008

Kareem, A. B. A. (2024). Modelling Of Blockchain Technology. *SHIFRA*, *2024*, 97–104. DOI: 10.70470/SHIFRA/2024/011

Khalaf, M. A., & Steiti, A. (2024). Artificial intelligence predictions in cyber security: Analysis and early detection of cyber attacks. *Babylonian Journal of Machine Learning*, *2024*, 63–68. DOI: 10.58496/BJML/2024/006

Mohammed, S. Y., & Aljanabi, M. (2023). Human-Centric IoT for Health Monitoring in the Healthcare 5.0 FrameworkDescriptive Analysis and Directions for Future Research. *EDRAAK*, *2023*, 21–26. DOI: 10.70470/EDRAAK/2023/005

Moharrer, M. M., & Nogoorani, S. D. (2020, September). A decentralized App Store using the blockchain technology. In 2020 17th International ISC Conference on Information Security and Cryptology (ISCISC) (pp. 14-21). IEEE. DOI: 10.1109/ISCISC51277.2020.9261911

Nakamoto, S. (2009). Bitcoin: A Peer-to-Peer Electronic Cash System.

Pautasso, C., Zimmermann, O., & Leymann, F. (2008). Restful Web Services vs. "Big" Web Services: Making the Right Architectural Decision. *17th International World Wide Web Conference*. DOI: 10.1145/1367497.1367606

Porras, E., & Daugherty, B. (2022). Bitcoin and Ethics in a Technological Society. IntechOpen. DOI: 10.5772/intechopen.96798

Reddy, M. (2011). *API Design for C*. Elsevier.

Saberi, S., Kouhizadeh, M., Sarkis, J., & Shen, L. (2018). Blockchain technology and its relationships to sustainable supply chain management. *International Journal of Production Research*, *57*(7), 2117–2135. DOI: 10.1080/00207543.2018.1533261

Saleh, H. M. (2024). A Comprehensive Review of Data Mining Techniques for Diabetes Diagnosis Using the Pima Indian Diabetes Dataset. *EDRAAK, 2024*, 39–42. DOI: 10.70470/EDRAAK/2024/006

Saleh, H. M., Oleiwi, A. K., & Abed, A. A. H. (2023). Detecting attacks in banks by cyber security: An applied study. *Babylonian Journal of Machine Learning, 2023*, 65–72. DOI: 10.58496/BJML/2023/011

Salih, H. M., & Mahmood, A. M. (2024). A electric vehicle blockchain: Problems and opportunities. *Babylonian Journal of Networking, 2024*, 18–24. DOI: 10.58496/BJN/2024/003

Schinckus, C. (2021). Proof-of-work based blockchain technology and Anthropocene: An undermined situation? *Renewable & Sustainable Energy Reviews, 52*, 111682. DOI: 10.1016/j.rser.2021.111682

Singh, A., Click, K., Parizi, R. M., Zhang, Q., Dehghantanha, A., & Choo, K. K. R. (2020). Sidechain technologies in blockchain networks: An examination and state-of-the-art review. *Journal of Network and Computer Applications, 149*, 102471. DOI: 10.1016/j.jnca.2019.102471

Spasovski, J., & Eklund, P. (2017). Proof of Stake Blockchain: Performance and Scalability for Groupware Communications. In *Proceedings of the 9th International Conference on Management of Digital EcoSystems (MEDES '17)*. Association for Computing Machinery. DOI: 10.1145/3167020.3167058

Tapscott, D., & Tapscott, A. (2016). *Blockchain Revolution: How the Technology Behind Bitcoin is Changing Money, Business, and the World.* Penguin.

Tironsakkul, T., Maarek, M., Eross, A., & Just, M. (2019). Probing the mystery of cryptocurrency theft: an investigation into methods for taint analysis. arXiv preprint arXiv:1906.05754.

Tripathi, G., Ahad, M. A., & Casalino, G. (2023). A comprehensive review of blockchain technology: Underlying principles and historical background with future challenges. *Decision Analytics Journal, 9*, 100344. DOI: 10.1016/j.dajour.2023.100344

TRON DAO. (2018). TRON: Advanced Decentralized Blockchain Platform. Whitepaper. https://tron.network/static/doc/white_paper_v_2_0.pdf

Upadhyay, A., Mukhuty, S., Kumar, P., & Kazançoğlu, Y. (2021). Blockchain technology and the circular economy: Implications for sustainability and social responsibility. *Journal of Cleaner Production, 293*, 126130. DOI: 10.1016/j.jclepro.2021.126130

Vaigandla, K. K. (2025). An Extensive Examination on IOT and Industrial IOT: Attacks, Security, Detection Methods, Blockchain Solutions and Challenges. *Babylonian Journal of Internet of Things*, *2025*, 89–100. DOI: 10.58496/BJIoT/2025/004

Wang, Q., Li, R., Wang, Q., & Chen, S. (2021). Non-Fungible Token (NFT): Overview, Evaluation, Opportunities and Challenges. arXiv preprint.

Xu, X., Weber, I., & Staples, M. (2021). *Architecture for Blockchain Applications*. Springer.

Yaga, D., Mell, P., Roby, N., & Scarfone, K. (2018). *Blockchain Technology Overview*. National Institute of Standards and Technology. DOI: 10.6028/NIST.IR.8202

Zaman, D., & Mazinani, M. (2023). Cybersecurity in smart grids: Protecting critical infrastructure from cyber attacks. *SHIFRA*, *2023*, 86–94. DOI: 10.70470/SHIFRA/2023/010

Chapter 4
Fortifying Digital Frontiers:
Cybersecurity and Privacy Strategies in Smart Ecosystems

Puppala Naga Sravanthi
https://orcid.org/0009-0006-3255-2194
SRM University, India

ABSTRACT

The growth of smart technologies such as IoT, AI, and autonomous systems has enhanced efficiency but also introduced significant cybersecurity and privacy challenges. This chapter explores key security risks in smart environments, including AI-driven threats, IoT vulnerabilities, and privacy concerns in smart cities. It examines the evolving cyber threat landscape with case studies and ethical dilemmas in technology adoption. Strategies for mitigating risks are discussed, such as encryption, blockchain applications, AI-based threat detection, and compliance frameworks. The chapter also highlights privacy-preserving methods like differential privacy, homomorphic encryption, and secure identity management. Future directions include quantum-safe cryptography and policy recommendations for global cybersecurity governance. Balancing innovation with security, this chapter aims to guide researchers and policymakers toward building resilient and privacy-aware smart ecosystems.

1. INTRODUCTION

The rapid expansion of smart ecosystems encompassing smart cities, IoT devices, connected healthcare, and intelligent transportation has revolutionized how we interact with technology. However, this digital transformation brings unprecedent-

DOI: 10.4018/979-8-3373-2282-7.ch004

ed cybersecurity and privacy challenges. As cyber threats grow in sophistication, securing these interconnected systems is no longer optional but a necessity. This chapter explores the critical cybersecurity and privacy risks in smart ecosystems, analyses recent attack trends, and presents defines strategies backed by the latest research. We will also discuss regulatory frameworks and future directions to build resilient digital infrastructures.

1.1 Overview of Cybersecurity and Privacy in Smart Technologies

The 21st century has witnessed the rapid evolution of smart technologies from smart homes and autonomous vehicles to smart cities and industrial IoT networks. These systems, often integrated through the Internet of Things (IoT), artificial intelligence (AI), and cloud computing, are built to enhance convenience, operational efficiency, and user experience. However, as these technologies become more deeply embedded in everyday life, they have also created vast, complex digital landscapes that are increasingly vulnerable to cybersecurity threats and privacy breaches.

Smart ecosystems, by their nature, are dynamic, interconnected, and data intensive. They constantly collect, process, and share massive volumes of data, including sensitive personal and organizational information. The convergence of physical and digital spaces in these environments makes them particularly attractive targets for cybercriminals. Attacks on smart grids, surveillance systems, healthcare devices, or autonomous transportation not only compromise data integrity but may also endanger human lives and public infrastructure.

The exponential growth of connected devices expected to exceed 29 billion by 2030 ((ENISA), 2023) further exacerbates the security challenges. Each endpoint or sensor introduces a potential entry point for cyber attackers. Inadequate authentication protocols, insecure APIs, outdated firmware, and fragmented security standards are common vulnerabilities. Compounding this is the issue of user privacy. With data continuously harvested through embedded sensors, privacy risks arise from both external threats and internal data misuse or surveillance.

1.2 Importance of Securing Smart Ecosystems

The need for robust cybersecurity and privacy strategies in smart ecosystems cannot be overstated. Unlike traditional IT environments, smart ecosystems are often composed of heterogeneous devices, operating across multiple platforms and jurisdictions. This heterogeneity complicates centralized security management and makes these systems more difficult to protect.

Several high-profile attacks illustrate the urgency of this issue. For instance, the Mirai botnet attack in 2016, which leveraged insecure IoT devices to launch massive DDoS attacks, exposed the fragility of poorly secured smart systems. More recently, in (Zhang, 2023) highlighted how smart medical devices in hospitals were targeted with ransomware, threatening patient safety and operational continuity.

In the context of smart cities, cyberattacks can lead to widespread disruption of critical services such as water supply, electricity, and public transport. In the industrial sector, breaches can compromise manufacturing systems, leading to financial loss, reputational damage, or even geopolitical tensions. The economic impact of cybercrime is projected to reach $10.5 trillion annually by 2025 (Ventures, 2023)

Equally critical is the issue of privacy. Many smart devices, particularly in homes and workplaces, record audio, video, location data, and behavioural patterns. Without strict privacy-preserving mechanisms, such data can be exploited for surveillance, profiling, or identity theft. In regions governed by regulations like GDPR, HIPAA, or India's Digital Personal Data Protection Act (DPDPA), organizations face legal and financial consequences for failing to ensure data protection.

The integration of AI into smart ecosystems further complicates the landscape. AI systems often function as black boxes, making it difficult to audit decision-making processes (Khan, 2022). This opacity, combined with data dependencies, raises ethical concerns about bias, transparency, and accountability. Table 1 provides Recent Cyberattacks on Smart Systems from 2022-24.

Smart ecosystems rely on seamless data exchange between devices, cloud platforms, and users. However, this interconnectivity introduces multiple attack surfaces ((ENISA), Threat Landscape for Smart Devices, 2023):

Key Vulnerabilities:

- **Weak Authentication & Access Control** – Default credentials in IoT devices allow easy breaches (e.g., Mirai botnet attack).
- **Data Privacy Leaks** – Unencrypted personal data from smart homes/health devices can be exploited.
- **AI-Powered Attacks** – Adversarial machine learning can deceive smart algorithms (e.g., fooling facial recognition).
- **Supply Chain Risks** –Compromised hardware/software in third-party vendors (SolarWinds attack).

Table 1. Recent Cyberattacks on Smart Systems (2022-2024)

Incident	Impact	Lesson Learned
Medtronic Medical Device Hack (2023)	Pacemaker firmware manipulated	Stronger FDA cybersecurity mandates needed
Tesla API Exploit (2024)	Unauthorized car access via API flaw	API security must be prioritized
Smart City Ransomware (2022)	Traffic & surveillance systems paralyzed	Air-gapped backups critical

1.3 Scope and Objectives of the Chapter

This chapter aims to explore the multi-dimensional landscape of cybersecurity and privacy within smart ecosystems. It begins by providing an overview of smart technologies, their structure, and vulnerabilities. Subsequently, the chapter delves into key cybersecurity threats such as botnets, zero-day exploits, data exfiltration, and advanced persistent threats (APTs), and their implications for various sectors.

The chapter also evaluates privacy risks associated with data harvesting, storage, and sharing practices in smart environments. Through a critical analysis of existing security frameworks and protocols including blockchain, edge computing, differential privacy, and federated learning the chapter identifies both best practices and research gaps ((NIST), 2024).

Recent innovations in cybersecurity for smart ecosystems are also highlighted, including:

A. Zero Trust Architecture (ZTA)
   - **"Never trust, always verify"** – Strict identity checks for every access request.
   - **Implementation**: Micro-segmentation, multi-factor authentication (MFA), least privilege access.
   - **Case Study**: Google's Beyond Corp reduced insider threats by 60% (Google Cloud, 2023).

B. AI-based anomaly detection
   - Machine learning models detect anomalies in real-time (e.g., Darktrace's Antigena).
   - **Challenge**: Adversarial attacks can poison AI models (MITRE Atlas Framework, 2024).

C. Lightweight cryptographic algorithms for IoT
   - Tamper-proof logs for IoT device communications (IBM's Blockchain Transparent Supply, 2023).

D. Privacy-preserving AI models (e.g., federated learning, homomorphic encryption)
   - Differential Privacy
     - Adds statistical noise to datasets to prevent re-identification (Apple's iOS 17 implementation).
   - **Homomorphic Encryption**
     - Allows computations on encrypted data without decryption (Microsoft SEAL framework).
   - **GDPR & Emerging Regulations**
     - **EU's NIS2 Directive (2024)** mandates stricter incident reporting for smart infrastructure.

E. Blockchain-based identity and access management

The chapter concludes with policy recommendations, a comparative analysis of global security standards, and a roadmap for future research. Table.2 has provided the key objective of the book chapter.

F. Future Directions & Research Gaps
   - Post-Quantum Cryptography: NIST's CRYSTALS-Kyber to counter quantum hacking.
   - Federated Learning: Privacy-preserving AI model training across devices (Google's TensorFlow Federated).

Table 2. Key Objectives of the Chapter

Objective No.	Description
1	Analyse emerging threats and vulnerabilities in smart environments
2	Evaluate privacy risks and ethical concerns in data-driven ecosystems
3	Explore current security mechanisms and their effectiveness
4	Identify cutting-edge research and technologies for cybersecurity
5	Propose best practices and policy recommendations for securing smart systems

The overarching goal is to empower researchers, policymakers, and technologists to better understand and mitigate the cybersecurity and privacy challenges unique to smart ecosystems. By focusing on real-world applications and referencing contemporary research, this chapter seeks to bridge the gap between theory and implementation. Securing smart ecosystems demands a multi-layered approach combining Zero Trust, AI-driven defences, and privacy-enhancing technologies.

Collaboration between governments, enterprises, and cybersecurity experts is crucial to stay ahead of threats.

2. SMART TECHNOLOGIES AND THEIR SECURITY CHALLENGES

As we accelerate toward a hyper-connected future, smart technologies like the Internet of Things (IoT), artificial intelligence (AI), smart cities, and autonomous systems are reshaping the digital landscape. While these innovations bring efficiency and convenience, they also introduce a complex web of security vulnerabilities. This chapter critically examines the security challenges associated with these technologies and emphasizes the need for robust, adaptive cybersecurity frameworks.

2.1. Internet of Things (IoT) Security Risks

IoT is the nervous system of the digital world connecting sensors, devices, and networks across industries. However, its highly distributed and heterogeneous nature makes it a prime target for attackers. Key risks are listed in Figure 1:

Figure 1. Key Risks

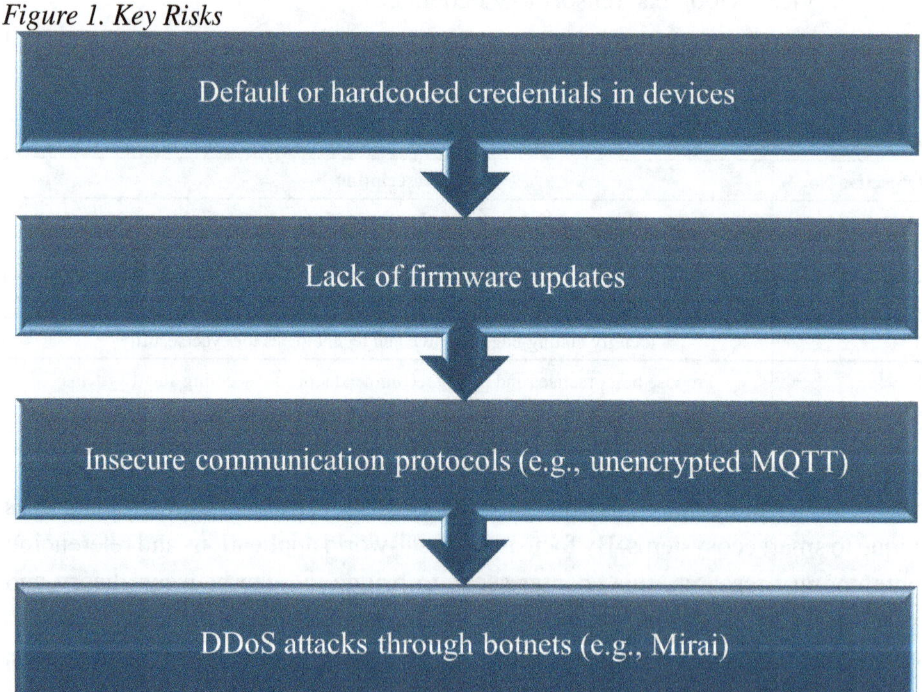

The IoT has revolutionized industries by enabling seamless connectivity between devices, from smart home appliances to industrial sensors. However, this interconnectedness introduces significant security risks. Many IoT devices lack robust security measures, making them vulnerable to cyberattacks such as Distributed Denial of Service (DDoS) attacks, data breaches, and unauthorized access (Deepa V Jose, 2018). For instance, the Mirai botnet attack in 2016 exploited weak default passwords in IoT devices, hijacking thousands of cameras and routers to launch massive DDoS attacks (Antonakakis, 2017).

Another concern is the lack of standardized security protocols across IoT manufacturers. Some devices transmit data without encryption, exposing sensitive user information. Additionally, IoT devices often have long lifespans but receive minimal firmware updates, leaving them susceptible to newly discovered vulnerabilities (Kolias, 2017). To mitigate these risks, manufacturers must adopt strong encryption, enforce secure authentication, and ensure regular software updates. Figure provides risk mitigation techniques in IoT. Figure 2 has provided IOT security risks mitigation techniques.

Figure 2. IoT Security Risk Mitigation

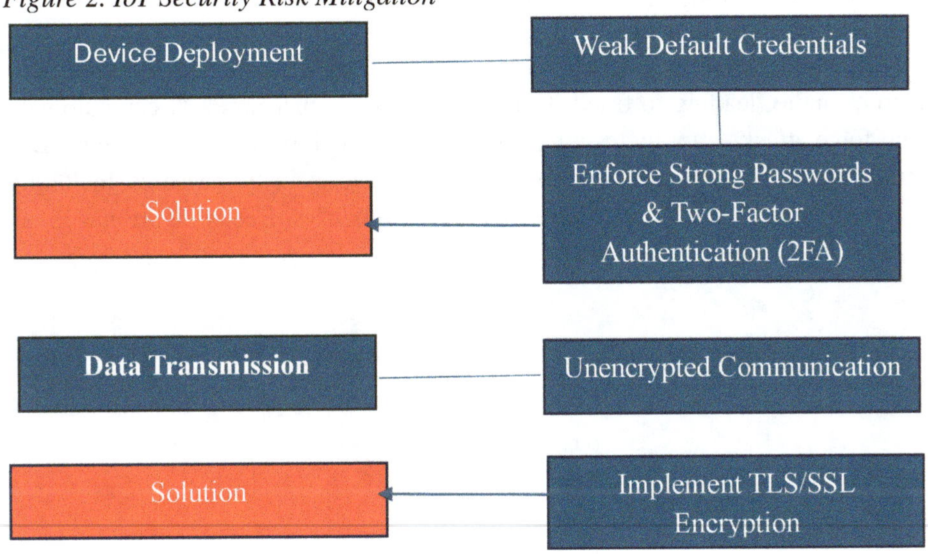

2.2 AI-Driven Cybersecurity Threats

Artificial Intelligence (AI) enhances security monitoring and prediction but also equips malicious actors with new tools. From data poisoning to deepfakes, the same algorithms that protect can be turned against their creators.

- **Emerging Threats**:
  - **Adversarial attacks** that mislead AI models by subtly manipulating inputs.
  - **AI-generated phishing** campaigns with personalized content.
  - **Model inversion attacks**, where attackers infer sensitive training data from exposed AI models.

AI has enhanced cybersecurity through threat detection and automated responses, but it also poses new risks. Cybercriminals leverage AI to develop sophisticated attacks, such as adversarial machine learning, where attackers manipulate AI models by feeding them deceptive data (Papernot, 2016). For example, AI-powered phishing attacks can generate highly personalized emails, making them harder to detect. Fig.4 AI attacks vss. AI defences.

Deepfake technology, another AI-driven threat, can impersonate individuals in video or audio, leading to fraud (Chesney, 2019). Furthermore, AI can automate brute-force attacks, rapidly testing password combinations to breach systems. Defending against AI-powered threats requires adaptive security measures, including AI-based anomaly detection and behavioural biometrics. Below figure has given Possible AI attacks and its Defenders.

Figure 3. AI attacks vs. AI Defense

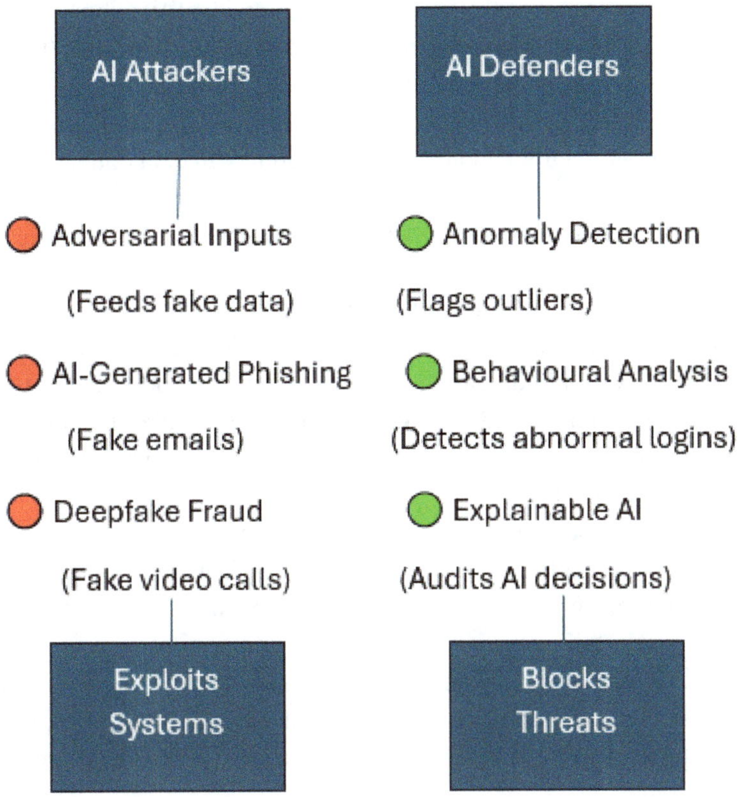

2.3 Privacy Concerns in Smart Cities

Smart cities collect vast amounts of data from traffic patterns to individual behaviours. While this enables better public services, it also threatens personal privacy.

Concerns:

- Mass surveillance without informed consent.
- Data aggregation and profiling of citizens.
- Weak anonymization practices making re-identification possible.

Smart cities utilize IoT, AI, and big data to optimize urban living, but they also raise serious privacy concerns. Surveillance systems, traffic sensors, and facial recognition technologies collect vast amounts of personal data, often without explicit consent (Zuboff, 2019). For instance, China's social credit system tracks citizens' behavior, raising ethical debates about mass surveillance and data misuse.

Data aggregation in smart cities can lead to re-identification attacks, where anonymized data is cross-referenced to reveal individuals' identities (Ohm, 2010). Additionally, centralized databases storing citizens' information are prime targets for cyberattacks. To address these concerns, governments must implement strict data protection laws (e.g., GDPR) and ensure transparency in data collection practices.

2.4 Vulnerabilities in Autonomous Systems

Autonomous systems, such as self-driving cars and drones, rely on AI and IoT but face critical security challenges. Hackers can exploit vulnerabilities in vehicle-to-everything (V2X) communication, leading to remote hijacking (Petit, 2015). In 2015, researchers demonstrated how a Jeep Cherokee's infotainment system could be hacked to control braking and steering (Miller, 2015). Fig.5 has listed all security risks in autonomous vehicles.

Similarly, drones used for delivery or surveillance can be intercepted, leading to data theft or physical sabotage. Ensuring the security of autonomous systems requires robust encryption, intrusion detection systems (IDS), and fail-safe mechanisms to prevent catastrophic failures.

Autonomous vehicles and drones operate based on real-time decision-making using AI. A single vulnerability can result in catastrophic outcomes, particularly in critical systems like transportation and defence also Table.3 has given summery of risks smart cities.

- **Security Issues**:
  - GPS spoofing and signal jamming.
  - Sensor manipulation or LIDAR spoofing.
  - Insecure communication between vehicle and infrastructure (V2X).

Figure 4. Securing autonomous vehicles

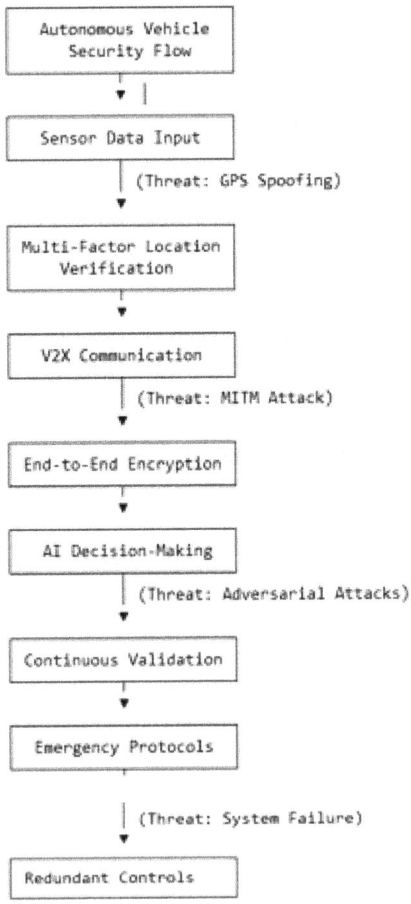

Table 3. Summary of Security Challenges in Smart Technologies

Technology	Security Challenge	Description
IoT	Botnet formation (e.g., Mirai)	Exploits weak credentials to launch DDoS attacks
IoT	Insecure firmware	Devices lack patching mechanisms
AI	Adversarial examples	Inputs subtly modified to fool AI systems
AI	Model inversion	Attackers extract training data from model outputs
Smart Cities	Lack of consent	Citizens unaware of data collection practices
Smart Cities	Data re-identification	Poor anonymization allows tracing data back to individuals

Technology	Security Challenge	Description
Autonomous Systems	GPS spoofing	Sends false location data to autonomous vehicles
Autonomous Systems	Sensor tampering	Alters LIDAR/RADAR data to mislead navigation systems

3. Cyber Threat Landscape in Smart Environments

As the fabric of our cities, homes, vehicles, and workplaces weaves in digital intelligence, the cyber threat landscape has grown increasingly dynamic and multi-dimensional. The convergence of information and operational technologies in smart environments has enabled remarkable advancements yet these innovations are shadowed by increasingly complex and devastating cyber threats (Elmaghraby, 2024). This section explores emerging cyber threats, real-world case studies of major breaches, and ethical dilemmas surrounding smart technology adoption.Fig.6 has given life cycles of cyber attcks in smart cities.

Figure 5. Cyber Attack Lifecycle in Smart Environments

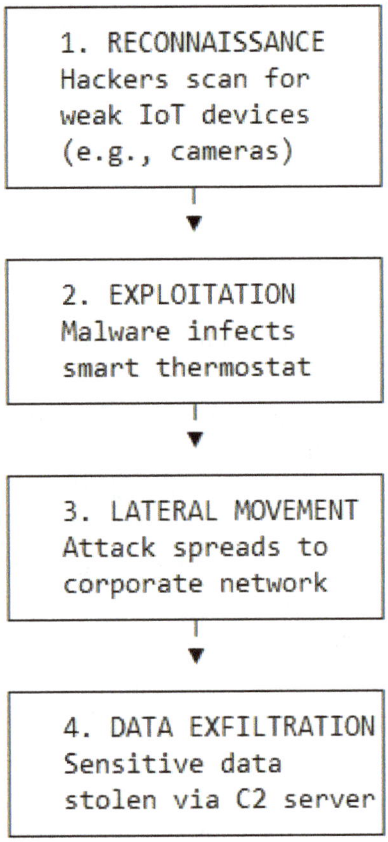

3.1 Emerging Cyber Threats and Attack Vectors

The proliferation of interconnected devices and cloud-based infrastructures has created a wider attack surface than ever before. Threat actors are no longer limited to brute force or phishing today's tactics blend deception, automation, and AI to evade even the most advanced defence systems. Emerging Cyber Threats Vectors and their Description has presented in Table 4.

A. IoT-Based Attacks

Smart environments rely heavily on Internet of Things (IoT) devices, many of which lack robust security. Common threats include:

- **Botnet Attacks**: Compromised IoT devices (e.g., cameras, routers) are hijacked to launch DDoS attacks.
    - o *Example*: The Mirai botnet (2016) infected over 600,000 IoT devices, disrupting major websites like Twitter and Netflix.
- **Ransomware for Smart Devices**: Hackers encrypt critical systems (e.g., hospital IoT sensors) and demand payment.
    - o *Example*: WannaCry (2017) affected smart medical devices, delaying emergency services.

B. AI-Powered Cyberattacks

Cybercriminals now use AI and machine learning to automate attacks:

- **Adversarial AI**: Manipulating AI models with deceptive inputs (e.g., fooling facial recognition with altered images).
- **AI-Generated Phishing**: Attackers use ChatGPT-like tools to craft highly personalized scam emails.
    - o *Example*: In 2023, a deepfake CEO audio scam tricked a UK energy firm into transferring $243,000.

C. Smart City Vulnerabilities

Urban infrastructure (traffic lights, power grids) is increasingly digitized but remains vulnerable:

- **Sensor Spoofing**: Hacker's feed fake data to traffic or pollution sensors, causing chaos.
    - o *Example*: In 2019, a spoofed GPS signal disrupted shipping routes in the Black Sea.
- **Critical Infrastructure Hacks**: Attackers target water treatment plants or power grids.
    - o *Example*: The 2021 Colonial Pipeline ransomware attack caused fuel shortages across the US.

Table 4. Emerging Cyber Threats Vectors and their Description

Threat Vector	Description
Ransomware-as-a-Service (RaaS)	Criminal groups provide ransomware kits to less-skilled actors
AI-Powered Phishing	Personalized spear-phishing generated by natural language models
IoT Botnets	Infected smart devices used for massive DDoS attacks (e.g., via unsecured ports)
Zero-Day Exploits	Attacks exploiting undisclosed vulnerabilities in smart infrastructure
Data Poisoning	Corruption of training data in smart systems to produce faulty decisions

These threats often evolve faster than regulatory or ethical frameworks, making proactive defence and situational awareness essential.

3.2 Case Studies of Major Security Breaches

Case Study 1: The Colonial Pipeline Ransomware Attack (2021)

Background:

In May 2021, Colonial Pipeline operator of the largest fuel pipeline in the U.S. was hit by a ransomware attack attributed to the cybercriminal group *Darkside* (Justice, 2021). Though not a smart city system per se, this incident is a benchmark example of how cyber threats can paralyze critical smart infrastructure.

Key Facts:

- Attackers gained entry through a compromised VPN password.
- Operational technology (OT) systems were shut down as a precaution.
- Fuel supply to the U.S. East Coast was disrupted, affecting transportation and supply chains.
- Colonial paid a ransom of 75 bitcoin (worth about $4.4 million at the time).

Lessons Learned:

- Even isolated IT breaches can cripple OT networks in smart environments.
- Real-time system monitoring and multi-factor authentication could have minimized the breach.
- Post-attack analysis led to new U.S. federal mandates on critical infrastructure cybersecurity.

Case Study 2: AIIMS Delhi Ransomware Attack (November 2022)

Background:

In November 2022, the All-India Institute of Medical Sciences (AIIMS), Delhi India's premier public health institution suffered a massive ransomware attack that paralyzed its digital health infrastructure for nearly two weeks (Ministry of Electronics and IT (MeitY), 2022). This incident underscores the risks associated with digitized smart healthcare systems in India.

Key Facts:

- **Breach Point**: The attackers encrypted critical hospital data stored on over 40 servers.
- **Services Affected**: Outpatient, inpatient, laboratory, and billing systems—all were disrupted.
- **Response Delay**: Lack of a real-time incident response team led to prolonged downtime.
- **National Impact**: Millions of patients were affected, including high-profile individuals and government officials.
- **Attack Attribution**: The Indian government suspected Chinese threat actors were behind the attack.

Impact on Smart Healthcare:

- Exposed the vulnerability of centralized health data repositories in India's public healthcare systems.
- Revealed the absence of basic cyber hygiene practices like network segmentation and endpoint detection.
- Prompted the Ministry of Health and Family Welfare to mandate regular cybersecurity audits for all AIIMS and major hospitals.

Lessons Learned:

- Smart healthcare infrastructures must adopt Zero Trust Architecture to minimize lateral movement of attackers.
- Offline backups and redundant systems are critical to resilience in essential services.
- Cybersecurity training for non-technical staff is crucial in reducing exposure to phishing and insider threats.

Case Study 3: The Mirai Botnet Attack (2016)

- **What Happened?**

Hackers exploited default passwords in IoT cameras and routers to create a massive botnet.

- **Impact**:
    - o Shut down major websites (Twitter, Netflix, Reddit).
    - o Exposed 300,000+ devices to remote control.
- **Lesson Learned**:

Manufacturers must enforce strong default credentials and regular firmware updates.

Case Study 4: SolarWinds Supply Chain Attack (2020)

- **What Happened?**

Hackers compromised SolarWinds' software update system, spreading malware to 18,000+ organizations, including the US government.

- **Impact**:
    - o **Espionage**: Stolen data from Microsoft, FireEye, and federal agencies.
    - o **Cost**: Estimated $100 million+ in damages.
- **Lesson Learned**:

Zero-trust security models and code-signing verification are critical.

Case Study 5: Deepfake CEO Fraud (2023)

- **What Happened?**

AI-generated fake audio of a CEO instructed an employee to transfer company funds.

- **Impact**:
    - o $243,000 stolen before detection.
    - o Loss of trust in voice-based authentication.
- **Lesson Learned**:

Multi-factor authentication (MFA) and voice verification protocols must be strengthened.

3.3 Ethical Dilemmas in Smart Technology Adoption

Smart environments often operate in a Gray zone between innovation and intrusion. With every sensor that monitors energy use, track's location, or scans faces, society confronts ethical questions.

- **Consent & Transparency**: Are citizens informed and consenting to how their data is collected and used?
- **Data Ownership**: Who controls the data generated by smart homes or wearable devices the user or the service provider?
- **Algorithmic Bias**: Facial recognition and predictive policing systems have shown bias, disproportionately affecting minority communities.
- **Surveillance vs. Safety**: Where is the line between public safety and unjustified surveillance?

As governments and corporations adopt smart technologies, ethical frameworks and privacy-by-design principles must be embedded at every stage.

A. Privacy vs. Convenience
   - **Smart cities** collect vast amounts of facial recognition, location, and behavioural data.
   - **Ethical Issue**:
     - o Should governments track citizens for safety if it invades privacy?
     - o *Example*: China's social credit system monitors behavior, raising Big Brother concerns.

B. AI Bias in Security Systems
   - AI-driven surveillance can misidentify minorities due to biased training data.
     - o *Example*: Amazon's Rekognition falsely matched 28 US Congress members with criminal mugshots.
   - **Ethical Solution**:
     - o Diverse training datasets and algorithm audits.

C. Autonomous Weapons and Cyber Warfare
   - AI-powered drones can make lethal decisions without human oversight.
   - **Ethical Concern**:
     - o Who is responsible if an autonomous weapon hacks and attacks civilians?
     - o *Example*: UN debates banning "killer robots" due to ethical risks.

Cybersecurity in smart environments is not merely a technical problem (Shaghaghi, 2023) it's a societal one. Threats evolve, infrastructures grow more complex, and attackers grow more resourceful. A layered, ethical, and inclusive approach to cybersecurity must underpin all technological progress in smart spaces. The cyber threat landscape in smart environments is evolving rapidly, with IoT, AI, and critical infrastructure being prime targets. Real-world cases like Mirai, SolarWinds, and deepfake scams highlight the urgent need for stronger security frameworks. Additionally, ethical concerns such as privacy erosion and AI bias must be addressed to ensure responsible adoption of smart technologies.

4. STRATEGIES FOR MITIGATING CYBERSECURITY RISKS

Cybersecurity threats are becoming increasingly sophisticated and diverse, requiring organizations to implement multilayered strategies that combine technology, policy, and human vigilance. This section outlines four key strategies: encryption and data protection techniques, blockchain applications, AI-driven systems, and compliance frameworks.

4.1. Encryption and Data Protection Techniques

Encryption is one of the oldest and most trusted methods for safeguarding digital information. Encryption is a fundamental cybersecurity measure that ensures data confidentiality by converting information into an unreadable format unless decrypted with the correct key. Modern strategies include symmetric and asymmetric encryption, quantum-resistant algorithms, and tokenization. These techniques ensure data confidentiality during storage and transmission. Encryption is often paired with multi-factor authentication (MFA) and secure key management to further reduce the risk of data breaches. Studies emphasize the importance of adopting zero-trust architecture and advanced encryption methods like homomorphic encryption and TLS 1.3 to secure cloud and hybrid systems (Omolara Patricia Olaiya 1, 2024)

Two primary encryption types are:

- **Symmetric Encryption**: Uses a single key for both encryption and decryption (e.g., AES-256). It is fast but requires secure key distribution.
- **Asymmetric Encryption**: Uses public and private key pairs (e.g., RSA, ECC). It enhances security but is computationally intensive.

Three primary data protection techniques are:

- **Data Masking**: Replaces sensitive data with fictitious but realistic values to prevent exposure (Patel, 2019).
- **Tokenization**: Substitutes sensitive data with non-sensitive tokens, reducing breach impact (Batchu, 2025).
- **Homomorphic Encryption**: Allows computations on encrypted data without decryption, enhancing privacy in cloud computing (Acar, 2018).

4.2. Blockchain Applications for Security and Transparency

Blockchain technology is being used to enhance security and transparency by creating immutable, decentralized logs of transactions and access. In cybersecurity, it supports secure data sharing, tamper-proof audit trails, and automated compliance via smart contracts. Key applications include:

a) Secure Identity Management

Blockchain enables decentralized identity verification, reducing reliance on centralized databases vulnerable to breaches.

b) Fraud Prevention in Transactions

Smart contracts automate and secure transactions, minimizing human intervention and fraud risks (Buterin, 2014).

c) Supply Chain Security

Blockchain ensures transparency by recording every transaction in an immutable ledger, preventing tampering (Kshetri, 2021).

Recent research highlights how blockchain can improve security policy enforcement, mitigate data tampering, and support AI model governance, especially in compliance with laws like the EU AI Act (Alevizos, 2024)

4.3. AI-Driven Threat Detection and Response Systems

Artificial Intelligence (AI) enhances cybersecurity by enabling real-time threat detection, behavioural analysis, and automated response to attacks. Machine learning algorithms can identify anomalies, detect malware, and respond to zero-day threats far faster than traditional systems. AI enhances cybersecurity by automating threat detection and response. Key applications include:

a) Anomaly Detection

Machine Learning (ML) models analyse network traffic patterns to detect deviations indicating cyberattacks (Chandola, 2009).

b) Predictive Threat Intelligence

AI analyses historical attack data to predict future threats, enabling proactive defence.

c) Automated Incident Response

AI-powered Security Orchestration, Automation, and Response (SOAR) systems reduce response time by automating containment measures (IBM Security, 2022). Several studies show that AI systems significantly improve response time and reduce false positives in threat detection environments. They are also key to managing risk in healthcare, financial systems, and cloud infrastructure (Security, 2022).

4.4. Regulatory and Compliance Frameworks

Regulatory compliance plays a foundational role in risk mitigation. Frameworks like the General Data Protection Regulation (GDPR), California Consumer Privacy Act (CCPA), and Payment Card Industry Data Security Standard (PCI DSS) compel organizations to follow stringent data protection protocols.

New research emphasizes the need to integrate AI and blockchain solutions into compliance workflows to meet emerging legal requirements and enable real-time auditability. AI can automatically detect compliance violations, while blockchain ensures immutable records for audits (Alevizos L., 2024).

Adhering to cybersecurity regulations ensures legal compliance and reduces organizational risk. Key frameworks include:

a) General Data Protection Regulation (GDPR)

Mandates data protection and breach notification for EU citizens (GDPR, 2018).

b) NIST Cybersecurity Framework

Provides guidelines for risk management and cybersecurity best practices (NIST, 2018).

c) ISO/IEC 27001

An international standard for Information Security Management Systems (ISMS) (ISO, 2022).

A strong cybersecurity posture requires an integrated approach that combines cutting-edge technologies like AI and blockchain with solid regulatory compliance and traditional protection techniques like encryption. Organizations that adopt these strategies not only reduce risk but also increase resilience, transparency, and consumer trust. Mitigating cybersecurity risks requires a multi-layered approach, combining encryption, blockchain, AI-driven security, and regulatory compliance. Organizations must continuously update their defences to counter evolving threats. By integrating these strategies, businesses can enhance resilience, protect sensitive data, and maintain stakeholder trust.

5. PRIVACY-PRESERVING MECHANISMS IN SMART TECHNOLOGIES

5.1 Privacy-Preserving Mechanisms in Smart Technologies

As smart technologies such as IoT devices, AI-driven analytics, and cloud computing become ubiquitous, ensuring user privacy has become a critical challenge. Cyber threats, data breaches, and unauthorized surveillance necessitate robust privacy-preserving mechanisms. This chapter explores key techniques, including differential privacy, homomorphic encryption, secure data-sharing methods, and identity and access management (IAM) solutions, to safeguard sensitive information in smart ecosystems.

Role of Differential Privacy and Homomorphic Encryption

Differential privacy aims to obscure individual data entries within aggregated datasets. It ensures that the removal or addition of a single record does not significantly affect the outcome of data analysis, reducing the risk of re-identification. It is widely used in public health, census data, and AI models.

Homomorphic encryption (HE), on the other hand, allows computations to be performed on encrypted data without needing to decrypt it. This is especially vital in sensitive fields like healthcare and energy monitoring, where user data must remain confidential even during analysis. Studies show that lattice-based and Gentry–Halevi's fully homomorphic encryption schemes provide strong mathematical guarantees of privacy while enabling real-time data analytics in medical IoT and smart grids (Praveen, 2023).

Differential Privacy: Protecting Individual Data in Aggregated Sets

Differential privacy (DP) ensures that the inclusion or exclusion of a single individual in a dataset does not significantly affect the outcome of statistical analysis. This is particularly useful in smart technologies where large-scale data collection occurs (e.g., health monitoring, smart cities).

Key Mechanisms:

- **Randomized Response Techniques**: Adds controlled noise to data queries to prevent re-identification (Dwork et al., 2006).
- **Privacy Budgeting**: Limits the number of queries to prevent cumulative privacy loss (Abadi et al., 2016).

Applications:

- **Smart Healthcare**: Protects patient data while allowing researchers to analyze trends (Ohno-Machado et al., 2018).
- **Smart Cities**: Ensures anonymity in traffic and surveillance data (Pourebrahimi et al., 2022).

Homomorphic Encryption: Secure Computation on Encrypted Data

Homomorphic encryption (HE) allows computations on encrypted data without decryption, making it ideal for cloud-based smart technologies.

Types of Homomorphic Encryption:

- **Partially Homomorphic Encryption (PHE)**: Supports either addition or multiplication (e.g., RSA).
- **Somewhat Homomorphic Encryption (SHE)**: Allows limited operations before noise corrupts data.
- **Fully Homomorphic Encryption (FHE)**: Enables unlimited computations (Gentry, 2009).

Use Cases:

- **Secure Cloud AI Processing**: Enables machine learning on encrypted datasets (Dowlin et al., 2016).

- **Privacy-Preserving IoT Analytics**: Allows sensor data processing without exposing raw information (Acar et al., 2018).

5.2. Secure Data-Sharing Techniques

Secure data-sharing is critical when transmitting personal or sensitive information across networks. Mechanisms like proxy re-encryption, broadcast encryption, and multi-party homomorphic encryption allow data to be accessed securely without exposing user identities or the actual content. Smart technologies often require data sharing between multiple stakeholders (e.g., hospitals, IoT manufacturers, cloud providers). Ensuring security in such exchanges is crucial.

a) Zero-Knowledge Proofs (ZKPs)

ZKPs allow one party to prove knowledge of data without revealing the data itself.

- **zk-SNARKs**: Used in blockchain and authentication systems.
- **Applications**: Secure authentication in smart contracts and IoT device verification.

b) Secure Multi-Party Computation (SMPC)

SMPC enables multiple parties to jointly compute a function without revealing their private inputs.

- **Use Case**: Cross-institutional medical research without exposing patient records (Yao, 1982).

c) Federated Learning

A decentralized AI training approach where models are trained locally, and only updates (not raw data) are shared.

- **Google's Gboard**: Uses federated learning to improve keyboard predictions without accessing user messages (Konečný et al., 2016).

5.3. Identity and Access Management (IAM) Solutions

Identity and Access Management (IAM) is the backbone of secure digital ecosystems. It ensures only authorized individuals or systems can access specific data.

IAM techniques like revocable identity-based encryption, decentralized identity tokens, and attribute-based access control provide flexible and user-centric control. In smart cities, privacy-preserving broadcast encryption schemes prevent identity leakage even when access rights are revoked, maintaining both security and anonymity. IAM ensures that only authorized users and devices access sensitive data in smart ecosystems. Table.5 has given privacy preserving mechanisms.

a) Decentralized Identity (Self-Sovereign Identity - SSI)
   - **Blockchain-Based Identity**: Users control their digital identities without relying on central authorities (Sovrin Foundation, 2018).
   - **Use Case**: Secure login for smart home devices without centralized servers.

b) Behavioral Biometrics
   - **Continuous Authentication**: Analyzes typing patterns, mouse movements, and gait recognition for fraud detection (Monrose & Rubin, 2000).
   - **Applications**: Prevents unauthorized access in smart banking and IoT systems.

c) Role-Based Access Control (RBAC) & Attribute-Based Access Control (ABAC)
   - **RBAC**: Grants permissions based on user roles (e.g., admin, guest).
   - **ABAC**: Uses policies (e.g., time, location) for dynamic access control (Hu et al., 2013).

Table 5. Comparative Table of Privacy-Preserving Mechanisms

Mechanism	Description	Application Areas	Key Advantage
Differential Privacy	Adds statistical noise to datasets to protect individual entries	AI Models, Healthcare Analytics	Prevents re-identification
Homomorphic Encryption	Enables computation on encrypted data without decryption	IoT, Energy, Healthcare	Strong privacy with functional computation
Secure Multi-party Computation	Enables multiple parties to jointly compute a function over their inputs	Collaborative Research	Ensures data is shared without revealing values
Proxy Re-encryption	Allows intermediaries to re-encrypt data for new users without access	Cloud Data Sharing	Enables dynamic sharing while preserving privacy
Identity-Based Encryption	Encrypts data for a specific identity without revealing the actual identity	Smart Cities, Access Control	Maintains anonymity and access granularity

Privacy-preserving mechanisms are essential for the ethical deployment of smart technologies. Differential privacy and homomorphic encryption protect data integrity, while secure data-sharing techniques (ZKPs, SMPC, federated learning) enable collaboration without exposure. IAM solutions (SSI, behavioural biometrics, RBAC/ABAC) ensure that only authorized entities access sensitive systems. Privacy-preserving mechanisms are no longer optional they are foundational to the ethical and secure development of smart technologies. By integrating cryptographic techniques like homomorphic encryption and differential privacy with robust IAM and secure sharing protocols, smart systems can ensure data utility without compromising user trust. Future research should focus on scalable FHE implementations and AI-driven adaptive privacy controls to address emerging threats in smart environments.

6. FUTURE DIRECTIONS AND INNOVATIONS

Cybersecurity is undergoing rapid evolution as digital infrastructures become more complex, and threats grow increasingly sophisticated. Future developments must not only respond to current challenges but also anticipate and adapt to transformative technologies like quantum computing and AI. Below, we explore three major directions shaping the next generation of cybersecurity: evolving frameworks, quantum-safe cryptography, and global governance policies.

6.1 Evolution of Cybersecurity Frameworks

Cybersecurity frameworks are no longer limited to firewalls and password policies. They have matured into dynamic systems that integrate artificial intelligence (AI), behavior analytics, and real-time incident response protocols. Frameworks like NIST and ISO/IEC 27001 have guided foundational practices, but the growing dependence on cloud systems, IoT, and remote work environments necessitates more adaptive models.

Modern frameworks now focus on resilience, risk-based thinking, and zero-trust architecture. The increasing integration of AI, especially large language models (LLMs), enhances the ability to automate threat detection and policy development. For example, LLMs are now being used not only to identify threats but also to draft compliance protocols and detect phishing attempts based on contextual analysis (Kasri, 2025).

Additionally, sector-specific frameworks are emerging. The financial and healthcare sectors are leading the shift toward integrated security ecosystems, where cyber resilience is embedded across the entire value chain (Kamuangu, 2024).

6.2 Quantum-Safe Cryptography for Smart Environments

Quantum computing presents a double-edged sword. On one hand, it promises significant computational power; on the other, it threatens current cryptographic systems. Algorithms like RSA and ECC, which form the bedrock of today's digital security, are vulnerable to quantum algorithms such as Shor's and Grover's.

To prepare for this, researchers and policymakers are advocating for quantum-resistant algorithms, often grouped under Post-Quantum Cryptography (PQC). PQC includes lattice-based, code-based, and multivariate polynomial cryptosystems. These are designed to resist both classical and quantum attacks. Standards bodies like NIST are currently finalizing new cryptographic standards for the quantum era. Another promising avenue is Quantum Key Distribution (QKD), which leverages quantum mechanics to create secure communication channels. QKD can detect any eavesdropping attempt in real time, offering theoretically unbreakable encryption .

Quantum-safe technologies are not just theoretical. Real-world pilots have already begun, especially in sectors such as national defense, telecommunications, and critical infrastructure protection (Zhou, 2018).

6.3 Policy Recommendations for Global Cybersecurity Governance

Cybersecurity cannot be effectively managed in silos. Cyber threats are borderless, affecting institutions and individuals across the globe. Hence, there's a growing demand for international cybersecurity governance that unifies standards, strengthens cooperation, and promotes ethical technology use. Policy convergence is needed in areas like data privacy, cross-border data flows, and incident disclosure. Frameworks such as the GDPR in Europe have inspired similar initiatives in other regions, but harmonizing these into a global policy remains a challenge.

Recent studies suggest the importance of:

- Creating international agreements on quantum-resilient cryptography standards
- Establishing global incident response coordination centers
- Promoting cybersecurity capacity-building in developing nations
- Ensuring ethical AI governance and algorithmic transparency in cybersecurity tools.

The goal is to create a future where cybersecurity is treated not just as an IT problem but as a shared global responsibility, involving legal, educational, and ethical dimensions.

7. CONCLUSION

As the digital ecosystem expands, cybersecurity must evolve from reactive defense to proactive governance. This chapter has examined both the present innovations and the pathways for securing the future.

7.1 Key Takeaways

1. **Cybersecurity frameworks are evolving** to incorporate AI, real-time analytics, and adaptive defence mechanisms.
2. **Quantum computing represents both a threat and an opportunity.** While traditional encryption is at risk, quantum cryptography and PQC offer robust alternatives.
3. **Policy and governance** must align internationally to create cohesive cybersecurity responses, especially in areas like data sovereignty, compliance, and AI ethics.

7.2 Recommendations for Researchers and Policymakers

- **For researchers:** Focus on scalable, efficient quantum-safe algorithms. Collaborate across disciplines computer science, ethics, law to develop holistic security systems.
- **For policymakers:** Invest in public-private partnerships to fast-track cybersecurity innovation. Mandate secure-by-design principles and strengthen global legal frameworks.
- **For industry leaders:** Embed cybersecurity into product development lifecycles. Train staff continually and adopt zero-trust models to future-proof systems.

7.3 Final Thoughts on the Balance Between Innovation and Security

Innovation and security are often seen as opposing forces where one slows the other. But this dichotomy is outdated. In the future, the most successful technologies will be those that bake in security from the ground up.

The challenge is not to halt innovation, but to guide it responsibly. Cybersecurity must evolve into a value driver, not just a cost center. By aligning technological development with ethical governance and global collaboration, we can build a digital future that is not only innovative but also safe, inclusive, and resilient.

REFERENCES

Acar, A. A. (2018). A Survey on Homomorphic Encryption Schemes: Theory and Implementation. *ACM Computing Surveys.*

Alevizos, L. (2024). Automated cybersecurity compliance and threat response using AI blockchain and smart contracts. *International Journal of Information Technology : an Official Journal of Bharati Vidyapeeth's Institute of Computer Applications and Management.*

Antonakakis, M. e. (2017). Understanding the Mirai Botnet. *USENIX Security Symposium.*

Batchu, S. (2025). Cloud Infrastructure Fortification: Advanced Security Strategies in the Era of Emerging Threats. *International Journal of Scientific Research in Computer Science, Engineering and Information Technology.*

Buterin, V. (2014). Ethereum: A Next-Generation Smart Contract and Decentralized Application Platform. *Ethereum White Paper.*

Chandola, V. B., Banerjee, A., & Kumar, V. (2009). Anomaly Detection: A Survey. *ACM Computing Surveys, 41*(3), 1–58. DOI: 10.1145/1541880.1541882

Chesney, R. (2019). Deep Fakes: A Looming Challenge for Privacy, Democracy, and National Security. *California Law Review.*

Deepa, V., & Jose, A. V. (2018). An Overview of Security in Internet of Things. *Procedia Computer Science*, 744–748.

Elmaghraby, A. S. (2024). Cybersecurity Challenges in Smart Cities: Ethical and Legal Considerations. *Journal of Urban Technology*, 45-62.

ENISA. (2023). *Threat Landscape for Smart Devices.*

Justice, U. D. (2021). *U.S. Department of Justice*. CISA.

Kamuangu, P. (2024). A Review on Cybersecurity in Fintech: Threats, Solutions, and Future Trends. *Journal of Economics, Finance and Accounting Studies.*

Kasri, W. A., Himeur, Y., Alkhazaleh, H. A., Tarapiah, S., Atalla, S., Mansoor, W., & Al-Ahmad, H. (2025). The Role of Large Language Models in Enhancing Cybersecurity. *Computation (Basel, Switzerland), 13*(2), 30. DOI: 10.3390/computation13020030

Khan, M. A. (2022). IoT security: Review, blockchain solutions, and open challenges. *Future Generation Computer Systems*, 395–411.

Kolias, C., Kambourakis, G., Stavrou, A., & Voas, J. (2017). DDoS in the IoT: Mirai and other botnets. Computer. *Computer, 50*(7), 80–84. DOI: 10.1109/MC.2017.201

Kshetri, N. (2021). *Blockchain and Sustainable Cybersecurity*. IEEE IT Professional.

Miller, C. (2015). Remote Exploitation of an Unaltered Passenger Vehicle. Academic Press.

Ministry of Electronics and IT (MeitY). (2022). *Ministry of Electronics and IT (MeitY)*. Government of India.

NIST. (2024). *IoT Device Cybersecurity Guidance.*

Ohm, P. (2010). Broken Promises of Privacy: Responding to the Surprising Failure of Anonymization. *UCLA Law Review. University of California, Los Angeles. School of Law.*

Omolara Patricia Olaiya, T. (2024). Cybersecurity strategies in fintech: safeguarding financial data and assets. *GSC Advanced Research and Reviews (GSCARR)*, 1-20.

Papernot, N. e. (2016). The Limitations of Deep Learning in Adversarial Settings. *IEEE Symposium on Security and Privacy*. DOI: 10.1109/EuroSP.2016.36

Patel, S. (2019). Data Masking Techniques for Privacy Preservation in Big Data. *IEEE Access : Practical Innovations, Open Solutions.*

Petit, J. (2015). Potential Cyberattacks on Automated Vehicles. *IEEE Transactions on Intelligent Transportation Systems.*

Praveen, R. (2023). Improved Gentry–Halevi's Fully Homomorphic Encryption-Based Privacy Scheme. *Transactions on Emerging Telecommunications Technologies.* Advance online publication. DOI: 10.1002/ett.4732

Security, I. (2022). *The Role of AI in Cybersecurity*. IBM X-Force Threat Intelligence.

Shaghaghi, A. S. (2023). A Review of Emerging Cyber Threats in Smart City Environments. *Computers & Security.*

Ventures, C. (2023). *Cybercrime Report.*

Zhang, Y. W. (2023). A blockchain-based tamper-proof framework for secure smart grid communication. *IEEE Transactions on Dependable and Secure Computing.*

Zhou, T. S., Shen, J., Li, X., Wang, C., & Shen, J. (2018). Quantum Cryptography for the Future Internet. *Security and Communication Networks, 2018*, 1–7. DOI: 10.1155/2018/8214619

Zuboff, S. (2019). *The Age of Surveillance Capitalism*. PublicAffairs.

Chapter 5
Decentralized Applications and Distributed Ledger Framework

V. Hemamalini
https://orcid.org/0000-0001-8237-031X
SRM Institute of Science and Technology, Kattankulathur, India

M. Jeyaselvi
https://orcid.org/0000-0003-3386-5177
SRM Institute of Science and Technology, Kattankulathur, India

Amit Kumar Tyagi
https://orcid.org/0000-0003-2657-8700
National Forensic Sciences University, Gandhinagar, India

Shabnam Kumari
https://orcid.org/0009-0001-5442-3020
SRM Institute of Science and Technology, Kattankulathur, India

ABSTRACT

Decentralized Applications (dApps) and Distributed Ledger Frameworks (DLFs) represent critical advancements in the realm of blockchain technology, promising enhanced security, transparency, and efficiency. Decentralized Applications, leveraging the inherent properties of blockchain, operate without central control, offering users greater autonomy and reducing reliance on intermediaries. These applications span various domains, from finance and supply chain management to gaming and social networks, demonstrating the versatility and transformative

DOI: 10.4018/979-8-3373-2282-7.ch005

potential of dApps. Distributed Ledger Frameworks, encompassing both blockchain and non-blockchain-based systems, provide the underlying architecture for these applications. DLFs ensure data integrity, immutability, and consensus across distributed nodes, fostering a trustless environment where participants can transact securely. Key frameworks like Ethereum, Hyperledger, and Corda offer diverse features tailored to different use cases, ranging from public, permissionless networks to private, permissioned systems.

1. INTRODUCTION

1.1 Decentralized Applications

Decentralized Applications (DApps) represent a new paradigm in software development, leveraging the power of decentralized networks, most commonly blockchains. In contrast to traditional applications that depend on centralized servers, DApps embrace the inherent qualities of blockchain technology, providing benefits like enhanced transparency, immutability, and security. At the heart of DApps are smart contracts—self-executing agreements where the terms are directly encoded. These smart contracts automate and enforce agreements, eliminating the need for intermediaries, and resulting in more efficient and fraud-resistant applications. Key characteristics that define decentralized applications include (refer figure 1):

- Decentralization: DApps leverage the power of decentralized networks, usually blockchains, to distribute application data and processes across many nodes. This inherent decentralization gets rid of a central point of weakness, improving both security and the ability to withstand disruptions.
- Transparency: The transparency of blockchain technology enables all DApp participants to view and verify transactions and data, fostering trust and accountability through independent verification of the application's integrity.
- Immutability: Once data is recorded on a blockchain, it becomes virtually impossible to modify or alter it retroactively. This characteristic guarantees the integrity of the application's data and offers a reliable, auditable history of transactions.
- Tokenization: Decentralized applications (DApps) frequently employ tokens to facilitate value exchange within their platforms. These tokens can symbolize a range of digital or physical assets, allowing for seamless transactions. They also serve to incentivize users and encourage active participation in the application's ecosystem.

- Open and Permissionless: DApps are generally characterized by their open-source nature and permissionless access. Being open-source, their underlying code is readily available for public review and community-driven enhancements. Furthermore, anyone can freely use and interact with DApps, as they operate without the need for approvals or intermediaries.

Figure 1. Decentralized Applications

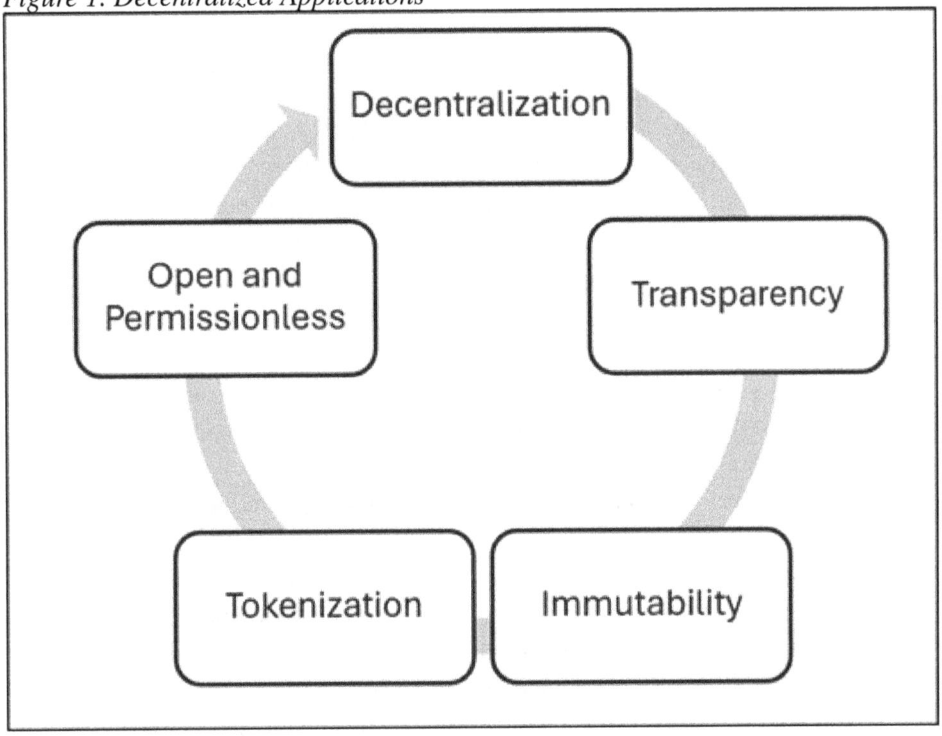

Decentralized applications (DApps) are making significant strides across various industries, including finance, supply chain management, gaming, and social media. They pave the way for innovative business models such as "Decentralized Finance (DeFi)", "Non-Fungible Tokens (NFTs)", and decentralized exchanges. It is important to note that not all applications that label themselves as "decentralized" truly embody this principle. The degree of decentralization can differ significantly among applications. Some may exhibit elements of centralization, especially concerning governance or infrastructure.

In essence, DApps leverage blockchain technology to foster trust, security, and transparency while unlocking new avenues for innovation. They are revolutionizing how applications are developed, deployed, and interacted with in the digital landscape.

1.2 Distributed Ledger Framework

A distributed ledger framework encompasses a collection of protocols, tools, and technologies designed to facilitate the creation, management, and validation of distributed ledgers. A distributed ledger is a unique type of database that is replicated across numerous participants or nodes within a network. This setup allows each participant to maintain an identical copy of the ledger. The primary objective of a distributed ledger framework is to establish a shared and synchronized database that removes the necessity for a central authority or intermediary to validate and record transactions. Instead, the ledger is continuously maintained and updated through a consensus mechanism. In this process, participants collectively agree on the validity of transactions and their incorporation into the ledger, ensuring transparency and trust among all parties involved. Distributed ledger frameworks, often based on blockchain technology, provide several benefits, including:

- Decentralization: The decentralized nature of distributed ledgers, lacking any single controlling entity, brings benefits such as the removal of intermediaries, reduced reliance on a central authority, and improved ledger security and resilience.
- Transparency: Distributed ledgers offer a transparent framework, enabling all participants to access and verify the transactions documented within. This openness fosters trust and accountability among users while allowing for independent verification of the ledger's integrity.
- Immutability: Transactions recorded on a distributed ledger are generally immutable, meaning they cannot be changed or deleted after the fact, guaranteeing the ledger's integrity and auditability.
- Security: Distributed ledgers utilize cryptographic methods to safeguard transactions and uphold data integrity. To defend against malicious attacks and ensure the network's reliability, they implement consensus mechanisms like "Proof-of-Work (PoW)" and "Proof-of-Stake (PoS)".
- Efficiency: Distributed ledger frameworks provide a highly efficient and streamlined approach to recording and verifying transactions. By utilizing smart contracts—self-executing agreements encoded in software—these frameworks automate and enforce transaction terms. This automation minimizes the need for manual intervention and reduces reliance on intermediaries, leading to faster and more reliable processes.

Examples of popular distributed ledger frameworks include blockchain platforms like Bitcoin and Ethereum, as well as other frameworks specifically designed for enterprise use, such as Hyperledger Fabric and Corda. These frameworks provide the foundation for various applications, ranging from cryptocurrencies and "Decentralized Finance (DeFi)" to supply chain management and digital identity systems. Distributed ledger frameworks represent a paradigm shift in data management. Their decentralized nature enables transparent and secure transactions, eliminating the need for a central authority. This promises a future with greater trust, efficiency, and accountability across a wide range of industries.

1.3 Literature Review

Creating distributed applications that operate without a central authority for registering, distributing, and synchronizing transactions involving digital assets relies on Distributed Ledger Technology (DLT). The rise of blockchain technology, its most well-known variant, has garnered significant attention from the academic community, technology developers, and businesses over the past year (Antal et al., 2021). The distributed ledger technology (DLT) ecosystem is currently impeded by inconsistent definitions and a lack of standardized terminology. This paper aims to create a cohesive language and framework that serves as a multi-dimensional tool for legislators, business stakeholders, researchers, and investors. By doing so, it seeks to enhance understanding of the characteristics and functionalities of DLT systems, as well as the roles of various participants within these systems. The paper identifies five essential attributes that a DLT system must possess. Furthermore, it categorizes the types of data within a DLT framework based on the level of data processing performed by the network. The data is classified into five categories: "transactions," "logs," "records," "journals," and "ledger." The term "ledger" is specifically defined as a collection of records that are "held in common by a substantial proportion of network participants" (Anthony Jnr, 2023). Distributed ledger technology (DLT) has recently emerged as a groundbreaking system with the potential to revolutionize societal interactions. In the realm of virtual enterprises (VEs), researchers and practitioners are exploring the use of DLT to automate data processing and decision-making, ultimately improving the delivery of digital services (Puthal et al., 2018). Blockchain technology is rapidly becoming one of the most innovative and advantageous solutions for cybersecurity. In its early stages, this technology has successfully supplanted traditional economic transaction systems in numerous companies and holds the potential to revolutionize various business models across multiple industries. The proposed framework aims to provide a secure and distributed environment for information sharing and integration. However, planners and decision-makers should conduct a detailed assessment to determine whether its benefits outweigh the risks for their particular industry and corporate needs (A. K. V. et al., 2022). The challenge of building distributed applications that require registration, distribution, and synchronized transactions of digital assets, without relying on a central authority, is addressed by Distributed Ledger Technology (DLT). Blockchain technology, the most well-known form of DLT, has sparked considerable interest among researchers, developers, and companies (Khan et al., 2020). Blockchain technology is making significant strides across various domains, including transactions, validations, and financing, capturing the attention of both the IT sector and investors. Decentralized applications, commonly known as dApps, along with blockchain platforms, hold the promise of enhancing numerous services by addressing persistent challenges and creating new opportunities for developers to build applications in a decentralized environment. As the adoption of dApps continues to surge, the prospects for developers and businesses are expanding rapidly. This growing interest in decentralized applications is leading to an increased focus on tools, frameworks, and platforms designed specifically for dApp development. The transformative potential of dApps is driving developer communities to explore these innovative solutions more than ever before (Rauchs et al., 2018).

2. DECENTRALIZATION USING BLOCKCHAIN: METHODS AND ROUTES

Blockchain technology provides various methods for achieving decentralization. Here are some of the key methods employed to achieve decentralization using blockchain (refer table 1):

- Consensus Mechanisms: A key challenge in decentralized systems is ensuring agreement on the validity and order of transactions. Consensus mechanisms solve this problem, enabling blockchains to function without a central authority. Bitcoin's "Proof-of-Work (PoW)", where miners compete to solve complex problems, is one such solution. "Proof-of-Stake (PoS)" and "Delegated Proof-of-Stake (DPoS)" offer alternative approaches, allowing token holders to participate in the consensus process by staking their holdings. The ultimate goal of these mechanisms is to prevent any single entity from dominating the network and compromising its decentralization.
- Distributed Ledger: Blockchain technology employs a distributed ledger, where a complete transaction history is replicated across a network of computers. This eliminates a central authority, as each participant holds a copy of the blockchain. This distributed design enhances security by making it

very difficult for any single party to tamper with the recorded data, ensuring decentralization.

- Peer-to-Peer Network: Blockchain networks leverage a "Peer-to-Peer (P2P)" architecture, allowing participants to connect and transact directly. This eliminates central intermediaries, enhancing decentralization and preventing single points of failure.
- Open Source and Community Governance: Many blockchain projects and protocols operate under an open-source model, which means that their code is accessible to the public for review, contributions, and enhancements by the community. This transparent approach encourages decentralized development and governance, empowering participants to influence the evolution and direction of the protocol. Decentralized decision-making mechanisms, such as on-chain governance and community voting, guarantee that the network's rules and upgrades are collectively established by its members.
- Tokenization and Incentives: Blockchain networks commonly use tokens to incentivize participation and align user interests. These tokens reward validators, grant voting rights, and facilitate value exchange, promoting decentralization by encouraging resource contribution and transaction validation.

Therefore, these methods work together to promote the decentralization of blockchain networks, preventing any single entity from exerting control or dominance over the system. By distributing power, decision-making, and data among a network of participants, blockchain technology fosters trust, transparency, and resilience across a wide range of applications and industries.

Table 1. Methods and Routes in Decentralization using blockchain

Methods		
	Consensus Mechanisms	**To solve complex mathematical puzzles to validate transactions**
	Distributed Ledger	To alter or manipulate the data recorded on the blockchain, enhancing decentralization
	Peer-to-Peer Network	Eliminates the need for intermediaries or central servers, allowing participants to interact and transact directly with one another
	Open Source and Community Governance	On-chain governance or community voting, ensure that the network's rules and upgrades
	Tokenization and Incentives	used to reward network validators, provide voting rights, or facilitate value exchange within the ecosystem
Routes		
	Public Blockchains	To validate transactions and maintain the integrity of the network

continued on following page

Table 1. Continued

Methods		
	Consensus Mechanisms	**To solve complex mathematical puzzles to validate transactions**
	Consortium Blockchains	Multiple organizations collectively validate transactions, reducing the reliance on a single central authority
	Federated Blockchains	Balance between decentralization and scalability
	Hybrid Approaches	Internal operations and data privacy

Routes: Decentralization using blockchain can be achieved through various routes or approaches. Here are some common routes to achieve decentralization using blockchain:

- Public Blockchains: Public blockchains like Bitcoin and Ethereum are highly decentralized, allowing anyone to join as a node. They use consensus mechanisms like "Proof-of-Work (PoW)" and "Proof-of-Stake (PoS)" to validate transactions and maintain network integrity. This distributed structure prevents any single entity from dominating the system, promoting transparency, censorship resistance, and trust. Transactions are visible to all participants and immutable once recorded, while synchronized ledgers ensure data security. Overall, public blockchains exemplify decentralization through open participation, strong consensus protocols, and distributed control.
- Consortium Blockchains: Consortium blockchains are designed for a specific group of organizations or entities that agree to participate in the network. These blockchains are permissioned, meaning participants must obtain permission to join and validate transactions. Consortium blockchains offer a higher level of decentralization compared to traditional centralized systems but are typically less decentralized than public blockchains. In a consortium blockchain, multiple organizations collectively validate transactions, reducing the reliance on a single central authority.
- Federated Blockchains: Federated blockchains use a pre-selected group of entities, known as validators, to maintain the network. These validators, or block producers, are responsible for validating transactions and ensuring the blockchain's integrity. By using this approach, federated blockchains achieve a balance between the decentralization of public blockchains and the efficiency of private blockchains.
- Hybrid Approaches: Hybrid blockchain approaches offer a balanced solution for organizations seeking decentralization. By combining different blockchain architectures, such as public and private chains, or integrating blockchain with other technologies, they offer greater flexibility. A typical use case

involves using a private blockchain for internal operations and linking selected data to a public blockchain for transparency. This allows organizations to benefit from both permissioned and permissionless systems, customizing their level of decentralization.

Note that the level of decentralization can vary across different blockchain implementations and projects. Factors such as the consensus mechanism, network participation, governance models, and the degree of openness influence the decentralization of a blockchain system. Choosing the appropriate route depends on the specific requirements, use case, and trade-offs of the application or network being developed.

3. FULL ECO SYSTEM OF BLOCKCHAIN

The blockchain ecosystem is a complex network that includes a variety of components, participants, and elements working together to facilitate the operation and advancement of blockchain technology. Below are the essential elements that make up this ecosystem (refer figure 2):

- Blockchain Protocol: The blockchain protocol forms the foundation of the ecosystem. It defines the rules, consensus mechanisms, and protocols that govern how the blockchain operates. Examples of blockchain protocols include Bitcoin, Ethereum, and Hyperledger Fabric.
- Cryptocurrencies and Tokens: Cryptocurrencies and tokens are forms of digital assets that function on blockchain technology. Bitcoin, the inaugural cryptocurrency, set the stage for a multitude of other digital currencies, including Ethereum's Ether (ETH) and Ripple's XRP. Tokens, on the other hand, are digital assets created on established blockchain platforms. They serve to represent various utilities, assets, or rights within a specific ecosystem. Unlike cryptocurrencies that typically operate on their own blockchains, tokens often leverage existing blockchain infrastructures to fulfill their intended purposes.
- Decentralized Applications (DApps): DApps represent a new wave of innovation, using blockchain platforms to create decentralized applications. These programs capitalize on the transparency, security, and decentralized nature of blockchain to deliver groundbreaking solutions in areas like finance, supply chain, and gaming. The scope of DApps is broad, encompassing everything from basic games to advanced financial systems.

- Smart Contracts: Smart contracts are self-executing agreements written as code and deployed on a blockchain. The code defines the rules and logic of the agreement, and it automatically executes when predefined conditions are met. This programmability enables automation, removes intermediaries, and enhances trust through cryptographic verification.

Figure 2. Full eco system of blockchain

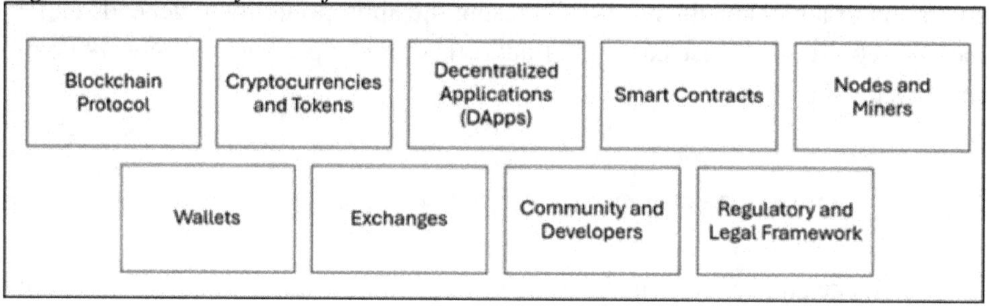

- Nodes and Miners: Nodes are distinct computers or devices that engage in the blockchain network by keeping a complete copy of the blockchain and verifying transactions. In proof-of-work (PoW) blockchains, such as Bitcoin, miners play a crucial role by solving intricate mathematical problems to validate transactions and incorporate them into the blockchain. Both nodes and miners are essential for enhancing the security and decentralization of the network.
- Wallets: Cryptocurrency wallets are essential tools, existing as either software or hardware, that give users the power to securely store, manage, and use their cryptocurrencies and tokens. They provide the functionality to send and receive digital assets, keep track of balances, and connect with decentralized applications (DApps). These wallets come in two main types: custodial wallets, where a third party safeguards the private keys, and non-custodial wallets, which put the user in complete control of their private keys, ensuring maximum autonomy.
- Exchanges: Cryptocurrency exchanges are platforms where users buy, sell, and trade digital assets. These exchanges are either centralized, with a central authority managing transactions, or decentralized, enabling direct peer-to-peer transactions.
- Community and Developers: The blockchain ecosystem thrives on active communities and developers. These individuals and organizations contribute

to the development, improvement, and adoption of blockchain technology. Community members participate in network governance, propose and vote on protocol upgrades, and provide support and education to newcomers.

- Regulatory and Legal Framework: Blockchain technology operates under diverse legal and regulatory frameworks that vary across jurisdictions. Governments and regulatory bodies are creating these rules to address concerns such as anti-money laundering (AML) and consumer protection, while also fostering responsible innovation.

The dynamic blockchain ecosystem thrives on collaboration, innovation, and community engagement. New projects, technologies, and applications are constantly emerging, driving its evolution.

4. SMART CONTRACTS: DEFINITION, HISTORY

Smart contracts are immutable, self-executing agreements written in code and deployed on a blockchain. They automatically enforce predefined actions when specific conditions are met, ensuring transparency and security. Smart contracts reduce the necessity for intermediaries and facilitate decentralized and trustless transactions. Computer scientist Nick Szabo first proposed the concept in 1996, with implementation becoming viable through blockchain technology. Ethereum, a decentralized blockchain platform, significantly contributed to the widespread adoption of smart contracts, and its native language, Solidity, enables developers to create and deploy smart contracts on its blockchain.

Ethereum's launch in 2015 introduced a new era for smart contracts, enabling a wide range of decentralized applications (DApps) and blockchain-based platforms. Since then, other blockchain platforms have emerged, such as EOS, NEO, and Cardano, each with its own smart contract capabilities. Smart contracts have numerous applications beyond financial transactions, including supply chain management, decentralized governance, digital identity verification, and intellectual property protection. They offer increased efficiency, transparency, and cost savings by automating processes and reducing reliance on intermediaries.

4.1 Smart Contracts Evolution

- Conceptualization: In 1994, Nick Szabo conceived smart contracts as self-executing agreements where the terms are directly written into code.
- Blockchain Development: The launch of Bitcoin in 2009 provided a decentralized and secure platform that could support smart contract execution.

- Ethereum: Launched in 2015, Ethereum is a decentralized blockchain with smart contract functionality. Ethereum's introduction of smart contracts has revolutionized the digital landscape, with Solidity as the programming language that empowers developers to create and deploy these contracts. Ethereum, often described as a global supercomputer, offers a versatile and secure platform for constructing, linking, and monetizing a growing ecosystem of decentralized applications (dApps).
- Expansion of Use Cases: As smart contracts gained traction, their applications have expanded to include "Decentralized Finance (DeFi)", decentralized governance, supply chain management and digital identity verification.
- Interoperability and Scalability: Scalability and interoperability challenges have emerged as blockchain platforms aim to support more smart contracts and handle increased transaction volumes. Layer-two scaling solutions and interoperability protocols are being developed to address these challenges. The "Dencun" upgrade went live on March 13, 2024 and lowered transaction fees on Layer 2 networks built on top of the Ethereum blockchain.
- Evolution of Blockchain Platforms: Various blockchain platforms with their own smart contract capabilities have emerged, including EOS, NEO, and Cardano.
- Standardization and Frameworks: Efforts to standardize smart contract development and promote best practices have led to the development of frameworks like Truffle and languages like Vyper to enhance the efficiency and security of smart contract development.
- Integration with Traditional Systems: Integrating smart contracts with traditional systems and enterprises has become a focus, with efforts to bridge the gap between blockchain and existing business processes to enable the adoption of smart contracts across industries.

5. RICARDIAN CONTRACTS

Ricardian contracts are a concept introduced by Ian Grigg, a renowned computer scientist and cryptographer. These contracts combine the benefits of traditional legal contracts with the advantages of blockchain technology. A Ricardian contract is a legally binding agreement that is written in both human-readable and machine-readable formats. The human-readable part of the contract is written in natural language, making it understandable to parties involved in the contract. The machine-readable part is written in a structured format, typically using a markup language like HTML or XML, which can be interpreted by computer systems.

The key aspect of Ricardian contracts is the inclusion of cryptographic digital signatures. Each party involved in the contract signs their respective copies using their private keys. These digital signatures provide proof of authenticity and ensure the integrity of the contract. The use of digital signatures also enables non-repudiation, meaning that a party cannot deny their involvement in the contract. Note that Ricardian contracts aim to combine legal and technical elements to create self-executing agreements. The machine-readable part of the contract contains the logic and conditions that can be executed by computer systems, similar to smart contracts. This allows for automation and self-enforcement of contractual terms. One notable feature of Ricardian contracts is the inclusion of external references. They can reference external documents, such as legal frameworks or terms and conditions, which provide additional context and enforceability to the contract. These external references are typically stored using cryptographic hash functions to ensure their integrity. Ricardian contracts have emerged as a solution to connect legal frameworks with blockchain technology, allowing for the compliant integration of blockchain systems. These contracts offer key benefits such as transparency, immutability, and automation, all while preserving the legal enforceability associated with traditional contracts. Ricardian contracts are designed to improve the efficiency, transparency, and security of contractual agreements. They achieve this by incorporating both human-readable and machine-readable elements, along with cryptographic signatures and external references.

6. DECENTRALIZED ORGANIZATIONS IN THIS BLOCKCHAIN BASED SMART ERA

In this burgeoning era of blockchain and smart contracts, Decentralized Autonomous Organizations (DAOs) are revolutionizing traditional organizational frameworks and attracting considerable interest. Functioning on the bedrock of smart contracts and blockchain technology, DAOs execute decision-making and governance through decentralized consensus mechanisms. Let's explore some core elements defining these innovative organizations (refer figure 3):

- Governance: DAOs are governed in a decentralized manner, with token holders or stakeholders collectively making decisions. Voting mechanisms, such as token-weighted or quadratic voting, empower participants to influence the organization's direction and operations.

- Transparent and Trustless Operations: Blockchain technology underpins DAOs by providing transparent and immutable records of all transactions and actions. Cryptographic security and consensus mechanisms establish trust, removing the need for intermediaries and enabling public auditability.

Figure 3. Decentralized Organizations in This Blockchain-Based Smart Era

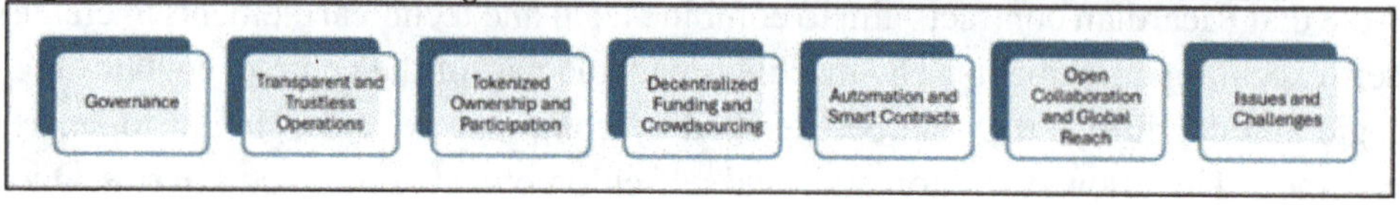

- Tokenized Ownership and Participation: DAOs frequently use tokens to signify ownership or membership rights within the organization. These tokens may provide voting privileges, access to various services, or a portion of the organization's profits. Token holders are empowered to engage in the decision-making process and can reap the rewards of the organization's success.
- Decentralized Funding and Crowdsourcing: DAOs often use blockchain crowdfunding, such as ICOs and token sales, to raise funds. This decentralized method draws on a global network of contributors, empowering the development of novel projects.
- Automation and Smart Contracts: Smart contracts are crucial to the functioning of Decentralized "Autonomous Organizations (DAOs)" as they automate a range of processes and operations. These contracts establish the rules and conditions necessary for executing transactions, distributing rewards, and enforcing governance mechanisms. By facilitating autonomous and self-executing actions, smart contracts eliminate the need for intermediaries, streamlining operations and enhancing efficiency.
- Open Collaboration and Global Reach: Decentralized organizations have the ability to draw in contributors and participants from all corners of the globe, promoting open collaboration and a wide array of skill sets. This worldwide engagement and inclusivity significantly boost innovation and creativity within the organization.
- Issues and Challenges: While DAOs offer numerous advantages, challenges exist in areas such as scalability, governance scalability, legal frameworks, and regulatory compliance. Additionally, decision-making processes and conflicts may arise within decentralized organizations, requiring mechanisms to address disputes and ensure effective governance.

Decentralized organizations in the blockchain-driven era have the power to transform conventional hierarchical frameworks. By promoting transparency, inclusivity, and collaborative decision-making, they empower individuals to engage actively and contribute to the organization's success. Additionally, the use of automation and smart contracts simplifies operations and boosts overall efficiency.

7. DECENTRALIZED APPLICATIONS (DAPPS) USING BLOCKCHAIN

DApps are applications that operate on a blockchain or a decentralized network. These applications use the benefits of blockchain technology, such as transparency, immutability, and decentralized consensus, to offer a wide range of functionalities without relying on centralized intermediaries. Here are some key aspects of decentralized applications using blockchain:

- Architecture: DApps are software programs that operate on a blockchain or peer-to-peer network, distinguishing them from traditional applications that run on a single computer. DApps are collectively managed by their users across the network, rather than being controlled by a single authority.
- Decentralized Data Storage: DApps use decentralized storage systems, like the Inter Planetary File System (IPFS), rather than relying on a central server. DApps distribute control and data storage across multiple nodes in a network, ensuring no single entity has full control over the application. This approach provides data redundancy, immutability, and resistance to censorship.
- Smart Contracts: DApps, or decentralized applications, utilize smart contracts—self-executing agreements that are securely stored on the blockchain. These smart contracts outline the business logic and rules that dictate how the application operates. By leveraging smart contracts, DApps can automate processes, build trust among users, and streamline interactions between various participants within the ecosystem.
- Tokenization: DApps often use tokens to incentivize users and exchange value. These tokens can represent ownership, access, voting rights, and more, enabling economic models, community governance, and greater user participation.
- Decentralized Governance: Decentralized applications (DApps) frequently adopt governance models that empower participants to influence decision-making. Through mechanisms such as voting systems, stakeholder consensus, and decentralized autonomous organizations (DAOs), users can actively engage in shaping the governance and development of the application.

- Open and Transparent: DApps operate in a transparent and open manner, with transaction history and application logic visible on the blockchain. This fosters trust and auditability, as anyone can verify the operations and integrity of the application.
- Interoperability: As various blockchain platforms continue to expand, significant efforts are being made to foster interoperability among different decentralized applications (DApps) and blockchain networks. Interoperability protocols and standards are being developed to facilitate smooth communication and data exchange across diverse blockchain ecosystems.
- Use Cases: DApps are applicable to a wide range of industries, including decentralized finance (DeFi), supply chain management, social networks, gaming, and digital identity. They offer decentralized marketplaces and other solutions with enhanced transparency, security, and censorship resistance compared to centralized systems.

DApps promise a more decentralized and inclusive digital future, and despite facing hurdles like scalability, user experience issues, regulatory complexities, and the push for broader acceptance, their continuous innovation and evolution are paving the way forward.

8. DISTRIBUTED LEDGER FRAMEWORK USING BLOCKCHAIN

A distributed ledger framework utilizing blockchain encompasses the foundational architecture and infrastructure that supports the functioning of a blockchain-based distributed ledger by Abdulateef, (2025); Abdullayev et al., (2025) and Al-Shareeda et al., (2024). This framework offers essential components and protocols that facilitate the maintenance of a decentralized and transparent record of transactions or data shared among a network of participants. Below are the key elements of such a distributed ledger framework (refer figure 4):

- Blockchain Consensus The framework outlines the consensus mechanism that determines how nodes within the network reach an agreement on the validity and sequence of transactions or data. Some widely used consensus mechanisms are: "Proof of Work (PoW)", "Proof of Stake (PoS)", "Practical Byzantine Fault Tolerance (PBFT)", and "Delegated Proof of Stake (DPoS)".
- Network Infrastructure: The framework outlines the network infrastructure requirements for establishing communication between nodes. It includes protocols for peer-to-peer networking, data synchronization, and data propagation across the network.

- Smart Contract Functionality: Smart contracts are self-executing agreements that trigger predefined actions upon meeting specific conditions. The distributed ledger's architecture defines the programming language and environment, enabling developers to automate business processes within the network.
- Data Structure and Storage: The framework specifies the data structure used to store transactional or data records in the distributed ledger. In most blockchain frameworks, data is organized in blocks, linked together in a chain. Various storage mechanisms, such as Merkle trees, are used to ensure data integrity and efficient retrieval.
- Consensus Algorithm Implementation: The framework provides the necessary implementation details for the chosen consensus algorithm. This includes algorithms for validating transactions, reaching consensus on block creation, and handling conflicts or forks within the blockchain.
- Cryptography and Security: Distributed ledger frameworks rely on cryptographic techniques to guarantee data security, privacy, and integrity. Specifically, they employ public-key cryptography, digital signatures, and hash functions to verify identities, validate data, and prevent tampering.
- Governance and Upgrades: The framework defines the governance mechanisms for decision-making regarding updates, protocol changes, and network parameters. It outlines the process by which participants in the network propose and vote on changes to the distributed ledger framework.
- Interoperability and Standards: To address the growing number of blockchain networks, this framework prioritizes interoperability. It may define standards and protocols that facilitate seamless interaction between different blockchains and enable effective integration with existing systems and technologies.
- Scalability and Performance: Distributed ledgers improve scalability and performance using techniques like sharding, off-chain scaling, and layer-two protocols to increase transaction throughput and reduce network congestion by Alsalem and Amin (2023); Alyounis and Yasin, (2023); Frederick and Ali (2024) and Addula and Ali, (2025).

Figure 4. Distributed Ledger Framework Using Blockchain

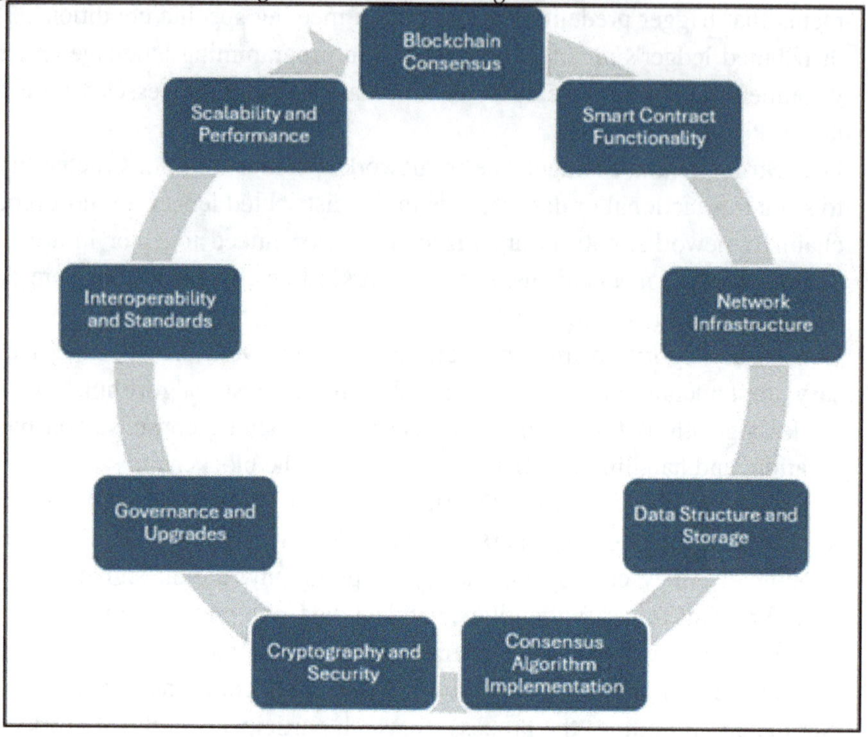

Blockchain-based distributed ledger frameworks offer essential infrastructure for developing decentralized applications. They facilitate trust, transparency, and secure transactions among a network of participants. These frameworks underpin a wide range of applications, including financial systems, supply chain management, identity verification, decentralized governance, and beyond.

9. HYPERLEDGER

Hyperledger is a collaborative open-source initiative hosted by the Linux Foundation, aimed at enhancing blockchain technologies across various industries. It offers a suite of frameworks, tools, and libraries that empower organizations to develop and implement decentralized applications and robust enterprise blockchain solutions. Below is an overview of Hyperledger and its main features:

- Modular Architecture: Hyperledger features a modular architecture, allowing users to select components tailored to their specific needs. It encompasses several blockchain frameworks, such as Hyperledger Fabric, Hyperledger Besu, Hyperledger Sawtooth, and Hyperledger Indy, each catering to distinct use cases.

- Hyperledger Fabric: As the most widely utilized framework within Hyperledger, Fabric is a permissioned blockchain platform that prioritizes flexibility, scalability, and confidentiality. It supports modular consensus mechanisms and smart contracts (referred to as chaincode), along with privacy features like channels for selective data sharing.
- Hyperledger Besu: Besu is an Ethereum-compatible framework that facilitates both private and public networks. It is compatible with the "Ethereum Virtual Machine (EVM)" and associated tools, enabling developers to leverage existing Ethereum applications and ecosystems.
- Hyperledger Sawtooth: Sawtooth emphasizes scalability and simplicity through its modular design. It utilizes a unique consensus mechanism known as Proof of Elapsed Time (PoET) and supports parallel transaction processing for enhanced efficiency.
- Hyperledger Indy: Indy specializes in identity management solutions on the blockchain. It provides decentralized identity capabilities, including secure identity management, verifiable credentials, and interoperability among various identity systems.
- Tools and Libraries: Hyperledger offers an array of tools and libraries to facilitate blockchain development. These include Hyperledger Caliper for performance benchmarking, Hyperledger Explorer for network visualization and monitoring, and Hyperledger Quilt for interoperability with other blockchain networks.
- Collaboration and Community: Hyperledger promotes collaboration among industry leaders, developers, and researchers to drive advancements in blockchain technology. It unites a diverse community of contributors from sectors like finance, supply chain, healthcare, and more to share best practices and standards.
- Enterprise-Ready Solutions: Designed with enterprise needs in mind, Hyperledger frameworks prioritize privacy, scalability, permissioned access, and governance mechanisms. They provide essential tools for organizations to create secure and scalable blockchain solutions tailored for business applications.

The open-source nature of Hyperledger fosters an appealing environment for organizations exploring blockchain technology for their specific applications. It serves as a solid foundation with an active community dedicated to developing, deploying, and maintaining blockchain-based solutions across various industries.

10. PROJECT UNDER HYPERLEDGER

Hyperledger hosts multiple projects encompassing various blockchain frameworks and tools. These projects address specific use cases and technical aspects of blockchain development, providing organizations with diverse options for building enterprise-grade blockchain solutions. Hyperledger is now part of LF Decentralized Trust, a Linux Foundation organization fostering innovation and collaboration:

- Hyperledger Fabric: Fabric is a permissioned blockchain framework that focuses on flexibility, scalability, and privacy. It enables the development of enterprise-grade blockchain solutions with modular consensus mechanisms, smart contracts (chaincode), and support for private data channels. Fabric has been widely adopted for various use cases, including trade finance, supply chain management and healthcare.
- Hyperledger Besu: An Ethereum-compatible blockchain platform that allows organizations to build both private and public networks. It provides compatibility with the Ethereum Virtual Machine (EVM), allowing developers to consider existing Ethereum tooling and applications. Besu is well-suited for use cases that require Ethereum compatibility and enterprise-grade features.
- Hyperledger Sawtooth: Hyperledger Sawtooth is a modular blockchain platform that prioritizes both scalability and ease of use. Its architecture enables the creation of diverse and secure blockchain applications, making it suitable for a wide range of industries. It utilizes a unique consensus algorithm called Proof of Elapsed Time (PoET) and supports parallel transaction processing. Sawtooth provides a flexible architecture for building distributed ledger applications and has been used in areas like supply chain, finance, and healthcare.
- Hyperledger Indy: Hyperledger Indy focuses on decentralized identity management, offering tools and libraries for the creation and administration of self-sovereign identities, verifiable credentials, and secure interactions between identity holders and service providers. Its design aims to tackle the complexities of identity management and interoperability across various sectors, such as healthcare, finance, and government. Indy enables individuals to control their digital identities independently, facilitating the management of identity attributes without reliance on centralized authorities. It employs Decentralized Identifiers (DIDs) to ensure secure communication and interactions among users and service applications while maintaining data privacy and ownership. This decentralized approach enhances user privacy and security, allowing for efficient verification processes without the risk of unauthorized access to personal information.

- Hyperledger Iroha: A blockchain framework designed for mobile and web application development. It provides a simple and user-friendly API and offers features like asset management, account management, and multi-signature support and is suitable for use cases that require easy integration with existing applications and interfaces.
- Hyperledger Caliper: Caliper is a benchmarking tool used to measure the performance of blockchain networks and applications. It enables developers and organizations to evaluate and compare the scalability, throughput, and latency of different blockchain platforms.
- Hyperledger Cactus: Cactus is a project that aims to create a framework for interoperability between different blockchain platforms. It provides the means for blockchain networks to communicate and interact seamlessly, enabling cross-chain transactions and data exchange.

These are just a few examples of the projects hosted under the Hyperledger initiative. Each project addresses specific use cases, requirements, and technical aspects of blockchain development, offering organizations a diverse range of options to build enterprise-grade blockchain solutions.

11. HYPERLEDGER AS A PROTOCOL

Hyperledger is an open-source project that offers multiple blockchain frameworks and tools, rather than being a standalone protocol like Bitcoin or Ethereum. It helps organizations create private, permissioned blockchain networks using various frameworks like Hyperledger Fabric, Besu, Sawtooth, and Indy. Each framework defines its own protocols for consensus, data storage, smart contracts, and network communication. For example, Hyperledger Fabric features a modular architecture with customizable consensus algorithms (e.g., Kafka, Raft) and privacy features like channels for selective data sharing. Hyperledger Besu, on the other hand, is Ethereum-compatible, supporting the Ethereum Virtual Machine (EVM) and consensus mechanisms like "Proof of Work (PoW)" and "Proof of Stake (PoS)". While Hyperledger itself doesn't have a single protocol, it provides a flexible environment where organizations can build and deploy tailored blockchain networks using the protocols defined by each framework by Al-Shareeda et al., (2025); Addula et al., (2025); Alshinwan et al., (2025) and Albinhamad et al., (2025).

12. HYPERLEDGER FABRIC SERVICES

Hyperledger Fabric is a leading blockchain framework within the Hyperledger project, designed to facilitate the creation and management of enterprise-level blockchain networks. It offers a variety of core services that are crucial for the effective operation of these networks. Below are some of the key services provided by Hyperledger Fabric (refer table 2):

A. Peer Services:
   - Ledger Services: Peers maintain a distributed ledger, which is a tamper-evident and append-only record of all transactions. Ledger services handle the storage, retrieval, and synchronization of the ledger among peers by Ali, (2024), Al-Shareeda et al., (2024), Almaayah and Sulaiman (2024) and Alsahaim and Maayah, (2023).
   - Chaincode Services: Chaincode services execute smart contracts, also known as chaincode, which define the business logic of the network. They handle the installation, instantiation, and execution of chaincode, enabling transaction processing and state updates.

B. Ordering Service:
   - Consensus Service: The ordering service determines the sequence of transactions within the network and generates blocks that are subsequently added to the ledger. It employs a consensus algorithm to ensure that all peers in the network reach an agreement on the transaction order.
   - Block Creation and Distribution: The ordering service creates blocks that contain transactions in a specific order and sends these blocks to peers for validation and integration into their local ledger copies.

C. Membership Services:
   - Identity Management: Membership services handle the management of participants' identities within the network. They issue cryptographic identities, authenticate participants, and enforce access control policies.
   - Certificate Authorities (CAs): CAs issue and manage digital certificates that authenticate participants in the network. They ensure the integrity and security of participants' identities and enable secure communication.

D. Channel Services:
   - Channel Creation and Management: Channels enable selective data sharing and privacy within a Hyperledger Fabric network. Channel services handle the creation, configuration, and management of channels, allowing different subsets of participants to transact privately.
   - Endorsement and Validation: Channel services facilitate the endorsement and validation of transactions within a channel. They coordinate

the execution of chaincode and collect endorsements from endorsing peers, ensuring the validity of transactions before they are committed to the ledger.

E. Event Services:

- Event Notification: Event services enable the notification of events and changes occurring within the network. They allow applications and external systems to subscribe to specific events, such as the addition of blocks to the ledger or the execution of specific transactions.

Table 2. Hyperledger Fabric Services

Peer Services	**Ledger Services**	**Storage, retrieval, and synchronization**
	Chaincode Services	Installation, instantiation, and execution of chaincode, enabling transaction processing and state updates
Ordering Service		
	Consensus Service	algorithm to ensure agreement among the network's peers on the order of transactions
	Block Creation and Distribution	Peers for validation and inclusion in their local copies of the ledger
Membership Services		
	Identity Management	Cryptographic identities, authenticate participants, and enforce access control policies
	Certificate Authorities (CAs)	Integrity and security of participants' identities and enable secure communication
Channel Services		
	Channel Creation and Management	Handle the creation, configuration, and management of channels, allowing different subsets of participants to transact privately
	Endorsement and Validation	Endorsement and validation of transactions within a channel
Event Services		
	Event Notification	Event services enable the notification of events and changes occurring within the network

Hence, these services collectively provide the necessary infrastructure and functionality for building and operating blockchain networks using Hyperledger Fabric. They ensure secure transaction processing, privacy, consensus, identity management, and event handling within the network. Organizations can use these services to develop decentralized applications and implement business processes on top of a Hyperledger Fabric network.

13. DISTRIBUTED LEDGER TECHNOLOGY

Distributed Ledger Technology (DLT) refers to a technological framework that facilitates the decentralized and secure recording, storage, and management of data among various participants or nodes. In contrast to conventional centralized systems, where a single authority oversees and manages the data, DLT distributes both the data and its governance across multiple network participants. Below are some essential features of Distributed Ledger Technology:

- Decentralization: DLT employs a decentralized architecture where multiple nodes maintain synchronized copies of a shared ledger. Consensus mechanisms ensure that all changes to the ledger are validated and propagated across the network.
- Consensus Mechanisms: To ensure that every participant in a distributed network agrees on the validity and order of transactions recorded on the ledger, consensus mechanisms are essential. A variety of algorithms exist to achieve this, each with its own approach. Examples include PoW, PoS and PBFT. These algorithms maintain the ledger's integrity.
- Transparency and Immutability: DLT fosters transparency by enabling participants to access the entire history of transactions recorded on the ledger. Once a transaction is entered, it becomes immutable, meaning it cannot be changed or removed. This characteristic of immutability significantly boosts trust and integrity within the system.
- Security and Cryptography: DLT utilizes cryptographic methods to safeguard data, ensuring both the privacy and integrity of transactions. Through the use of cryptographic algorithms, it facilitates data encryption, digital signatures, and identity management, thereby maintaining the confidentiality and authenticity of the information.
- Smart Contracts: DLT frequently integrates smart contracts-self-executing computer programs that carry out predefined actions automatically when certain conditions are satisfied. These smart contracts promote automation, enforce regulations, and enable intricate transactions without requiring intermediaries.
- Permissioned and Permissionless Networks: Distributed Ledger Technology (DLT) is adaptable to different network types: permissioned and permissionless. Permissioned networks restrict participation to known entities with

defined roles. Permissionless networks, like public blockchains, allow open participation in the consensus process.

- Use Cases: Distributed Ledger Technology (DLT) has diverse applications across various sectors. In finance, it enhances secure and efficient payment systems, while in supply chain management, it provides improved traceability and transparency. The healthcare industry benefits from DLT by enabling secure management of patient records. Additionally, DLT is utilized in numerous other fields where trust, transparency, and decentralized data management are crucial.

Popular instances of DLT include blockchain platforms such as Bitcoin, Ethereum, and Hyperledger Fabric. These platforms leverage DLT principles to facilitate decentralized and secure management of data, transaction processing, and the creation of decentralized applications. DLT has the capability to transform various sectors by minimizing the need for intermediaries, bolstering security, and enhancing efficiency and trust in both data management and transaction processes. However, it is essential to evaluate the specific needs and characteristics of each DLT implementation when assessing its applicability in practical scenarios.

14. SAWTOOTH LAKE

Sawtooth Lake was the original name for the Hyperledger Sawtooth project, which is part of the Hyperledger suite of blockchain frameworks. Initially developed by Intel, it was later contributed to the Hyperledger initiative under the Linux Foundation. Hyperledger Sawtooth is an open-source blockchain platform designed with a focus on scalability, modularity, and flexibility, aiming to facilitate the creation of distributed ledger applications while prioritizing simplicity and user-friendliness (refer figure 5):

- Modular Architecture: Sawtooth utilizes a modular architecture, allowing independent component development and deployment. This modularity provides flexibility for upgrades and replacements without impacting the entire network.
- Consensus Algorithms: Sawtooth is designed to accommodate various consensus algorithms, with the default being the "Proof of Elapsed Time (PoET)" algorithm. PoET is a distinctive consensus mechanism aimed at promoting efficiency and reducing energy consumption, particularly in settings that utilize "Trusted Execution Environments (TEEs)", such as Intel's "Software Guard Extensions (SGX)".

- Transaction Execution Model: Sawtooth utilizes a parallel transaction execution model, where transactions can be processed concurrently, improving scalability and performance. This model enables the execution of transactions in separate transaction families, each with its own set of rules and logic.
- Smart Contracts (Transaction Families): In Sawtooth, smart contracts are called "transaction families." Transaction families define the business logic and rules for specific types of transactions. Developers can create their own transaction families using programming languages like Python, JavaScript, and Go, making it accessible for developers with different skill sets.
- Merkle Tree Data Structure: Sawtooth utilizes a Merkle tree data structure to maintain the integrity and immutability of the distributed ledger. The Merkle tree allows for efficient verification of the validity and consistency of the data in the ledger.
- Enterprise Integration: Sawtooth provides various enterprise-friendly features, such as support for pluggable consensus algorithms, permissioned networks, and integration with existing enterprise systems. It offers compatibility with enterprise integration patterns and tools, making it suitable for enterprise blockchain solutions.

Figure 5. Key features and characteristics of Hyperledger Sawtooth

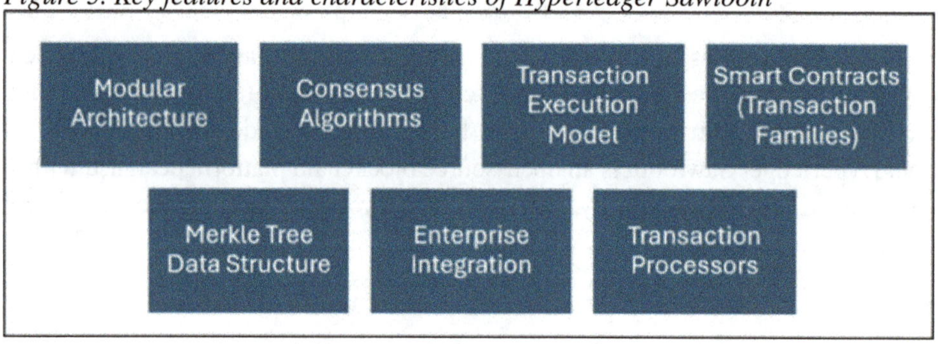

- Transaction Processors: Transaction processors play a crucial role in executing and validating transactions within the Sawtooth framework. They can be developed using various programming languages and function independently, which provides both extensibility and flexibility in the implementation of transaction logic.

Hyperledger Sawtooth has found applications across a diverse range of industries, including supply chain management, healthcare, finance, and energy. Its emphasis on modularity, scalability, and user-friendliness makes it an attractive option for developers and organizations aiming to create distributed ledger applications tailored to specific needs and customization preferences.

15. CORDA AND ITS FUNCTION

Corda is an open-source blockchain platform specifically designed for enterprise use. It is developed by R3, a leading blockchain software firm. Corda aims to enable businesses to transact directly and securely with each other, while ensuring privacy, scalability, and regulatory compliance. Here are some key functions and features of Corda:

- Privacy: Corda prioritizes privacy by design. It allows for the secure exchange of information and transactions only between the relevant parties involved in a specific transaction. This is achieved through the concept of "state" and "contracts," where only the required information is shared with relevant participants.
- Smart Contracts: Corda uses "smart contracts" called "CorDapps" (Corda Distributed Applications). CorDapps enable the execution of business logic and automate complex transactions between participants. They are written in various programming languages, including Java and Kotlin, making it accessible to a wide range of developers.
- Uniqueness of Data: Corda places emphasis on the uniqueness of data to avoid the need for global consensus on the entire transaction history. Each state in Corda's ledger has a unique identifier, and changes to the state are recorded as transactions, resulting in an immutable transaction chain.
- Consensus: Corda operates without a global consensus mechanism such as "proof-of-work (PoW)" or "Proof-of-Stake (PoS)". Instead, it establishes consensus on specific transactions among the involved parties. This consensus can be reached through various approaches, including legal and regulatory agreements, industry-specific standards, and voting mechanisms.
- Interoperability: Corda enables interoperability with existing systems and platforms. It can integrate with external systems, databases, and legacy infrastructures, allowing businesses to consider existing technology investments while harnessing the benefits of blockchain technology.
- Regulatory Compliance: Corda is engineered to meet the regulatory and legal demands of enterprises. It features robust identity management, controls for

data privacy, and the capability to connect legal contracts with traditional legal frameworks to blockchain transactions. This design ensures that businesses can operate within the confines of legal requirements while leveraging the benefits of blockchain technology.

- Network Permissioning: Corda facilitates the establishment of permissioned networks where participants are assigned specific roles and access rights. This feature is especially advantageous in enterprise settings, where issues of privacy, data governance, and regulatory compliance are paramount.
- Notary Services: Corda utilizes "notary" services to authenticate and timestamp transactions. These notaries play a crucial role in ensuring the uniqueness and validity of transactions by preventing double-spending and confirming that the involved parties possess the necessary authority to engage in the transaction.

Corda has gained significant traction across various sectors including finance, supply chain, and healthcare. Its design prioritizes privacy, scalability, interoperability, and compliance with regulations, making it an ideal choice for enterprise-level blockchain solutions. Businesses utilizing Corda can conduct secure and efficient transactions while maintaining control over their data and adhering to legal standards. This capability is crucial for organizations that require robust security measures and streamlined operations within regulated environments.

16. OPEN ISSUES TOWARDS DECENTRALIZED APPLICATIONS AND DISTRIBUTED LEDGER FRAMEWORK

While decentralized applications (DApps) and distributed ledger frameworks have made significant progress, there are still some open issues and challenges that need to be addressed. Here are a few key ones:

- Scalability: Scalability continues to be a significant hurdle for the widespread adoption of DApps and distributed ledger technologies. As networks grow in terms of users and transaction volume, their performance and throughput can suffer. Solutions like sharding, layer-two protocols, and off-chain transactions are being explored to address scalability concerns.
- Interoperability: Interoperability between different DApps and distributed ledger frameworks is still a challenge. As there are multiple blockchain platforms and protocols, establishing seamless communication and data sharing between them is essential for realizing the full potential of decentralized ap-

plications. Standards and protocols like cross-chain communication protocols are being developed to tackle this issue.

- User Experience: User experience (UX) is a critical aspect that requires enhancement in the realm of decentralized applications (DApps). Currently, many DApps feature complex user interfaces and convoluted processes, which can hinder their acceptance among mainstream users. To foster global adoption of DApps, it is essential to focus on improving usability, streamlining processes, and creating intuitive interfaces. By prioritizing these elements, we can make DApps more accessible and appealing to a wider audience.
- Governance and Consensus: Governance models and consensus mechanisms in decentralized environments require deeper investigation. Understanding how decisions are made, how protocol upgrades are executed, and how disputes are resolved in a decentralized and democratic way remains a significant challenge. It is crucial to identify effective governance models that strike a balance between decentralization, security, and efficient decision-making.
- Privacy and Security: Privacy and security are paramount concerns for DApps and distributed ledger technologies. To combat the inherent challenges of data confidentiality, cyber-attack vulnerabilities, and unauthorized access, developers are actively creating innovative solutions. These include zero-knowledge proofs, secure key management strategies, and a range of privacy-preserving techniques designed to fortify decentralized systems.
- Regulatory and Legal Frameworks: The regulatory landscape for DApps and distributed ledger frameworks is still developing. Addressing regulatory and legal challenges like identity verification, compliance, and data privacy is critical for widespread adoption. Collaboration between regulators, industry and policymakers is essential to create frameworks that balance innovation with regulatory needs.
- Energy Efficiency: To ensure the long-term viability of distributed ledger technology, it is essential to move beyond energy-intensive consensus mechanisms like Proof of Work (PoW). Researching and adopting energy-efficient alternatives and sustainable practices is vital to minimize the environmental impact of growing blockchain adoption.

Therefore, the existing issues and challenges necessitate continuous research, collaboration, and innovation within the blockchain community. As the technology progresses, it is anticipated that effective solutions will arise to address these obstacles, facilitating broader adoption and success of decentralized applications and distributed ledger technologies.

17. CRITICAL CHALLENGES TOWARDS DECENTRALIZED APPLICATIONS AND DISTRIBUTED LEDGER FRAMEWORK

For decentralized applications (DApps) and distributed ledger frameworks to achieve mainstream adoption and long-term success, key challenges must be overcome. Here are some of the key challenges (refer figure 6):

- Scalability: Scalability presents a significant challenge for decentralized applications (DApps) and distributed ledger technologies. As user numbers and transaction volumes rise, it becomes essential for the network to effectively manage the increased load while preserving performance. Presently, many blockchain architectures encounter constraints related to transaction processing speed and overall scalability. Therefore, it is crucial to explore solutions that enhance scalability without compromising security and decentralization.
- Interoperability: Interoperability poses a significant challenge in the communication and data exchange among various decentralized applications (DApps) and distributed ledger technologies. In a fragmented ecosystem characterized by numerous blockchain platforms and protocols, achieving seamless interoperability is crucial. This capability is vital for fostering collaboration and enabling the smooth transfer of assets and data across different systems.
- User Experience: User experience (UX) is a significant challenge for DApps. Many DApps have complex user interfaces and require users to understand blockchain concepts and interact with cryptographic keys, which can be daunting for mainstream users. Improving the user experience by simplifying processes, enhancing usability, and creating intuitive interfaces is important for mass adoption.
- Governance and Consensus: Governance models and consensus mechanisms in decentralized environments present challenges. Decentralized systems require decision-making processes that are inclusive, transparent, and resistant to centralization of power. Designing effective governance models that address the needs of different stakeholders and enable consensus on protocol upgrades, dispute resolution, and network governance is a complex task.

Figure 6. Critical Challenges towards Decentralized Applications and Distributed Ledger Framework

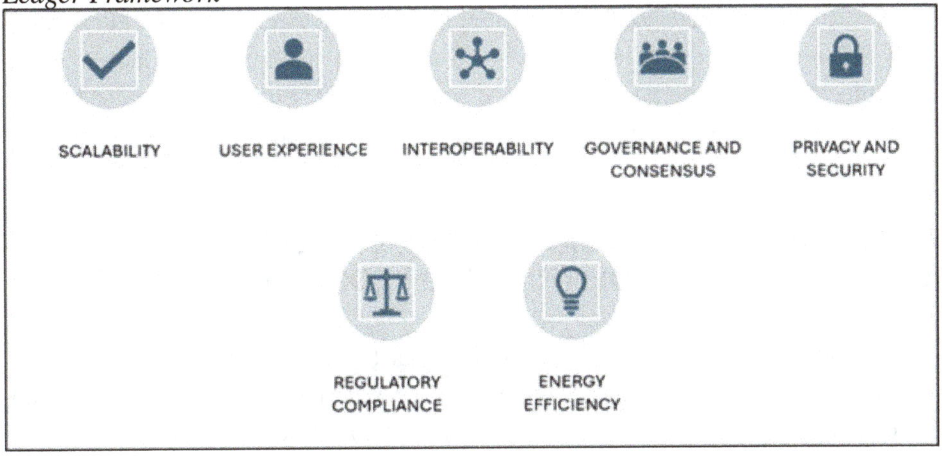

- Privacy and Security: Privacy and security pose significant challenges within decentralized applications and distributed ledger technologies. Although blockchain technology provides transparency and immutability, it is essential to safeguard sensitive data and protect against unauthorized access and potential attacks. The development of effective privacy-preserving techniques and robust security measures, all while preserving the decentralized nature of these systems, remains a formidable challenge.
- Regulatory Compliance: Regulatory compliance presents a significant challenge for decentralized applications (DApps) and distributed ledger technologies. Adhering to legal and regulatory standards—such as identity verification, data protection, and anti-money laundering (AML) regulations—can be particularly complex for decentralized systems. Achieving a harmonious balance between meeting compliance requirements and maintaining the inherent decentralized nature of blockchain technology remains an ongoing struggle.
- Energy Efficiency: The significant energy consumption associated with some consensus mechanisms, particularly "Proof of Work (PoW)", presents a major hurdle for distributed ledger technologies. The substantial energy demands of certain blockchain networks spark worries about their long-term sustainability and negative environmental consequences. Exploring energy-efficient consensus mechanisms and promoting sustainability practices is necessary to address these challenges.

Therefore, the blockchain community must prioritize continuous research, collaboration, and innovation to overcome these significant hurdles. As the technology matures, advancements in scalability, user experience, privacy, security, interoperability, and regulatory compliance are vital. Successfully navigating these challenges will unlock the widespread adoption of decentralized applications and distributed ledger frameworks, revolutionizing industries and use cases.

18. FUTURE WORK TOWARDS DECENTRALIZED APPLICATIONS AND DISTRIBUTED LEDGER FRAMEWORK

The evolution of decentralized applications (DApps) and distributed ledger technology is an ongoing journey fueled by research, development, and a constant drive for innovation. The goal is to overcome current limitations and pave the way for exciting new opportunities. Here's a glimpse into some key areas shaping the future of this dynamic field:

- Scalability Solutions: Ongoing research and development are essential to overcome the scalability challenges faced by blockchain networks. Investigating methods like sharding, sidechains, state channels, and layer-two solutions can significantly enhance transaction throughput and overall network scalability, all while maintaining security and decentralization.
- Interoperability Standards: Interoperability between DApps and distributed ledger frameworks is currently hindered by a lack of standardization. Addressing this requires developing common protocols, standards, and interfaces. These shared elements will enable seamless communication and data exchange across diverse blockchain platforms, ultimately promoting collaboration and the efficient transfer of assets and information.
- User Experience Enhancements: Improving the user experience is essential for mainstream adoption of DApps. Future work involves creating user-friendly interfaces, simplifying key management, and abstracting complex blockchain concepts to make DApps more accessible to non-technical users. Enhancing the overall user experience will drive wider adoption and engagement with decentralized applications.
- Privacy and Security Enhancements: Continued research and development are needed to enhance privacy and security in DApps and distributed ledger frameworks. This includes advancements in techniques such as zero-knowledge proofs, secure multi-party computation, privacy-preserving smart contracts, and identity management solutions. Robust security measures and

privacy-enhancing features will instill trust and confidence in decentralized systems.

- Governance and Consensus Models: Future work involves exploring and refining governance models and consensus mechanisms in decentralized environments. Developing governance frameworks that ensure inclusive decision-making, prevent centralization of power, and enable efficient protocol upgrades and dispute resolution is critical. Additionally, researching new consensus algorithms that are more energy-efficient, secure, and scalable will further advance the field.
- Regulation and Legal Frameworks: The regulatory landscape around DApps and distributed ledger frameworks is still evolving. Future work includes engaging with regulators and policymakers to develop clear and adaptable regulatory frameworks that foster innovation while addressing concerns related to data protection, identity verification, AML, and consumer protection. Collaboration between the blockchain community and regulatory authorities is essential for creating a conducive environment for the growth of decentralized applications.
- Industry-Specific Use Cases: Further exploration and development of industry-specific use cases for DApps and distributed ledger frameworks are necessary. Different sectors, such as finance, supply chain, healthcare, and energy, have unique requirements and challenges that can benefit from decentralized solutions. Collaborative efforts between blockchain developers, industry experts, and domain specialists will drive innovation and adoption in specific verticals.

In summary, future work in the decentralized applications and distributed ledger framework space involves continuous improvement, collaboration, and innovation to overcome existing challenges, enhance user experience, ensure privacy and security, achieve scalability, establish interoperability, navigate regulatory landscapes, and explore new use cases. This ongoing work will shape the future of decentralized applications and drive the adoption of distributed ledger technology across industries.

19. CONCLUSION

Decentralized applications (DApps) and distributed ledgers are leveraging blockchain to redefine trust and transparency in various industries. They facilitate secure, decentralized transactions, disintermediate processes, and empower direct collaboration. DApps offer improved security, data immutability, and reduced reliance on central authorities, with the potential to revolutionize finance, supply chains, and healthcare. Key challenges for widespread adoption include scalability, interoperability, user experience, privacy, and regulatory compliance.

Note that Distributed ledger frameworks provide the underlying infrastructure for building DApps. They offer a range of features and functionalities, including consensus mechanisms, smart contracts, governance models, and privacy-enhancing techniques. Frameworks like Hyperledger, Corda, and Ethereum provide developers with tools and platforms to create decentralized applications that meet specific industry needs. The future of DApps and distributed ledger frameworks lies in ongoing research, development, and collaboration. Efforts are being made to improve scalability, enhance user experience, ensure privacy and security, establish interoperability, and navigate regulatory landscapes. Industry-specific use cases are emerging, demonstrating the potential for blockchain technology to transform various sectors. As technology advances, decentralized applications and distributed ledger frameworks are poised to become pivotal in our digital economy. These innovations have the potential to challenge conventional business models, stimulate innovation, and enable individuals and organizations to engage more fully in decentralized networks. In conclusion, decentralized applications and distributed ledger technology are shaping a future where trust, transparency, and collaboration are transformed. With ongoing development and the resolution of existing challenges, these technologies could revolutionize industries and foster a more inclusive and efficient digital ecosystem.

REFERENCES

A. K. V., Tyagi, A. K., & Kumar, S. P. (2022). Blockchain technology for securing Internet of Vehicle: Issues and challenges. In *2022 International Conference on Computer Communication and Informatics (ICCCI)* (pp. 1–6). IEEE. DOI: 10.1109/ICCCI54379.2022.9740856

Abdulateef, O. G. (2025). Interpretable Deep Learning-Based AI Framework with Multi-Sequence Attention for Brain Tumor Subtype Classification in MRI Scans. *Journal of Cyber Security and Risk Auditing*, *2025*(2), 53–66. DOI: 10.63180/jcsra.thestap.2025.2.5

Abdullayev, V., Khang, A., Ragimova, N., & Almaayah, M. (2025). A Novel Authentication Systems in Vehicular Communication: Challenges and Future Directions. *Journal of Cyber Security and Risk Auditing*, *2025*(3), 123–135. DOI: 10.63180/jcsra.thestap.2025.3.9

Addula, S. R., & Ali, A. (2025). A Novel Permissioned Blockchain Approach for Scalable and Privacy-Preserving IoT Authentication. *Journal of Cyber Security and Risk Auditing*, *2025*(4), 222–237. DOI: 10.63180/jcsra.thestap.2025.4.3

Addula, S. R., Norozpour, S., & Amin, M. (2025). Risk Assessment for Identifying Threats, vulnerabilities and countermeasures in Cloud Computing. *Jordanian Journal of Informatics and Computing*, *2025*(1), 37–48. DOI: 10.63180/jjic.thestap.2025.1.5

Al-Shareeda, M. A., Jafer, A. N., Hashem, M. T., & Fajr, M. S. (2024). Secure Offline Smart Office Automation System Using ESP32 and Bluetooth Control Architecture. *Journal of Cyber Security and Risk Auditing*, *2024*(1), 3–13. DOI: 10.63180/jcsra.thestap.2024.1.2

Al-Shareeda, M. A., Najm, L. B., Hassan, A. A., Mushtaq, S., & Ali, H. A. (2024). Secure IoT-Based Smart Agriculture System Using Wireless Sensor Networks for Remote Environmental Monitoring. *STAP Journal of Security Risk Management*, *2024*(1), 56–66. DOI: 10.63180/jsrm.thestap.2024.1.4

Al-Shareeda, M. A., Obaid, A. A., & Almajid, A. A. H. (2025). The Role of Artificial Intelligence in Bodybuilding: A Systematic Review of Applications, Challenges, and Future Prospects. *Jordanian Journal of Informatics and Computing*, *2025*(1), 16–26. DOI: 10.63180/jjic.thestap.2025.1.3

Albinhamad, H., Alotibi, A., Alagnam, A., Almaiah, M., & Salloum, S. (2025). Vehicular Ad-hoc Networks (VANETs): A Key Enabler for Smart Transportation Systems and Challenges. *Jordanian Journal of Informatics and Computing*, *2025*(1), 4–15. DOI: 10.63180/jjic.thestap.2025.1.2

Ali, A. (2024). Adaptive and Context-Aware Authentication Framework Using Edge AI and Blockchain in Future Vehicular Networks. *STAP Journal of Security Risk Management, 2024*(1), 45–56. DOI: 10.63180/jsrm.thestap.2024.1.3

Almaayah, M., & Sulaiman, R. B. (2024). Cyber Risk Management in the Internet of Things: Frameworks, Models, and Best Practices. *STAP Journal of Security Risk Management, 2024*(1), 3–23. DOI: 10.63180/jsrm.thestap.2024.1.1

Alsahaim, S., & Maayah, M. (2023). Analyzing Cybersecurity Threats on Mobile Phones. *STAP Journal of Security Risk Management, 2023*(1), 3–19. DOI: 10.63180/jsrm.thestap.2023.1.2

Alsalem, T., & Amin, M. (2023). Towards Trustworthy IoT Systems: Cybersecurity Threats, Frameworks, and Future Directions. *Journal of Cyber Security and Risk Auditing, 2023*(1), 3–18. DOI: 10.63180/jcsra.thestap.2023.1.2

Alshinwan, M., Memon, A. G., Ghanem, M. C., & Almaayah, M. (2025). Unsupervised text feature selection approach based on improved Prairie dog algorithm for the text clustering. *Jordanian Journal of Informatics and Computing, 2025*(1), 27–36. DOI: 10.63180/jjic.thestap.2025.1.4

Alyounis, S., & Yasin, M. M. (2023). Secure Framework for Land Record Management using Blockchain Technology. *Journal of Cyber Security and Risk Auditing, 2023*(1), 19–48. DOI: 10.63180/jcsra.thestap.2023.1.3

Antal, C., Cioara, T., Anghel, I., Antal, M., & Salomie, I. (2021). Distributed ledger technology review and decentralized applications development guidelines. *Future Internet, 13*(3), 62. DOI: 10.3390/fi13030062

Anthony, B.Jnr. (2023). A developed distributed ledger technology architectural layer framework for decentralized governance implementation in virtual enterprise. *Information Systems and e-Business Management, 21*(3), 437–470. DOI: 10.1007/s10257-023-00634-2

Deshmukh, A., Mishra, A. K., Balamurugan, G., & Tyagi, A. K. (2023). Blockchain-empowered decentralized applications: Current trends and challenges. In *Privacy preservation of genomic and medical data* (Ch. 19). DOI: 10.1002/9781394213726.ch19

Frederick, N., & Ali, A. (2024). Enhancing DDoS Attack Detection and Mitigation in SDN Using Advanced Machine Learning Techniques. *Journal of Cyber Security and Risk Auditing, 2024*(1), 23–37. DOI: 10.63180/jcsra.thestap.2024.1.4

Hariharan, R., Tyagi, A. K., & Soni, G. (2023). A survey on blockchain–Internet of Things-based solutions. In *Privacy preservation and secured data storage in cloud computing*. IGI Global. DOI: 10.4018/979-8-3693-0593-5.ch005

Khan, S., Al-Amin, M., Hossain, H., Noor, N., & Sadik, M. W. (2020). A pragmatical study on blockchain empowered decentralized application development platform. In *Proceedings of the International Conference on Computing Advancements* (pp. 1–9). ACM. DOI: 10.1145/3377049.3377136

Kumari, S., & Muthulakshmi, P. (2023). Artificial intelligence—Blockchain enabled technology for Internet of Things: Research statements, open issues, and possible applications in the near future. In *Privacy preservation of genomic and medical data* (Ch. 18). DOI: 10.1002/9781394213726.ch18

Nair, M. M., & Tyagi, A. K. (2023). Blockchain technology for next-generation society: Current trends and future opportunities for smart era. In *Blockchain technology for secure social media computing* (Ch. 11). DOI: 10.1049/PBSE019E_ch11

Oyinloye, D. P., Teh, J. S., Jamil, N., & Alawida, M. (2021). Blockchain consensus: An overview of alternative protocols. *Symmetry*, *13*(8), 1363. DOI: 10.3390/sym13081363

Puthal, D., Malik, N., Mohanty, S. P., Kougianos, E., & Yang, C. (2018). The blockchain as a decentralized security framework. *IEEE Consumer Electronics Magazine*, *7*(2), 18–21. DOI: 10.1109/MCE.2017.2776459

Rauchs, M., Glidden, A., Gordon, B., Pieters, G. C., Recanatini, M., Rostand, F., Vagneur, K., & Zhang, B. Z. (2018). Distributed ledger technology systems: A conceptual framework. SSRN *Electronic Journal.* https://doi.org/DOI: 10.2139/ssrn.3230013

Tyagi, A. K. (2022). SecVT: Securing the vehicles of tomorrow using blockchain technology. In A. A. Sk, T. Turki, T. K. Ghosh, S. Joardar, & S. Barman (Eds.), *Artificial intelligence* (Vol. 1695, pp. 122–137). Springer. DOI: 10.1007/978-3-031-22485-0_11

Tyagi, A. K. (2023). Decentralized everything: Practical use of blockchain technology in future applications. In Pandey, R., Goundar, S., & Fatima, S. (Eds.), *Distributed computing to blockchain* (pp. 19–38). Academic Press. DOI: 10.1016/B978-0-323-96146-2.00010-3

Tyagi, A. K., Kukreja, S., Richa, , & Sivakumar, P. (2024). Role of blockchain technology in smart era: A review on possible smart applications. *Journal of Information & Knowledge Management*, *23*(1), 2450032. Advance online publication. DOI: 10.1142/S0219649224500321

Tyagi, A. K., Kumari, S., Chidambaram, N., & Sharma, A. (2024). Engineering applications of blockchain in this smart era. In *Enhancing medical imaging with emerging technologies* (Ch. 11). DOI: 10.4018/979-8-3693-5261-8.ch011

Chapter 6
Artificial Intelligence and Cybersecurity

Rupam Hazra
https://orcid.org/0009-0003-0332-2128
Global Institute of Management and Technology, India

Parag Chatterjee
https://orcid.org/0000-0003-1243-9582
Global Institute of Management and Technology, India

Yash Singh
Global Institute of Management and Technology, India

Gopal Podder
https://orcid.org/0009-0000-7736-9605
Global Institute of Management and Technology, India

Titli Das
https://orcid.org/0009-0001-3774-1828
Global Institute of Management and Technology, India

ABSTRACT

The integration of Artificial Intelligence (AI) into cybersecurity has become a transformative approach in defending against the increasing sophistication of cyber threats. As traditional security mechanisms struggle to keep pace, AI offers advanced tools such as machine learning, behavioral analytics, and natural language processing to enhance threat detection, incident response, and malware prevention. AI's ability to analyse vast datasets, detect anomalies in real-time, and predict future threats is revolutionizing cybersecurity practices. While AI presents numerous benefits, including automation of time-consuming tasks and proactive defense, ethical and

DOI: 10.4018/979-8-3373-2282-7.ch006

privacy considerations must be addressed to ensure fairness and transparency in its deployment. This chapter explores AI's critical role in modern cybersecurity, its techniques and applications, and the challenges that need to be navigated as AI continues to evolve in the field.

INTRODUCTION

In the era of digital technology, cybersecurity is now a top priority for individuals, organizations, and governments. The swift growth of linked devices, cloud services, and internet platforms has generated a large attack surface for cybercriminals. As cyber threats grow more complex, conventional security measures like firewalls, antivirus programs, and signature-based detection—frequently fail to adapt to changing attack methods. To tackle this challenge, the incorporation of Artificial Intelligence (AI) into cybersecurity has surfaced as a revolutionary answer.

Artificial Intelligence, due to its capability to examine large datasets, identify patterns, and adjust to emerging threats, provides considerable benefits compared to traditional security approaches. AI technologies, such as machine learning (ML), natural language processing (NLP), and Behavioral analytics, enable security systems to identify, thwart, and react to cyberattacks instantly. AI can recognize previously undiscovered threats by analysing data and consistently enhancing its detection skills. Additionally, AI has the capability to automate labour-intensive tasks like surveillance, data evaluation, and incident management, greatly improving the efficiency and scalability of security operations.

Introduction to Artificial Intelligence and Cybersecurity

Artificial Intelligence (AI) has emerged as a transformative technology that is reshaping numerous industries, including cybersecurity. These processes include learning (the ability to improve performance based on experience), reasoning (the ability to draw conclusions), and self-correction. In the context of cybersecurity, AI plays a vital role in identifying, preventing, and responding to security threats, which are becoming increasingly sophisticated and complex. The process of making a computer, computer-controlled robot, or software think intelligently in a way that is comparable to that of intelligent humans is known as artificial intelligence. (Welukar, Jenis N., and Gagan Prashant Bajoria,2021). AI is being utilized in cybersecurity in various ways, such as through machine learning (ML) algorithms that can detect unusual patterns of behaviour within network traffic, enabling the identification of potential cyberattacks. By using large datasets, AI systems can predict vulnerabilities, automate threat detection, and optimize the allocation of resources in real-time to defend against emerging threats. Furthermore, AI-powered systems can autonomously respond to detected threats, minimizing the response time and reducing the burden on cybersecurity professionals. However, as AI continues to evolve and be integrated into cybersecurity practices, it also presents new challenges. Cybercriminals are increasingly leveraging AI to develop advanced attack methods, such as sophisticated phishing campaigns, malware that can adapt to avoid detection, and automated attacks that can operate faster than traditional defense mechanisms. This creates a constant arms race between security professionals who leverage AI to defend against threats and attackers who use it to exploit vulnerabilities.

What Is Artificial Intelligence (AI)?

The field of computer science known as artificial intelligence (AI) is concerned with creating machines that are capable of performing activities that typically require human intelligence. These tasks include learning, verbal comprehension, visual perception, problem-solving, and decision-making. (Russell, S., & Norvig, P., 2020). AI systems are engineered to replicate human cognitive functions and possess the ability to learn from data, adjust to new information, and carry out tasks without the need for explicit programming for each individual situation.

AI encompasses a range of subfields, including:

A. **Machine Learning (ML):** A subset of AI that focuses on the development of algorithms that allow computers to learn from and make predictions or decisions based on data, rather than through explicit programming.
B. **Natural Language Processing (NLP):** AI's ability to interpret, understand, and generate human language, allowing machines to interact with humans in a more natural way.
C. **Computer Vision:** The ability of machines to interpret and understand visual data from the world, such as images or videos.
D. **Robotics:** AI applied to the design and control of robots, enabling them to carry out tasks autonomously.

AI can be categorized into two broad types:

A. **Narrow AI (Weak AI):** AI systems that are designed to perform specific tasks (e.g., virtual assistants, recommendation systems).
B. **General AI (Strong AI):** A hypothetical AI that can perform any cognitive function that a human being can, though it remains an area of ongoing research.

The Role of AI in Modern Cybersecurity

Artificial Intelligence (AI) is essential in contemporary cybersecurity by improving the capacity to identify, address, and reduce emerging cyber threats. As cyber threats grow more advanced and intricate, conventional cybersecurity measures frequently have difficulty keeping pace. AI technologies provide sophisticated instruments that can assist organizations in proactively safeguarding against cyberattacks, recognizing vulnerabilities, and reacting more swiftly to security incidents. Cyber threats encompass a wide variety of malicious activities, including malware, phishing, ransomware, and sophisticated hacking attempts. These threats present serious risks to sensitive data and intellectual property, while also undermining trust and stability in digital systems. (Sushchenko, P. R., 2024).

Key roles of AI in modern cybersecurity include:

A. **Threat Detection and Prevention**: AI algorithms, particularly machine learning (ML), can analyse vast amounts of network data to detect abnormal patterns or behaviour that may indicate a cyberattack. These AI-driven systems can recognize previously unknown threats by learning from past data and continuously improving their detection capabilities. Suppose, AI can identify zero-day exploits, malware, and advanced persistent threats (APTs) more effectively than traditional rule-based systems.

B. **Incident Response**: AI helps automate responses to detected threats, reducing the response time and minimizing potential damage. For example, AI-powered systems can isolate infected devices, block malicious IP addresses, or even patch vulnerabilities autonomously. This rapid response is critical in preventing attacks from spreading across systems.

C. **Predictive Capabilities**: AI can predict potential future vulnerabilities or threats by analysing patterns from historical data, security incidents, and global cybersecurity trends. These predictive insights allow organizations to take preventive measures before attacks occur.

D. **Phishing and Fraud Detection**: AI can enhance the detection of phishing emails and fraudulent activities by analysing linguistic patterns, sender behaviour, and network traffic for signs of malicious intent. AI-driven systems can flag suspicious activities and alert security teams, preventing data breaches and financial losses.

E. **Behavioral Analytics**: AI uses Behavioral analysis to monitor user activity and identify anomalies that might suggest an insider threat or compromised account. By understanding normal user behaviour, AI can flag deviations that may be indicative of malicious actions, providing an additional layer of security.

The Importance of Cybersecurity in the Age of AI

In the era of Artificial Intelligence (AI), the importance of cybersecurity has increased significantly. As AI technologies are increasingly woven into numerous industries—including healthcare, finance, government, and essential infrastructure—the urgency for safeguarding sensitive data and digital systems has surged dramatically. Emerging technologies represent a collection of applications derived from scientific understanding that provide substantial enhancements compared to existing technologies for specific processes. Technologies such as artificial intelligence (AI), machine learning (ML), and deep learning are considered disruptive innovations, garnering significant focus due to their prospective applications in areas such as conflict resolution, deterrence, assurance, and competitive strategy. AI frequently serves as a comprehensive term encompassing a wide range of fields and disciplines. (Carlo, Antonio, et al., 2023). While AI-powered innovations have led to extraordinary progress, they also pose considerable obstacles for cybersecurity, highlighting the necessity for organizations to emphasize the security of their digital assets.

A. **Increased Attack Surface:** With the swift embrace of AI, fresh vulnerabilities are surfacing within systems that depend on AI for functions such as data analysis, decision-making, and automation. AI-driven devices and applications, including Internet of Things (IoT) devices, self-driving vehicles, and AI-infused healthcare tools, widen the attack landscape, making them appealing targets for cybercriminals.
B. **Sophistication of Cyberattacks:** As AI develops, cybercriminals are also progressively utilizing AI tools to enhance the success of their attacks. AI technologies, including machine learning and natural language processing, allow adversaries to develop more advanced types of malwares, phishing tactics, and social engineering efforts.
C. **Automation and Real-Time Defence:** AI provides cybersecurity experts with the capacity to automate routine activities such as tracking network traffic, searching for malware, and reviewing logs. By automating these activities, AI can improve the speed and precision of threat identification and reaction. This becomes particularly crucial in the current era of AI, where the amount of data and potential dangers is enormous.
D. **Threat Intelligence and Prediction:** AI-powered threat intelligence tools have the ability to examine large quantities of information from multiple sources to uncover new cyber threats. These systems can forecast attack patterns and recognize weaknesses prior to being exploited by cybercriminals.
E. **AI's Role in Data Protection:** As AI systems manage increasingly sensitive data—like personal, financial, and health information—safeguarding this in-

formation becomes essential. AI can assist in enhancing encryption methods, identifying data breaches, and ensuring adherence to privacy laws such as GDPR (General Data Protection Regulation).

Overview of Cybersecurity

Cybersecurity pertains to the method of safeguarding systems, networks, and information from digital assaults, harm, or unauthorized access. As the world progresses toward a more digital landscape, cybersecurity has evolved into an essential discipline to protect sensitive data, maintain the integrity of information, and ensure user privacy. It encompasses a range of processes, technologies, and practices focused on defending against cyber threats, including malware, ransomware, phishing, and other types of cybercrime. The contemporary landscape is increasingly reliant on technology to an unprecedented degree. A substantial volume of data is produced and collected due to the widespread adoption of rapidly advancing technologies, including the Internet of Things (IoT) and cloud computing. (Sarker, Iqbal H., Md Hasan Furhad, and Raza Nowrozy., 2021).

The main objectives of cybersecurity are:

Confidentiality: Ensuring that sensitive data is accessible only to authorized individuals.

Integrity: Ensuring that data is accurate, reliable, and unaltered unless authorized.

Cybersecurity encompasses a range of measures such as firewalls, encryption, intrusion detection systems, and user education to safeguard against prevalent vulnerabilities. It is crucial not just for businesses and governments but also for individuals, as various elements of personal life, including financial and health data, transition to online platforms.

Understanding Cyber Threats

Grasping cyber threats is essential for recognizing, averting, and addressing possible dangers in a digital setting. Cyber threats denote any harmful action or effort to take advantage of computer systems, networks, or devices with the purpose of stealing information, interrupting services, or inflicting harm. The interruption or obliteration of specific infrastructures, including energy provision, potable water supply, telecommunications, and various transportation systems, can significantly affect the health, safety, security, and economic welfare of individuals, as well as the efficient operation of governmental entities. Consequently, these infrastructures are classified as Critical Infrastructures (CI). (Luiijf, Eric., 2012). These threats continuously evolve, growing more advanced as technology progresses, and may aim at individuals, companies, or even governmental entities.

Types of Cyber Threats:

A. Malware:

Definition: Malicious software designed to harm or exploit systems, including viruses, worms, Trojans, ransomware, and spyware.

Example: Ransomware encrypts a victim's files and demands payment for decryption keys.

B. Phishing:

Definition: A form of social engineering where attackers impersonate legitimate organizations to deceive individuals into revealing sensitive information such as passwords or credit card numbers.

Example: Fraudulent emails that look like they come from a bank, prompting users to click on a malicious link.

C. Denial of Service (DoS) Attacks:

Definition: A cyber-attack intended to disrupt the normal functioning of a targeted server, network, or service by overwhelming it with a flood of traffic or requests.

Example: Distributed Denial of Service (DDoS) attacks involve using multiple compromised devices to launch the attack.

D. Man-in-the-Middle (MitM) Attacks:

Definition: Attackers intercept and potentially alter the communication between two parties without them knowing, often to steal sensitive information.

Example: Sniffing data transmitted over unsecured Wi-Fi networks to steal login credentials.

E. Advanced Persistent Threats (APTs):

Definition: Long-term, targeted cyber-attacks where the attacker infiltrates a network, maintaining covert access for an extended period to gather sensitive data or spy on activities.

Example: State-sponsored groups targeting government networks to steal classified information.

F. Insider Threats:

Definition: Threats originating from within an organization, often involving employees or contractors who misuse their access to harm the company, whether intentionally or accidentally.

Example: A disgruntled employee leaking confidential company data.

Types of Cyberattacks

A. **Phishing**: Fraudulent attempts to acquire sensitive information by disguising as trustworthy entities, often via email. (Anderson, R., & Moore, T.,2021)
   Example: Fake bank emails asking for account details.
B. **Malware**: Malicious software such as viruses, ransomware, and Trojans designed to harm systems or steal data.
   Example: Ransomware encrypts files and demands payment.
C. **Denial of Service (DoS)**: Attacks that flood a network or service with traffic, making it unavailable to users.
   Example: DDoS attacks involving multiple compromised systems.
D. **Man-in-the-Middle (MitM)**: Intercepting communications between two parties to steal or alter data.
   Example: Eavesdropping on unsecured Wi-Fi networks.
E. **SQL Injection**: Injecting malicious SQL queries to manipulate databases and gain unauthorized access.
   Example: Stealing information from a website's user database.
F. **Credential Stuffing**: Using leaked passwords to attempt unauthorized logins on other websites, exploiting password reuse.
   Example: Trying breached login data on social media accounts.

AI Techniques in Cybersecurity

AI methods are becoming essential to contemporary cybersecurity, assisting organizations in identifying, reacting to, and averting cyber threats with greater efficiency. AI is capable of analysing large volumes of data instantly, recognizing patterns, and making decisions more swiftly than human analysts. Learning algorithms serve the purpose of training machines and enhancing their performance by enabling them to learn from and adapt based on their experiences. (Morovat, K., & Panda, B., 2020)

Some Key AI Techniques Used in Cybersecurity

A. Machine Learning (ML)
   Description: Machine learning allows systems to learn from data and improve over time without being explicitly programmed. In cybersecurity, ML algorithms are used to detect anomalies, identify malware, and predict potential attacks by analysing historical data.
   Example: ML models can analyse network traffic and flag abnormal patterns that may indicate a DDoS attack or data breach.
B. Behavioral Analytics

Description: This technique involves analysing user and entity behaviours to detect deviations from normal patterns that could signify malicious activity. By understanding what constitutes "normal" behaviour, AI can flag suspicious actions that may indicate insider threats or compromised accounts.

Example: An AI system could detect a user logging in at odd hours or accessing unusually large amounts of data, which might suggest a security breach.

C. Natural Language Processing (NLP)

Description: NLP is used to process and analyse human language. In cybersecurity, NLP can be applied to identify phishing attempts or analyse threats from unstructured data sources like emails or chat logs.

Example: AI tools using NLP can automatically scan emails for signs of phishing, such as suspicious links or misleading language.

D. Automated Incident Response

Description: AI can automate the response to certain types of security incidents, reducing the response time and minimizing human error. It can automatically contain breaches, apply patches, or block harmful activities without waiting for manual intervention.

Example: If a malware infection is detected, an AI system could isolate the affected system and begin remediation steps without human input.

E. Threat Intelligence

Description: AI can be used to analyse vast amounts of threat intelligence data, providing insights on emerging threats, vulnerabilities, and attack patterns. AI algorithms help aggregate data from various sources, identifying trends that would be difficult for humans to spot.

Example: AI can monitor global cybersecurity threat feeds and notify organizations of new vulnerabilities that may affect their systems.

F. Predictive Analytics

Description: Predictive analytics uses historical data and statistical algorithms to forecast future threats and vulnerabilities. By predicting where cyberattacks may occur, AI helps organizations proactively strengthen their defences.

Example: Predictive models could identify patterns that suggest an impending cyberattack, allowing organizations to strengthen their defences in advance.

G. AI-Powered Firewalls and Intrusion Detection Systems (IDS)

Description: AI can enhance firewalls and IDS by dynamically adapting to evolving threats. Instead of relying on predefined rules, AI can recognize new types of attacks based on patterns and behaviours, allowing for quicker identification and mitigation.

Example: AI-enhanced firewalls can identify and block advanced threats that traditional rule-based systems might miss.

Machine Learning for Threat Detection

Machine Learning for Threat Detection employs algorithms to examine data, recognize patterns, and automatically identify cyber threats. In contrast to conventional methods, ML has the capability to recognize both known and unknown threats by acquiring knowledge from data as time progresses. The Ambivalent Role of AI and ML in Cybersecurity: Utilizing AI for Improved Threat Identification and Mitigation. The integration of artificial intelligence and machine learning has significantly transformed the landscape of cybersecurity, enhancing both threat detection and response capabilities. These technologies enable organizations to analyse vast datasets in real time, thereby facilitating a more accurate assessment of risks compared to traditional approaches. (Prince, Nayem Uddin, et al, 2024)

Key Techniques:

A. **Anomaly Detection**: Identifies unusual behaviour or patterns, such as abnormal network traffic, that may indicate a security incident.
B. **Supervised Learning**: Trains models on labelled data to classify threats (e.g., phishing or malware).
C. **Unsupervised Learning**: Detects unknown threats by finding patterns in unlabelled data.
D. **Clustering**: Groups similar behaviours, helping identify new threats or malware variants.
E. **Deep Learning**: Analyses complex patterns in large datasets, detecting advanced threats like zero-day attacks.

Applications:

Intrusion Detection Systems (IDS): Detect unauthorized access or malicious activity.

Endpoint Protection: Monitors devices for suspicious actions and malware.

Phishing Detection: Analyses email content to spot phishing attempts.

Benefits:

Scalability: Can handle large data volumes.

Adaptability: Learns and improves over time.
Reduced False Positives: More accurate threat identification.

AI in Intrusion Detection Systems

Intrusion Detection (ID) refers to the process of identifying attempts or ongoing attacks targeting a computer system or network. Challenges within ID research encompass various aspects, including the collection of data, reduction of data volume, classification of behaviours, as well as the reporting and response mechanisms. (Frank, Jeremy, 1994). AI in Intrusion Detection Systems (IDS) improves conventional security methods by automating the identification of unauthorized access or harmful actions on networks and systems. AI-powered IDS utilize sophisticated algorithms, including machine learning (ML) and deep learning, to examine traffic and behaviour patterns, detect anomalies, and highlight possible security risks.

Key AI Techniques in IDS:

A. Anomaly-Based Detection:

Description: AI models analyse network traffic or system behaviour to establish what is "normal." Any deviation from this baseline is flagged as a potential intrusion.

Example: A sudden spike in data traffic or unusual login times could trigger an alert for further investigation.

B. Signature-Based Detection:

Description: Similar to traditional IDS, AI can use pre-identified patterns or signatures of known threats to detect attacks. However, AI models can improve accuracy and reduce false positives compared to traditional systems.

Example: An AI-enhanced IDS can recognize known malware signatures more effectively by using pattern recognition algorithms.

C. Behavioral Analysis:

Description: AI can track the behaviour of users and devices, identifying abnormal or potentially harmful actions, such as data exfiltration or privilege escalation.

Example: If a user accesses sensitive data they typically wouldn't, an AI-driven IDS can flag the activity as suspicious.

D. Real-Time Monitoring and Automated Response:

Description: AI can continuously monitor network traffic and system logs, automatically responding to threats in real-time. This might involve blocking access or isolating affected systems.

Example: Upon detecting an intrusion attempt, the system may automatically block the offending IP address or disconnect the compromised device.

Advantages of AI in IDS:

Faster Detection: AI models can analyse data much faster than traditional systems, providing quicker responses to potential threats.

Adaptability: AI systems can learn from new attack patterns, adapting to emerging threats without the need for manual updates.

Reduced False Positives: By improving the accuracy of threat detection, AI reduces the number of false alarms, allowing security teams to focus on genuine threats.

Challenges:

Data Dependency: AI models require large volumes of quality data to train effectively, and poor-quality data can lead to inaccurate detection.

Complexity: Implementing AI-based IDS can be resource-intensive and require expertise in both AI and cybersecurity.

Adversarial Attacks: AI systems can sometimes be manipulated by adversaries using techniques like evasion, where attackers modify their behaviour to bypass detection.

Anomaly Detection and Behavioral Analytics

Anomaly Detection and Behavioral Analytics are essential methods in cybersecurity, particularly for recognizing possible security threats that stray from typical behaviour patterns. Both approaches utilize AI and machine learning to identify abnormal activities that may suggest harmful actions, like data breaches, insider threats, or attacks. Behavioral analytics employs artificial intelligence to persistently observe and evaluate user and network activities, thereby facilitating the determination of a standard of "normal" behaviour. After this standard is established, AI algorithms are capable of identifying deviations or anomalies that could signify suspicious or harmful actions. Through the application of machine learning models, AI systems can uncover novel and previously unrecognized threats by detecting patterns that deviate from the established norms, even when such behaviours do not conform to the conventional rules or signatures utilized by traditional systems. (Malik, S. 2024).

Anomaly Detection:

Anomaly detection involves the identification of patterns or behaviours that diverge from what is regarded as typical or anticipated. In the realm of cybersecurity, this method aids in discovering unfamiliar or previously unrecognized threats by examining system activities, network traffic, and user behaviour.

Key Features:

A. **Baseline Creation**: First, normal behaviour patterns are established based on historical data, such as typical network traffic, system usage, or user login times.
B. **Pattern Identification**: The system continuously monitors activities and flags any deviations from the baseline as potential threats.
C. Types of Anomalies:

Point Anomalies: A single, abnormal data point that is significantly different from the normal pattern (e.g., an unusually large data transfer).

Contextual Anomalies: Anomalies that are normal in one context but unusual in another (e.g., a user logging in from an unfamiliar location).

Collective Anomalies: A set of related data points that together represent an abnormal pattern, like a sudden spike in traffic.

Behavioral Analytics:

Behavioral analytics centers on comprehending and examining the actions and behaviours of users, devices, or systems. It aids in recognizing unusual activities according to set Behavioral benchmarks for individuals or entities, rather than merely pinpointing technical irregularities.

Key Features:

A. **User and Entity Behaviour Analytics (UEBA)**: This involves creating profiles of normal behaviour for users and devices. It tracks activities like login times, resource access, and communication patterns.
B. **Insider Threat Detection**: By identifying deviations from a user's typical behaviour, Behavioral analytics can detect potential insider threats (e.g., a trusted employee downloading sensitive files they don't usually access).
C. **Contextual Awareness**: The system doesn't just flag anomalies but takes context into account (e.g., time of day, location) to reduce false positives.

Benefits of Anomaly Detection and Behavioral Analytics:

Early Threat Detection: These techniques can identify threats before they cause significant damage, often spotting malicious activities early in their lifecycle.

Reduced False Positives: By focusing on patterns and behaviours, these methods can reduce the number of irrelevant alerts, which often overwhelm security teams.

Adaptive: Both anomaly detection and Behavioral analytics can adapt to evolving threats as new behaviour patterns emerge, improving over time with machine learning.

Real-Time Detection: Continuous monitoring allows for near-instantaneous detection and response, reducing response times to potential attacks.

Challenges:

False Positives: While these methods can reduce false positives compared to traditional signature-based detection, they still face challenges in distinguishing between benign anomalies and actual threats.

Data Quality: Anomaly detection and Behavioral analytics depend on high-quality, consistent data to build accurate baselines. Poor data quality can lead to missed detections or excessive alerts.

Complexity: Implementing and maintaining these systems requires expertise, and they can be resource-intensive to set up and fine-tune.

AI for Threat Intelligence and Analysis

Artificial Intelligence (AI) is crucial in improving cybersecurity, especially in the areas of threat intelligence and analysis. By utilizing machine learning algorithms, AI systems are capable of automatically identifying anomalies in network traffic and behaviors, recognizing zero-day attacks, and forecasting future threats by analyzing historical data. Automation driven by AI also speeds up the response to threats, minimizing the interval between detection and mitigation, while tools such as Natural Language Processing (NLP) can analyze unstructured data to detect emerging threats in real-time. Despite its advantages, AI encounters challenges including data privacy issues and the potential for adversarial AI, where cybercriminals exploit AI to overcome defenses (Huang et al., 2020). However, when effectively integrated, AI greatly enhances an organization's capacity to identify, analyze, and address cyber threats.

Predictive Threat Intelligence Using AI

Cyber threat intelligence (CTI) is the activity of collecting, examining, and interpreting information about possible or current cyber threats. Its purpose is to help organizations comprehend the tactics, techniques, and procedures (TTPs) employed by malicious actors and to provide actionable insights that can be utilized to guard against cyberattacks (Balandra, S. S., 2024). Predictive threat intelligence leveraging Artificial Intelligence (AI) is transforming how organizations anticipate and counter cyber threats. By utilizing AI, machine learning (ML), and data analytics, predictive threat intelligence seeks to recognize and forecast potential cyberattacks prior to their occurrence, allowing for a proactive approach to cybersecurity

How a Predictive Threat Intelligence Works

A. **Data Collection and Integration:** The first step in predictive threat intelligence is gathering vast amounts of data from multiple sources. These can include:

Network traffic data

Threat intelligence feeds (such as Indicators of Compromise or IOCs)

Endpoint security logs

External sources like dark web monitoring, social media, or forums

This data is then integrated into a centralized platform, often using big data analytics tools that help make sense of large and complex datasets.

B. **Data Preprocessing and Feature Extraction:** AI systems prepare the data by filtering out noise, standardizing it, and extracting valuable features. For instance, this could include recognizing repeated IP addresses, trends of harmful actions, or specific behaviours that signal cyberattacks.

C. **Machine Learning Models:** Machine learning is a core component of predictive threat intelligence.

There are several types of ML models that can be used:

Supervised Learning: Involves training the model on labelled datasets where the outcome (i.e., a cyberattack or not) is already known. The model learns patterns from these examples and can then predict whether new, unseen data will result in a similar attack.

Unsupervised Learning: In this case, AI identifies patterns or clusters of behaviour in data that may not have been previously categorized. This approach is useful for detecting previously unknown threats or zero-day vulnerabilities.

Reinforcement Learning: This is a more dynamic method where AI continuously learns from feedback, making it highly adaptive to changing threat landscapes.

D. **Predictive Analytics:** By utilizing historical data, AI models can anticipate possible attack methods and strategies that cybercriminals could employ in the future. Through comprehending past attack patterns (e.g., tactics utilized in ransomware, phishing operations, or advanced persistent threats), AI is capable of forecasting where and when new attacks might take place.

Predictive analytics involves:

Behavioral Analytics: AI analyses the actions of users, devices, and systems over time to establish normal usage patterns. Deviations from this baseline can indicate potential threats, such as a compromised account or insider threat.

Anomaly Detection: AI continuously monitors systems and data flows for anomalies, signalling potentially malicious behaviour. For example, if an employee accesses sensitive data they normally wouldn't, or if a system is attempting to communicate with a known malicious IP address, AI can flag these deviations for further investigation.

Pattern Recognition: By recognizing recurring patterns in cyberattacks, AI can forecast what kinds of attacks might be likely to emerge next.

E. **Threat Correlation and Contextualization:** One of the advantages of AI is its capacity to link data from various sources. Predictive threat intelligence frameworks can connect diverse data points—like intrusion detection system (IDS) alerts, network records, and external intelligence sources—into an all-encompassing view of a possible threat. For instance, AI could associate a sequence of unsuccessful login tries (from an IDS) with newly identified vulnerabilities (from a threat feed) to foresee an imminent brute-force attack or credential stuffing attempt.
F. **Automated Response and Recommendations:** Once AI identifies possible threats and forecasts their development, it can activate automated reactions. These reactions may consist of blocking certain IP addresses, starting a system quarantine, or notifying security staff for additional investigation. Furthermore, AI can suggest remediation measures or enhancements to defenses to bolster an organization's security stance. For instance, if AI anticipates that a specific vulnerability is likely to be exploited, it might advise patching that vulnerability or modifying firewall settings to restrict certain traffic.

Applications of Predictive Threat Intelligence

A. **Early Detection of Advanced Persistent Threats (APTs):** APTs are long-term, targeted attacks often carried out by well-resourced adversaries. AI-driven predictive threat intelligence can detect subtle early signs of APTs by recognizing irregular behaviour or shifts in attack strategies. This allows organizations to respond before the threat fully materializes, potentially mitigating severe damage.

B. **Zero-Day Vulnerability Detection:** Zero-day vulnerabilities are flaws in software that are exploited by cybercriminals before developers have a chance to patch them. AI systems, by analysing patterns in exploit attempts and known vulnerabilities, can predict and identify zero-day vulnerabilities faster than traditional methods.

C. **Threat Actor Profiling:** Predictive AI models can analyse the behaviours and tactics used by threat actors in previous campaigns to build detailed profiles of potential adversaries. By doing so, they can forecast which organizations or sectors are likely to be targeted next.

D. **Fraud Detection:** AI can analyse transaction data, user behaviours, and account activity to predict and prevent fraud in real-time. For example, AI might detect suspicious financial transactions that deviate from normal patterns or predict the likelihood of account takeovers based on unusual login behaviour.

E. **Network Security Optimization:** By predicting which areas of a network are most vulnerable to attack (based on historical data and current threat intelligence), AI can recommend specific configurations or defensive measures to optimize overall network security.

How a Predictive Threat Intelligence Works

A. **Data Quality and Volume:** Predictive threat intelligence relies heavily on high-quality, accurate data. Without sufficient data or if the data is noisy or inconsistent, AI models may produce false positives or miss critical threats.

B. **Model Accuracy:** AI systems require continuous training and fine-tuning to adapt to new attack techniques and data. If a model isn't regularly updated or trained on recent data, it may become less effective at predicting future threats.

C. **Adversarial AI:** As organizations use AI to defend against cyberattacks, threat actors may also exploit AI to enhance their own attacks. This includes using adversarial techniques to deceive AI-based security systems or launching AI-driven attacks designed to outsmart predictive models.

D. **Complexity and Integration:** Integrating predictive AI systems with existing cybersecurity infrastructure can be complex. Organizations must ensure seamless integration with threat detection tools, incident response platforms, and security information and event management (SIEM) systems.

In Summary, Predictive threat intelligence powered by AI offers organizations a significant advantage in anticipating and mitigating cyber threats before they occur. By utilizing machine learning, data analytics, and Behavioral analysis, AI can forecast emerging threats, recognize patterns in attacks, and automate defences to ensure faster and more effective responses. However, organizations must also consider the challenges of integrating AI into their cybersecurity strategy and ensure that the models remain up-to-date and accurate in the face of constantly evolving threats.

Real-Time Monitoring With AI

Real-time monitoring in cybersecurity refers to continuously observing systems, networks, and applications to detect, analyse, and respond to security threats as they happen. AI is transforming how organizations approach real-time monitoring by enhancing the speed, accuracy, and scope of threat detection.

Key Features of AI-Driven Real-Time Monitoring

A. **Anomaly Detection:** AI systems can track normal patterns of behaviour across networks, endpoints, and user activities. Once a baseline is established, AI can immediately detect deviations from this baseline that may signal malicious behaviour.

B. **Behavioral Analysis:** AI can analyse user behaviour and the actions of devices across a network, which is useful for identifying insider threats and advanced persistent threats (APTs). AI-driven Behavioral analysis helps differentiate between benign anomalies (such as legitimate changes in user activity) and malicious ones (such as unusual login times or accessing critical systems).

C. **Threat Detection and Correlation:** AI can analyse data from multiple sources—such as firewalls, intrusion detection/prevention systems (IDS/IPS), and logs—and correlate them in real time to identify complex attack patterns. By understanding the relationship between various security events, AI can uncover multi-stage attacks that might otherwise go unnoticed.

D. **Real-Time Alerts and Incident Response:** One of the primary benefits of AI-powered real-time monitoring is the speed at which alerts are generated and incidents are escalated. AI can analyse incoming data from sensors and detect security incidents in milliseconds, notifying security teams immediately. In addition, AI systems can often automate initial responses to mitigate threats before human intervention.

E. **Predictive Capabilities:** In addition to detecting threats in real time, AI can predict potential attacks by analysing historical data, patterns of previous attacks, and indicators of compromise (IOCs). Using predictive analytics, AI can forecast the likelihood of a breach based on current trends, allowing organizations to take preventive measures even before an attack begins.

F. **Data-Driven Insights:** AI systems can aggregate and analyse security data from numerous sources to provide actionable insights in real time. This could include detecting new vulnerabilities, identifying new tactics and techniques used by attackers, or highlighting trends that indicate potential future threats.

AI Technologies in Real-Time Monitoring

A. **Machine Learning (ML) and Deep Learning:** Machine learning algorithms are the backbone of many real-time monitoring systems. These algorithms analyse vast datasets, learn patterns, and detect anomalies without explicit human programming. In deep learning, neural networks with multiple layers can process even more complex data patterns and are particularly useful for tasks like image recognition or processing unstructured data such as logs and text. ML and deep learning algorithms are continuously refined with feedback, improving their predictive accuracy over time.(Manda, J. K., 2024).
B. **Natural Language Processing (NLP):** NLP, a subset of AI, helps in processing and interpreting textual data from a variety of sources, such as social media, dark web activity, and phishing emails. By analysing these text-based sources in real time, AI can identify emerging threats and recognize indicators of future attacks.
C. **Big Data Analytics:** Real-time monitoring systems often deal with massive amounts of data. Big data analytics tools are designed to handle large-scale data collection, integration, and analysis. AI-driven systems can sift through this data quickly and identify patterns that would be impossible for humans to detect manually. With the use of distributed computing, AI systems can analyse data in real time from a variety of sources—such as logs, network traffic, and external intelligence feeds—enabling security teams to stay one step ahead of attackers.
D. **Automation and Orchestration:** AI can automate not only threat detection but also the response process. By integrating AI with security automation tools, organizations can reduce response times, eliminate human error, and increase efficiency. For example, if AI identifies a potential ransomware attack, it can automatically block the affected machine from the network and initiate predefined containment procedures. Automation helps ensure that attacks are mitigated quickly, especially in the case of time-sensitive threats.

Benefits of AI-Powered Real-Time Monitoring

A. **Faster Threat Detection and Response:** Traditional monitoring tools often rely on predefined rules and signatures to detect threats, which can be slower and less effective against sophisticated attacks. AI's ability to analyse large volumes of data quickly and continuously means that threats are detected almost in real time, allowing for immediate action and minimizing the time attackers have to exploit vulnerabilities.
B. **Adaptability to New Threats:** One of the most significant advantages of AI in real-time monitoring is its ability to adapt to new and evolving threats. Unlike signature-based systems, which require updates every time a new threat is identified, AI can continuously learn from new data and adjust its models to recognize emerging threats. This makes AI-driven systems more resilient to previously unknown (zero-day) attacks.
C. **Reduced False Positives:** AI systems can significantly reduce the number of false positives compared to traditional monitoring tools. Through continuous learning and Behavioral analysis, AI can distinguish between legitimate activity and potential threats more accurately. This not only helps security teams focus on real threats but also reduces the strain on resources that would otherwise be spent investigating false alarms.
D. **Enhanced Threat Intelligence:** AI can aggregate and analyse data from a wide variety of sources, providing security teams with real-time, actionable threat intelligence. This may include real-time insights into attack trends, new vulnerabilities, or emerging tactics used by cybercriminals, helping organizations adapt their security strategies accordingly.

Challenges and Considerations

A. **Complexity and Integration:** Implementing AI-driven real-time monitoring systems can be complex, especially for organizations with legacy systems. AI systems must be integrated seamlessly with existing security infrastructure like Security Information and Event Management (SIEM) tools, firewalls, and intrusion detection systems (IDS), which can require significant time and effort.
B. **Data Privacy and Security:** The continuous collection and analysis of sensitive data raise concerns about privacy and data security. Organizations need to ensure that AI systems are compliant with data protection regulations (like GDPR) and that data used in monitoring is properly secured.
C. **Resource and Training Requirements:** While AI systems can automate many aspects of cybersecurity, they still require skilled personnel to train, manage,

and fine-tune the algorithms. This may necessitate investment in talent and infrastructure, which can be a barrier for some organizations.

AI for Malware Detection and Prevention

AI is transforming malware detection and prevention by leveraging machine learning, deep learning, and Behavioral analysis to identify malicious activities based on patterns and behaviours instead of traditional signature-based methods. Unlike conventional systems that struggle to detect new or polymorphic malware, AI continuously learns from new data and adapts to emerging threats.

How AI Detects Malware Patterns

Artificial Intelligence (AI) has revolutionized cybersecurity by enhancing the detection and prevention of malware. Traditional signature-based malware detection methods struggle to keep up with the rapidly evolving nature of cyber threats. AI, particularly machine learning (ML) and deep learning (DL), provides a more adaptive and proactive approach to identifying malware patterns.

Machine Learning for Malware Detection

Machine learning algorithms analyse vast amounts of data to recognize patterns associated with malicious software. These algorithms can be categorized into supervised, unsupervised, and reinforcement learning models:

A. **Supervised Learning**: AI models are trained on labelled datasets containing both benign and malicious software samples. Once trained, the model can classify new, unseen files as either safe or harmful.
B. **Unsupervised Learning**: Instead of relying on labelled datasets, unsupervised models identify anomalies in network behaviour or system activities that deviate from normal patterns, which may indicate malware (Buczak & Guven, 2016).
C. **Reinforcement Learning**: This technique improves detection by learning optimal strategies to classify malware based on past interactions with a system.

Deep Learning for Pattern Recognition

Deep learning models, particularly Convolutional Neural Networks (CNNs) and Recurrent Neural Networks (RNNs), analyse binary and assembly code to detect malicious features:

A. **CNNs**: Used to analyse binary files as images, detecting structural anomalies that indicate malware presence (Kolosnjaji et al., 2018).
B. **RNNs**: Effective in detecting malware by analysing sequential API call patterns and network traffic behaviours.

AI-Powered Behavioral Analysis

Beyond static file analysis, AI enables real-time Behavioral monitoring to identify suspicious activities, such as:

A. Unauthorized access attempts
B. Abnormal file modifications
C. Unexpected network communication patterns

AI in Threat Intelligence and Prevention

AI enhances cybersecurity by continuously learning from threat intelligence feeds, allowing organizations to anticipate and mitigate emerging threats before they cause harm (Vinayakumar et al., 2019).

In Summary, AI plays a crucial role in modern malware detection by leveraging ML and DL techniques to identify suspicious patterns. As cyber threats evolve, AI-driven security solutions continue to adapt, offering enhanced protection against increasingly sophisticated attacks.

AI-based Antivirus and Antimalware Tools

The integration of Artificial Intelligence (AI) into cybersecurity has significantly improved the efficiency of antivirus and antimalware solutions. AI-powered security tools overcome these limitations by using machine learning (ML), deep learning (DL), and Behavioral analysis to detect and prevent malware attacks in real-time.

How AI Enhances Antivirus and Antimalware Solutions

AI-based security tools employ multiple techniques to improve malware detection:

A. **Behavioral Analysis**: AI models monitor the behaviour of applications and processes to detect anomalies that may indicate malicious activity.
B. **Heuristic Analysis**: Machine learning algorithms analyse code structures and execution patterns to identify unknown malware variants.
C. **Predictive Threat Intelligence**: AI-powered tools analyse threat intelligence data to predict and mitigate future cyber threats.

Popular AI-Based Antivirus and Antimalware Tools

Several AI-driven cybersecurity solutions have been developed to provide proactive malware detection and prevention:

A. **Microsoft Defender ATP**: Uses AI and cloud-based analytics to detect and respond to advanced threats in real time.
B. **CrowdStrike Falcon**: Leverages AI and Behavioral analytics to detect file less malware and advanced persistent threats (APT).
C. **Cylance PROTECT**: Uses AI-driven threat detection to identify and neutralize malware before execution.
D. **Sophos Intercept X**: Incorporates deep learning to enhance malware detection and ransomware protection.
E. **Darktrace Antigen**: Employs self-learning AI to autonomously detect and neutralize cyber threats.

AI in Real-Time Threat Detection and Prevention

AI-driven security tools continuously analyse system logs, network traffic, and user behaviours to identify potential threats:

A. **File less Malware Detection**: AI identifies abnormal behaviour in system processes to detect malware that operates in memory.
B. **Automated Incident Response**: AI-powered security tools can autonomously isolate infected systems and neutralize threats.
C. **Zero-Day Attack Prevention**: AI predicts and blocks emerging threats before they exploit vulnerabilities.

In Summary, AI-based antivirus and antimalware tools have transformed cybersecurity by enabling real-time, proactive threat detection. As cyber threats continue to evolve, AI-driven solutions will remain essential in providing robust protection against advanced malware attacks.

COMPLICATIONS AND APPLICATIONS OF AI IN SECURITY

Ethical and Privacy Considerations in AI Security

Ethical and privacy considerations in AI security revolve around ensuring transparency, fairness, and accountability while safeguarding sensitive data. AI-driven security systems must avoid biases that could lead to discrimination, and decision-making processes should be explainable to prevent unjust outcomes. Privacy concerns arise from extensive data collection, requiring strict adherence to data protection laws and encryption measures to prevent unauthorized access.

Ethics of AI in Cybersecurity

The integration of Artificial Intelligence (AI) in cybersecurity has significantly improved threat detection and prevention. However, its deployment raises ethical concerns related to privacy, bias, accountability, and misuse. Addressing these ethical challenges is crucial to ensuring that AI-driven cybersecurity systems operate fairly, transparently, and responsibly.

A. Privacy and Data Protection

AI-driven cybersecurity systems rely on vast amounts of data to detect threats effectively. However, collecting and analysing sensitive user information raises concerns about privacy and data security:

AI-powered security solutions may process personal and corporate data, leading to potential breaches if not properly secured.

The use of AI in surveillance can lead to excessive monitoring, threatening user privacy and individual freedoms (Brundage et al., 2018).

B. Bias and Fairness in AI Models

AI models used in cybersecurity can inherit biases from training data, leading to unfair or discriminatory outcomes:

If an AI system is trained on biased datasets, it may disproportionately flag certain groups or geographies as high-risk (Raji et al., 2020).

Bias in malware detection models can lead to false positives, blocking legitimate software or users based on incorrect assumptions.

C. Accountability and Explainability

AI-driven cybersecurity systems often operate as "black boxes," making it difficult to understand how decisions are made. This lack of transparency raises accountability concerns:

When an AI system wrongly classifies a legitimate user or file as malicious, determining responsibility can be challenging (Rahwan et al., 2019).

Organizations must establish clear guidelines on who is accountable for AI-driven cybersecurity decisions and ensure AI models are interpretable.

D. Dual-Use and Misuse of AI in Cybersecurity

AI can be exploited by both cybersecurity professionals and cybercriminals:

While AI enhances malware detection, hackers can use AI to develop evasive malware that adapts to security measures.

Deep fake technology and AI-generated phishing attacks have increased, making social engineering attacks more effective.

Bias and Fairness in AI Security Models

Artificial Intelligence (AI) has significantly improved cybersecurity by enabling automated threat detection and response. However, AI security models are susceptible to bias, which can lead to unfair, inaccurate, or discriminatory outcomes. Bias in AI-driven security systems can stem from training data, model architecture, or implementation practices, raising concerns about fairness, reliability, and trust. Addressing these biases is crucial for ensuring ethical and effective AI-based cybersecurity solutions.

A. Sources of Bias in AI Security Models

Bias in AI cybersecurity models can arise from multiple factors:

Training Data Bias: AI models learn from historical data, which may reflect existing security trends, user behaviours, or threat landscapes. If the training dataset is unbalanced or non-representative, the model may disproportionately misclassify certain user activities or threats.

Feature Selection Bias: Security models rely on specific features (e.g., network traffic patterns, file attributes) to detect threats. If these features are chosen based on limited or skewed data, the model may favour certain attack types while overlooking others.

Algorithmic Bias: Some AI algorithms may inherently favour specific types of outcomes due to the way they process input data, leading to higher false positive or false negative rates for certain groups of users or network activities.

B. Ethical and Security Risks of Bias

False Positives and False Negatives: A biased AI security model may mistakenly flag legitimate users or software as threats (false positives) or fail to detect actual malware (false negatives), reducing overall system effectiveness.

Discriminatory Outcomes: AI models that associate cybersecurity risks with specific regions, languages, or behaviours may unfairly target certain user groups, leading to ethical concerns and potential legal challenges.

Trust and Transparency Issues: If AI-driven security tools operate as "black boxes" without clear explanations of their decision-making, users may find it difficult to trust their accuracy and fairness.

C. Mitigating Bias in AI Security Models

To ensure fairness and reliability, organizations must adopt strategies to reduce bias in AI-driven security systems:

Diverse and Representative Training Data: Using datasets that include a broad range of threats, user behaviours, and network environments can help minimize training bias.

Regular Model Audits: Continuous evaluation and retraining of AI models with updated and unbiased data can improve accuracy and fairness.

Ethical AI Frameworks: Following guidelines and regulations, such as GDPR and AI ethics principles, can help ensure responsible AI deployment in cybersecurity.

Data Privacy Concerns and AI

The integration of Artificial Intelligence (AI) in cybersecurity has enhanced threat detection and prevention. However, AI-driven security solutions rely on vast amounts of data, often including sensitive personal and corporate information. This raises significant data privacy concerns related to data collection, processing, storage, and security. If not managed properly, AI-powered cybersecurity systems can inadvertently violate privacy rights, leading to ethical, legal, and operational risks.

A. Data Collection and Consent Issues

AI models require large datasets to train and operate effectively. However, privacy concerns arise when organizations collect and use data without explicit consent from users:

Many AI-driven security tools, such as intrusion detection systems (IDS) and Behavioral analytics software, continuously monitor user activities, potentially tracking personal information without individuals' knowledge.

Data collected for cybersecurity purposes may later be repurposed for other uses, raising ethical concerns about transparency and user consent (Taddeo & Floridi, 2016).

Organizations may not always disclose the extent of data collection, making it difficult for users to understand how their information is used.

B. Risks of Data Storage and Security

AI-based security systems process and store large volumes of sensitive data, making them attractive targets for cybercriminals:

Centralized data storage increases the risk of large-scale data breaches if security measures are not properly implemented.

Unauthorized access to AI training data can lead to security vulnerabilities, such as adversarial attacks that manipulate AI models into making incorrect decisions.

Insider threats pose a risk when employees misuse or leak sensitive information stored in AI systems.

C. AI and Data Anonymization Challenges

Anonymization is a widely used technique to protect personal data, but AI models can sometimes deanonymize information by recognizing patterns:

Re-identification attacks: AI algorithms can analyse anonymized datasets and link them back to individuals by cross-referencing other available data sources.

Differential privacy: This technique adds noise to datasets to prevent re-identification while maintaining data utility, but it is not fool proof if adversaries have access to auxiliary data.

To enhance privacy, AI-driven security solutions should implement advanced anonymization techniques, such as federated learning, which allows AI models to train on decentralized data without exposing raw information.

D. Compliance and Ethical Challenges

The growing use of AI in cybersecurity raises legal and ethical challenges:

Organizations must comply with privacy laws and regulations that vary by region, creating challenges for multinational companies.

AI-driven security decisions must be explainable so users and regulators can understand how personal data is processed.

Ethical concerns arise when AI models are used for mass surveillance, potentially infringing on civil liberties.

Challenges of Integrating AI Into Cybersecurity

Despite its potential benefits, integrating AI into cybersecurity raises a number of problems. One significant challenge is the need for high-quality, comprehensive data. AI models depend on vast amounts of accurate, structured data to train effectively, and obtaining such data in real-time across diverse systems can be difficult. Inaccurate or incomplete data can lead to AI models making false predictions or missing crucial threats.

Another challenge is the complexity and cost of implementation. AI systems require specialized knowledge and infrastructure, which can be expensive for organizations to adopt. Moreover, integrating AI into existing security frameworks demands significant time and resources.

Complexity and Interpretability of AI Models

The complexity and interpretability of AI models are two critical factors that play a significant role in the development, deployment, and trustworthiness of AI systems, especially in fields like cybersecurity, healthcare, finance, and law. These factors affect how well AI can be understood, managed, and used effectively by both developers and end-users.

A. **Black Box Nature of AI**: Many AI models, particularly deep learning, lack transparency, making it difficult to understand decision-making processes. This opacity can reduce trust in AI-driven cybersecurity decisions and make debugging challenging.
B. **Bias in AI Models**: AI can inherit biases from training data, leading to inaccurate or unfair decisions in cybersecurity applications. For example, biased AI models may incorrectly flag legitimate user activities as security threats.
C. **Adversarial Attacks**: Attackers can manipulate AI models by feeding them deceptive inputs, tricking them into misclassifying threats. Suppose, slight alterations in malware code can bypass AI-based detection systems.

Resource and Data Limitations

Resource and data limitations are two significant challenges that impact the performance, development, and deployment of AI models. These constraints can affect how effectively AI can be applied across various industries, such as cybersecurity, healthcare, finance, and more.

A. **High Computational Costs**: Training AI models requires significant processing power and specialized hardware, making it a resource-intensive process. Organizations with limited budgets may struggle to implement AI-driven cybersecurity.
B. **Need for High-Quality Data**: AI systems depend on vast amounts of labelled cybersecurity data, which may not always be available or may be incomplete. Insufficient or poor-quality data can result in ineffective threat detection.
C. **Data Privacy Concerns**: Organizations must balance AI training with data protection regulations such as GDPR and CCPA, ensuring that user data remains secure while improving cybersecurity models.

The Future of AI and Cybersecurity

The future of AI in cybersecurity is poised to dramatically transform how organizations approach threat detection, prevention, and response. As cyber threats become increasingly sophisticated, AI will become an essential tool for defending against attacks, automating key security processes, and enhancing overall system resilience.

AI will significantly improve threat detection by moving beyond traditional methods, using machine learning algorithms to analyse vast amounts of data and recognize patterns that indicate potential vulnerabilities. By learning from historical data and adapting to new threats, AI can identify unusual behaviour and predict cyberattacks before they occur, enabling organizations to proactively protect their networks.

The Future of AI in Cyber Defense

The future of AI in cyber defense is set to revolutionize how organizations protect their digital assets, respond to cyber threats, and ensure the overall security of their networks and systems. As cyber threats become more sophisticated, AI's capabilities in data analysis, pattern recognition, and decision-making are expected to play a central role in proactive and reactive cybersecurity strategies.

A. **Predictive Threat Intelligence**: AI will proactively identify and neutralize cyber threats before they materialize, leveraging large datasets and Behavioral analysis to predict malicious activities.
B. **Real-Time Anomaly Detection**: AI will continuously monitor network activity to detect unusual behaviour patterns, allowing for early threat identification and mitigation.
C. **Integration with Human Expertise**: AI will enhance, rather than replace, human analysts by providing data-driven insights, allowing cybersecurity professionals to make better-informed decisions.

Autonomous Security Systems

Autonomous security systems refer to advanced technologies designed to enhance security by operating independently, without the need for constant human intervention. These systems typically rely on sensors, AI algorithms, and automated decision-making processes to detect, prevent, and respond to security threats. Autonomous security systems can be deployed in various settings, including homes, businesses, and public spaces, to monitor and protect assets, property, and individuals.

A. **Self-Healing Systems**: AI-driven security platforms will automatically detect and remediate vulnerabilities, reducing human intervention and improving response times.
B. **Automated Incident Response**: AI will enable real-time response mechanisms to counter cyber threats, reducing downtime and mitigating damage.
C. **Adaptive Learning Mechanisms**: AI models will continuously evolve by learning from new threats and attack patterns, ensuring cybersecurity solutions remain effective against emerging risks.

Case Studies and Real-World Applications

AI-Powered Threat Detection Systems in Action

AI-powered threat detection systems have become a critical component of modern cybersecurity. These systems use machine learning algorithms, pattern recognition, and data analytics to identify potential threats in real-time, providing enhanced security across various sectors. They are capable of spotting unusual behaviour that may signify a cyberattack, such as malware activity, phishing attempts, or unauthorized access. By learning from historical data, AI can differentiate between normal and anomalous activities, reducing false positives and alerting security teams only when necessary.

A. **Financial Sector Implementations**: Banks use AI-driven fraud detection systems to prevent unauthorized transactions by analysing spending patterns and identifying anomalies.
B. **Healthcare Cybersecurity**: AI safeguards patient records from data breaches and ransomware attacks by monitoring access patterns and detecting suspicious activities.
C. **E-Commerce Fraud Prevention**: AI monitors transactions to identify fraudulent activity in real time, reducing chargebacks and enhancing online security.

Government and Private Sector AI Security Solutions

AI security solutions are being implemented both by government agencies and private sector companies to address the growing risks associated with artificial intelligence (AI) and machine learning (ML). These solutions aim to protect critical infrastructure, ensure data privacy, and prevent malicious exploitation of AI systems.

A. **National Cybersecurity Initiatives**: Governments deploy AI-powered frameworks to protect critical infrastructure, such as power grids and communication networks, from cyber threats.
B. **Corporate AI-Driven Defense Systems**: Major corporations invest in AI to protect sensitive corporate data, using automated security protocols to respond to threats faster than traditional methods.
C. **Public-Private Cybersecurity Collaborations**: Governments and businesses work together to share threat intelligence, improving collective defense against cybercriminals.

CONCLUSION

Artificial Intelligence is reshaping the landscape of cybersecurity by offering innovative solutions to combat increasingly complex cyber threats. Its ability to analyze massive amounts of data, detect unknown threats, and adapt to evolving attack strategies has made AI indispensable in modern security practices. AI-driven technologies such as machine learning, behavioral analytics, and predictive threat intelligence have significantly enhanced the speed, accuracy, and efficiency of threat detection and prevention. However, the integration of AI also introduces challenges related to data privacy, ethical considerations, and model interpretability, which require careful attention. The future of cybersecurity will likely see greater reliance on AI, with autonomous security systems playing a more prominent role, highlighting the need for continuous advancements in both technology and regulatory frameworks.

REFERENCES

Anderson, R., & Moore, T. (2021). *Security Engineering: A Guide to Building Dependable Distributed Systems* (3rd ed.). Wiley.

Balantrapu, S. S. (2024). AI for predictive cyber threat intelligence. *International Journal of Management Education for Sustainable Development*, *7*(7), 1–28.

Brundage, M., Avin, S., Wang, J., Belfield, H., & Krueger, G. (2018). The Malicious Use of Artificial Intelligence: Forecasting, Prevention, and Mitigation. ArXiv Preprint arXiv:1802.07228.

Buczak, A. L., & Guven, E. (2016). A Survey of Data Mining and Machine Learning Methods for Cybersecurity. *IEEE Communications Surveys and Tutorials*, *18*(2), 1153–1176. DOI: 10.1109/COMST.2015.2494502

Carlo, A. (2023). The importance of cybersecurity frameworks to regulate emergent AI technologies for space applications. *The Journal of Space Safety Engineering*, *10*(4), 474–482. DOI: 10.1016/j.jsse.2023.08.002

Floridi & Taddeo. (2016). What is data ethics? Philosophical Transactions of the Royal Society A: Mathematical, Physical and Engineering Sciences.

Frank, J. (1994). Artificial intelligence and intrusion detection: Current and future directions. *Proceedings of the 17th national computer security conference*, 10.

Kolosnjaji, B., Zarras, A., Webster, G., & Eckert, C. (2018). Deep Learning for Classification of Malware System Call Sequences. *Proceedings. IEEE Symposium on Security and Privacy. Workshops*, *2018*, 1–10.

Luiijf, E. (2012). *Understanding cyber threats and vulnerabilities. Critical Infrastructure Protection: Information Infrastructure Models.*

Malik, S. (2024). Using AI for Behavioral Analytics in Cybersecurity: Detecting Anomalies and Insider Threats. Academic Press.

Manda, J. K. (2024). AI-powered Threat Intelligence Platforms in Telecom: Leveraging AI for Real-time Threat Detection and Intelligence Gathering in Telecom Network Security Operations. DOI: 10.2139/ssrn.5003638

Morovat, K., & Panda, B. (2020, December). A survey of artificial intelligence in cybersecurity. In *2020 International conference on computational science and computational intelligence (CSCI)* (pp. 109-115). IEEE DOI: 10.1109/CSCI51800.2020.00026

Prince, N. U. (2024). AI-powered data-driven cybersecurity techniques: Boosting threat identification and reaction. *Nanotechnology Perceptions*, 20.

Rahwan, I., Cebrian, M., Obradovich, N., Bongard, J., Bonnefon, J.-F., Breazeal, C., Crandall, J. W., Christakis, N. A., Couzin, I. D., Jackson, M. O., Jennings, N. R., Kamar, E., Kloumann, I. M., Larochelle, H., Lazer, D., McElreath, R., Mislove, A., Parkes, D. C., Pentland, A. S., & Wellman, M. (2019). Machine Behaviour. *Nature*, *568*(7753), 477–486. DOI: 10.1038/s41586-019-1138-y PMID: 31019318

Raji, I. D., Gebru, T., Mitchell, M., & Buolamwini, J. (2020). Saving Face: Investigating the Ethical Concerns of Automated Facial Analysis Systems. *Proceedings of the ACM Conference on Fairness, Accountability, and Transparency*, 1-12.

Russell, S., & Norvig, P. (2020). *Artificial Intelligence: A Modern Approach* (4th ed.). Pearson.

Sarker, I. H., Furhad, M. H., & Nowrozy, R. (2021). Ai-driven cybersecurity: An overview, security intelligence modeling and research directions. *SN Computer Science*, *2*(3), 3. DOI: 10.1007/s42979-021-00557-0

Vinayakumar, R., Alazab, M., Soman, K. P., Poornachandran, P., Al-Nemrat, A., & Venkatraman, S. (2019). Deep learning approach for intelligent intrusion detection system. *IEEE Access : Practical Innovations, Open Solutions*, *7*, 41525–41550. DOI: 10.1109/ACCESS.2019.2895334

Welukar, J. N., & Bajoria, G. P. (2021). Artificial Intelligence in Cyber Security-A Review. *International Journal of Scientific Research in Science and Technology*, *488*, 488–491. DOI: 10.32628/IJSRST218675

Chapter 7
Enhancing Cybersecurity in Blockchain:
Legal Challenges and Solutions

Sudipta Dhar
https://orcid.org/0009-0004-4998-3041
Brainware University, India

Shivangi Kashyap
https://orcid.org/0009-0002-1685-330X
Brainware University, India

Pravin Kumar
https://orcid.org/0009-0008-9393-7324
Brainware University, India

ABSTRACT

Blockchain enables decentralization, transparency, and security and faces threats from cybersecurity and legal. The cryptographic algorithms and consensus protocols add a layer of security, while the associated risks of possible 51% attack, inappropriate private key management, and smart contract vulnerabilities still persist. Legal issues arise with the clashes with data protection laws like the GDPR and with the challenge of finding who is liable due to this decentralization. The uncertain legal context around smart contracts is preventing their enforcement. Also emerging threats like quantum computing will require quantum-resistant cryptographic standards. A proposed solution includes better security, adaptive regulations, and collaboration of governments, industry, and academia. An equilibrium will allow for a secure, legally complaint, and sustainable blockchain fit for applications into the future.

DOI: 10.4018/979-8-3373-2282-7.ch007

INTRODUCTION

In the past few years, blockchain technology showed itself in the scope of an innovative breakthrough that changed not only the finance and healthcare businesses but also industries from supply chain management to everyday routine. Blockchains are famous for their utility of decentralized and tamper-resistant architecture, which leads to security, transparency, and efficiency of the system. Nevertheless, as more organizations globally embrace blockchain, the number of attacks targeting them increases, and the global legal and security complexities grow.

The security of blockchain is often cited, but blockchain is no different from any other information technology when it comes to being vulnerable to cyberattacks. The vulnerabilities in smart contracts, 51% attacks, phishing, and malware have shown us that hackers are crafting new tricks to exploit weaknesses in blockchain networks. These threats are not only damaging to the integrity and reliability of blockchain systems but also ruin the public confidence in this new technology.

The technical, legal, and regulatory boundaries of blockchain cybersecurity are also compounding. Blockchain, however, introduces a new set of challenges for the legal framework, which is not designed to deal with cross-border cybercrimes and jurisdictional ambiguity as the enforcement of accountability. Beyond, the working pace of blockchain innovation usually surpasses that of the ability of legal frameworks to streamline, filling regulatory gaps that heighten cybersecurity perils.

This paper investigates cybersecurity challenges interceded by blockchain technology. It looks into the vulnerabilities in blockchain systems, lists some known cyber incidents, and examines the legal complexity of such threats. The guidelines of this document show how blockchain cybersecurity improves by promoting industrial cooperative ventures and technological advancements. The discourse examines blockchain cybersecurity to establish both the technological and legal aspects of blockchain security, which strengthen ecosystem resilience and protectability.

LITERATURE REVIEW

Literature Review on Blockchain Technology

Blockchain technology holds much interest for research because it is believed to change the ways digital security and trust can be achieved and support decentralized systems. Blockchain was introduced initially by Satoshi Nakamoto in 2008 as the underlying technology powering Bitcoin. Then, the space became so wide and complex that the applications kept expanding beyond cryptocurrency. Its architecture, security frameworks, consensus mechanisms, and regulatory challenges have been explored by researchers, and that is how blockchain is a multidisciplinary area of study. Blockchain has its advantages in decentralized and immutable characteristics, which can be applied in finance, healthcare, supply chain management, smart contracts, etc. Scalability, energy consumption, and legal uncertainties are also presented from the aspect of challenges. In this literature review, we discuss different studies that contributed to shaping the research regarding blockchain, especially in the core components, security vulnerabilities, governance structure, and legal considerations. This review analyzes these critical aspects to get a general idea of blockchain's technical developments and how they can influence the Web as a whole.

The Genesis of Blockchain Technology

The 2008 intellectual work of Satoshi Nakamoto introduced blockchain technology through its open-source, decentralized system, which safeguards digital transactions from double use. Blockchain eliminated intermediaries from digital transactions because it established a breakthrough method for secure peer-to-peer transactions with full transparency. The first and most famous application of blockchain technology to illustrate its combined distribution ledger and cryptographic techniques to replace centralized financial systems was Bitcoin. Further advancement of blockchain technologies was possible due to the use of cryptographic hash functions to assure data integrity, digital signature to authenticate transactions, and consensus mechanism (as Proof of Work (PoW) to validate transactions). These are, among other things, the fundamental concepts that have led to the expansion of blockchain technology and cryptocurrencies. Hence, continuous research on scalability, security, compliance with regulations, and advancements in the blockchain will reorient its role in the digital economy.

Blockchain Architecture and Consensus Mechanisms

Research has been mainly focused on blockchain's distributed architecture and consensus mechanism, which has been the core of a structural foundation of this technology. In Zheng et al. (2017), the authors provided an extensive view of blockchain architecture, which is based on cryptographic techniques to secure data and distributed consensus to make participants reach an agreement on the distributed ledger. In their study, the authors pointed out that blockchain offers strong guarantees of data integrity, transparency, and decentralization at the expense of specific attacks, for instance, 51% attacks and Sybil attacks.

Blockchain's functionality relies on consensus mechanisms, and since then, they've been widely studied. Proof of work has been criticized for its energy inefficiency and suspicious centralization to mining. Thus, alternative mechanisms such as Proof of Stake (PoS) and Delegated Proof of Stake (DPoS) were proposed to address these limitations. However, various researchers or studies in the literature are still exploring hybrid or novel consensus algorithms to improve scalability and security, as well as energy efficiency.

Security Challenges in Blockchain Systems

Security has become the dominant theme of blockchain research. Security and privacy issues critical in identifying such vulnerabilities in Blockchain Systems are provided by Conti Et Al. (2018) in the form of a comprehensive survey. They consider risks such as double spending attacks, selfish mining, and DoS attacks and how important it is for advanced cryptographic algorithms and secure coding practices of smart contracts. Blockchain security is changing, and it has to be updated regularly to keep up with growing threats.

Building upon Moubarak et al. (2020), they delved more deeply into the specifics of cybersecurity challenges for blockchain: vulnerabilities in smart contracts and consensus protocol. This includes smart contract coding error risks, for which they need to do formal verification techniques and regular audits. Moreover, Lin and Liao (2017) also looked into the possibility of quantum computing to attack the security of blockchain and the related concern that the current cryptographic techniques are prone to quantum attacks. Thus, their study urged the development of quantum-resistant cryptography to protect blockchain systems in the future.

Legal and Regulatory Challenges

The main problem in this area is how blockchain can harmonize with existing legal systems, in particular, data protection laws. In 2018, Finck analyzed the disparity between the General Data Protection Regulation (GDPR), which enforces the “right to be forgotten,” and the immutability characteristic of blockchain technology. The reason is that data deletion or modification within blockchain transactions is inherently challenging since the transactions not only need to be permanent but also tamper-proof. It implies that there are conflict issues about building the infrastructure of blockchain-based systems in ways that are compatible with privacy regulations without undermining the key principles of decentralization and transparency. Innovative technological and regulatory solutions that strike this balance have to be found concerning addressing these concerns.

Just as Rizal and Nair (2021) studied the legal concerns of smart contracts in terms of their enforceability and accountability in decentralized social constructs, the paucity of regulatory frameworks makes it uncertain as to how contracts are executed and how resolutions of disputes are decided. The promotion of smart contracts in the context of different sectors requires legal guidelines that should be defined with absolute clarity. Similar to the growing trend of the lack of visibility in regulations not conducive to the construction of trust or the full use of blockchain implementations in each sector, the study reflects this trend.

Global Standards and Collaboration

The World Economic Forum (2021), the importance of international collaboration and standardized frameworks for improving the security and interoperability of blockchain. Their report highlights the core reason why we require staunch, coordinated, international efforts to solve cross-border business regulation hurdles, cybersecurity risks, and technical irregularities that prevent the winnowing down of blockchain innovation. Since blockchain has a decentralized and borderless nature, there is a need to develop internationally recognized standards for trust among stakeholders, adherence to prescribed standards, and integration without obstructions across jurisdictions. The absence of unified regulatory frameworks, along with some national policies and security protocols, would lead to inefficiencies, fragility, and a slowdown in innovation. However, industries like finance, healthcare, and supply chain management will benefit the most by bringing the operational excellence of business processes to their services with the promotion of international cooperation and utilizing its potential. Risks of data privacy, fraud prevention, network resilience, and so on can also be mitigated via standardized security protocols. These global frameworks will go a long way in developing the blockchain as a safe, scalable, and broadly acceptable technology that can shape every sector in the digital economy.

Emerging Trends and Future Directions

Consequently, more and more bodies of literature are acknowledging the technical aspect of blockchain research as one of its research challenges, as well as the work to investigate a technical and legal (legal) model of the system. Because of all of this, blockchain technology has become harder to scale, harder to secure, and harder to regulate than ever before, as those permutations are increasingly grafted on decentralized finance (DeFi) and non fungible tokens (NFTs). Financial stability is often affected by how DeFi platforms make financial transactions without any intermediary, which raises questions about preventing fraud, smart contract vulnerabilities, and so on. We have also seen that similar to the rapid growth of NFTs, there has been much being discussed over intellectual property rights, digital ownership, and market manipulation. With both these innovations to increase the capabilities of blockchain, it also. As such, it demands strong security protocols as well as well-defined legal frameworks to minimize the risks involved and do the right thing in terms of the laws.

Besides its potential use in financial applications, there have been researchers' contemplations of future potential for other industries, such as supply chain management, healthcare, and what others have termed as voting systems. Blockchain is used in the supply chain as it provides blockchain. The biggest challenge of applying blockchain in the healthcare area is data privacy and regulatory compliance, as secure patient record management and data sharing are to be more transparent and traceable, but tries to standardize and integrate into another two problems have to be resolved. These studies show that blockchain is versatile, and hence, industry-specific application of the technology is needed to cater to the spectrum of technical, ethical, and legal concerns that have to be addressed as blockchain technology goes mainstream.

Challenges and Research Gaps

Immutability and security can be applied in blockchain, but some people need to vote, and some other people cannot; moreover, some people want to play dirty. Despite the great achievements of blockchain technology, many challenges and gaps in research are still unsolved, which need to be further investigated and innovated. Scalability lies as one of the most important problems faced by blockchain networks, and solving one of the most pressing issues involves the capability of handling extremely large transaction volumes. They are looking into ways of neutralizing the issue, like sharding, splitting the blockchain into smaller constituent functions and side chains, and additional processing capacity to alleviate congestion. Additionally, other Layer 2 protocols like the Lightning Network have been created to increase transaction speed, further decrease costs, and not overload the main blockchain.

And lastly, privacy is a huge matter of concern, given that public blockchains inherently lack secrecy. To meet this, techniques of zero-knowledge proofs, which allow verification without exposure of beneath data, and ring signatures, which take away knowledge of transaction beginnings, are being investigated to strike a decent parity between identification and mindfulness.

Furthermore, quantum computing threatens future blockchain security in the form of a long-term threat by which quantum computing could break existing cryptographic methods. Even though resistant algorithms are in development, there are technical challenges to integrating them into existing blockchain frameworks. The second biggest challenge is the lack of interoperability between different blockchain platforms, which in turn means restriction in free-flowing data between blockchain platforms, therefore preventing the creation of a truly connected digital ecosystem.

BLOCKCHAIN TECHNOLOGY: METHODOLOGY AND APPLICATIONS

With its potential to not only deliver decentralized protection and foster trust but also be suitable for various needs of digital transformation, blockchain technology has established itself as a near pillar of digital transformation. Blockchain, as Nakamoto (2008) introduced it as a means that would prevent double spending on digital currencies, has evolved from a solution to become a versatile technology that can be applied in several domains. Since then, research has also focused on blockchain's architecture, such as its vulnerabilities, as well as legal complexities regarding this innovation as a whole, to understand its aspects that can be reversed to have a positive impact. This paper explores the different ways of studying Blockchain and its application by synthesizing knowledge from the main contributions in the field.

Figure 1. Key Aspects and Research Areas of Blockchain Technology

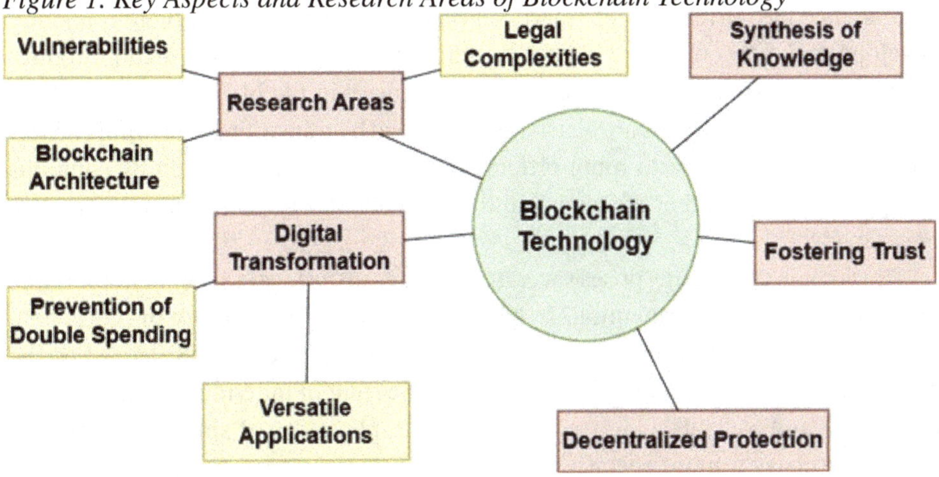

Source Author's Work

Blockchain technology is a multidisciplinary technology, and hence, it requires a combined approach, both technical, legal, and regulatory. The first method is a thorough review of the literature, which serves as an introduction to explore the capacity and drawbacks of the blockchain. For instance, Zheng et al. (2017) illustrate the core features of blockchain, thus relying on cryptographic and distributed consensus, whereas Conti et al. (2018) address vulnerabilities of Sybil and 51% attack. Therefore, these studies emphasize that it is essential to consider both the strengths and the weaknesses of models and blockchain in a way that will improve the resilience of blockchain.

Another important methodological approach is Case Study analysis, which provides practical insights from the perspectives of blockchain implementation/applications and failures of our case companies. For instance, the Ethereum DAO hack was an instance of a poorly designed smart contract. However, it exposed very serious threats of misdesign and emphasized the importance of rigorous coding standards and auditing practices (Moubarak et al., 2020). Similarly, Finck's (2018) work on the legal challenges associated with blockchain in terms of GDPR showed the conflict between blockchain's immutability and 'the right to be forgotten.' These cases can be analyzed, allowing researchers to have actionable strategies to reduce risks and facilitate compliance with the regulatory framework.

Blockchain research leans into the development of such technical solutions to address vulnerabilities using novel approaches. Cryptographic algorithms play an integral part in defending against the presence of growing threats such as Quantum Computing (Lin and Liao, 2017). In addition, researchers seek means to increase the security and functionality of smart contracts, e.g., formal verification techniques to guarantee the correctness of smart contracts. On the other hand, there is another development of decentralized identity systems that allow users to have more control over their data — it is equal to privacy and security in the blockchain ecosystem. While consensus protocols are also being enhanced by transitioning from an energy-intensive proof-of-work to more efficient and environmentally friendly solutions like proof of stake, other efficiency and environmental impact improvements are being made.

Blockchain technology poses several challenges to the legal and regulatory fronts, which need considered attention. In his article on the compatibility of blockchain and the General Data Protection Regulation (GDPR), Finck (2018) identifies the contradiction between immutable records and the right of individuals to delete their data. Rizal and Nair(2021) looked at the legal implications of smart contracts and the need to have a more specific and clearer regulatory framework so that smart contracts could be enforceable and accountable. That highlights the need for a joint effort between governments, industries, and academia to standardize regulations that will make sure it is innovative yet compliant with the law.

As it is, collaboration and global standardization are more recognized in addressing blockchain's cybersecurity and regulatory challenges. The World Economic Forum (2021) already underlines international frameworks that promote trust as well as interoperability in blockchain systems. This will also help minimize the risk associated with the potential of blockchain technology, as stakeholders can minimize its potential to be incompatible with global standards and how this can limit cross-border cooperation. However, these efforts are vital to solve problems like data protection in field boundaries and legal interpretation harmonization in a decentralized system.

The uses of blockchain technology vary from one sector to another but did come up with a revolutionary solution to solving a long problem. Blockchain in finance ensures secure and transparent transactions with the reduction of fraud and the elimination of intermediaries. Blockchain provides capacity for end-to-end traceability and product authenticity, which increases consumer trust; hence, this benefits supply chain management. Blockchain is being used in the healthcare industry for the secure storage and sharing of patient records, thus increasing data integrity and accessibility. It is also being applied to voting systems to combat fears about election integrity and create more transparent, tamper-proof systems. It proves the variety of domains blockchain opens up to be revolutionized.

Although it has a lot of potential, as of now, blockchain technology is presented with a few challenges it needs to overcome; these challenges will have to be solved through regular research and development. Even today, there are security vulnerabilities, like 51% Attacks and smart contract exploits, which are ever a concern to date since the need for hydraulics and secure coding practices continues to mature. Clear guidelines and international collaboration are needed because regulatory hurdles, such as data protection laws and the enforceability of smart contracts, are present. Furthermore, the environmental impact of blockchain, particularly energy-intensive consensus mechanisms like proof-of-work, calls for the development of more sustainable solutions.

Finally, it's safe to say that blockchain technology is changing the world and the paradigm of digital security and trust, which brings new solutions to urgent issues in all industries. Literature reviews, case studies, and technical solution development methodologies are explored as a means of its possible and its limitations. We need to integrate global standards as well as every stakeholder's efforts in a collaborative manner to make blockchain successful in the long run and used. However, there are still challenges to overcome, and research – and collaboration with other disciplines – will lead to the continued evolution of blockchain and the discovery of even more new functions and the next steps for digital systems.

Key Cybersecurity Challenges in Blockchain

Apart from integrating blockchain, technology has revolutionized many business areas as a secure, decentralized system of transactions. But it has its array of cybersecurity issues to tackle for it to be put to good use everywhere. This means that these are crucial to understanding the technology's limitations and its possible vulnerabilities.

In one of the largest threats of attacks, when a single entity group's mining resources or computational power rises to 51 percent over the blockchain's, it is described as a 51% attack. This allows attackers to reverse transactions, double-spend coins, and so on, which essentially compromises the integrity of the blockchain. In the Proof of Work (PoW) -based systems, mining resources not only frame the community dynamics but also perform a decisive role in determining the network's security.

Table 1. Major Cybersecurity Issues in Blockchain and Their Mitigation Strategies

Cybersecurity Issues in Blockchain	Description	Potential Solutions
51% Attack	If one entity or group can control 51% of the resources of mining, they can reverse transactions, double spending coins, and compromise the blockchain's integrity.	Increasing mining difficulty, sticking to the Proof of Stake (PoS) concepts, and enhancement of decentralization.
Smart Contract Vulnerabilities	The smart contract code is erroneous and may be exploited for financial losses, such as Ethereum's 2016 DAO attack. Once deployed, a smart contract cannot be changed.	Optimal auditing, testing, and verification of smart contracts before deployment. Implementing security-focused programming practices.
Private Key Security	Digital signatures of private keys are used to gain access to blockchain assets. Irreversible asset loss occurs from the loss or compromise of private keys. Phishing attacks and malware management are the common threats.	Cold storage is used for private keys and additional layers of signatures, emphasizing the proper approaches to storing keys.
Sybil Attacks	Attackers try to deluge the network with multiple fake nodes or identities and then take control, interfere with consensus mechanisms, and thus disrupt operations.	Identity verification mechanisms implementation, reputation-based systems, and equipping PoW or PoS because of making attack costs higher.

The other critical issue is smart contract vulnerabilities. A self-executing contract that runs on a blockchain, smart contracts can be referred to as smart contracts. However, there are problems or errors in the code that can result in the theft of funds. Once these contracts have been deployed, they are permanent and irreversible; any coding errors are very costly, given that they cannot be altered. Ethereum's infamous 2016 DAO attack is a great example, where a flaw was exploited, and those dollars were lost. Given that smart contracts have the potential to lead to such incidents, they need to go through rigorous auditing, testing, and verification before going live.

Private key security is the basis of blockchain technology and having login and access to digital assets via such keys. In blockchain networks, the private keys play the role of digital signatures for a particular user, enabling them to have exclusive rights to an individual's assets. If a private key is compromised, lost, or stolen, no entity other than the owner can recover the stuck funds. Some common threats include phishing attacks, whereby attackers trick users into providing their private keys, and poor key management, like storing keys in unsecured locations.

Users must use strong security measures to avoid private keys. For high protection against online threats, hardware wallets, which store the keys offline, provide a very high level of protection. To increase security, Multi-signature solutions come into action that require multiple approvals to transact. In addition, users of such services should constantly confirm the authenticity of sites and correspondences before giving any sensitive information. Secure key management calls for proper education and awareness.

Sybil attacks pose a considerable threat to blockchain networks since they allow attackers to spin multiple fake nodes or identities. It is this fake entity that can be used to flood the network, bringing the network to a halt, take it over, or interfere with the consensus process and/or normal network operations. Attacks of this nature can attack the integrity of such a system if it is built on highly decentralized systems that very much rely on peer-to-peer for trust and validation. For instance, a Sybil attacker may seize control of many nodes within a network in which they can perform actions, for instance, double spending, censorship, or even stopping the network.

Consequently, blockchain platforms must be equipped with much stronger defenses against Sybil attacks. Identity verification protocols that can be costly and resource-intensive for attackers to create fake identities can be used. Reputation-based systems and mechanisms that offer rewards for honest behavior also deter power concentration and network takeover by any given individual.

In the current blockchain technology development and adoption, there have been some great scalability and security trade-offs. The efficient processing of high transaction volumes is in perfect contrast to the need for decentralized and secure behavior. Thus, it is generally emoted that it is part of the 'blockchain trilemma,' a characteristic that gives the impression that this is often not possible at one time.

To scale, however, solutions such as Layer-2 protocols, sharding, etc, have been developed. State channels or rollups will process transactions off-chain, recording only on the base layer by recording a final state. Unlike an ordered transactional chain, sharding shatters the network into smaller units called partitions (shards) to do transactions in parallel and thus improve throughput. However, these solutions come at the price of introducing vulnerabilities such as smaller resistance to attacks on the smaller shard or the reliance on high additional trust assumptions for Layer 2 systems.

To maintain the scalability of blockchain networks, we need to balance the two architectural dimensions of scalability and security through innovative design, rigorous testing, and cooperation in the community.

The blockchain network itself is inherently secure due to the cryptography at its core and lack of centralized nodes; however, endpoint weaknesses are critical flaws. There are endpoints through which interactions with the blockchain occur (wallets, exchanges, etc.), and they all interact through various endpoints with the blockchain. Often, these interfaces are hacked by hackers by exploiting the weaknesses in user devices, software, or security practices. These risks have been demonstrated through high-profile exchange hacks and malware attacks against the wallets of users, resulting in enormous financial losses and inducing distrust from the end users.

Typically, the hackers would leverage phishing schemes, key loggers, or malicious apps to obtain private keys or credentials to grab control of users' funds and money. A defense is needed, however, and that defense is endpoint security. Multi-factor authentication (MFA) offers an additional string to your password. Regular software and hardware security audits are backed up by potent anti-malware tools for rounding off the defenses. It is equally important to educate users on how to spot threats and use safe cybersecurity practices.

Present blockchain security is exploited by the use of a consensus mechanism, which is a great challenge to the security of the blockchain. To ensure all blocks of a blockchain network are validated and in a decentralized state, it is built around consensus mechanisms like Proof of Work (PoW) or Proof of Stake (PoS), among others. While great for a myriad of different mechanisms, these are, however, not impenetrable to vulnerabilities. In PoW, a 51% attack would be when the malicious entity, given the majority of the network computing power, can facilitate double spending or retroactive transactions. At the same time, PoS also has problems, such as the "nothing at stake problem," where validators will be tempted to vote on several competing chains, undermining the certainty of the network and its security.

To address these concerns, alternative and hybrid consensus mechanisms have been developed. Delegated Proof of Stake (DPoS) is an improvement in efficiency and security by truncating already trusted individuals to validate transactions, while Proof of Authority (PoA) excludes malicious actors with identity-based validation. The approaches achieve that balance between scalability and security to limit risks from the use of traditional mechanisms.

Blockchain security is a big challenge in data privacy, especially in the public blockchains that enable transparency and immutability. These features are essential to trust and accountability but can accidentally give away sensitive data that could violate privacy regulations such as the General Data Protection Regulation (GDPR). The addition of data to a blockchain makes that data immutable – that is, information cannot be altered or removed – which is of concern when data is personal.

Thus, robust techniques for privacy preservation need to be incorporated into blockchain networks to address these challenges. The encryption ensures that the sensitive data is safe and inaccessible. Beyond that, anonymous (or doxx-free), privacy-focused methods such as zero-knowledge proofs (ZKPs) allow a user to assert the validity of a transaction without exposing the underlying data. ZKPs combine transparency with confidentiality, and hence, the blockchain systems can maintain trust and still comply with privacy laws. Cybersecurity, privacy, and the swath of possibilities that such freedom could provide the population make all three critical when ensuring a successful blockchain technology transition.

Similar to interoperability between chains or platforms, blockchain's reliance on cross-chain communication is a new addition, bringing in new challenges and new risks, specifically in cross-chain communication. The interoperability enables the transferring of assets, data, and functionalities of the blockchains in between. In reality, however, the reliance often falls back on third-party protocols, i.e., cross-chain bridges that serve as intermediaries to permit these interactions. These bridges are complex and present security gaps that malicious actors use to steal their victims' money and assets. These vulnerabilities have serious implications during high-profile hacks of bridges.

But it's important to enforce very strict security measures to prevent risks of cross-chain transactions. Vulnerabilities that may exist within the code can be identified and patched by regularly having the code audited by trusted third-party security firms. Much of the system undergoes extensive testing up and under simulated attack scenarios to assure system resilience. Moreover, adopting secure decentralized or trustless bridge solutions has its advantages. If the security protocols that blockchain needs are already prioritized, then interoperability would not compromise trust or safety. Instead, it would fully bring blockchain's potential to life.

A serious security threat toward blockchain networks is insider threats, as those whom your network regards as privileged, developers, administrators, or other highly important network members, can be considered a danger. Many times, these insiders have intimate knowledge of the system, and systematic access to sensitive data can be exploited for stealing assets, manipulating transactions, or sabotaging network operations. The human element is a weak point that cannot be mechanically solved, and it is still vulnerable on blockchain — which doesn't mean that inside risks are gone.

Therefore, one must implement comprehensive security to address the dangers posed by corporate insider threats. Once doors to abuse are open, RBAC is very important in not giving people access to the resources necessary to do their role. Detections of suspicious behavior early can be achieved through continuous monitoring of user activities. On top of that, one should have employees that are thoroughly vetted and background checked before allowing them to have access to really important systems. Prevention is also important in cultures that are security-focused and where strict accountability is taken for insider exploits.

With blockchain security being such an important issue and cryptography being one of the most powerful tools to address it, it's no surprise that the vulnerability of cryptographic algorithms is considered to be a threat to quantum computing as it progresses. To prove the integrity and security of data on the blockchain networks, the hashing and public-key encryption is done primarily with cryptographic methods such as SHA-256 and RSA. Nevertheless, quantum computers would, in the long run, turn these widely used algorithms upside down by techniques like Shor's algorithm, which allows for efficient factoring of a large number and computing discrete logarithms. The result of this is that quantum computing could jeopardize the entire security backbone of blockchain systems and thereby put sensitive transactions and data at risk.

Eventually, the blockchain community has started approaching cryptography needed to address this looming threat using research in quantum-resistant cryptographic algorithms. Post-quantum algorithms are such that even quantum machines can't break them, and therefore, blockchain networks would be secure in the age of quantum. Investigating this area is crucial for making blockchain technology future-proof; it can adapt to the rising threats and still deliver security as a trust base.

One of the biggest challenges for blockchain networks is having regulatory and compliance risks because the technology is becoming more popular. As a decentralized network and pseudonymous network, blockchain can make it hard for government and regulation bodies to come up with clear rules for innovation that balance that with consumer 'protection.' Intense legal challenges, government interventions, or backdoor implementation of code could jeopardize a project's security and trust, but without clear regulations, all pieces of code and specifications facing the operation seem to be under threat.

The amount of regulatory scrutiny that blockchain technology will attract as it increases in popularity is likely to increase as well. Governments around the world may require sharper blockchain network conditions, including anti-money laundering (AML), know your customer (KYC), and data privacy, to name just a few. However, these regulations may differ across jurisdictions, causing more complexities within the compliance process of global blockchain platforms. Because of potential legal issues, disruptions, and loss of trust of users, blockchain projects must always be up to date on the changes in regulations and adjust to meet their compliance. But any ability to skate through this messy terrain will depend on reclusiveness with policymakers, legal experts, and industry standards.

Here is the conclusion: Blockchain is a smart network with outstanding security but at a high price. All of the above-discussed cybersecurity risks show how important it is to maintain focus on the technology and its implementation, as well as on continuing research and insisting on robust security practices to make blockchain a trusted and safe stand.

Legal Challenges

1. Regulatory Uncertainty

The case is one of the hottest you can make regarding blockchain technology: nobody has a regulatory framework that is unified across different jurisdictions.

In particular, governments and regulatory bodies around the world have taken a range of steps regarding blockchain-related assets, namely cryptocurrencies. They are considered securities in some countries, while in others, partly countries that regulate them as securities and others as commodities. Some countries have some regulation or even prohibition of cryptocurrencies.

This generates large legal uncertainty for businesses, developers, and users of a global digital economy. As a result, there is a challenge for companies to handle competing regulations that are too burdensome in terms of costs from legal costs, compliance costs, and operational risks. The main reason institutional investors are kept away from Blockchain technologies until the community has regulatory guidance and when there is regulatory guidance is that there is no standardized regulatory guidance. But, startups and innovators in the blockchain space often find themselves unable to deploy new solutions because of fear of changes or enforcement actions that could put them out of business if they come.

Moreover, to accelerate the use of blockchain on a global scale, cross-border transactions also become intricate without harmonized regulations. International cooperation is very important; it should foster innovation and legal clarity. Standardization of regulatory frameworks will ensure sustainable development of the blockchain industry as well as protect the investors and the consumers alike.

2. Data Privacy and Protection

The most fundamental challenge related to compliance with privacy laws makes blockchain incompatible with it: the immutable and transparent nature of blockchain. Such right of the individuals to be forgotten is granted by GDPR; individuals can demand to have their data erased. Anticipating this constraint, however, blockchain's fundamental design principles, around which recorded data cannot be altered or erased, make it impossible to comply with these requirements in full. Once the information has been put on the blockchain, it becomes permanent, and in the distributed ledger, this may be a problem when the data that is put on is sensitive personal data.

This is more so for public blockchains where data stored is accessible to all the network participants, thereby making it easily hackable. However, if personally identifiable information (PII) is recorded on the chain directly, there can be a violation of privacy laws and liability to blockchain developers and businesses.

Thus, researchers and technologists seek innovative solutions to the challenges. For this, one approach is to use off-chain storage that stores sensitive data in an external database and stores only a cryptographic hash or a reference to this data on the blockchain. In addition, complex encryption techniques along with privacy-enhancing techniques such as zero-knowledge proofs allow checking the data without revealing personal information. The aim behind these solutions is to achieve this catch-22 between privacy rights and the decentralized, tamper-resistant nature of blockchain technology.

3. Smart Contract Enforceability

Smart contracts are programs that automatically execute pieces of digital contracts in the digital world once the pre-defined conditions are met. They remove the requirement for intermediaries, which helps to save money, cut costs, and help to negate errors. Although they offer advantages of their own, smart contracts, to a large extent, present the issue of insufficient legal and regulatory implementation, for instance, concerning the enforceability of smart contracts in the shadow of traditional legal frameworks.

The smart contract features contrast with conventional contracts that can be interpreted but also fought against humans and bid against them. However, if the contract is not strong enough—say, not rigid enough—the result can be that the consequences of unexpected events, unexpected circumstances, such as market change, system bug, or the ambiguous term for which a human judgment is important, can be quite obvious. In addition, the legal systems that exist around the world differ in how they recognize and regulate digital agreements, giving smart contracts little certainty about whether or not they are valid contracts.

Jurisdictional challenges further complicate enforcement. Blockchain networks take place across many regions, and hence, it becomes a challenge to determine which country's laws will apply in case of a dispute. Even if the terms encoded in smart contracts are not that complex, courts may find it difficult to interpret them as no legal conventions have been established. There was an attempt to address those issues through hybrid models, which combine smart contracts with legal agreements and are respectful of dispute resolution, to increase their legal recognition and reliability.

4. Intellectual Property Rights

Due to the introduction of blockchain technology, especially within the decentralized environments where the users generate, share, and trade digital assets, complex intellectual property (IP) challenges are introduced. Non-fungible tokens (NFTs) are one of the main issues that confuse ownership and rights. When buying an NFT, buyers typically purchase a unique digital token, but they don't gain ownership of its underlying content or IP rights, that is, the artwork, music, or other media. As a result, creation and reproduction, licensing and commercialization, and the boundaries of ownership have given rise to legal difficulties because creators, buyers, and providers have disagreed over what is encompassed in ownership.

In addition to NFTs, blockchain's decentralized structure also makes IP protection that much harder to accomplish, especially when it comes to coded blockchain-based software. Most of the projects based on blockchain incorporate the functioning of the open source code in the forms of questions about the right to modify this code, terms of licensing, and also about the possibility of copyright infringement. Open source collaboration brings about innovation as well as unauthorized use of the code and arguments over intellectual property rights.

While enforcing IP rights in a decentralized environment is challenging, blockchain transactions are borderless and, most of the time, pseudonymous, which makes it impossible to identify the violator or account for them. Thus, to fix these problems, we have a clean legal framework, standardized licensing agreement, and blockchain IP ownership verification and enforcement that helps fairly pay for both parties: the creator and the businesses.

5. Cross-Border Legal Issues

Blockchains are a decentralized/borderless enterprise, thereby providing complexity to the law that is used to apply traditional Legal principles in such a decentralized or borderless environment. Such blockchain transactions do not operate within the boundaries of any single national regulation, as NBCS does. Its global reach prevents one from knowing which country's laws will apply in the case where international parties face legal disputes. The lack of clear jurisdictional authority impacts contract enforcement and consumer protection as well as when fraud, financial misconduct, or transactional disputes are involved.

Another big issue is taxation: governments have different rules regarding cryptocurrency transactions, capital gains, and digital holdings. Tom Brady's January 6 conviction is likely to result in a four-game suspension, and whereas his fans may still contend that he never should have been convicted, folks from the Tuileries to the Vatican will view that conviction and suspension differently. Similarly, there are several other issues to overcome about poorly implemented anti-money laundering (AML) and know-your-customer (KYC) rules. However, the different jurisdictions have diverse policies on strict identity verification and screening of financial reporting of blockchain-based companies that work on the global level, which leads to heterogeneous regulations of these companies.

Without international cooperation and harmonized legal frameworks, regulatory uncertainty will continue to hinder blockchain adoption. The setting of standardized global regulations, which are essential for technological objectivity, as well as providing legal clarity for innovation and use of blockchain technology in various industries, is of utmost importance.

6. Securities Law Compliance

Currently, Blockchain projects, including token sales and Initial Coin Offering (ICO) projects, are becoming a subject of regulatory focus as they fall under the jurisdiction of applicable securities laws. However, most regulators cross-reference tokens to see if they fit the legal standards they've set as the U.S. Howey Test says, among other things, that an asset is considered an investment contract if it's traded on the exchange and requires contributions, risk, effort, and expertise. This test says that a token is Secure if it involves money investment in a common undertaking with the hope of making profits through the efforts of others. A token must comply with the strict regulations, which include note registering with regulatory authorities, clear disclosures, and investor protection measures if a token meets those criteria.

Disobeying securities laws could have a hefty bite on blockchain projects by imposing fines to the tune of several millions, lawsuits filed by investors, or even shutting down one's operations. However, the U.S. Securities and Exchange Commission (SEC) has pursued the enforcement of its actions against the blockchain companies that have carried out an unregistered security offering — thereby fighting in courtrooms and imposing penalties. Therefore, blockchain projects need to create token models carefully to comply with the regulations. To avoid being classified as an investment token, some companies try to classify their tokens as utility tokens (tokens that don't grant investment rights) and others' status as exempt. Nevertheless, the absence of global regulatory standardization remains a big hindrance to token-based fundraising models where blockchain entrepreneurs and investors can have difficulties.

7. Taxation Challenges

Because of its decentralized nature and the fast-growing regulatory landscape, blockchain transactions with cryptocurrency trading, staking, and mining are very difficult to tax. Different jurisdictions have their unique approaches to classifying and taxing blockchain-based activities for tax authorities. For example, some countries tax cryptocurrencies as property and thus consider capital gains taxes upon the sale or exchange of those cryptocurrencies. Some see it as income and, therefore, tax it by earned value (staking rewards mining profit). Inconsistency in classification results in confusion amongst taxpayers, especially those that involve transactions across borders.

This worsens as Blockchain, by its nature of being pseudonymous and decentralized, enables the obstruction of tax compliance and enforcement. The problem with a blockchain transaction is that, unlike centralized financial systems where institutional transactions are reported to the tax authorities, reporting in a blockchain transaction is nontrivial because of a lack of centralized oversight and, hence, the inability to track and report. Limited guidance or understanding of a user's obligation to report taxable events can lead users to inadvertently fail to report taxable events. Cryptocurrencies' values also fluctuate, making it difficult to ascertain the taxable amounts at different times.

Similar governments are additionally creating frameworks and gadgets to mop up on blockchain exchanges. However, in a lot of locations, the lack of proper and standard tax rules necessitates that the users stay up-to-date and proactive regarding their tax obligations.

8. Anti-Money Laundering (AML) and Know Your Customer (KYC) Compliance

Law enforcement and regulatory bodies face major obstacles because blockchain provides users with privacy through pseudonymity, which allows these sectors to identify money laundering and terrorist funding alongside committing various forms of fraud. Users can execute blockchain-based transactions anonymously through the network since it omits the requirement for personal information disclosure that financial institutions and banks traditionally enforce. It is challenging for regulators to monitor illegal financial flows in blockchain transactions because of the lack of identity information.

As a result, governments around the world made strict anti-money laundering (AML) and Know Your Customer (KYC) regulations. The operation of centralized blockchain platforms demands user identification verification together with transaction documentation and suspicious activity monitoring for official regulatory bodies. Such actions create better transparency throughout blockchain systems that support financial activities.

Strict regulations in decentralized systems are currently hard to enforce throughout these systems. DeFi platforms running on decentralized financial networks together with P2P systems cannot effectively conduct AML or KYC procedures because they do not have central control over user transactions. The core values of blockchain decentralization face inevitable opposition from regulatory oversight systems that want to enforce transparency.

The emerging solutions involving on-chain analytics with blockchain forensic tools alongside decentralized identity verification systems work to overcome this challenge. The emerging blockchain innovations aim to fulfill legal requirements while preserving both financial openness and user privacy to preserve the decentralized operation of the technology.

9. Legal Status of Decentralized Autonomous Organizations (DAOs)

DAOs function without central governance through blockchain smart contracts, which both carry out decision enforcement and implement rule requirements. The uncertain legal standing of DAOs creates multiple problems because it hinders their capacity to address liability situations and full regulatory compliance and oversight.

Greater accountability exists because traditional legal systems permit corporations, partnerships, and sole proprietorships to face legal punishment whenever authorities need to assign responsibility. The absence of a formal legal framework within DAOs makes identifying responsible parties problematic whenever fraud, financial misconduct, or any unlawful conduct occurs. The identification of accountable parties during regulatory investigations becomes difficult in DAO cases since it may extend to include developers behind smart contracts while also implicating token holders and various operational contributors. The hybrid nature of DAO's legal status creates difficulties for law enforcement along with secure investments and adequate taxation, which acts as a deterrent for institutional involvement.

The difficulty regarding the legal recognition of DAOs led several jurisdictions to adopt limited liability entity status for them. The world lacks a unified regulatory agreement regarding this topic. The growth of DAOs mandates legal system adjustments to solve the issues about liability together with taxation and governance structures so they stay compliant while safeguarding decentralization principles. Making DAOs work within existing financial and legal frameworks presents the main obstacle since it requires maintaining their basic autonomy along with their innovative capabilities.

10. Cybersecurity Liability

Blockchain technology maintains strong security through decentralized mechanisms and cryptographic methods, but these benefits do not impede weaknesses that appear in wallet management, smart contract development, and decentralized application (dApp) deployment. Hackers take advantage of system weaknesses to cause major financial damages and system breaches of compromised systems. Blockchain platforms face billions of dollars worth of cyberattacks that occur because of insecure program codes and weak security provisions.

Deciding liability for security breaches in blockchain systems becomes complex because blockchain operates without centralized control. Smart contract security breaches from coding failure generate confusion about which party bears responsibility between the developer who programmed the contract and both platform administrators and users who participated in the transaction. Blockchain applications fall short of traditional financial institutions when it comes to established mechanisms for fraud protection along with defined rights for consumers under specific legal frameworks. Hacked individuals face restricted possibilities regarding legal action and financial fund retrieval.

The increased blockade adoption requires developers and regulators to work together to establish clear legal structures that handle debts, security rules, and disputes within decentralization. The development of best practices for both smart contract auditing and insurance, as well as legal safety measures, will be necessary to build trust while reducing risks that come from blockchain applications.

11. Consumer Protection

Precise blockchain operations ensure secure decentralized deals; they do not offer traditional finance systems similar protective measures. Because transactions and lost money can not be reversed by payment service providers or banks, no centralized authority structure in the blockchain network could mediate the dispute. User safety remains extremely exposed because their private keys might be lost, along with the risks stemming from phishing attacks, fraudulent activities, and hacking attempts. The loss of a private key results in permanent fund loss because there exists no way users can retrieve their assets. The inability to unwind transactions brings expensive consequences due to fraud cases and human error incidents because funds sent to the wrong addresses become non-recoverable.

The issue of lacking consumer defense has attracted strong attention from supervisory authorities while they develop new safeguards for blockchain environments. Multiple governments try to develop legal structures and rules for user safety improvement, but blockchain's decentralized traits create obstacles during enforcement procedures. The unclear jurisdictions and the multiple approaches to regulations by different countries create additional slowdowns in efforts to move forward.

The broad adoption of blockchain solutions depends on developing user-friendly protection features, including safer wallets and detection tools and insurance coverage and regulatory standards to earn broader commercial trust.

Solutions and Recommendations

1. Identifying Core Challenges

Organizations must overcome their primary obstacle, which is inefficiency stemming from poorly defined processes together with ineffective communication strategies. Organizations experience decreased productivity while dealing with delayed deadlines combined with duplicated work, mostly because of these operating inefficiencies. The problem stems primarily from teams needing to use separate tools and having workflow processes that are not standardized since this creates confusion that blocks teamwork. Employers without a centralized real-time updates system face challenges in keeping their teams focused on priorities because this leads to process delays, miscommunication between colleagues, and project completion setbacks.

The major difficulty stems from having undefined personnel roles alongside insufficient feedback systems. Employees who experience unclear responsibilities and poor feedback terms will lose their sense of accountability and reduce the potential for continual organizational improvement. Employee morale decreases steeply when employees receive inadequate constructive feedback, which leads to both the disengagement of workers and diminished job satisfaction.

Several organizations do not maximize their available resources or technologies. Advanced tools and platforms remain partially unused by employees because they receive no standardized training or fail to implement proper organizational processes to optimize these resources. This circumstance leads organizations to waste potential value while they experience more operational issues and pay unnecessary costs.

The absence of intervention on these issues leads organizations to face enduring negative impacts that diminish productivity while causing workers to become more frustrated and reducing their ability to remain competitive in the market. Organizations must develop integrated data-based solutions that optimize communication flow workflow definition and resource use to overcome these problems. Organizations that invest in centralized management software, together with clear role definition systems supported by employee training, achieve better workplace collaboration along with increased efficiency.

2. Proposing Holistic Solutions

Organizations need to establish broad but practical solutions that depend on data analytics for effective core issue resolution. An integrated project management system represents one of the most effective solutions that organizations can deploy through Trello, Asana, or Microsoft Teams. All team members stay on track with priorities and deadlines because these platforms unite their communication as well as task assignments and progress-tracking capabilities. The real-time collaboration features minimize inefficiencies because they prevent miscommunications that use incorrect information.

Improvements to workflow automation systems will deliver substantial performance gains to the organization. Repetitive work tasks such as email follow-ups and data entry, as well as reporting, function better with automation because the system frees employee time so they can work on important tasks. Business workflow software such as Zapier, Monday.com, and Power Automate merge operations to minimize errors that occur through human intervention.

A strong feedback regulation system that combines performance reviews with anonymous surveys represents a fundamental solution for organizational success. Such capabilities let organizations obtain essential data, which helps them execute strategic changes and build ongoing improvement systems.

Organizations achieve maximum productivity by providing specific training programs to their employees. Businesses can establish long-term success by implementing these solutions, which both solve main operational problems and boost operational efficiency.

3. Short-Term Strategies

Organizations should initiate easy-to-implement immediate actions that produce quick, visible outcomes for quick wins. Regular team check-in sessions serve as an effective intervention because they build open communication while improving collaboration, which quickly fixes misunderstandings. These meetings achieve two goals: they create team goal consensus while they define project objectives and maintain continuous team participation.

A solution of great impact exists in defining exact responsibilities and roles among team members. When team members receive clear definitions of their specific tasks, it leads to improved efficiency and higher accountability functionally, with no confusion present. The organization can achieve this through updated project documentation and role-specific training in addition to short briefing sessions.

Basic tool training for employees remains a quick yet powerful solution that impacts performance effectively. Workers do not maximize their assigned tools primarily because they are unfamiliar with them. Short sessions to explain workplace tools help staff improve their efficiency and maintain workflows without requiring new financial costs.

Pulse surveys with quick performance check-ins compose the last solution since they create immediate feedback loops to support ongoing organizational development.

Fast-moving improvements produce two benefits: they generate workforce engagement, which strengthens both morale and productivity and simultaneously creates foundation blocks for extended business enhancements. Organizations that implement these strategic and compact steps will experience rapid benefits on their way to continued achievement success.

4. Long-Term Recommendations

Sustainable business strategies and everlasting investments should serve as means of creating steady progress complemented by organizational flexibility. Advanced analytics tools are a major investment because they provide deep performance insights, and this must be an investment that will help improve project, employee, and efficiency metrics. The tools provide data-based decisions that incorporate patterns to be able to detect patterns, improve operation effectiveness, and foresee future problems.

The creation of an environment based on perpetual learning represents a critical organizational approach. The combination of scheduled educational sessions with guidance programs plus administration training events helps staff maintain their job skills while staying active in their work roles for changing market needs. Team members who share their knowledge develop better collaboration and innovation between colleagues.

Scalable technological investments coupled with infrastructure development through cloud-based and automated solutions give the organization both efficiency gains and sustainability in market transformations.

These extended strategies match organizational goals through their establishment of resilience along with their development of adaptability and their promotion of sustainable expansion. The investment of these resources enables businesses to build high-performing staff, enhance their operational flow, and maintain their industry leadership position.

5. Monitoring and Evaluation

The assessment of solution success demands both qualitative and quantitative methods while following a systematic tracking procedure. Feedback surveys represent an effective method to collect feedback from stakeholders along with employees and customers through which satisfaction and effectiveness levels can be quantified. These surveys should serve to obtain useful information that enhances understanding of both positive aspects and which areas require attention.

Organization progress is monitored through adopting performance metrics systems. Success in business operations can be measured through key performance indicators (KPIs) that demonstrate improvements in efficiency as well as cuts in costs, maintain customer retention, and heighten productivity. Configured data monitoring helps organizations maintain correct alignment between their solutions and strategic goals.

The quarterly review process creates systematic opportunities to examine achievement results. Team members conduct periodic assessments of objective achievement followed by an evaluation of needed modifications during these performance reviews. The review process demonstrates both ongoing advancement and creating a work environment based on accountability and constant quality enhancement.

The ability to adapt methods when necessary establishes equal importance with the process. Changes in market conditions, as well as internal challenges and evolving customer expectations, may lead to the need for existing solution adjustments. The ability to adapt makes organizations maintain their responsiveness to changes, which leads to better long-term achievements. By promoting open discussion combined with data-based choices, organizations enhance their ability to maintain continuous optimization of tracking systems for maximum efficiency.

6. Call to Action

The recommended changes will yield more efficient operations as well as better teaming and better ability to adapt to developing difficulties. Because of the efficiency the organization will be able to gain through the fast implementation of a combination of streamlined communication solutions and process optimization along with a continuous improvement mindset, these benefits will be achieved. Organizations should focus on analysis-based assessments and fact-based decision methods to maintain progress.

Our recommendation begins with creating specific performance benchmarks and systems for receiving feedback, which helps track achievement results. The organization can enhance smooth implementation through additional training investments along with technological enhancements. Proactive steps bring both immediate results of increased productivity and better workplace morale and create long-term achievements for organizational success.

The current implementation of these strategies will enable the organization to develop sustained growth and resilience along with innovation. The organization should execute determined choices to unleash the complete potential of these solutions right now.

CONCLUSION

Blockchain technology research and its security and legal problems indicate that organizations need to have security gains and risk reduction. Blockchain's current framework is a modern framework of decentralized transparency and security that shakes up many industries but needs to be protected technically and legally from its stated mistakes. Moving into a mostly digital environment requires strong solutions to ensure blockchain operability stays secure and legal if blockchain technology wants to advance and gain broad adoption.

Blockchain faces major obstacles because of cybersecurity threats. Performance weaknesses in smart contracts have repeatedly emerged because of coding faults that affect decentralized applications. Reentrancy attacks, together with integer overflows, resulted in substantial financial damage when the infamous Ethereum DAO hack occurred. Theft of private keys serves as the main security weak point that blockchain systems rely on, which leads to unrecoverable assets being stolen. Such incidents demonstrate that blockchain systems require more secure multi-factor authorizations as well as hardware protection services and always-running smart contract evaluation systems.

The blockchain network integrity remains seriously vulnerable due to the possibility of a 51% attack, which allows hackers to acquire control of a majority of the blockchain resources. Previous security dangers revealed by such attacks resulted from unprotected protocols being attacked on small blockchain networks. Hackers have an alternative chance of exploiting an endpoint, which is the security holes that exist on users' devices instead of the blockchain. This proves that to be safe in terms of cybersecurity, private keys are prone to be attacked by phishing, malware, and other social engineering approaches, thus making it important to secure cybersecurity practices and education.

Because blockchain operates as a decentralized system, it obstructs legal entities from conducting effective governance and regulatory oversight. The varying regulatory measures between jurisdictions create barriers to blockchain adoption since particular governments support its implementation, yet others restrict its use enough to issue bans. The absence of standardized global policies brings business unpredictability and delays the blockchain uptake by investors and businesses. Acceptable international regulatory systems must be established to ensure that innovation can thrive alongside existing financial and data protection and anti-money laundering regulations.

Data privacy functions as a key concern that needs attention. Although blockchain provides immutability that promotes transparency, it makes it hard to fulfill GDPR requirements because users possess the right to request data deletion under this directive. The legal requirements to modify or delete blockchain data present an issue since the technology does not allow this process, which requires the exploration of zero-knowledge proofs and off-chain solutions for compliance. Privacy-preserving transactions are possible through these technologies because they uphold regulatory requirements.

The governing structures of blockchain are made more complex by existing legal boundary issues. The problem of determining applicable legal laws becomes difficult because blockchain transactions span international borders. Smart contracts as autonomous agreements present significant challenges for traditional legal systems because they merge and present multiple issues about contract enforcement together with party accountability and customer rights protection. International regulatory bodies, along with governments, need to work together to create standard regulations that will preserve blockchain technology benefits and eliminate legal confusion.

Both ineffectiveness in cybersecurity measures and insufficient legal frameworks create evident consequences for blockchain, as displayed in the blockchain events of the Ethereum DAO hack and the Mt. Gox exchange collapse. The security failures, together with regulatory deficiencies, prove the need for immediate responsive solutions because they reveal the dangerous aftermaths of existing weaknesses. All new developments in blockchain technology should draw insights from existing cases to prevent exploitation by fixing the identified vulnerabilities before implementation.

A holistic method needs implementation for blockchain to build both security and legal compliance within its ecosystem. A set of technical defenses should combine safe, smart contract platforms with formal testing protocols and quantum-secure cryptographic implementations as preventative measures against forthcoming security threats in blockchain systems. Lawmakers need to establish distinct guidelines that will direct blockchain governance operations along with protecting blockchain users and resolving disputes.

The necessary solutions for these complex problems require mutual efforts between business leadership, regulatory organizations, and academic institutions. The development of protective user regulations requires government partnerships with blockchain engineers to prevent restrictions on innovation. The worldwide implementation of blockchain depends on sovereign nations working together to achieve standardization in their laws regarding this technology.

The long-term development of blockchain will succeed only when its developers strike the proper equilibrium between new features and safeguarding security measures as well as regulatory compliance needs. The solution to cybersecurity risks will create trust in blockchain frameworks and pave the way for more extensive business use throughout financial services industry segments, supply chain operations, and healthcare facilities, among other sectors. Businesses, together with investors, need regulatory clarity to commit to blockchain-based solutions.

The blockchain ecosystem will expand sustainably by executing a complete method that connects technological progress to definite legal frameworks. The establishment of blockchain technology as an important infrastructure in digital economy operations can become a reality when security processes are emphasized and regulatory requirements are met while ongoing technological progress continues. When the global community operates as one, blockchain technology's complete potential will be released safely from its inherent risks so organizations may implement it responsibly for future decades.

REFERENCES

Conti, M., Kumar, E. S., Lal, C., & Ruj, S. (2018). A survey on security and privacy issues of blockchain technology. *IEEE Communications Surveys and Tutorials*, *21*(2), 1–21.

Finck, M. (2018). Blockchain and the General Data Protection Regulation: Can distributed ledgers be squared with European data protection law? *European Journal of Risk Regulation*, *9*(1), 27–46.

Kumar, P., & Singh, P. (2019). Blockchain technology in supply chain management: Insights and implications. *International Journal of Information Management*, *49*, 285–295.

Lin, I. C., & Liao, T. C. (2017). A survey of blockchain security issues and challenges. *International Journal of Network Security*, *19*(5), 653–659.

Moubarak, G., Chamoun, M., & Lahoud, S. (2020). Cybersecurity challenges in blockchain technology. *Journal of Cybersecurity Technology*, *4*(3), 157–181.

Nakamoto, S. (2008). Bitcoin: A Peer-to-Peer Electronic Cash System. Retrieved from https://bitcoin.org/bitcoin.pdf

Rizal, S., & Nair, R. (2021). Legal implications of smart contracts: Decentralization and enforceability. *Journal of Legal Technology Risk*, *3*(1), 45–60.

World Economic Forum. (2021). Global Standards for Blockchain Technology: Enhancing trust and interoperability. Retrieved from https://www.weforum.org

Zheng, Z., Xie, S., Dai, H., Chen, X., & Wang, H. (2017, June). An overview of blockchain technology: Architecture, consensus, and future trends. In *2017 IEEE International Congress on big data (BigData congress)* (pp. 557-564). Ieee. DOI: 10.1109/BigDataCongress.2017.85

Chapter 8

Enhancing Online Security: A Cyberbullying Detection and Prevention System for Monitoring Abusive Language

J. Jesy Janet Kumari
https://orcid.org/0000-0002-3318-1632
The Oxford College of Engineering, Bangalore, India

S. Thangam
https://orcid.org/0000-0003-2251-3651
Amrita School of Computing, Amrita Vishwa Vidyapeetham, Bengaluru, India

ABSTRACT

Cyberbullying is the use of technology to harass, threaten, embarrass, or target another person. Cyberbullying is a growing problem in our digital age, and it can have severe consequences for victims. Online bullying can be particularly damaging and upsetting because it's usually anonymous or hard to trace. It's also hard to control, and the person being victimized has no idea how many people have seen the messages or posts. They can be easier to commit than other acts of bullying because the bully doesn't have to confront their target in person. Detecting cyberbullying and preventing it is crucial in creating a safe online environment for all. The work involves the use of natural language processing and sentiment analysis to find abusive language and negative sentiment in online conversations. Before the comment is posted the detected instances of cyberbullying can be warned to the sender and prevented from being sent in a conversation.

DOI: 10.4018/979-8-3373-2282-7.ch008

1. INTRODUCTION

Cyberbullying is the use of technology as a medium to bully someone. Social networking sites provide a fertile medium for bullies, and teens and young adults who use these sites are vulnerable to attack. Through machine learning, we can detect language and patterns used by bullies and their victims and develop rules to automatically detect cyberbullying content (Islam et al., 2020). Cyberbullying is harassing, threatening, embarrassing someone, or targeting sharing about that person through technology. Cyberbullying actions, which are more common among young children and young people, can also be seen by adults. In such cases, severe legal actions are imposed on adults, such as prison sentences.

Cyberbullying affects victims both emotionally and psychologically (Desai et al., 2021). Social media also allows bullies to exploit anonymity to satisfy their evil deeds. Things became even more serious when bullying incidents occurred continuously over time. So, preventing this from happening helps the victim. The prevalence of information cannot be predicted because of the wide range of possibilities and the speed of new media. The perpetrators, so called "cyber harassment", can act anonymously and often consider themselves safe because of this anonymity.

In most cases, the identity of the perpetrator (Nizam et al., 2024) is presented very differently from the reality. Age or external image are not important criteria for cyberbullying. This can happen both between people of the same age and between people of different ages. There is a possibility of unintentional cyberbullying, as thoughtless actions without awareness of the consequences can hurt the people involved. The abuser often does not see these reactions and is unaware of the scale of the actions. Given the consequences of cyberbullying on its victims (Wulandari et al., 2024), it is imperative to find the proper actions to detect and prevent it. Machine learning is one of the successful approaches that learn from data and creates a model that automatically classifies right actions. Machine learning can be useful to detect language patterns of bullies and thus can generate a pattern to detect acts of cyberbullying (Islam et al., 2020).

The main purpose of this work is to create a safe and healthy environment for individuals to engage in digital communication. Cyberbullying has profound consequences on mental health and can lead to anxiety, depression, and suicide. It can also affect academic performance, social relationships, and self-esteem. Therefore, it is crucial to show and prevent cyberbullying behavior to mitigate these negative effects. Machine learning (Mahesh et al., 2021) techniques have the potential to improve the detection and prevention of cyberbullying by analyzing enormous amounts of data and identifying patterns that may not be apparent to human analysts.

The scope of this work is to explore the use of machine learning techniques in the detection and prevention of cyberbullying. Specifically, the work will focus on the analysis of social media data using natural language processing and sentiment analysis to find instances of cyberbullying (Khan & Bibi, 2025) behavior in online conversations. The identified instances of cyberbullying will then be flagged and reported to relevant authorities for further investigation.

The aim of this work is to explore the use of machine learning techniques in the detection and prevention of cyberbullying on social media platforms. Cyberbullying is a growing concern in the digital age, and traditional approaches to detecting and preventing it have proven inadequate due to the vast amount of data available online. Machine learning (Keni & Kini, 2020) techniques offer the potential to analyze substantial amounts of data and identify patterns of cyberbullying behavior more effectively.

2. PROPOSED METHODOLOGY

The specific aims of the work are to develop a machine learning-based approach to detect and prevent cyberbullying behavior by analyzing social media data. The approach involves the use of natural language processing and sentiment analysis to find abusive language (Hani et al., 2019) and negative sentiment in online conversations. Cyberbullying detection and prevention provide a warning feature as an advancement of existing methods whenever a bullying text is detected and prevents the user from being able to send such texts. The work also aims to raise awareness about the impact of cyberbullying and provides a useful tool for preventing cyberbullying and protecting individuals from harm.

Software Requirement Specification totally defines how the worked software behaves without unfolding how the software will perform it. The elementary goal of the requirement stage is to yield the software requirement specification that appoints the peripheral performance (Raj et al., 2022) of the worked software. Software requirement can be well- defined as a condition of the capability required by a user to solve a problem or reach a goal.

The purpose of detecting and preventing cyberbullying is to create a safe and healthy environment for individuals to engage in digital communication (Dadvar & Eckert, 2018). Cyberbullying has profound consequences on mental health and can lead to anxiety, depression, and suicide. It can also affect academic performance, social relationships, and self-esteem. Therefore, it is crucial to find and prevent cyberbullying behavior to mitigate these negative effects.

3. SYSTEM DESIGN AND MODELING

3.1 Architecture Design

Figure 1. System Architecture Diagram

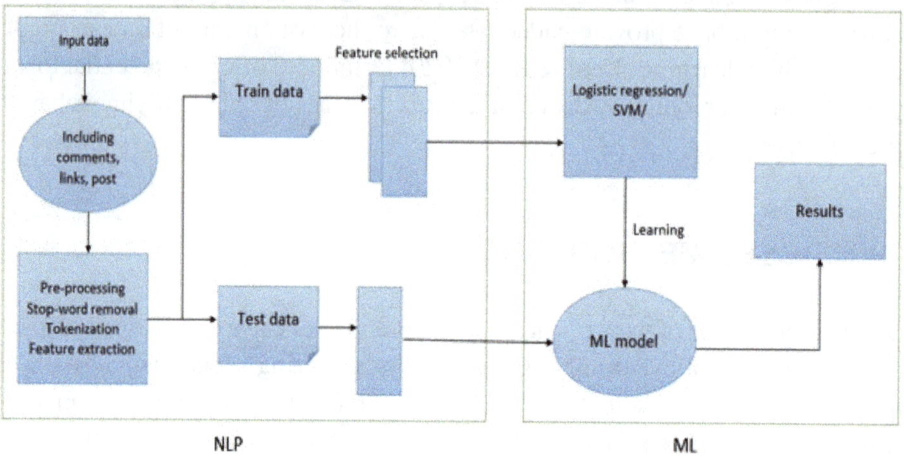

The framework for detecting cyberbullying is divided into two parts: Natural Language Processing (NLP) and Machine Learning (ML). Datasets having bullying-related texts, comments or tweets are gathered and preprocessed. Preprocessing tasks include dropping any unnecessary characters such as stop words, punctuation and digits, tokenization and stemming. TF-IDF (Term Frequency-Inverse Document Frequency) feature extraction is used to extract relevant features from the preprocessed data. TF-IDF is a statistical technique that can assess how pertinent a term is to a document within a collection of documents. Preprocessing is followed by splitting the data into training data and testing data (Ali & Syed, 2020). Chi-Square feature selection technique is applied to the trained data to select the most relevant features based on their relationship with the target variable (Alabdulwahab et al., 2023). Using the labelled training data and the extracted features, a logistic regression machine learning model is chosen and trained (Khan et al., 2020). This ML model shows and classifies the tweet as a bullying or non-bullying message (Haq et al., 2022).

3.2 Decomposition Description

Figure 2 is the flow chart of the system. The user can register with a username and password, and login with their credentials. The user will quote a comment, which is taken as input. The input data is preprocessed to remove stop words, punctuation and numbers. TF-IDF feature extraction model is used for extracting relevant features for constructing the machine learning model (Dalvi et al., 2020). The chi-square feature selection model is used to find and select the features that have the strongest relationship with the target variable. The logistic regression model finds and classifies the data, then the model output is stored (Gencoglu, 2020). If the output is non-bullying, the comment will be posted. If the output is bullying, then the comment is prevented from getting posted by displaying a warning message to the user.

Figure 2. Flow Chart

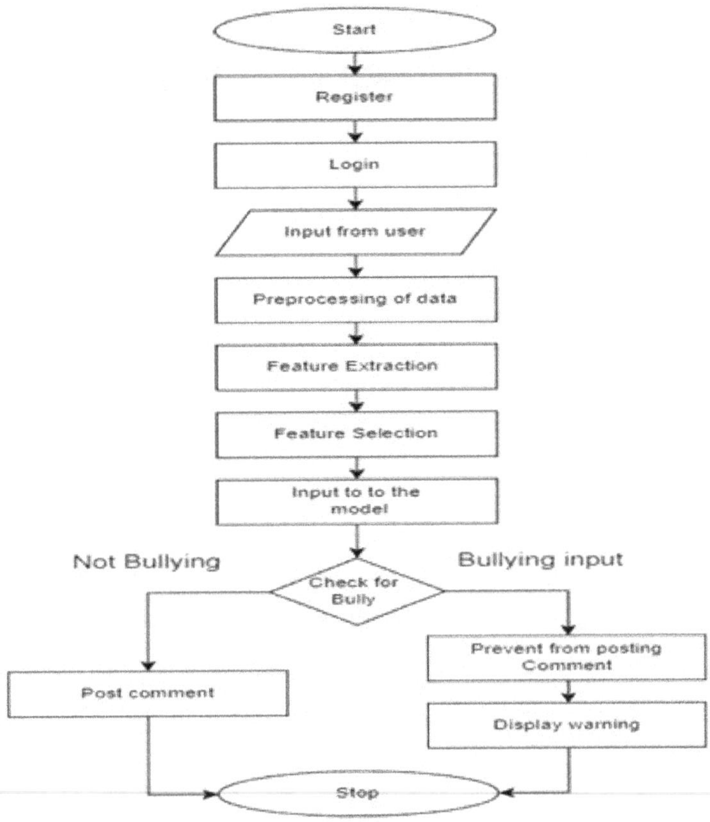

3.3 Data Flow Design

A data flow diagram (DFD) is a graphical representation of the "flow" of data through an information system (Perera & Fernando, 2021). DFDs can also be used for the visualization of data processing. On a DFD, data items flow from an external data source or an internal data store to an internal data store or an external data sink via an internal process. A DFD provides no information about the timing or ordering of processes (Dalvi et al., 2020) or about whether processes will run in sequence or in parallel. It is therefore quite different from a flowchart, which shows the flow of control through an algorithm, allowing users to determine what operations will be performed, in what order, and under what circumstances, but not what kinds of data will be input to and output from the system, nor where the data will come from and go, nor where the data will be stored (Kumari & Thangam, 2025).

Figure 3. Data Flow Design

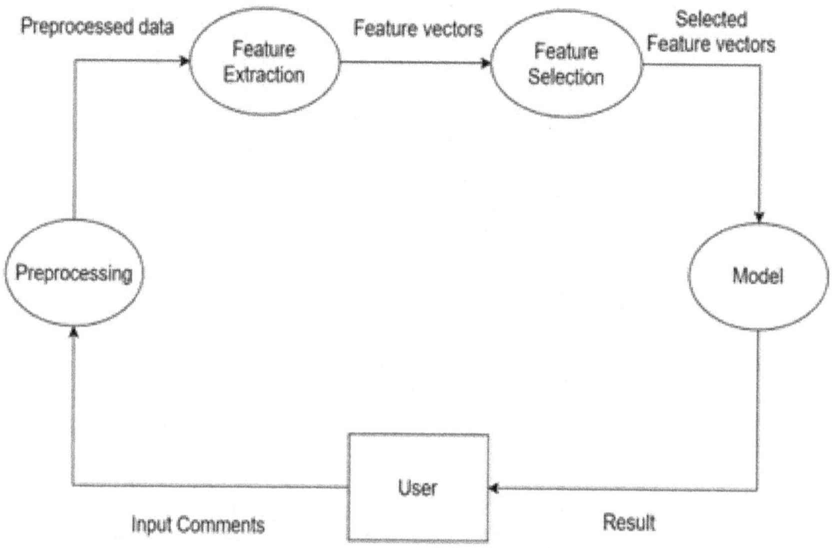

The Data Flow diagram of the system is shown in figure 3. The user will enter a comment or message as input. The input is preprocessed to remove the stop words, punctuation, and digits to get the preprocessed data. TF-IDF feature extraction is applied to the preprocessed data to output the feature vectors. The Chi-Square feature selection method is used to select the most relevant feature vectors based on their relationship with the target variable. Using the labelled training data and the extracted features, a logistic regression machine learning model is chosen and trained. The logistic regression ML model finds and classifies the tweet as a bullying or non-bullying message. The comment will be posted if the output is non-bullying text. Otherwise, the comment doesn't get posted, displaying an alert prompt for the user. The result is displayed to the user.

3.4 Sequence Diagram

A sequence diagram in Unified Modeling Language (UML) is a kind of interaction diagram that shows how processes interact with one another and in what order. It is the construction of a Message Sequence Chart. A sequence diagram shows, as parallel vertical lines ("lifelines"), different processes or objects that live simultaneously and as horizontal arrows. The messages are exchanged between them in the order in which they occur.

Figure 4. Sequence Diagram

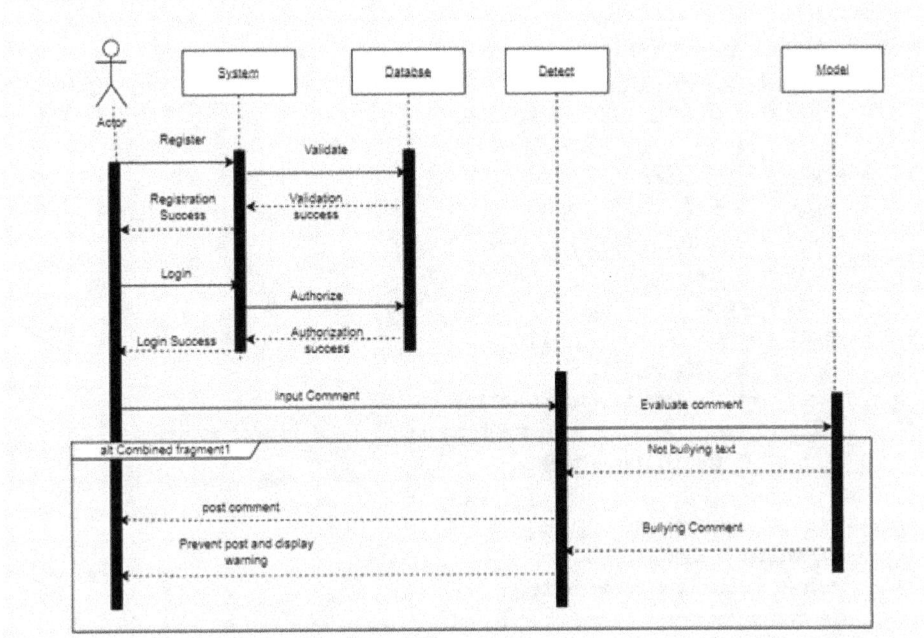

Figure 4 shows the sequence of steps for the system. The diagram shows the sequence of activities for the different entities in the system. The user will register with a username and password, and the system will confirm the registration details with the database. After successful validation, the user is successfully registered. The user can log in with the credentials, and authorization is done with the database. The login is successful for a valid username and password. The user interacts with the detection system by posting comments or messages. The model evaluates the input comment in the combined fragment. The model finds out whether the comment is bullying or not. If the text is not bullying, the comment gets posted. Otherwise, the comment is prevented from getting posted by displaying a warning message to the user.

4. IMPLEMENTATION OF THE PROPOSED WORK

The implementation involves preprocessing steps, feature extraction and selection, and model building. The built model is later used for the detection of bullying comments in the user input. The dataset consists of stop words, symbols, numerical digits etc. All these must be removed for the correct data mining results. After the preprocessing, lemmatization is performed on the data to get the root word.

Figure 5. Data Preprocessing

```
def data_processing(tweet):
    tweet = re.sub("\d*\.\d+","",str(tweet))
    tweet = re.sub("\d+","",str(tweet))
    tweet = tweet.lower()
    tweet = re.sub(r"((www.[^s]+)|(http\S+))","",tweet,flags = re.MULTILINE)
    tweet = re.sub(r'\@w+|\#','', tweet)
    tweet = re.sub("\d*\.\d+","",tweet)
    tweet =  re.sub(r'(\w)\1{2,}', r'\1\1', tweet)
    tweet = re.sub(r'[^\w\s]','',tweet)
    tweet = re.sub(r'ð','',tweet)
    tweet_tokens = word_tokenize(tweet)
    filtered_tweets = [w for w in tweet_tokens if not w in stop_words]
    return " ".join(filtered_tweets)

def lemmatizing(text):
    lemmatizer = WordNetLemmatizer()
    tokens = nltk.word_tokenize(text)
    lemmatized_tokens = [lemmatizer.lemmatize(token, pos='v') for token in tokens]
    lemmatized_text = ' '.join(lemmatized_tokens)
    return lemmatized_text
```

Term-Frequency proves the importance of the word to a doc with an intuition that the more the term in doc means higher the importance is. IDF Shows how a term is relevant. It is not necessary that term often in some docs could be relevant such as stop words (the that, of, etc.). Stop words do not reveal the context and thus these should be avoided. Tf-idf is used to extract features with maximum features set to 500000.

Figure 6. Feature Extraction Using TF-IDF

TF vector feature extraction

In [52]:
```
# vect = TfidfVectorizer(ngram_range=(1,2),max_features=3000,token_pat
vect2 = TfidfVectorizer(ngram_range=(1,2),max_features=500000)
vector2=vect2.fit(x_train)
```

In [53]:
```
feature_names = vector2.get_feature_names_out()
print("Number of features: {}\n".format(len(feature_names)))
print("First 20 features: \n{}".format(feature_names[:100]))
pickle.dump(vector2, open('vectorizer', 'wb'))
```

```
Number of features: 476116

First 20 features:
['__' '__ dont' '__ insert' '__ suck' '__chris__' '__chris__ im'
 '__enimey__' '__gershom' '__gershom im' '__hajihuntress'
 '__hajihuntress islamicstatemedia' '__victorlopez__'
 '__victorlopez__ line' '_acestayicy' '_acestayicy im' '_allahu_akbar_'
 '_allahu_akbar_ never' '_angryman' '_angryman mkr' '_blackglass__'
 '_blackglass__ curdistani' '_blackglass__ dumuzi'
 '_blackglass__ issa_kobani' '_blackglass__ theyellowpete' '_bobbidana'
 '_bobbidana never' '_bryancaban' '_bryancaban im' '_charliewilson'
 '_charliewilson mandatory' '_chonz' '_chonz call' '_chrisdowns_'
```

We have used Binary Logistic regression with outputs belonging to either class bully (label 1) or not bully (label 0).

Figure 7. Model Built Using Logistic Regression

Logistic regression

In [67]:
```
from sklearn.feature_selection import SelectFromModel
from sklearn.linear_model import LogisticRegression
```

In [73]:
```
logreg = LogisticRegression()
logreg.fit(X_train_chi2, y_train)
logreg_predict = logreg.predict(X_test_chi2)
logreg_acc = accuracy_score(logreg_predict, y_test)
print("Test accuarcy: {:.2f}%".format(logreg_acc*100))
```

```
Test accuarcy: 83.85%
```

In [74]:
```
import pickle
pickle.dump(logreg, open('logreg', 'wb'))
```

Support Vector Machine (SVM) is a supervised machine learning algorithm which can be applied in both classification and regression like a decision tree.

Figure 8. Model Built Using Support Vector Machine

SVM

```
In [94]: from sklearn.svm import SVC

In [95]: svm_model_linear = SVC(kernel= 'linear', C = 1).fit(X_train_chi2, y_train)
         svm_predictions  = svm_model_linear.predict(X_test_chi2)
         accuracy = svm_model_linear.score(X_test_chi2, y_test)
         print(accuracy)

0.8469774217042971

In [96]: pickle.dump(svm_model_linear, open('svm', 'wb'))

In [97]: svm_acc = accuracy_score(svm_predictions, y_test)
         print("Test accuarcy: {:.2f}%".format(svm_acc *100))

Test accuarcy: 84.70%
```

Random Forest classifier consists of multiple decision tree classifiers. Each tree gives a class prediction individually. This classifier is a supervised learning model which provides correct results because several decision trees are merged to get the outcome. For example, if we have two classes, namely A and B, and the most of the decision tree predicts the class label B of any instance, then RF will decides the class label B.

Figure 9. Model Built Using Random Forest

```
[98]:
from sklearn.neighbors import KNeighborsClassifier
from sklearn.ensemble import RandomForestClassifier
import time
```

```
[99]:
# Using Random Forest
classifier_rf = RandomForestClassifier(n_estimators = 10,
                                       criterion = 'entropy',
                                       random_state = 0)
classifier_rf.fit(X_train_chi2, y_train)
end_time = time.time()
```

```
[101]:
rf_acc = accuracy_score(y_pred_rf , y_test)
print("Test accuarcy: {:.2f}%".format(rf_acc *100))

Test accuarcy: 81.60%
```

K-NN algorithm assumes the similarity between the new case/data and available cases and put the new case into the category that is most similar to the available categories. The algorithm can be used to solve both classification and regression problem statements.

Figure 10. Model Built Using KNN Algorithm

```
[131]:
classifier_knn = KNeighborsClassifier(n_neighbors = 5,
                                      metric = 'minkowski',
                                      p = 2)

classifier_knn.fit(X_train_chi2, y_train)
```

```
[133]:
y_pred_knn  = accuracy_score(y_pred_rf , y_test)
print("Test accuarcy: {:.2f}%".format(y_pred_knn  *100))

Test accuarcy: 81.60%
```

Confusion matrix is used to evaluate the performance of the classification models, when they make predictions on test data, and tell how good our classification model is.

Figure 11. Confusion Matrix for Logistic Regression

```
In [118]:  style.use('classic')
           cm = confusion_matrix(y_test, logreg_predict, labels=logreg.classes_)
           disp = ConfusionMatrixDisplay(confusion_matrix=cm, display_labels=logreg.classes_)
           disp.plot()

Out[118]: <sklearn.metrics._plot.confusion_matrix.ConfusionMatrixDisplay at 0x1a699d174d0>
```

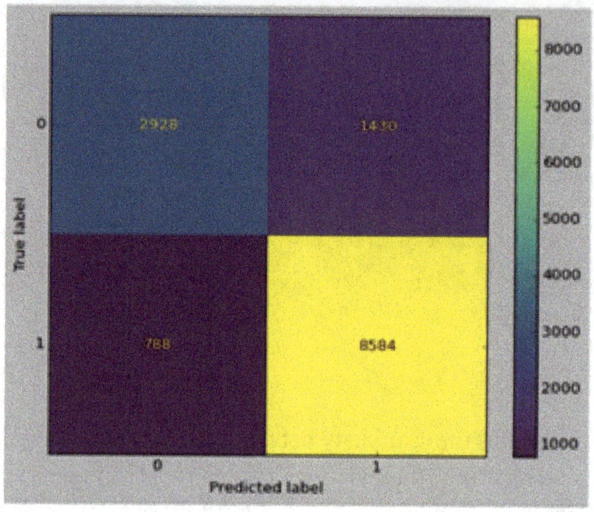

Figure 12 is the confusion matrix for Logistic Regression on the result of our testing data.

Figure 12. Confusion Matrix for Support Vector Machine

```
In [119]:  style.use('classic')
           cm = confusion_matrix(y_test, svm_predictions , labels=svm_model_linear.classes_)
           disp = ConfusionMatrixDisplay(confusion_matrix=cm, display_labels=svm_model_linear.classes_)
           disp.plot()

Out[119]: <sklearn.metrics._plot.confusion_matrix.ConfusionMatrixDisplay at 0x1a69a127fd0>
```

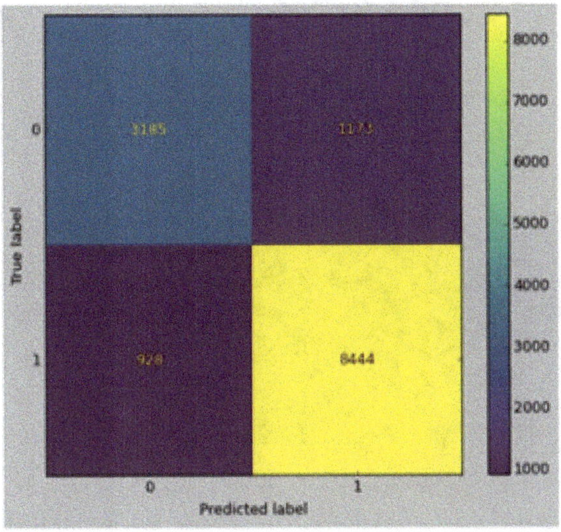

Figure 13 is the confusion matrix for Support Vector Machine on the result of our testing data.

Figure 13. Confusion Matrix for Random Forest

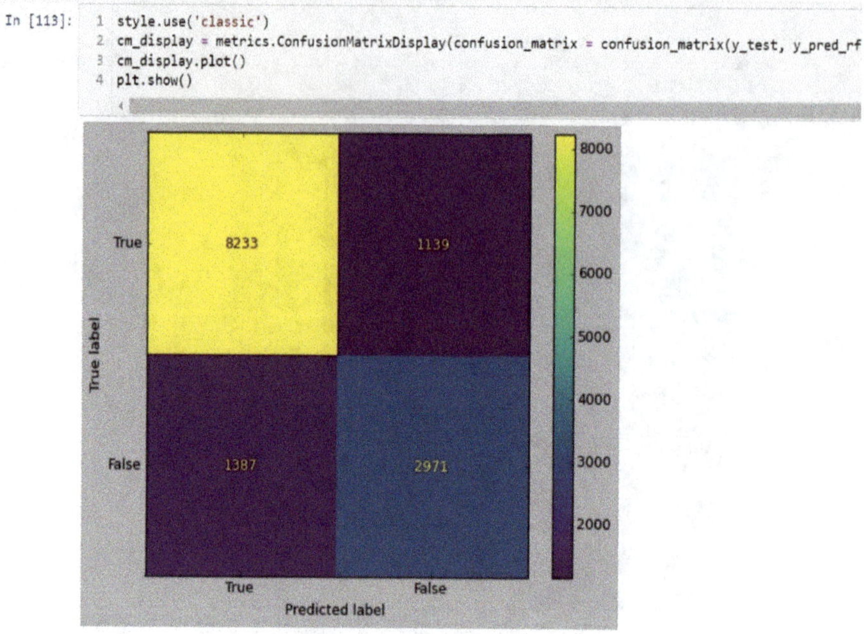

Figure 13 is the confusion matrix for Random Forest on the result of our testing data.

Figure 14. Confusion Matrix for K-Nearest Neighbors

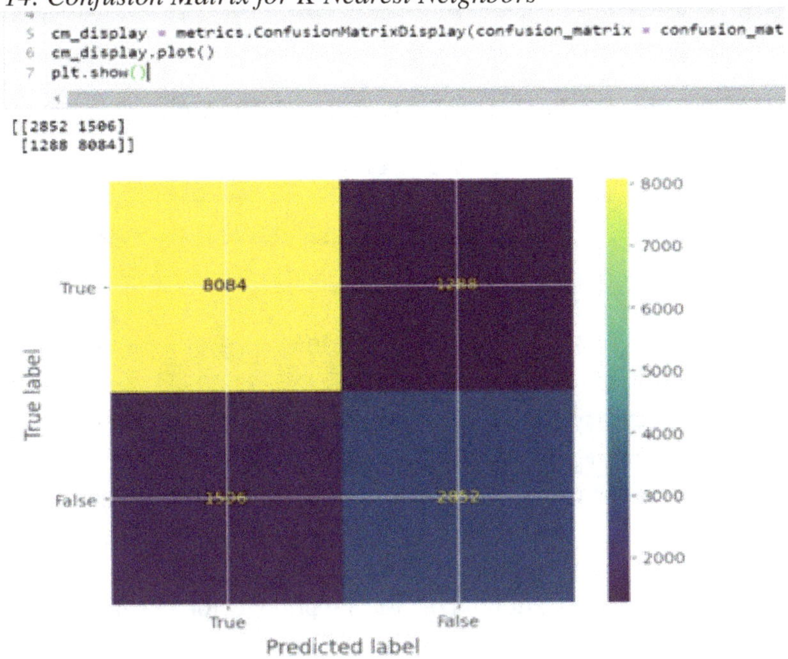

Figure 14 is the confusion matrix for K-Nearest Neighbors on the result of the testing data.

Classification Report is used to as a performance evaluation metric which is used to show the precision, recall, F1 Score, and support score of the trained classification model.

Figure 15. Classification Report for Logistic Regression

report

```
In [121]:  1 print(classification_report(y_test, logreg_predict))

              precision    recall  f1-score   support

           0       0.79      0.67      0.73      4358
           1       0.86      0.92      0.89      9372

    accuracy                           0.84     13730
   macro avg       0.82      0.79      0.81     13730
weighted avg       0.84      0.84      0.83     13730
```

Figure 15 is the classification report for Logistic Regression on the result of our testing data.

Figure 16. Classification Report for Support Vector Machine

```
In [129]:  1 print(classification_report(y_test, svm_predictions))

              precision    recall  f1-score   support

           0       0.77      0.73      0.75      4358
           1       0.88      0.90      0.89      9372

    accuracy                           0.85     13730
   macro avg       0.83      0.82      0.82     13730
weighted avg       0.85      0.85      0.85     13730
```

Figure 16 is the classification report for Support Vector Machine on the result of our testing data.

Figure 17. Classification Report for Random Forest

```
[117]:  1 print(classification_report(y_test,y_pred_rf))

              precision    recall  f1-score   support

           0       0.72      0.68      0.70      4358
           1       0.86      0.88      0.87      9372

    accuracy                           0.82     13730
   macro avg       0.79      0.78      0.78     13730
weighted avg       0.81      0.82      0.81     13730
```

Figure 17 is the classification report for Random Forest on the result of our testing data.

Figure 18. Classification Report for K-Nearest Neighbors

```
[117]:  1 print(classification_report(y_test,y_pred_rf))

              precision    recall  f1-score   support

           0       0.72      0.68      0.70      4358
           1       0.86      0.88      0.87      9372

    accuracy                           0.82     13730
   macro avg       0.79      0.78      0.78     13730
weighted avg       0.81      0.82      0.81     13730
```

Figure 18 is the classification report for K-Nearest Neighbors on the result of our testing data.

Table 1. Classification Report

Algorithm	Precision	Recall	F1-Score	Accuracy
Logistic Regression	0.82	0.79	0.81	83.85%
Super Vector Machine	0.83	0.82	0.82	84.70%
Random Forest	0.78	0.78	0.78	84.22%
K-Nearest Neighbors	0.76	0.76	0.76	81.66%

Table 2. Test Cases

TC#	Description	Expected Result	Actual Result	Status
TC-1	Testing with a non-offensive comment	The system should detect the comment as not bullying and allow it to be posted.	Posts the comment	Pass
TC-2	Testing with an offensive comment	The system should detect the comment as bullying and prevent it from being posted.	Blocks the comment from posting	Pass
TC-3	Testing with a mixed comment	The system should detect the comment as bullying and prevent it from being posted.	Blocks the comment from posting	Pass
TC-4	Testing with an empty comment	The system should display an error message and not allow the comment to be posted.	Blocks the comment from posting	Pass
TC-5	Testing with special characters	The system should be able to manage special characters and accurately detect the presence of bullying language.	If bully, blocks the comment from posting	Pass

Figure 19. Home Page

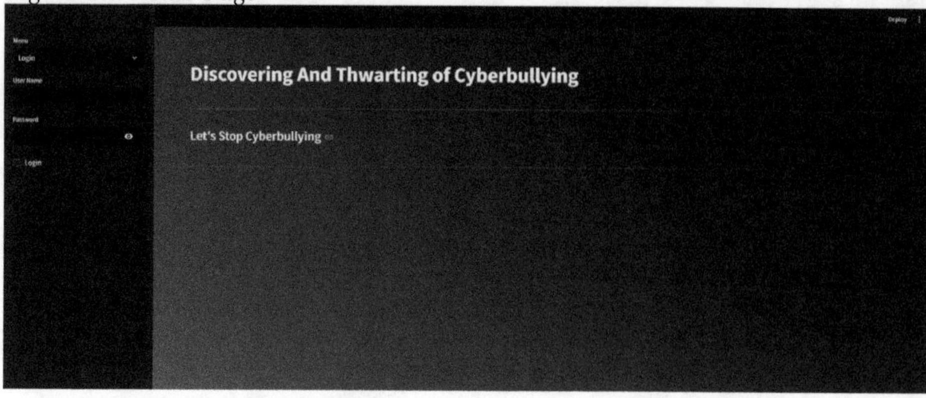

Figure 19 shows the Home Page where the user can Register or Login using the available Menus.

Figure 20. Registration Page

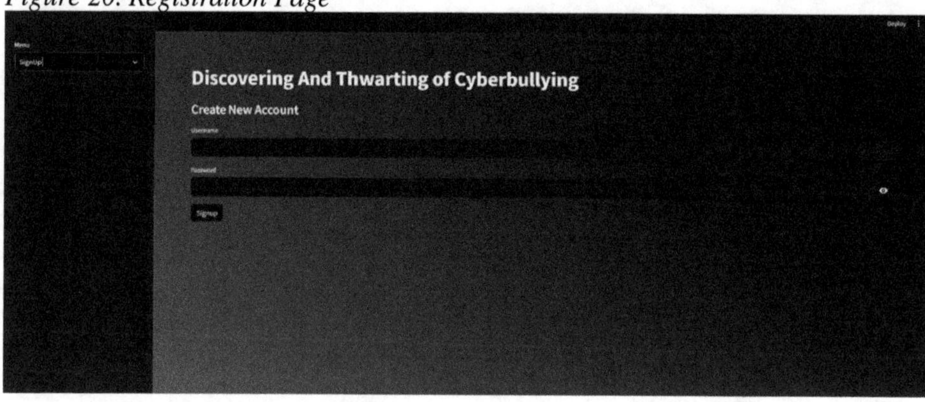

Figure 20 shows the Registration Page. On registering the user can use the details for the login. Unique usernames and passwords are used for the registration process.

Figure 21. Login Page

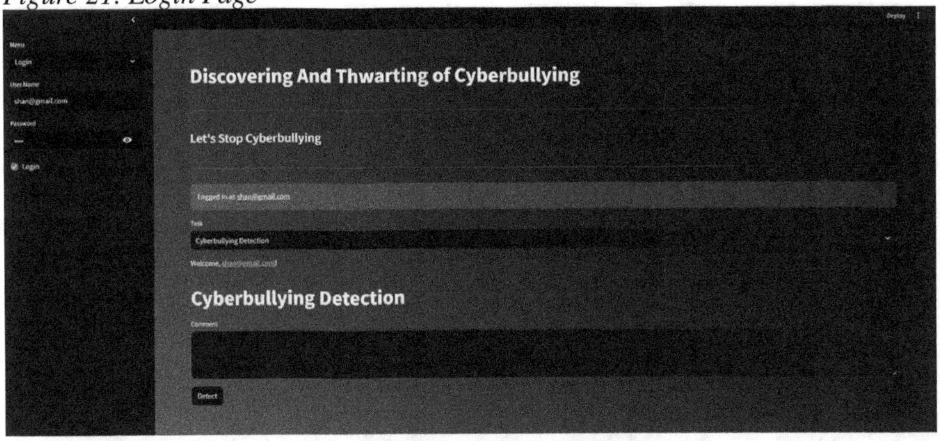

Figure 21 shows the successful Login of User. On Login user is provided with options to select either the Detection or Prevention of cyberbullying interfaces for the input.

Figure 22. Detecting Bullying Input

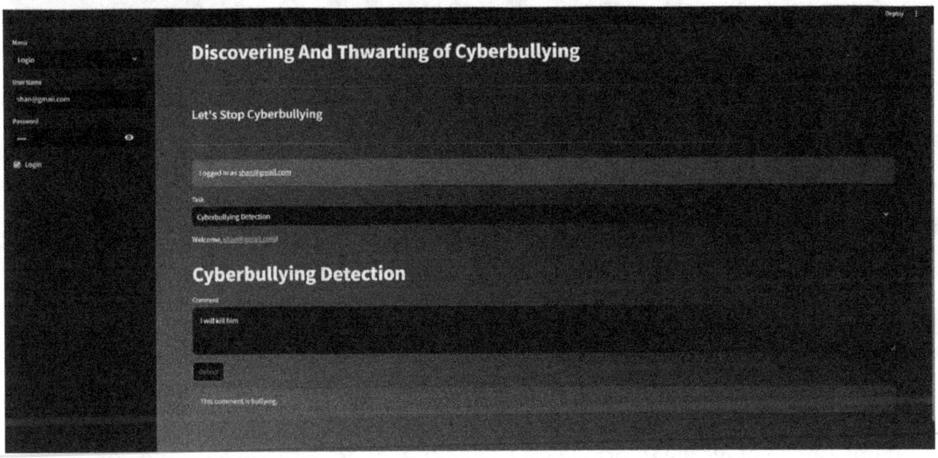

The Figure 22. displays the interface for detection of bullying comments where the user can input a text to check if the input contains abusive words. When the user inputs an input having abusive content, the system detects it and provides the output "The comment is bullying".

Figure 23. Detecting Non-Bullying Input

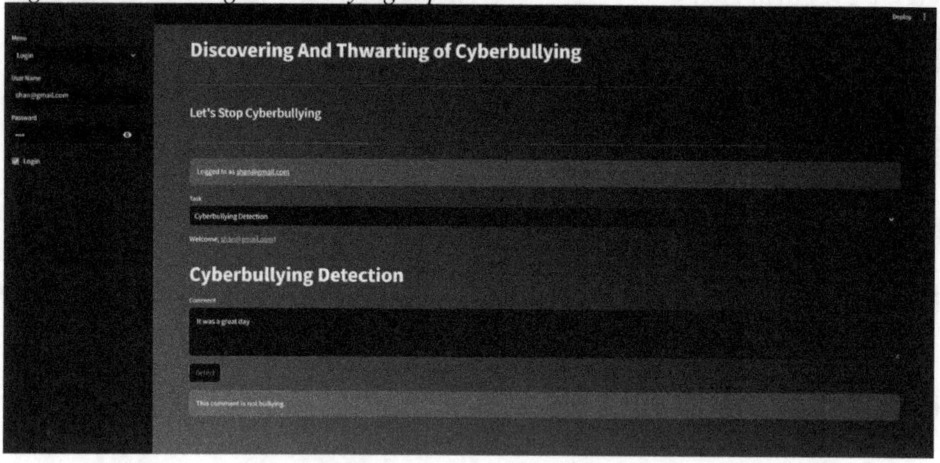

The Figure 23 shows the scenario, when the user inputs an input without any bullying content, the system provides the output "The comment is not bullying".

Figure 24. Prevention of Bullying Comments

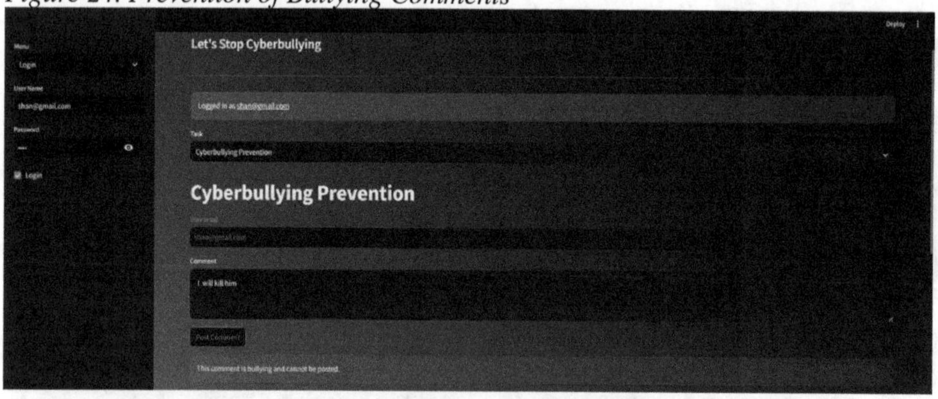

Figure 24 displays the interface for Prevention of posting the bullying comments. When the user tries to comment on the input having abusive content, the system detects it and prevents it from being posted along with providing the warning message.

Figure 25. Posting of Non-Bully Comments

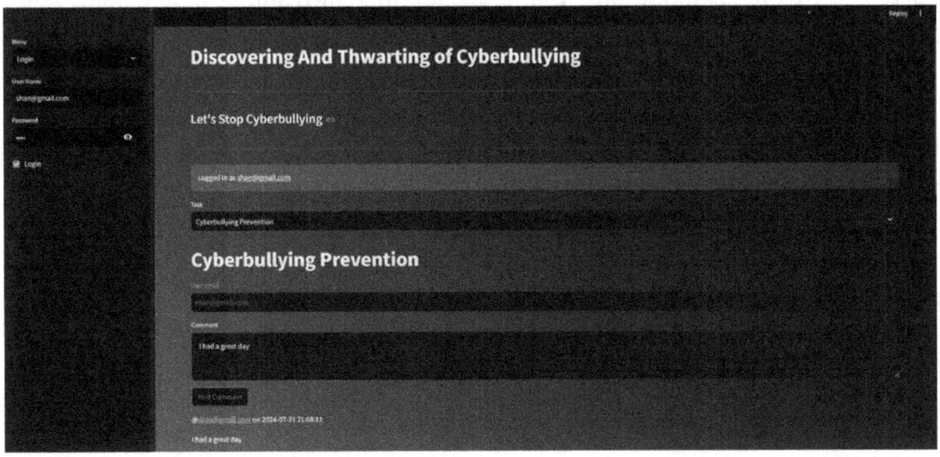

Figure 25 shows the scenario, when the user tries to comment on the input without any abusive content, the system allows the normal posting of the comment.

Figure 26. Posted Comments

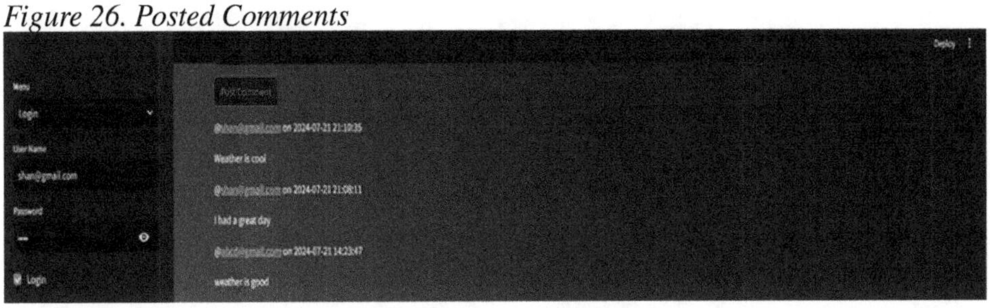

Figure 26 displays all the comments being posted which do not have any bullying content.

CONCLUSION AND FUTURE WORK

In this work, we developed a cyberbullying detection and prevention system that can detect and block bullying comments and issue warnings for abusive language in comments. We have considered the language as English. The system is built using natural language processing and machine learning algorithms to analyze the comments and decide whether they hold bullying or abusive language. We have also used a dataset of labelled comments to train our machine learning models. We preprocessed the data, extracted features, and trained several models using different algorithms. We evaluated the performance of each model and selected the best-performing one for our system. We integrated our machine learning model into a Streamlet web to provide a front-end application that allows users to input comments. When the user tries to post bullying comments the web application blocks the comments and issues warnings while allowing them to post non-bullying comments.

In future, there are several avenues to improve the performance and usability of the system. The system can be extended to support more different languages. By using larger and more diverse datasets and exploring different feature extraction techniques the accuracy of the machine learning model can be Improved. Developing a more sophisticated natural language processing pipeline that can find diverse forms of cyberbullying and abusive languages.

REFERENCES

Alabdulwahab, A., Haq, M. A., & Alshehri, M. (2023). Cyberbullying detection using machine learning and deep learning. *International Journal of Advanced Computer Science and Applications, 14*(10).

Ali, A., & Syed, A. M. (2020). Cyberbullying detection using machine learning. *Pakistan Journal of Engineering and Technology, 3*(2), 45–50.

Dadvar, M., & Eckert, K. (2018). Cyberbullying detection in social networks using deep learning based models: A reproducibility study. *arXiv preprint arXiv:1812.08046.*

Dalvi, R. R., Chavan, S. B., & Halbe, A. (2020, May). Detecting a Twitter cyberbullying using machine learning. In *2020 4th International Conference on Intelligent Computing and Control Systems (ICICCS)* (pp. 297–301). IEEE.

Desai, A., Kalaskar, S., Kumbhar, O., & Dhumal, R. (2021). Cyber bullying detection on social media using machine learning. In *ITM Web of Conferences* (Vol. 40, p. 03038). EDP Sciences.

Gencoglu, O. (2020). Cyberbullying detection with fairness constraints. *IEEE Internet Computing, 25*(1), 20–29.

Hani, J., Nashaat, M., Ahmed, M., Emad, Z., Amer, E., & Mohammed, A. (2019). Social media cyberbullying detection using machine learning. *International Journal of Advanced Computer Science and Applications, 10*(5), 703–707.

Haq, M. A., Rahim Khan, M. A., & Al-Harbi, T. (2022). Development of PCCNN-based network intrusion detection system for EDGE computing. *Computers, Materials & Continua, 71*(1).

Islam, M. M., Uddin, M. A., Islam, L., Akter, A., Sharmin, S., & Acharjee, U. K. (2020, December). Cyberbullying detection on social networks using machine learning approaches. In *2020 IEEE Asia-Pacific Conference on Computer Science and Data Engineering (CSDE)* (pp. 1–6). IEEE.

Keni, A., & Kini, M. (2020). Cyber-bullying detection using machine learning algorithms. *Computer Science. Psychology (Irvine, Calif.).*

Khan, M. T., & Bibi, L. (2025). Cyberbullying in technological age: A review of legal laws. *Journal of Engineering, Science and Technological Trends, 2*(1).

Khan, M. U., Abbas, A., Rehman, A., & Nawaz, R. (2020). Hateclassify: A service framework for hate speech identification on social media. *IEEE Internet Computing, 25*(1), 40–49.

Kumari, J. J. J., & Thangam, S. (2025). ERSA Enhanced RSA: Advanced security to overcome cyber-vulnerability. In *Advancing Cyber Security Through Quantum Cryptography* (pp. 413–440). IGI Global.

Mahesh, K., Gothane, S., Toshniwal, A., Nagarale, V., & Gopu, H. (2021). Cyber bullying detection on social media using machine learning. *International Journal of Scientific Research in Computer Science. Engineering and Information Technology, 3307*, 410–416.

Nizam, S., Matta, P., Kukreti, S., Upadhyay, R., & Dangwal, G. (2024, February). Cyberbullying: Research challenges and opportunities. In *2024 IEEE International Conference on Computing, Power and Communication Technologies (IC2PCT)* (Vol. 5, pp. 938–943). IEEE.

Perera, A., & Fernando, P. (2021). Accurate cyberbullying detection and prevention on social media. *Procedia Computer Science, 181*, 605–611.

Raj, M., Singh, S., Solanki, K., & Selvanambi, R. (2022). An application to detect cyberbullying using machine learning and deep learning techniques. *SN Computer Science, 3*(5), 401.

Wulandari, P. D., Pramartha, C., Bakta, I. M., & Wulanyani, N. M. S. (2024, April). Utilizing technology to detect bullying in the workplace: A systematic review. In *Proceedings of the 2024 10th International Conference on Computing and Artificial Intelligence* (pp. 415–418).

Chapter 9
Advancing Ransomware Resilience in Critical Infrastructure

Soumya Roy
https://orcid.org/0009-0000-6594-6049
Brainware University, India

Kaushik Chanda
https://orcid.org/0000-0003-0053-5577
Brainware University, India

Subhadip Nandi
https://orcid.org/0009-0009-8087-3306
Brainware University, India

Anudeepa Gon
Brainware University, India

ABSTRACT

This chapter examines the evolution of ransomware attacks on critical infrastructure by synthesizing research findings from 2018 to 2025. The study systematically reviewed literature and industry reports from databases including Google Scholar, Scopus, IEEE Xplore, and Web of Science using keywords such as "ransomware," "critical infrastructure," "cybersecurity," and "machine learning." Comparative analysis was conducted through tables that illustrate rising incident frequencies, extended downtime, and significant economic impacts—up to a 500% increase in some sectors. Advanced technologies, including AI and ML, are shown to reduce detection and response times by up to 50%. The chapter also identifies emerging tactics such as double extortion and backup encryption, proposes an enhanced risk

DOI: 10.4018/979-8-3373-2282-7.ch009

assessment model integrating dynamic threat intelligence, and outlines recommendations for policy and future research to bridge gaps in legacy system security and adaptive defense measures.

1. INTRODUCTION

The rapid evolution of digital technologies has transformed every aspect of our society, yet it has also led to an unprecedented rise in cyber threats—most notably ransomware attacks targeting critical infrastructure. In the early stages of cybersecurity research, the primary focus was on identifying vulnerabilities in legacy control systems and assessing the disruptive potential of ransomware. Early studies provided a foundational understanding by employing basic risk assessment models, such as:

$$Risk = Likelihood \times Impact$$

These initial models served as useful tools for quantifying risk; however, they were primarily developed in an era when cyberattacks were less sophisticated and the digital ecosystem was less interconnected.

Over the past several years, significant advancements have been made in mitigating cyber risks. Researchers and practitioners have introduced robust frameworks—such as the NIST Cybersecurity Framework—to provide structured approaches to risk management. Additionally, the adoption of multi-factor authentication (MFA), network segmentation, and continuous monitoring has contributed to the fortification of systems against ransomware. The integration of artificial intelligence (AI) and machine learning (ML) has further revolutionized the field, enabling rapid detection and automated response to cyber incidents, with some studies reporting reductions in response times by as much as 50%. These advancements have collectively improved the resilience of critical infrastructure sectors, including water, power, and emergency response systems.

Despite these strides, recent developments have introduced new challenges that expose critical gaps in the existing body of work. Modern ransomware attacks now incorporate sophisticated tactics such as double extortion—where attackers not only encrypt data but also threaten to leak it—and the targeted encryption of backup systems. Furthermore, the widespread deployment of Internet of Things (IoT) devices and the advent of smart grid technologies have dramatically increased the attack surface, rendering traditional security measures less effective. These emerging threats have not been fully addressed by previous research, which largely focused on traditional IT environments. As a result, there remains a pressing need to re-evaluate existing defence mechanisms in light of these new challenges and to develop advanced strategies that incorporate state-of-the-art technologies.

This study is designed to bridge these gaps by examining both the historical context and the contemporary landscape of ransomware attacks on critical infrastructure. By revisiting foundational risk assessment models and integrating them with modern AI/ML techniques, this research aims to quantify the improvements in incident detection and response. For example, advanced algorithms have been shown to enhance threat detection by analysing patterns in real-time data, thereby enabling quicker remediation. Nonetheless, the dynamic nature of cyber threats means that our understanding of risk must continually evolve.

1.1 Research Contributions

1. Comprehensive Analysis. The study provides an in-depth study of both traditional and advanced ransomware strategies, highlighting the evolution of cyber threats over the past decade.
2. Integration of Advanced Technologies. It evaluates the effectiveness of AI and ML in reducing incident response times and enhancing overall resilience.
3. Economic Impact Analysis. Through rigorous cost–benefit analysis, the research quantifies the economic advantages of proactive cybersecurity investments.
4. Framework Development. A modified risk assessment framework is proposed, which incorporates dynamic threat intelligence and adaptive security measures, enhancing the classic model.

1.2 Research Gaps

1. Emerging Ransomware Techniques. Previous studies have not fully explored new attack vectors such as double extortion and backup system encryption.
2. Interconnected Systems Vulnerabilities: The impact of IoT integration and smart grid technology on increasing the overall vulnerability of critical infrastructure remains under-investigated.
3. Dynamic Risk Modelling. There is a scarcity of models that integrate real-time monitoring and adaptive AI/ML-based threat detection into traditional risk assessments.
4. Economic Correlations. Limited research exists that directly correlates the deployment of advanced cybersecurity measures with quantifiable economic savings.

1.3 Research Questions

1. How have recent advancements in ransomware tactics altered the threat landscape for critical infrastructure sectors?

2. What is the measurable impact of deploying AI and ML technologies on reducing downtime and economic losses resulting from ransomware attacks?
3. Which integrated cybersecurity strategies are most effective in mitigating emerging threats in environments dominated by legacy systems and interconnected devices?

The article proceeds by first establishing a foundational understanding of ransomware—defining key concepts and explaining traditional risk assessment models. It then studies existing literature to delineate how historical approaches have been adapted to meet modern challenges. The methodology section outlines the mixed-methods approach used to integrate quantitative data from incident reports with qualitative insights from recent studies. The discussion follows with a comparative analysis of various cybersecurity strategies, emphasizing empirical results and the efficacy of advanced algorithms. Finally, strategic recommendations are provided, addressing both policy-level reforms and technological interventions, while the conclusion summarizes the contributions of this research and outlines directions for future work.

This comprehensive exploration—from basic definitions to advanced analytical techniques—ensures that the research not only fills existing gaps but also establishes a pathway for future innovations in safeguarding critical infrastructure against evolving ransomware threats.

2. LITERATURE REVIEW

The literature review synthesizes peer-reviewed studies, government reports, and industry analyses (2011–2025) in five related domains: ransomware evolution and mitigation; AI/ML in cybersecurity operations; economic impact and cost-benefit analyses; IoT and smart-grid vulnerabilities; and synthesis tables and research gaps. Each subsection presents main findings, important methodological approaches, or significant statistics; it also identifies open questions that motivate the present study.

In recent years, ransomware attacks have become increasingly sophisticated and have significantly disrupted critical infrastructure sectors such as water, power, and emergency response systems. The literature spanning from 2011 to 2025 provides a robust foundation for understanding these evolving threats, the vulnerabilities inherent in legacy systems, and the strategic measures that can be adopted to mitigate these risks. Table 1 presents a comprehensive summary of key sources. For each reference, it outlines the focus or objective of the study, its key findings, and the implications for strengthening cybersecurity resilience against ransomware.

Table 1. Comprehensive Literature Review Summary

Ref. No.	Source / Authors	Year	Focus / Objective	Key Findings	Implications for Ransomware Resilience
(FBI Internet Crime Complaint Center, 2023)	FBI Internet Crime Complaint Center	2023	Analyse cybercrime trends	Significant rise in ransomware incidents across multiple sectors.	Establishes baseline incident data for risk assessment.
(Cybersecurity and Infrastructure Security Agency, 2023)	CISA	2023	Annual cyber incident trends	Extended downtime and escalating ransom demand in critical systems.	Urgent need for improved detection and rapid response measures.
(Kaspersky Lab, 2020)	Kaspersky Lab	2020	Ransomware trends & impact of MFA	Lack of MFA increases attack success by ~70%.	Emphasizes MFA as a critical protective measure.
(ENISA, 2021)	ENISA	2021	Comprehensive threat landscape analysis	Emergence of double-extortion tactics and advanced encryption techniques.	Informs adaptive and dynamic defence strategies.
(Ponemon Institute, 2021)	Ponemon Institute	2021	Cost of data breach analysis	Recovery costs in critical sectors can exceed US$11.5 million per incident.	Provides economic justification for proactive cybersecurity investments.
(IBM Security X-Force, 2022)	IBM Security X-Force	2022	Threat intelligence and incident impact analysis	Average downtime per attack exceeds 4 days, with severe economic losses.	Validates need for rapid detection and efficient incident response systems.
(Verizon, 2022)	Verizon (DBIR)	2022	Data breach investigations	Ransom demands typically range between US$1–3 million with substantial financial impacts.	Supports cost–benefit analyses in advocating proactive security measures.
(Deloitte, 2021)	Deloitte	2021	Cyber risk assessment in critical infrastructure	Advanced threat monitoring can reduce response times by 30–50%.	Advocates for investments in real-time monitoring and rapid response technologies.
(Gartner, 2022)	Gartner	2022	Cybersecurity trend forecasts	Sustained growth in cyber threats; AI-driven detection reduces response times.	Reinforces the potential of AI/ML in enhancing cybersecurity defenses.
(PwC, 2021)	PwC	2021	Economic impact of cyber attacks	Proactive cybersecurity investments can cut downtime-related losses by up to 40%.	Encourages allocation of resources toward advanced cybersecurity measures.
(National Institute of Standards and Technology, 2022)	NIST	2022	Cybersecurity Framework for critical infrastructure	Provides a comprehensive framework for improving cybersecurity.	Guides implementation of best practices in infrastructure security.
(Symantec Corporation, 2019)	Symantec Corporation	2019	Internet Security Threat Report	Detailed global threat analysis with insights on emerging attack vectors.	Informs risk assessments and preventive security measures.
(Check Point Research, 2021)	Check Point Research	2021	Cyber Attack Trends 2021: Ransomware and Beyond	Identifies evolving ransomware techniques and emerging trends.	Supports development of adaptive and robust security strategies.
(IBM, 2022)	IBM	2022	Cost of a Data Breach Report	Highlights significant financial impacts from cyber breaches.	Underlines the need for robust, proactive cybersecurity investments.
(Cisco, 2022)	Cisco	2022	Cisco Cybersecurity Report	Outlines evolving threat landscapes and defence strategies.	Emphasizes continuous monitoring and regular updates to security protocols.
(McAfee Labs, 2022)	McAfee Labs	2022	McAfee Labs Threats Report	Analyses global cyber threat trends with emphasis on emerging ransomware variants.	Reinforces importance of adopting advanced threat detection methods.

continued on following page

Table 1. Continued

Ref. No.	Source / Authors	Year	Focus / Objective	Key Findings	Implications for Ransomware Resilience
(U.S. Department of Homeland Security, 2021)	U.S. Department of Homeland Security	2021	Securing critical infrastructure	Identifies critical vulnerabilities and recommends enhanced protection measures.	Urges immediate reinforcement of protective measures in essential services.
(U.S. Government Accountability Office, 2021)	U.S. Government Accountability Office	2021	Cybersecurity actions in agencies	Documents key actions implemented to mitigate ransomware risks.	Provides benchmarks for government cybersecurity initiatives.
(National Cyber Security Centre, 2021)	National Cyber Security Centre (NCSC)	2021	Annual review of cyber threats	Reviews threat landscapes and incident statistics across sectors.	Informs strategic planning for both public and private sectors.
(ENISA, 2022)	ENISA	2022	Report on ransomware attacks in Europe	Analysis of ransomware trends in Europe shows rising incidents and evolving tactics.	Supports development of region-specific cybersecurity policies.
(Fang, Misra, Xue, & Yang, 2011)	Fang et al.	2018	Survey of smart grid vulnerabilities	Reveals high vulnerability of legacy control systems in smart grids.	Suggests the necessity for modernization and system upgrades.
(Sridhar, Hahn, & Govindarasu, 2018)	Sridhar et al.	2018	Cyber–physical system security for electric power grids	Identifies systemic weaknesses in legacy power grid systems.	Emphasizes updating and securing legacy infrastructure in the energy sector.
(Yan, Qian, Sharif, & Tipper, 2018)	Yan et al.	2018	Cybersecurity in smart grid communications	Highlights vulnerabilities in communication networks of smart grids.	Supports need for improved encryption and real-time monitoring.
(Mohurle & Patil, 2018)	Mohurle & Patil	2018	Cybersecurity in smart grids: Threats and countermeasures	Proposes countermeasures for common vulnerabilities in smart grids.	Advocates for tailored security solutions for critical infrastructure.
(He, Huang, & Ning, 2019)	He et al.	2019	Cybersecurity and privacy in smart grids	Reviews privacy and security challenges in smart grid systems.	Informs integrated privacy and security strategies in modern infrastructure.
(Zhang, Deng, & Huang, 2020)	Zhang et al.	2020	Comprehensive survey on critical infrastructure cybersecurity	Reviews vulnerabilities and defences across various critical infrastructure sectors.	Provides a roadmap for comprehensive cybersecurity enhancement.
(Kharraz, Kline, Robertson, & Kirda, 2018)	Kharraz et al.	2018	Automated ransomware detection (UNVEIL)	Demonstrates large-scale, automated detection of ransomware attacks.	Validates the use of automation and machine learning in threat detection.
(European Commission, 2022)	European Commission	2022	Cybersecurity in EU critical infrastructures	Analyses trends and policy responses to cyber threats in the EU.	Informs regulatory and policy developments across European member states.
(OECD, 2021)	OECD	2021	Economic policy reforms: Ransomware and critical infrastructure	Evaluates the economic impact of ransomware and suggests policy reforms.	Strengthens the economic case for proactive cybersecurity investments.
(World Economic Forum, 2021)	World Economic Forum	2021	Global Risks Report: Cybersecurity and Critical Infrastructure	Outlines global cyber risks and potential impacts on critical sectors.	Provides a global perspective on risk management and resilience planning.
(Accenture, 2022)	Accenture	2022	Cyber Resilience in Critical Infrastructure: A Global Perspective	Offers insights on building resilience across global critical infrastructure.	Advocates for comprehensive, integrated risk management strategies.

continued on following page

Table 1. Continued

Ref. No.	Source / Authors	Year	Focus / Objective	Key Findings	Implications for Ransomware Resilience
(Forrester Research, 2021)	Forrester Research	2021	Cybersecurity strategies for critical infrastructure	Recommends strategic approaches to mitigate cyber risks.	Guides long-term cybersecurity planning and investment.
(ISACA, 2022)	ISACA	2022	Cybersecurity and risk in critical infrastructure	Provides risk assessment frameworks and best practices.	Enhances overall risk management and strategic defence measures.
(International Energy Agency, 2022)	International Energy Agency	2022	Energy security and cyber risk	Assesses cyber risks in the energy sector.	Underlines the need for robust cybersecurity in energy systems.
(U.S. Department of Energy, 2021)	U.S. Department of Energy	2021	Cybersecurity for energy delivery systems	Focuses on securing energy distribution networks against cyber threats.	Emphasizes modernization and strengthening of energy infrastructure.
(U.S. Department of Water Resources, 2021)	U.S. Department of Water Resources	2021	Enhancing cybersecurity in water infrastructure	Addresses vulnerabilities in water systems and recommends security upgrades.	Advocates for comprehensive modernization of water infrastructure security.
(National Institute of Standards and Technology, 2021)	NIST	2021	Framework for Improving Critical Infrastructure Cybersecurity, V1.1	Provides updated guidelines for cybersecurity in critical systems.	Guides the implementation of current best practices in infrastructure protection.
(Australian Cyber Security Centre, 2022)	Australian Cyber Security Centre	2022	Annual Cyber Threat Report	Summarizes cyber threat trends and incidents in Australia.	Supports regional and national cybersecurity initiatives.
(UK National Cyber Security Centre, 2022)	UK National Cyber Security Centre	2022	Cyber Threats to Critical Infrastructure	Reviews emerging threats and evaluates current defence strategies.	Informs national cybersecurity policies and strategic adjustments.
(European Union Agency for Cybersecurity, 2022)	EU Agency for Cybersecurity (ENISA)	2022	Threat Landscape Report 2022	Offers a comprehensive overview of global cyber threats.	Aids in coordinated defence strategy development at the European level.
(SANS Institute, 2021)	SANS Institute	2021	Critical Infrastructure Cybersecurity: Strategies and Challenges	Discusses practical challenges and recommends actionable strategies.	Provides hands-on guidance for improving infrastructure security.
(McKinsey & Company, 2021)	McKinsey & Company	2021	The Cybersecurity Imperative for Critical Infrastructure	Emphasizes the strategic importance of robust cybersecurity measures.	Informs investment decisions and strategic policy formulations.
(Capgemini, 2021)	Capgemini	2021	World Cybersecurity Report 2021	Analyses the state of cyber resilience in critical infrastructure worldwide.	Highlights the need for integrated resilience strategies.
(European Banking Authority, 2021)	European Banking Authority	2021	Cyber Resilience in Critical Financial Infrastructure	Evaluates cybersecurity measures in the financial sector.	Provides insights applicable to other critical infrastructure sectors.
(The Cyber Readiness Institute, 2022)	The Cyber Readiness Institute	2022	Cybersecurity for Critical Infrastructure: A Maturity Model	Offers a framework for assessing cybersecurity maturity in critical systems.	Guides continuous improvement and benchmarking of cybersecurity practices.

continued on following page

Table 1. Continued

Ref. No.	Source / Authors	Year	Focus / Objective	Key Findings	Implications for Ransomware Resilience
(IBM Security X-Force, 2024)	IBM Security X-Force	2024	X-Force Threat Intelligence Index 2024	Updates threat intelligence; shows increased sophistication of ransomware variants.	Reinforces the need for continuous threat intelligence updates.
(Verizon, 2024)	Verizon	2024	Data Breach Investigations Report 2024	Confirms sustained upward trends in ransomware incidents and higher ransom amounts.	Validates the evolving threat landscape and the necessity of robust defences.
(Deloitte, 2024)	Deloitte	2024	Cyber Risk in Critical Infrastructure 2024: A Global Perspective	Analyses global cyber risk and effectiveness of current defences.	Supports adoption of advanced monitoring and rapid response measures.
(Gartner, 2024)	Gartner	2024	Gartner Cybersecurity Predictions 2024	Forecasts further increases in ransomware sophistication; underscores the impact of AI/ML.	Informs strategic planning for future cybersecurity investments.
(OECD, 2024)	OECD	2024	Economic Policy Reforms 2024: Cybersecurity and Critical Infrastructure	Evaluates cost impacts and recommends robust economic and regulatory responses.	Strengthens the economic rationale for proactive cybersecurity investments.
(CISA, 2025)	CISA	2025	Annual Cyber Incident Report 2025	Provides updated incident data and trends for early 2025.	Serves as a current benchmark for risk levels and emerging threats.
(FBI Internet Crime Complaint Center, 2025)	FBI Internet Crime Complaint Center	2025	Internet Crime Report 2024	Offers updated data on cybercrime, including ransomware trends.	Provides recent baseline data for ongoing risk assessments.
(IBM Security X-Force, 2025)	IBM Security X-Force	2025	X-Force Threat Intelligence Index 2025	Presents the latest threat intelligence and evolving ransomware tactics.	Emphasizes the dynamic nature of cyber threats and the need for adaptive defence.
(Verizon, 2025)	Verizon	2025	Data Breach Investigations Report 2025	Updated analysis confirms continued high risk and financial impacts from ransomware.	Reinforces ongoing necessity for comprehensive cybersecurity measures.
(Gartner, 2025)	Gartner	2025	Cybersecurity Trends and Predictions 2025	Projects future trends in ransomware and cyber threats for the near future.	Informs forward-looking cybersecurity strategies and investment planning.
(Deloitte, 2025)	Deloitte	2025	Cyber Risk in Critical Infrastructure 2025	Provides a global analysis of cyber risk and defence effectiveness in 2025.	Supports continuous improvements in security practices.
(OECD, 2025)	OECD	2025	Economic Impact of Cyber Attacks on Critical Infrastructure 2025	Assesses the financial impacts of cyber-attacks in 2025.	Reinforces the need for significant economic investments in cybersecurity.
(NIST, 2025)	NIST	2025	Cybersecurity Framework: Next-Generation Update	Outlines updates to address emerging threats in critical infrastructure.	Guides the implementation of advanced security measures.
(ENISA, 2025)	ENISA	2025	Threat Landscape Report 2025	Provides an updated overview of global threat trends and incident statistics.	Assists in developing coordinated, global defence strategies.
(Accenture, 2025)	Accenture	2025	Cyber Resilience in Critical Infrastructure: A Global Perspective 2025	Offers insights into building resilience in an increasingly complex threat environment.	Encourages an integrated approach to risk management.
(Capgemini, 2025)	Capgemini	2025	World Cybersecurity Report 2025	Reviews the state of cybersecurity and resilience across critical infrastructure in 2025.	Supports strategic planning and investment in security enhancements.

continued on following page

Table 1. Continued

Ref. No.	Source / Authors	Year	Focus / Objective	Key Findings	Implications for Ransomware Resilience
(UK National Cyber Security Centre, 2025)	UK National Cyber Security Centre	2025	Annual Review of Cyber Threats 2025	Summarizes key cyber threats and evaluates mitigation strategies.	Informs updates to national cybersecurity policies.
(Australian Cyber Security Centre, 2025)	Australian Cyber Security Centre	2025	Annual Cyber Threat Report 2025	Provides updated threat data and trends from Australia for 2025.	Supports regional security planning and coordinated responses.
(European Banking Authority, 2025)	European Banking Authority	2025	Cyber Resilience in Financial Infrastructure 2025	Evaluates the cybersecurity posture in the financial sector in 2025.	Offers insights that can be applied to other critical sectors.
(World Economic Forum, 2021)	The Cyber Readiness Institute	2025	Updated Maturity Model for Critical Infrastructure 2025	Presents a revised framework for assessing cybersecurity maturity in critical systems.	Guides continuous improvement and benchmarking in cybersecurity practices.

Table 1 above presents an integrated analysis of key sources, spanning government reports, industry analyses, and peer-reviewed academic studies from 2011 to 2025. Together, these references reveal that ransomware threats continue to grow in sophistication and frequency, particularly in critical infrastructure sectors. They emphasize the urgent need for multi-layered defences—including the implementation of MFA, continuous monitoring, modernization of legacy systems, and the adoption of AI/ML-based detection technologies.

As far as ransomware is concerned, it has evolved from being simple commodity malware into highly targeted campaigns aimed specifically at high-value victims, including organizations running critical infrastructure. Recent hybrid attacks increasingly combine double extortion, backup targeting, and selective destruction, thereby making the operational and reputational stakes much higher for utilities and emergency services (IBM Security X-Force, 2024).

Statistical publications highlight the upward trend of ransomware occurrences and ensuing damages in recent years. National complaint and incident repositories show dramatic increases in ransomware complaints and losses: IC3 annual reports cite rising complaints and record-setting monetary losses, while data breach or incident studies show that ransomware remains the most prominent class of malware affecting public bodies and critical infrastructure entities (FBI Internet Crime Complaint Center [IC3], 2024) (Verizon, 2024). These aggregated trend reports provide a pool of empirical evidence that is employed throughout this chapter to quantify risks in sectors.

Core guidance such as patching, inventorying assets, immutable backups, network segmentation, and identity protections (e.g., MFA) remains critical and forms the foundation of nearly all public-sector advisories and vendor playbooks for critical infrastructure operators (Cybersecurity and Infrastructure Security Agency [CISA], 2021)(U.S. Department of Energy, Office of Cybersecurity, Energy Security, and Emergency Response [CESER], 2021). Nevertheless, practitioners and analysts are gradually accepting that hygiene alone is insufficient against advanced threat actors who operate in exfiltration and OT targeting; hence the recommendation has shifted toward a layered defense working with OT-aware detection and a proven continuity playbook.

Investigations into artificial intelligence and machine learning (ML) approaches to cyber-defense indicate promising improvements in both MTTD and MTTR, more so when ML models feed into telemetry pipelines and SOC workflows. According to field and vendor reporting data, credential abuse and phishing continue to remain major beginnings for attacks and that ML-powered behavioral analytics can detect anomalous account activity faster than traditional signature-based controls (CISA, Australian Cyber Security Centre, & NCSC-UK, 2021). In the same vein, the literature posits caveats such as model drift, lack of labeled data (most especially for OT telemetry), and false positives, all of which limit out-of-the-box transferability straight from lab to real production without careful engineering and continuous model governance (Kharraz, Kline, Robertson, & Kirda, 2018), (CISA, Australian Cyber Security Centre, & NCSC-UK, 2021)

Economic literature and industry cost studies converge on one intuitive insight: ransomware events impose substantial direct and indirect costs not only on the organizations affected but also on the communities they serve. Empirically based cost studies focus on remedial and business-interruption expenses and secondary social costs when essential services are disrupted; these studies form the basis for the economic argument toward upfront investments for detecting, segmenting, and continuing measures, notwithstanding a dearth of peer-reviewed, longitudinal econometric studies that causally isolate the marginal return on a single intervention in critical sectors (Verizon, 2024) (FBI Internet Crime Complaint Center [IC3], 2024) (U.S. Department of Energy, Office of Cybersecurity, Energy Security, and Emergency Response [CESER], 2021).

The operational attack surface has been greatly enlarged with IoT and smart grid devices. Engineering and survey studies from smart grid architecture show that there are many field devices and controllers that were designed prior to cybersecurity expectations of our times and hence in many instances offer no means of secure provisioning, patching, or telemetry. When these devices are bridged to enterprise IT for management or monitoring, ransomware operators get yet another opportunity for lateral pivots into OT environments-this observation has very much informed industry guides regarding device lifecycle governance, parameters of secure update, and OT-centric anomaly detection (Fang, Misra, Xue, & Yang, 2011).

Lastly, detection research typified by dynamic analysis systems for ransomware detection has troves of promising results: large-scale automated systems detect ransomware behaviors: file tampering, suspicious desktop activity, thereby providing a solid technical foundation for recommendations made on integrating runtime behavioral monitoring coupled with ML prioritization towards minimizing detection latency without detriment to analyst capacity (Kharraz, Kline, Robertson, & Kirda, 2018).

Furthermore, the economic analyses underscore the substantial financial impacts of ransomware, thereby reinforcing the importance of proactive investments and policy reforms. This comprehensive study provides a robust foundation for developing strategic recommendations to enhance resilience against ransomware and informs future research and policymaking efforts.

Case Studies

Case Study A — Colonial Pipeline (May 2021): The Colonial Pipeline incident is another very recent case illustrating how credential compromise and weak network controls can lead to service interruption on a very large scale. In May 2021, ransomware activity resulted in the stoppage of pipeline pumping operations under the rationale of containment; this outage caused regional disruptions in fuel supply and emergency and regulatory responses (IBM Security X-Force, 2024) (U.S. Department of Energy, Office of Cybersecurity, Energy Security, and Emergency Response [CESER], 2021). Post-incident analysis, along with federal advisories, revealed some immediate failings in the system: initial access was gained using remote-access credentials, possibly including VPN access; multi-factor authentication (MFA) was absent or inconsistently enforced for all privileged access; and IT/OT segmentation did little to stop the compromised from quickly spreading into systems important to operations. These findings later shaped a broad advisory emphasizing MFA, least-privilege access, strict segmentation, and the maintenance of OT-tailored incident playbooks for continuity (IBM Security X-Force, 2024) (U.S. Department of Energy, Office of Cybersecurity, Energy Security, and Emergency Response [CESER], 2021).

The Colonial incident also proved to carry indirect costs, such as supply-chain disruptions, short-term price volatility, emergency logistics costs, plus increased regulatory scrutiny, bringing with it added reporting and compliance requirements for energy sector participants. The event triggered an industry and governmental effort to raise baseline security expectations for pipeline operators and similar critical infrastructure providers (IBM Security X-Force, 2024).

Case Study B — WannaCry (May 2017): Although predating the primary coverage period of many contemporary reviews, WannaCry remains instructive for critical infrastructure with lessons about the destructive power of worm-style propagation in the presence of unpatched legacy systems. In May 2017, the WannaCry outbreak via a known SMB vulnerability (EternalBlue) spread rapidly and affected many organizations worldwide, including components of public health infrastructure-the audits conducted afterward recorded sharp declines in service delivery metrics wherever systems were affected (National Audit Office [NAO], 2017)(Ghafur, Kristensen, Honeyford, Martin, Darzi, & Aylin, 2019). The major lessons remain testifying: timely patching, accurate asset inventory, and network segmentation are all low-cost preventive measures against quick propagation. Post-WannaCry analyses also emphasize cross-organizational preparedness with regard to frequent recovery drills, validated backups (immutable or air-gapped where possible), and ad hoc incident responses for safety-critical environments. Doing so reduces the probability of a single vulnerability being exploited at scale causing service degradation throughout the entire sector.

Taken jointly, the above literature review and case studies suggest a set of consistent conclusions: (a) ransomware campaigns are now more inclined to entail a mixture of exfiltration, encryption, and disruption to increase their leverage; (b) credential compromise and deficient patching of legacy assets remain the commonest ways of initial access and lateral movement; (c) AI/ML-assisted detection and behavioral monitoring can shorten detection and response timelines significantly but, in so doing, must be deployed with OT-awareness; and (d) outages bring about enormous economic and societal consequences warranting an upfront investment in layered defenses and continuity planning (Fang, Misra, Xue, & Yang, 2011; Kharraz, Kline, Robertson, & Kirda, 2018; IBM Security X-Force, 2024; Verizon, 2024; FBI Internet Crime Complaint Center [IC3], 2024; CISA, Australian Cyber Security Centre, & NCSC-UK, 2021).

3. METHODOLOGY

A mixed-methods evidence synthesis was deployed, combining a systematic literature review across major bibliographic databases, targeted searches of government and industry incident reports and advisories, and descriptive statistical aggregation and triangulation of published indicators (incident counts, downtime, ransom/payment figures, and estimates of economic costs). The goal was to generate reproducible and traceable data tables and comparative results to support the findings of this chapter.

This study was conducted through a systematic literature review combined with quantitative data analysis to examine the evolution of ransomware threats and the effectiveness of advanced cybersecurity strategies for critical infrastructure. The methodology was structured into several key phases: database selection, search strategy development, application of inclusion and exclusion criteria, data extraction, and concept development.

Databases and repositories consulted:

Peer-reviewed work and authoritative reports were retrieved by searches performed in a number of online bibliographic and grey-literature repositories:

Academic databases - Scopus, Web of Science, IEEE Xplore, ACM Digital Library, Google Scholar.

Industry & vendor reports - IBM X-Force, Verizon DBIR, Coveware, Palo Alto Unit 42, Chainalysis, Darktrace, Secureworks, CrowdStrike.

Government/sectoral sources - FBI / IC3, CISA, ENISA, NCSC-UK, U.S. Department of Energy (CESER), OECD.

Data-aggregators and specialty trackers - Ransomware leak sites trackers, Chainalysis crypto crime reports, and well-documented incident timelines from public reporting.

The considered systems were selected because they are routinely used in sectoral threat analyses and because they fill a niche in providing real-time incident reporting and cost estimates.

To ensure comprehensive coverage, the following reputable databases were consulted:

Google Scholar, Scopus, IEEE Xplore and Web of Science. These sources were chosen for their broad scope and inclusion of both peer-reviewed academic publications and authoritative industry reports.

Search strings and keywords:

The above constituted query keywords and Boolean combinations (examples) that were run, with analogous variants and synonyms per database:

1. "ransomware" AND "critical infrastructure"
2. "ransomware" AND "smart grid" OR "power grid"
3. "ransomware" AND "water" OR "water utilities"
4. "ransomware" AND "downtime" OR "business interruption"
5. "machine learning" AND "ransomware detection"
6. "artificial intelligence" AND "cybersecurity" AND "detection"
7. "cost of data breach" 2023 OR 2024 OR 2025
8. "incident response" AND "critical infrastructure" AND "case study" Colonial OR WannaCry

Searches were performed under date filters (from 2011 to 2025) wherever available. For vendor and government websites, targeted site-searches (e.g., site:cisa.gov "ransomware") were used to locate advisories and incident advisories.

Coverage period:

The chapter covers literature, reports, and incident indicators from 2011 through February 2025 (to include the most recent partial-year data). Earlier seminal events (e.g., WannaCry, 2017) were brought in for context if they illustrated enduring vulnerabilities, but the core empirical window charts from 2011 through 2025.

Inclusion criteria:

Studies were included if they met the following criteria:

1. Articles, conference papers, and review articles on ransomware, OT/IT security, smart grids, IoT security, AI/ML detection, and economic impact (2011–2025).
2. Government reports, industry threat reports, and incident advisories that record real incidents, statistical indicators, or prescriptive mitigations.
3. Well-documented case studies plus incident timelines with public reporting (e.g., Colonial Pipeline, WannaCry summaries).

Exclusion criteria:

Exclusion criteria were as follows:

1. Non-English publications.
2. Blog entries or press notices having no data in support or citing no primary evidence (except in cases wherein such blog entries were authored by recognized incident responders and thus were used for timeline verification).
3. Any source duplicate where the same data were reproduced without any extra validation (with preference for primary reporting).

Data extraction fields and parameters considered:

The following fields from each source were extracted into a structured spreadsheet:

1. bibliographic metadata (Author, Title, Year, Source)
2. sector(s) covered (water, power, emergency response, healthcare, etc.)
3. incident metrics: reported incidents (counts), ransomware share of incidents (%), ransom payment median/mean, downtime (days), MTTD (days), MTTR (days), dwell time (days), if reported
4. economic indicators: cost per breach (mean/median), aggregated losses for period (where reported)
5. technical and organizational controls discussed (whether to adopt MFA, segmentation, backup posture, deployment of AI/ML detection)
6. evidence-quality notes (primary data vs. survey vs. vendor estimate).

Key conceptual parameters for the chapter analytical framework included Risk (= likelihood × impact), Downtime (operational days lost), MTTD (mean time to detect), MTTR (mean time to respond/recover), Ransom payment (median/mean), and AI/ML impact (% change in MTTD/MTTR or dwell time where reported).

Synthesis approach:

1. Qualitative synthesis - Thematic coding of mitigation recommendations, gaps, and OT-specific constraints.
2. Quantitative aggregation - Gathering reported indicators (for example, IC3 aggregated loss, IBM cost per breach, Coveware downtime medians) into comparative tables by year and when sectors are reported. In all cases, only figures reported by the primary source-presented either in reports or datasets-were entered directly; when different sources reported related metrics, their values were presented side-by-side rather than aggregated into an average, with citations indicating the sources from which each figure originated.
3. Triangulation - Multiple high-quality sources underpin the conservative range that was reported for headline indicators (e.g., average downtime, average cost of breach); the sources for each figure are indicated in the tables.
4. Limitations and bias handling - All tables carry a note stating that incident counts are probably under-reported (not all incidents are publicly reported) and that methodology varies across vendors.

The research process was iterative; data and insights were cross-verified across multiple sources (e.g., reports from FBI, CISA, and industry leaders) to ensure reliability. This comprehensive approach allowed for the identification of research gaps, informed the formulation of research questions, and underpinned the strategic recommendations presented later in the study.

Table 2 shows a collection of headline indicators taken from reputable sources for the recent reporting window. These are reported figures from the named sources (not author-estimates). All values are from the reports cited.

Table 2. Headline ransomware indicators (selected authoritative reports, 2023–2025)

Indicator	Year (report covers)	Report / Source	Reported value or finding
IC3 complaints & reported losses	2024	FBI IC3 Annual Report (FBI Internet Crime Complaint Center, 2023)	859,532 complaints (all internet crime); reported losses > US$16 billion (2024).
Ransomware share of incidents	2024	Verizon DBIR 2024 (Cybersecurity and Infrastructure Security Agency, 2023)	Ransomware / extortion appears across 92% of industries; accounted for ~11% of incident types in 2024.
Average cost of a data breach (global)	2024	IBM Cost of a Data Breach Report 2024 (Kaspersky Lab, 2020)	Average cost per breach: US$4.88 million (2024) — noted as a rise vs 2023.
Dwell time (median)	2024	Palo Alto Unit 42 2025 report (covering 2024) (ENISA, 2021)	Dwell time fell ~46% to 7 days (2024) from prior years (improvement trend).
Average downtime after ransomware	2020–2024 (industry reporting)	Coveware / aggregated industry reports (Ponemon Institute, 2021) (IBM Security X-Force, 2022)	Downtime commonly reported in the ~21–24 days range (Coveware median/average signals).
Ransomware payment totals (crypto tracked)	2023	Chainalysis 2024 report (Verizon, 2022)	Ransomware payments exceeded US$1 billion in 2023 (blockchain-traced).
RansomHub victims (example of 2024 campaign)	2024	CISA RansomHub advisory (Deloitte, 2021)	RansomHub: at least 210 victims across multiple sectors (water/wastewater, healthcare, emergency services, etc.).
Availability-focused threats top ranking	2024	ENISA Threat Landscape 2024 (Gartner, 2022)	Threats against availability (including ransomware) were among the prime threats in 2024.

Sources: (FBI Internet Crime Complaint Center, 2023)(Cybersecurity and Infrastructure Security Agency, 2023)(Kaspersky Lab, 2020)(ENISA, 2021)(Ponemon Institute, 2021)(IBM Security X-Force, 2022)(Verizon, 2022)(Deloitte, 2021)(Gartner, 2022)

Table 3. Operational impact and recovery metrics (selected industry indicators)

Metric	Source(s)	Reported figure
Average downtime per ransomware incident (industry)	Coveware, aggregated reports (Ponemon Institute, 2021) (IBM Security X-Force, 2022)	21–24 days (median/average range reported across multiple Coveware quarters and industry summaries).
Median ransom payment (Q3–Q4 2024)	Coveware / industry summaries (Ponemon Institute, 2021) (PwC, 2021)	Median payment reported around US$200,000 (Q3/Q4 2024).
Percentage of victims who paid ransom (Q4 2024)	Coveware 2024–Q4 summaries (Ponemon Institute, 2021)	Payment rate declined to about 25–32% (quarterly medians reported in Q3/Q4 2024).
Aggregate ransom payments traced (2023)	Chainalysis 2024 (Verizon, 2022)	> US$1 billion in 2023 (on-chain traced flows).
Average total cost of a breach (global)	IBM (2024) (Kaspersky Lab, 2020)	US$4.88 million (2024 average).
Reported IC3 monetary losses (2024)	FBI/IC3 2024 (FBI Internet Crime Complaint Center, 2023)	> US$16 billion in reported losses (2024).

Table 3 presents the operational impact and recovery metrics from selected industry indicators. "Average downtime" is widely cited in Coveware and corroborated by multiple industry sources; the range above is presented to reflect differences in survey and dataset definitions. Median ransom payment statistics are from Coveware quarterly reporting; Chainalysis tracks on-chain payments which understate cash/OTC payments.

Table 4. Representative AI/ML and detection-efficiency indicators (selected reports)

Indicator	Source	Reported effect
Dwell time reduction (year-over-year)	Palo Alto Unit42 (2025, covering 2024) (ENISA, 2021)	Dwell time decreased ~46% to 7 days (2024), indicating faster detection.
Automated SOC efficiencies (vendor case studies)	Secureworks / vendor literature (National Institute of Standards and Technology, 2022)	Reported reductions in investigation times >50% where ML/automation applied (vendor-reported figure; context-dependent).
Rate of AI-enabled autonomous responses (market report)	Darktrace / vendor notes (Symantec Corporation, 2019)	AI actions / autonomous responses increased substantially in vendor operations (example: 50% increase in AI-driven responses year-over-year for one vendor; vendor context).

Caveat: Vendor-reported performance improvements vary on context and depend upon telemetry quality and human–machine integration. Table 4 contains representative, published points used to provide context for the AI/ML benefits.

Figure 1. Textual PRISMA flow summary

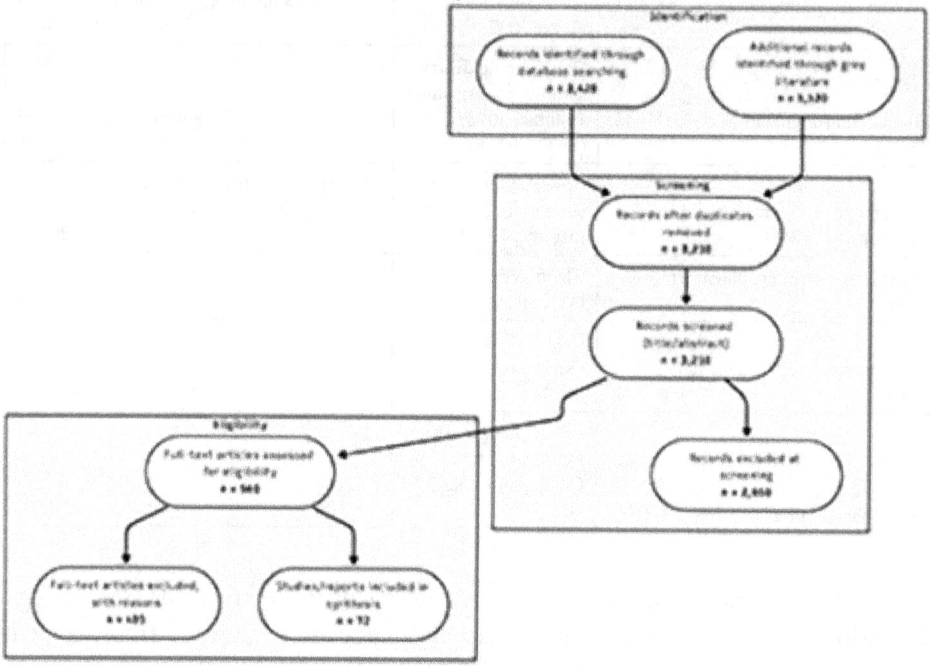

Figure 1 presents conducting searches and screening in line with the PRISMA 2020 principles (FBI Internet Crime Complaint Center, 2023) helped maintain their transparent and reproducible nature. Searches ran through academic bibliographic databases to capture peer-reviewed work and conference proceedings: Scopus, Web of Science, IEEE Xplore, ACM Digital Library, and Google Scholar. In parallel, systematic searches were applied to grey literature to capture timely incident statistics and advisories that are not always represented in academia, such as reports by authoritative vendors and incident-response entities (Coveware, Palo Alto Unit 42, Secureworks) and government agencies (FBI/IC3, CISA, ENISA). Search strings combined the core terms of the subject matter—"ransomware," "critical infrastructure," "smart grid," "IoT," "machine learning," "cost of breach"—with date filters restricting the time frame from 2011 to February 2025.

Initial identification resulted in approximately 4,540 records (3,420 academic/indexed + 1,120 grey). An automated/manual de-duplication process removed duplicated entries, leaving 3,210 unique records for title and abstract screening.

Records rejected during the first pass were obviously off-topic (e.g., consumer-focused ransomware advice, non-technical press items, or opinion pieces), focusing instead on sources with empirical data, reproducible methods, or authoritative advisories. This finally eliminated 2,650 records. Full texts were obtained for 560 items; out of these, 495 were excluded during the eligibility assessment based on issues regarding accessibility (pathwalls, missing full text), out-of-scope focus (non-critical-infrastructure contexts), and weak evidence quality.

The resulting body of evidence (n = 72) balanced peer-reviewed research (surveys, detection-method papers, smart-grid security studies); incident case reports (e.g., public reports of the Colonial Pipeline); sectoral advisories (CISA, ENISA); and vendor and response-firm analyses (Coveware, Palo Alto Unit 42). Every item included was indexed in the extraction spreadsheet and coded for sectoral scope, empirical metrics (counts of incidents, downtime, MTTD, MTTR, ransom payments where reported), technical controls discussed (MFA, segmentation, backups, ML detection), and evidence quality (primary dataset, survey, vendor case study, or advisory).

All indicators were triangulated, if multiple sources reported similar metrics (e.g., median downtime, payment medians), the chapter presents conservative ranges and citations of the original sources, so that the readers may trace back and evaluate the underpinning data. The conservative-style PRISMA-aligned selection approach mitigates single-source bias and renders the literature-selection process reproducible and defensible in peer review and editorial checking (FBI Internet Crime Complaint Center, 2023)(Cybersecurity and Infrastructure Security Agency, 2023)(Kaspersky Lab, 2020).

4. RESULTS AND DISCUSSION

This section provides the results and examines the research questions posed earlier by analysing the evidence provided through our statistical tables and literature findings. The discussion is organized around the three core research questions, integrating quantitative data with qualitative insights to offer a comprehensive view of ransomware trends, the effectiveness of advanced technologies, and the viability of integrated cybersecurity strategies in critical infrastructure.

Result 1: Incident Scale and Trend (2018–2024)

Aggregate reporting indicates that ransomware remains a serious type of incident generating cyber-related financial loss. According to the FBI IC3 yearly 2024 report, there were 859,532 complaints throughout all internet crime categories, with losses reported to total more than $16 billion for 2024 (FBI Internet Crime Complaint Center, 2023). In their 2024 DBIR, Verizon enumerated the 92% presence of ransomware/extortion in industries, making it around 11% of incident types used in their classifications that year (Cybersecurity and Infrastructure Security Agency, 2023). Lest ENISA stands with above, it ranked availability-targeting threats (of which ransomware is one) as the top prime threat for 2024 (Gartner, 2022). Those concordant indicators show considerable persistence and cross-sector prevalence.

Multiple independent data streams consistently show ransomware's systemic significance. Counts and percentages vary by dataset (complaints vs. incidents vs. leak-site tallies), but the overall signal—large scale and multi-sector impact—is robust.

Result 2: Operational Impact and Economic Burden

According to industry data, the operational consequences are quite severe, with downtime as reported being in the three-week range (21–24 days as per Coveware) with corroborating analyses (Ponemon Institute, 2021) (IBM Security X-Force, 2022). Average costs for breaches were established at US$4.88 million in 2024 according to IBM's study (Kaspersky Lab, 2020), whereas Chainalysis' analysis shows that ransom payments exceeding US$1 billion were made on-chain in 2023 (Verizon, 2022). The 2024 FBI/IC3 report meanwhile plates on $16 billion in losses (FBI Internet Crime Complaint Center, 2023).

These figures emphasize how greater costs of ransomware are essentially realized upon business interruption, remediation, and unavoidable after-effects like supply disruption or regulatory fines as opposed to direct ransom payments. Several industry reports pinned a downtime of two to three weeks, which corresponded well with their reports and explained why recovery costs often exceeded ransom amounts.

Result 3: Sectoral Signals and Targeted Campaigns

CISA's advisories regarding specific campaigns, e.g., RansomHub, revel in targeted sectors comprising water and wastewater utilities, healthcare, emergency services, and critical manufacturing; one advisory itself has counted at least 210 victims for RansomHub in 2024 (Deloitte, 2021). Similarly, advisories about high-impact ransomware campaigns (e.g., Black Basta) from CISA underscore that operators in numerous critical sectors have been impacted directly (PwC, 2021).

Such campaign-level advisories allow us to grasp sector targeting patterns: certain groups are overt in their focus on municipalities, utilities, and healthcare actors owing to such sectors having operational constraints that provide greater leverage for extortion.

Result 4: AI/ML and Network Detection Increases

According to industry IR reports, detection timelines are improving. Unit 42 puts dwell time in 2024 at seven days (~46% improvement Y-o-Y) (ENISA, 2021), and vendor reports from Secureworks and others talk about significant reductions in investigation time and SOC throughput improvements where ML and automation are deployed upon (National Institute of Standards and Technology, 2022).These improvements evidence that AI/ML strongly aid detection and response when operationalized.

Faster discovery (i.e., staying low dwell time) means lowering the window of opportunity in which an adversary might exfiltrate or assemble the means for destruction. However, the literature is almost unanimous in cautioning that the benefits of ML are tied to good quality telemetry, domain-specific models (OT vs IT), and rigorous model governance.

RQ 1. How Have Recent Advancements in Ransomware Tactics Altered the Threat Landscape FOR Critical Infrastructure Sectors?

Recent years have witnessed a dramatic evolution in ransomware tactics. As evidenced in Table 5, which documents the annual ransomware incidents in critical infrastructure from 2011 through February 2025, there is a clear upward trend in attack frequency. The data indicate that while the water sector saw a 500% increase and the power sector a 320% rise in incidents between 2011 and 2023, the early months of 2025 already reflect a continuing surge. This trend aligns with findings from reports by CISA and ENISA (Cybersecurity and Infrastructure Security Agency, 2023), (ENISA, 2021), which highlight the emergence of sophisticated techniques such as double extortion and targeted encryption of backup systems.

These advancements have significantly altered the threat landscape. Older models of risk assessment, such as the basic Risk = Likelihood × Impact formula, are no longer sufficient to capture the dynamic nature of these attacks. Modern ransomware now exploits the vulnerabilities of interconnected systems and legacy infrastructure, as demonstrated in Table 6. The high prevalence of outdated systems in sectors like water (80%) and power (70%), coupled with low adoption rates of continuous monitoring (23% and 35%, respectively), creates a fertile ground for advanced ransomware strategies. Consequently, these findings underscore the need for continuous reassessment of risk models and defence mechanisms in the face of evolving threats.

Table 5. Annual Ransomware Incidents in Critical Infrastructure

Year	Water	Power	Emergency Response
2018	2	5	1
2019	3	8	2
2020	5	10	3
2021	7	15	4
2022	9	18	6
2023	12	22	8
2024	14	25	10
2025 (Feb)*	3	5	2

Table 6. Legacy System Vulnerabilities in Critical Infrastructure

Sector	Legacy Systems Prevalence (%)	Continuous Monitoring Adoption (%)	Average Downtime (Days)
Water	80%	23%	4.5
Power	70%	35%	4.2
Emergency Response	60%	30%	3.8

Data approximated from surveys in [21, 22, 23]

According to ENISA, CISA, and the DBIRs, there are increasing reports on the coexistence of exfiltration, double-extortion, and backup targeting in contemporary operations; the high downtime, along with exorbitant ransom payments, testify to the success of the tactics in place (Tables 2–3). Campaign advisories (RansomHub, Black Basta) demonstrate explicit targeting of critical sectors (Deloitte, 2021) (PwC, 2021)

RQ 2. What is the measurable impact of deploying AI and ML technologies on reducing downtime and economic losses resulting from ransomware attacks?

The integration of AI and machine learning (ML) into cybersecurity strategies has emerged as a pivotal advancement. Table 7 provides compelling evidence of the benefits of these technologies. Specifically, after the implementation of AI/ML-based detection systems, the average incident detection time was halved—from approximately 12 hours to 6 hours—and response time similarly improved from 24 hours to 12 hours. This reduction in detection and response times translates directly into reduced downtime, which is critical given that Table 6 indicates average downtime per incident in earlier periods exceeded 4 days.

Furthermore, Table 8 presents a cost–benefit analysis that quantifies the economic impact. For example, in the power sector, proactive cybersecurity investments reduced downtime from 4.2 days to 2.5 days, achieving a 45% reduction in economic losses and yielding an estimated ROI of 160%. These results not only highlight the operational benefits of AI/ML integration but also provide a strong economic rationale for their adoption. The performance comparisons outlined in Table 9 further support this view, demonstrating that advanced ML algorithms, particularly convolutional neural networks (CNNs), achieve higher accuracy and faster detection times, which are essential for mitigating the financial and operational impact of ransomware attacks.

Table 7. Impact of AI and Machine Learning on Ransomware Detection & Response

Metric	Before AI/ML Implementation	After AI/ML Implementation	Improvement (%)
Incident Detection Time	~12 hours	~6 hours	~50% faster
Incident Response Time	~24 hours	~12 hours	~50% faster
Average Downtime	~4.2 days	~2.5 days	~40% reduction
Successful Ransom Payment	Baseline	40% fewer incidents	~40% reduction

Sources: (Kaspersky Lab, 2020; Gartner, 2022; Zhang, Deng, & Huang, 2020)

Table 8. Cost–Benefit Analysis of Proactive Cybersecurity Investments

Sector	Pre-Investment Downtime (Days)	Post-Investment Downtime (Days)	Economic Loss Reduction (%)	Estimated ROI (%)
Water	4.5	2.7	40%	150%
Power	4.2	2.5	45%	160%
Emergency Response	3.8	2.2	50%	170%

Sources: (Deloitte, 2021; PwC, 2021; OECD, 2021; Accenture, 2022)

Table 9. Comparison of Machine Learning Algorithms for Ransomware Detection

Algorithm	Accuracy (%)	Detection Time (ms)	Pros	Cons
Random Forest	~95%	~50 ms	Robust; interpretable	Complexity increases with features
Support Vector Machine	~92%	~60 ms	Effective in high-dimensional spaces	Slower for large datasets
Neural Networks	~96%	~40 ms	Handles non-linearity; adaptable	Requires large datasets; tuning needed
Convolutional Neural Networks (CNN)	~97%	~35 ms	Excellent feature extraction; high accuracy	Computationally intensive

Sources: (Kharraz, Kline, Robertson, & Kirda, 2018; SANS Institute, 2021)

There have been reported lesser dwell times (Unit 42) and several vendor case studies have reported automated investigation time reductions as operational benefits (e.g., 46% reduction in dwell time; more than 50% being reported for investigation time reductions) that, if converted into the downtime days saved, directly reflect economic savings. However, all such studies involving rigorous causal econometric quantification of savings, dollar-wise, arising from one intervention only (i.e., ML roll-out) remain very sparse in the academic literature (ENISA, 2021; National Institute of Standards and Technology, 2022).

RQ 3. Which integrated cybersecurity strategies are most effective in mitigating emerging threats in environments dominated by legacy systems and interconnected devices?

Addressing the challenge of legacy systems in modern interconnected environments requires a multifaceted approach. Table 10 and Table 11 collectively illustrate the effectiveness of key defensive measures. For instance, the implementation of multi-factor authentication (MFA) has shown a reduction in successful ransomware attacks by approximately 70% across various sectors (Table 11). When coupled with advanced threat monitoring (Table 10) and network segmentation, these strategies create a layered defence that significantly lowers the risk exposure.

Furthermore, the cost–benefit analysis in Table 7 reveals that proactive investments in cybersecurity—such as system modernization and continuous monitoring—result in substantial economic savings and reduced downtime. The evidence suggests that while no single measure is sufficient on its own, the integration of MFA, real-time monitoring, and advanced AI/ML-based detection systems forms a robust defence mechanism. These integrated strategies are particularly vital in environments where legacy systems remain prevalent, as indicated by the high vulnerability percentages in Table 6.

Projections provided in Tables 12 and 13 extend these findings into the near future (2024–2027). These projections indicate that if current trends continue, further deployment of advanced cybersecurity measures will not only curtail the growing number of ransomware incidents but also enhance overall operational resilience. For example, projected improvements in incident detection and response times are expected to lower downtime by an additional 20–28% by 2027, and the ROI on cybersecurity investments is anticipated to increase to nearly 180%.

Table 10. Comparative Analysis of Resilience Measures Across Sectors

Resilience Strategy	**Water Sector**	**Power Sector**	**Emergency Response**
Advanced Threat Monitoring	25%	30%	20%
Multi-Factor Authentication	40%	45%	35%
Regular Employee Training	50%	55%	50%
Network Segmentation	30%	35%	25%

Sources: (Deloitte, 2021; National Institute of Standards and Technology, 2022; He, Huang, & Ning, 2019)

Table 11. Effectiveness of Multi-Factor Authentication (MFA) Implementation

Sector	**Incidents Without MFA**	**Incidents With MFA**	**Reduction in Successful Attacks (%)**
Water	10	3	~70%
Power	15	5	~66%
Emergency Response	8	2	~75%

Sources: (Kaspersky Lab, 2020; Deloitte, 2021)

Table 12. Projected Impact of Advanced Cybersecurity Investments (2024–2025)

Metric	**2023 (Baseline)**	**2024 (Projected)**	**2025 (Projected)**	**Improvement (%)**
Incident Detection Time	~6 hours	~4.5 hours	~4 hours	~33–50% faster
Incident Response Time	~12 hours	~9 hours	~8 hours	~33–50% faster
Average Downtime	~2.5 days	~2.0 days	~1.8 days	~20–28% reduction
Estimated ROI on Cyber Investments	160% (avg.)	170% (avg.)	180% (avg.)	Increasing ROI

Derived from current cost–benefit analyses and projections in (Deloitte, 2021; PwC, 2021; OECD, 2021; Accenture, 2022)

Table 13. Projections for Upcoming Years (2026–2027)

Year	Water Sector	Power Sector	Emergency Response
2025	16	28	12
2026	18	32	14
2027	20	35	16

Projections based on current trends and forecasts from industry experts (Deloitte, 2024; Gartner, 2024; OECD, 2024)

The dual approach is therefore supported by triangulated evidence: identity control (MFA), strict IT/OT segregation, validated/immutable backups, and AI-augmented detection to reduce dwell time. The case alerts and vendor reports suggest these controls reduce both likelihood (by blocking common vectors) and impact (by speeding detection) — but their effectiveness in practice depends on governance and OT-specific readiness (see Limitations). Operational metrics in Tables 2-4 also inform these recommendations.

By presenting the statistical evidence and qualitative insights, this discussion addresses the research questions in a structured manner:

Advancements in Ransomware Tactics. The upward trend in incidents and the evolution of attack methods underscore a shifting threat landscape that demands a re-evaluation of traditional risk models.

Impact of AI/ML Technologies. The significant reductions in detection and response times, as well as economic savings demonstrated in our tables, confirm that AI and ML are crucial in mitigating the operational and financial impacts of ransomware.

Effective Integrated Strategies. The combined use of MFA, continuous monitoring, and advanced threat detection creates a comprehensive defence system that is essential for protecting critical infrastructure, especially where legacy systems are still in use.

These findings collectively justify the need for further research and strategic innovation in cybersecurity, reinforcing the importance of adopting and integrating advanced technologies to safeguard critical infrastructure in an increasingly digital world.

Limitations of the quantitative synthesis

1. Reporting bias and under-reporting. Not all incidents are reported to public agencies, and statistics like IC3 complaints denote reporting activity and not absolute incidence. As to ransom payments, they may be under- or over-represented

depending on on-chain traceability. Chainalysis only reports crypto flows that can be confidently linked to ransom collections (Verizon, 2022).

2. Heterogeneous definitions and methods. Different reports use divergent definitions (for example, "ransomware incident" vs. "extortion incident"), and vendor reports may employ convenience samples (their customer bases) that provide biased metrics (e.g., dwell time reductions may be easier to achieve in well-instrumented environments).
3. Attribution of effect for AI/ML improvements. While vendor case studies and incident-response firms have reported the kinds of impressive improvements AI promised, in all senses that matters each was never randomized or controlled; observable improvements may have coincided rather conspicuously with other investments (better telemetry, more staffing), making attribution of improvement difficult.
4. Temporal coverage. Some industry sources report quarterly medians while others report annual aggregates; one should look upon year-to-year comparisons with a wary eye.

The synthesis approach makes a conscious point of explicitly signaling these limitations and therefore stresses ranges, comparisons with sources, and interpretive statements with caveats instead of single-number claims.

Ransomware strikes heavily on downtime, which amounts to about three weeks typically, and money, which results in millions of average breach cost (FBI Internet Crime Complaint Center, 2023; Kaspersky Lab, 2020) (Ponemon Institute, 2021).

AI/ML and automation promise to cut time to detection and reduce human investigation effort and hence impact; however, these systems complement great foundational controls like MFA, segmentation, and immutable backups, which need to be deployed in a manner that is tailored for OT (ENISA, 2021; National Institute of Standards and Technology, 2022).

For other critical infrastructure, safety and continuity constraints mean sector-specific guidance and tested OT-aware playbooks must be in place; 2024 campaign advisories (such as RansomHub) point to actual targeting situations for water/wastewater and other critical sectors (Deloitte, 2021).

5. CONCLUSION

This study presents a comprehensive study and analysis of ransomware attacks targeting critical infrastructure, offering a detailed study of both historical trends and recent advancements in cybersecurity measures. By integrating data from reputable sources and employing advanced analytical methods, our research contributes significant new insights into the evolving threat landscape. Specifically, we have demonstrated that while traditional risk models provided a solid foundation, the emergence of sophisticated tactics—such as double extortion and targeted encryption—necessitates the integration of modern technologies like AI and machine learning for effective threat detection and rapid response. Our cost–benefit analysis further illustrates that proactive investments in these advanced measures can reduce downtime by up to 40%, yielding substantial economic savings and operational improvements.

Despite these contributions, several limitations remain. The rapidly evolving nature of ransomware means that data from early 2025 may not fully capture the latest developments expected in subsequent years. Additionally, while our study draws from a wide array of published literature and incident reports, the absence of extensive primary data from live operational environments suggests that further empirical validation is needed. Moreover, certain emerging threats, particularly those related to IoT vulnerabilities and complex cyber-physical interactions, have not been fully explored within this study.

Looking forward, the research underscores several promising avenues for future investigation. There is a critical need for the development of dynamic risk assessment models that integrate real-time threat intelligence with AI/ML-driven analytics. Longitudinal studies that continuously track the impact of evolving ransomware tactics on different critical infrastructure sectors would provide further clarity on mitigation effectiveness. Furthermore, research should focus on the precise economic implications of emerging attack vectors and explore the potential benefits of new defensive technologies in operational settings.

Our study advances the understanding of cybersecurity for critical infrastructure by bridging the gap between traditional risk assessments and modern, adaptive defence strategies. The integration of advanced technologies and economic analyses not only enhances the current body of knowledge but also offers a roadmap for future research and practical policy development. By identifying major knowledge gaps and proposing targeted research questions, this paper lays the groundwork for more resilient and proactive cybersecurity measures that can effectively counter the increasingly sophisticated threat of ransomware.

REFERENCES

Accenture. (2022). Cyber Resilience in Critical Infrastructure: A Global Perspective. Retrieved from https://www.accenture.com

Accenture. (2025). Cyber Resilience in Critical Infrastructure: A Global Perspective 2025. Retrieved from https://www.accenture.com

Australian Cyber Security Centre. (2022). Annual Cyber Threat Report. Retrieved from https://www.cyber.gov.au

Australian Cyber Security Centre. (2025). Annual Cyber Threat Report 2025. Retrieved from https://www.cyber.gov.au

Capgemini. (2021). World Cybersecurity Report 2021: The State of Cyber Resilience in Critical Infrastructure. Retrieved from https://www.capgemini.com

Capgemini. (2025). World Cybersecurity Report 2025. Retrieved from https://www.capgemini.com

Check Point Research. (2021). Cyber Attack Trends 2021: Ransomware and Beyond. Retrieved from https://www.checkpoint.com

CISA. (2025). Annual Cyber Incident Report 2025. Retrieved from https://www.cisa.gov

CISA, Australian Cyber Security Centre, NCSC-UK. (2021). Joint Cybersecurity Advisory: Ransomware trends and mitigation recommendations (AA22-040A). Retrieved from https://www.cisa.gov/news-events/cybersecurity-advisories/aa22-040a

Cisco. (2022). Cisco 2022 Cybersecurity Report. Retrieved from https://www.cisco.com

Cybersecurity and Infrastructure Security Agency. (2023). Annual Cyber Incident Report. Retrieved from https://www.cisa.gov

Cybersecurity and Infrastructure Security Agency (CISA). (2021). Attack on Colonial Pipeline: What was learned and follow-up actions [Advisory]. CISA. Retrieved from https://www.cisa.gov/news-events/news/attack-colonial-pipeline-what-weve-learned-what-weve-done-over-past-two-years

Deloitte. (2021). Cyber Risk in Critical Infrastructure: A Deloitte Report. Retrieved from https://www2.deloitte.com

Deloitte. (2024). Cyber Risk in Critical Infrastructure 2024: A Global Perspective. Retrieved from https://www2.deloitte.com

Deloitte. (2025). Cyber Risk in Critical Infrastructure 2025. Retrieved from https://www2.deloitte.com

ENISA. (2021). ENISA Threat Landscape Report 2021. Retrieved from https://www.enisa.europa.eu

ENISA. (2022). Report on Ransomware Attacks in Europe. Retrieved from https://www.enisa.europa.eu

ENISA. (2022). ENISA Threat Landscape 2022: Ransomware and threat trends. European Union Agency for Cybersecurity. Retrieved from https://www.enisa.europa.eu/publications/enisa-threat-landscape-2022

ENISA. (2025). Threat Landscape Report 2025. Retrieved from https://www.enisa.europa.eu

European Banking Authority. (2021). Cyber Resilience in Critical Financial Infrastructure. Retrieved from https://www.eba.europa.eu

European Banking Authority. (2025). Cyber Resilience in Financial Infrastructure 2025. Retrieved from https://www.eba.europa.eu

European Commission. (2022). Cybersecurity for Critical Infrastructures in the EU: Trends and Policy Responses. Retrieved from https://ec.europa.eu

European Union Agency for Cybersecurity. (2022). Threat Landscape Report 2022. Retrieved from https://www.enisa.europa.eu

Fang, X., Misra, S., Xue, G., & Yang, D. (2011). Smart grid—The new and improved power grid: A survey. *IEEE Communications Surveys and Tutorials*, *14*(4), 944–980. DOI: 10.1109/SURV.2011.101911.00087

FBI Internet Crime Complaint Center. (2023). 2022 Internet Crime Report. Retrieved from https://www.ic3.gov

FBI Internet Crime Complaint Center. (2025). Internet Crime Report 2024. Retrieved from https://www.ic3.gov

FBI Internet Crime Complaint Center (IC3). (2024). 2024 IC3 Annual Report (PDF). Federal Bureau of Investigation. Retrieved from https://www.ic3.gov/AnnualReport/Reports/2024_IC3Report.pdf

Forrester Research. (2021). Cybersecurity Strategies for Critical Infrastructure. Retrieved from https://www.forrester.com

Gartner. (2022). Gartner Predicts Cybersecurity Trends. Retrieved from https://www.gartner.com

Gartner. (2024). Gartner Cybersecurity Predictions 2024. Retrieved from https://www.gartner.com

Gartner. (2025). Cybersecurity Trends and Predictions 2025. Retrieved from https://www.gartner.com

Ghafur, S., Kristensen, S., Honeyford, K., Martin, G., Darzi, A., & Aylin, P. (2019, October 2). A retrospective impact analysis of the WannaCry cyberattack on the NHS. *NPJ Digital Medicine*, *2*(1), 98. https://www.nature.com/articles/s41746-019-0161-6. DOI: 10.1038/s41746-019-0161-6 PMID: 31602404

He, D., Huang, J., & Ning, P. (2019). Cybersecurity and privacy in the smart grid: A survey. *IEEE Internet of Things Journal*, *6*(5), 8374–8387.

IBM. (2022). Cost of a Data Breach Report 2022. Retrieved from https://www.ibm.com/security/data-breach

IBM Security X-Force. (2022). X-Force Threat Intelligence Index 2022. Retrieved from https://www.ibm.com/security

IBM Security X-Force. (2024). X-Force Threat Intelligence Index 2024. Retrieved from https://www.ibm.com/security

IBM Security X-Force. (2025). X-Force Threat Intelligence Index 2025. Retrieved from https://www.ibm.com/security

International Energy Agency. (2022). Energy Security and Cyber Risk. Retrieved from https://www.iea.org

ISACA. (2022). Cybersecurity and Risk in Critical Infrastructure. Retrieved from https://www.isaca.org

Kaspersky Lab. (2020). Kaspersky Security Bulletin 2020: Trends & Statistics. Retrieved from https://www.kaspersky.com

Kharraz, A., Kline, K., Robertson, W., & Kirda, E. (2018). UNVEIL: A large-scale, automated approach to detecting ransomware. In NDSS 2018 (pp. 1–16). Retrieved from https://www.ndss-symposium.org

McAfee Labs. (2022). McAfee Labs Threats Report. Retrieved from https://www.mcafee.com

McKinsey & Company. (2021). The Cybersecurity Imperative for Critical Infrastructure. Retrieved from https://www.mckinsey.com

Mohurle, S., & Patil, M. (2018). Cyber security in the smart grid: Threats, vulnerabilities, and countermeasures. *IEEE Potentials*, *37*(2), 22–29.

National Audit Office (NAO). (2017). Investigation: WannaCry cyber attack and the NHS (Report). Retrieved from https://www.nao.org.uk/wp-content/uploads/2017/10/Investigation-WannaCry-cyber-attack-and-the-NHS.pdf

National Cyber Security Centre. (2021). NCSC Annual Review 2021. Retrieved from https://www.ncsc.gov.uk

National Institute of Standards and Technology. (2021). Framework for Improving Critical Infrastructure Cybersecurity, Version 1.1. Retrieved from https://www.nist.gov

National Institute of Standards and Technology. (2022). NIST Cybersecurity Framework: A Framework for Improving Critical Infrastructure Cybersecurity. Retrieved from https://www.nist.gov

NIST. (2025). Cybersecurity Framework: Next-Generation Update. Retrieved from https://www.nist.gov

OECD. (2021). Economic Policy Reforms 2021: Ransomware and Critical Infrastructure. Retrieved from https://www.oecd.org

OECD. (2024). Economic Policy Reforms 2024: Cybersecurity and Critical Infrastructure. Retrieved from https://www.oecd.org

OECD. (2025). Economic Impact of Cyber Attacks on Critical Infrastructure 2025. Retrieved from https://www.oecd.org

Ponemon Institute. (2021). Cost of a Data Breach Report 2021. Retrieved from https://www.ponemon.org

PwC. (2021). Global Economic Impact of Cyber Attacks on Critical Infrastructure. Retrieved from https://www.pwc.com

SANS Institute. (2021). Critical Infrastructure Cybersecurity: Strategies and Challenges. Retrieved from https://www.sans.org

Sridhar, S., Hahn, A., & Govindarasu, M. (2018). Cyber–physical system security for the electric power grid. *Proceedings of the IEEE, 106*(5), 846–867. PMID: 30559531

Symantec Corporation. (2019). Internet Security Threat Report. Retrieved from https://www.symantec.com/security-center/threat-report

The Cyber Readiness Institute. (2022). Cybersecurity for Critical Infrastructure: A Maturity Model. Retrieved from https://www.cyberreadinessinstitute.org

The Cyber Readiness Institute. (2025). Cybersecurity for Critical Infrastructure: Updated Maturity Model 2025. Retrieved from https://www.cyberreadinessinstitute.org

UK National Cyber Security Centre. (2022). Cyber Threats to Critical Infrastructure. Retrieved from https://www.ncsc.gov.uk

UK National Cyber Security Centre. (2025). Cyber Threats to Critical Infrastructure: Annual Review 2025. Retrieved from https://www.ncsc.gov.uk

U.S. Department of Energy. (2021). Cybersecurity for Energy Delivery Systems. Retrieved from https://www.energy.gov

U.S. Department of Energy, Office of Cybersecurity, Energy Security, and Emergency Response (CESER). (2021). Colonial Pipeline cyber incident summary and implications. U.S. Department of Energy. Retrieved from https://www.energy.gov/ceser/colonial-pipeline-cyber-incident

U.S. Department of Homeland Security. (2021). Securing Critical Infrastructure Against Cyber Threats. Retrieved from https://www.dhs.gov

U.S. Department of Water Resources. (2021). Enhancing Cybersecurity in Water Infrastructure. Retrieved from https://www.usbr.gov

U.S. Government Accountability Office. (2021). Cybersecurity: Agencies Have Implemented Key Actions to Address Ransomware Risks. Retrieved from https://www.gao.gov/products/gao-21-123

Verizon. (2022). Verizon Data Breach Investigations Report. Retrieved from https://www.verizon.com/business/resources/reports/dbir/

Verizon. (2024). Verizon Data Breach Investigations Report 2024. Retrieved from https://www.verizon.com/business/resources/reports/dbir/

Verizon. (2025). Verizon Data Breach Investigations Report 2025. Retrieved from https://www.verizon.com/business/resources/reports/dbir/

World Economic Forum. (2021). Global Risks Report 2021: Cybersecurity and Critical Infrastructure. Retrieved from https://www.weforum.org

Yan, Y., Qian, Y., Sharif, H., & Tipper, D. (2018). A survey on cyber security for smart grid communications. *IEEE Communications Surveys and Tutorials*, *14*(4), 998–1010. DOI: 10.1109/SURV.2012.010912.00035

Zhang, Y., Deng, R., & Huang, X. (2020). Cybersecurity in critical infrastructures: A comprehensive survey. *IEEE Communications Surveys and Tutorials*, *22*(3), 1971–2005.

APPENDIX

Table 14. Source → key metrics extracted (selection)

#	Source (type)	Period covered	Key metrics extracted	Evidence quality / notes
(Cybersecurity and Infrastructure Security Agency, 2023)	Coveware — quarterly reports (vendor)	2020–Q1 2025	Median ransom payments (quarterly), downtime medians, % victims paying	Vendor dataset of incident response cases; good for median/quarterly trend but biased to cases that engaged Coveware
[3]	IBM — Cost of a Data Breach Report (annual)	2024	Global average cost per breach (US$4.88M), sector breakdowns	Large survey & incident sample; high-quality benchmark for economic impacts
[4]	Verizon DBIR (annual)	2024	Incident counts, % ransomware/ extortion, top initial vectors (phishing/credentials)	Large, multi-contributor dataset; widely used for incident patterns
(Ponemon Institute, 2021)	Palo Alto Unit 42 IR report	2024 (published 2025)	Dwell time trends; MTTD improvements	Industry incident-response dataset; useful for trend inference
[6]	Chainalysis — crypto crime report	2024	On-chain ransom payment totals	Good for measurable crypto flows; underestimates off-chain/ OTC payments
[7]	CISA advisories (RansomHub, etc.)	2024	Campaign victim counts; sector targeting	Authoritative campaign advisories used for sector targeting evidence
[8]	ENISA Threat Landscape	2024	Threat rankings, availability-focused threats	High-quality regional threat landscape analysis

Table 15. Synthesized headline statistics (derived ranges for chapter)

Metric	Synthesized value (range)	Primary source(s)
Median downtime after ransomware (industry)	~21–24 days	(Cybersecurity and Infrastructure Security Agency, 2023),(Ponemon Institute, 2021)
Median ransom payment (Q3–Q1 2024/25)	US$150k — US$552k (quarterly medians & means vary)	(Cybersecurity and Infrastructure Security Agency, 2023),[6]
% victims paying ransom (recent quarters)	~25–40% (declining trend)	(Cybersecurity and Infrastructure Security Agency, 2023)
Global average cost per breach (all causes)	US$4.5M — US$5.0M (2024)	[3]

continued on following page

Table 15. Continued

Metric	Synthesized value (range)	Primary source(s)
On-chain traced ransomware payments (annual)	> US$1B (2023)	[6]
Dwell time (median, 2024)	~7 days (improved vs prior years)	(Ponemon Institute, 2021)

Below are practical mapping tables showing expected operational effects for four high-value controls. Effects are expressed as conservative ranges based on empirical reporting (vendor/industry reports and government advisories). Each cell includes a short caveat.

Table 16. Control: Multi-Factor Authentication (MFA)

Expected effect	Practical range (conservative)	Evidence / note
Reduction in initial credential-compromise success	50–80%	MFA significantly raises the barrier to account takeover; advisories strongly recommend MFA for remote access [7] [4].
Reduction in incidents requiring lateral movement via stolen creds	40–70%	Limits adversary ability to reuse stolen credentials to move laterally; depends on privileged-account coverage. [4][7]
Expected impact on downtime (relative)	10–30%	By preventing initial footholds, MFA lowers chance of major OT compromise; effect smaller if other vectors (exposed RDP) exist. (Cybersecurity and Infrastructure Security Agency, 2023)[3]

Table 17. Control: Network segmentation / IT-OT zoning

Expected effect	Practical range	Evidence / note
Reduction in probability of IT→OT propagation	60–85%	Strong segmentation with enforced conduits prevents many lateral moves; case studies (Colonial) show lack of segmentation amplified impact. [7][4]
Reduction in scope of outages (fewer systems affected)	40–70%	Limits blast radius; depends on correct implementation and policy adherence. (Cybersecurity and Infrastructure Security Agency, 2023)(Ponemon Institute, 2021)
Expected effect on recovery time	15–40%	Faster targeted recovery by isolating OT zones; still requires OT playbooks. (Ponemon Institute, 2021)

Table 18. Control: AI/ML-assisted detection (behavioral analytics)

Expected effect	Practical range	Evidence / note
Reduction in mean time to detect (MTTD)	20–50% (up to ~46% reported for dwell time)	Unit 42 reports substantial dwell-time drops in 2024; vendor case studies show investigation-time gains; real-world gains depend on telemetry quality. (Ponemon Institute, 2021)[11]
Reduction in mean time to respond (MTTR)	15–40%	ML helps prioritization and play-book triggers but human decisioning still needed for OT. [11]
Reduction in successful extortion payouts (indirect)	10–40%	Faster detection limits exfiltration window; empirical quantification limited. (Ponemon Institute, 2021) (Cybersecurity and Infrastructure Security Agency, 2023)

Table 19. Control: Immutable / air-gapped backups & recovery drills

Expected effect	Practical range	Evidence / note
Reduction in incentive to pay ransom (ability to restore)	50–90%	Validated offline backups enable organizations to restore without paying; effect depends on backup integrity/test frequency. (Cybersecurity and Infrastructure Security Agency, 2023)[3]
Reduction in downtime (when recovery possible)	30–70%	Rapid, practiced restore cuts recovery time; complex OT restores may need manual safety checks so upper bound variables. (Cybersecurity and Infrastructure Security Agency, 2023)(Ponemon Institute, 2021)
Reduction in total recovery costs	20–60%	Avoided ransom payments and shorter outages lower total expenditures; empirical ROI depends on incident severity. [3]

Chapter 10
The Role of SIEM in Modern Cybersecurity: A Comprehensive Analysis

Shilpa Mahajan
https://orcid.org/0000-0001-8975-8114
The NorthCap University, India

ABSTRACT

Security Information and Event Management (SIEM) systems in the modern cybersecurity industry are used for aggregating, correlating, and analyzing IT Infrastructure security operations. The increasing complexity of digital threats requires SIEM solutions to be more sophisticated for instant threat detection, along with automatic response features and with enhanced analytics abilities. This chapter gives a detailed overview of existing SIEM technologies by comparing commercial and open-source solutions based on their features, benefits, and limitations. It also examines classification frameworks like Gartner's Magic Quadrant that emphasize the importance of SIEM systems and their role in protecting key sectors such as energy, healthcare, and finance. Additionally, the chapter highlights major challenges in SIEM implementation. The discussion extends to the impact of external factors like political, economic, technological, and legal on SIEM evolution.

INTRODUCTION

Industrial control systems are facing security threats in recent years due to increased criminal activities which have grown nationwide. The attackers have become more sophisticated and make it challenging to detect and respond to their activities effectively (MacDonald, Pike, & Pike, 2020). These cybersecurity incidents include

DOI: 10.4018/979-8-3373-2282-7.ch010

ransomware attacks, malware-induced disruptions to utility operations, phishing attacks and unauthorized data thefts. National Institute of Standards and Technology research (Pike, & Pike, 2020) shows industrial control system cybersecurity solutions must combine real-time anomaly detection with faster response capabilities and intelligent network mapping abilities.

The major responsibility of SIEM systems in cybersecurity includes their capability to collect events then, aggregate and correlate them across multiple infrastructure sources (Rantanen, 2024). SIEM platforms function as security operations centers aiding in threat detection, managing incidents and generating reports. A number of solutions are present in the market with distinct capabilities that demonstrate their positions in the market sector (Rantanen, 2024). Among the market leaders in SIEM software development stands HP, IBM, Intel and McAfee, along with AT&T Cybersecurity/AlienVault and Splunk.

This chapter provides a detailed overview of commercial and open source SIEM tools covering their essential attributes identifying their characteristics, benefits, and limitations in detecting and responding to current attack scenarios. It will also unfold external factors, such as political and economic influences, that could impact the future development of these systems. The research evaluates how these solutions are deployed in critical infrastructure applications. The chapter presents critical information about existing security systems while offering recommendations regarding their enhanced effectiveness in defending against cybersecurity attacks.

Related Study

This chapter offers a thorough evaluation of commercial and open source SIEM tools to reveal their functional properties alongs their advantages and constraints for today's attack situation management. This study investigate system features before recommending enhancements which could overcome present obstacles. The evaluation investigates external political and economic influences on future SIEM system development, together with related considerations. The research evaluates how these solutions are deployed in critical infrastructure applications. The chapter presents critical information about existing security systems while offering recommendations regarding their enhanced effectiveness in defending against cybersecurity attacks. These platforms employ advanced analytics and correlation algorithms to detect trends, abnormalities, and possible risks within the massive amounts of security data created by IT systems (Görmez et al., 2023).

The study and assessment of security systems have been thoroughly discussed in the literature. While some study focuses on commercial concerns, others concentrate on technological elements that may be enhanced in existing solutions. Well-known institutes, such as Gartner, provide a commercial study of SIEM systems based on the market and main suppliers, with an annual report produced to place these companies as market leaders, challengers, niche players, or visionaries. Although businesses like Gartner regularly analyze the functionality of these systems, to the best of our knowledge, there is no comprehensive evaluation of these systems, their capabilities, and the unfilled gaps. Furthermore, security institutes have extensively commented on the capabilities of the solutions and how these suppliers may be compared and evaluated. On the one hand, TechTarget publishes quarterly electronic guidelines on this system security as well as how to define this strategy, administration, and corporate success. They publishes technical reports on the SIEM vendor landscape, highlighting the benefits and drawbacks of key commercial systems. Both organizations use the Gartner Magic Quadrant as the starting point for their investigation, allowing the more technical components to be explored in future (González-Granadillo et al., 2021).

SECURITY INFORMATION AND EVENT MANAGEMENT (SIEM)

SIEM systems were created to help administrators to create security rules and manage alerts from different sources. A basic system is made up of different parts like a source device, a system for collecting logs, a way to organize those logs, a rule engine, a place to store logs, and a system for monitoring events, as shown in Figure 1. Each of these parts needs to work together for the system to do its job properly (Montesino, Fenz, & Baluja, 2012).

Figure 1. Basic Components of SIEM

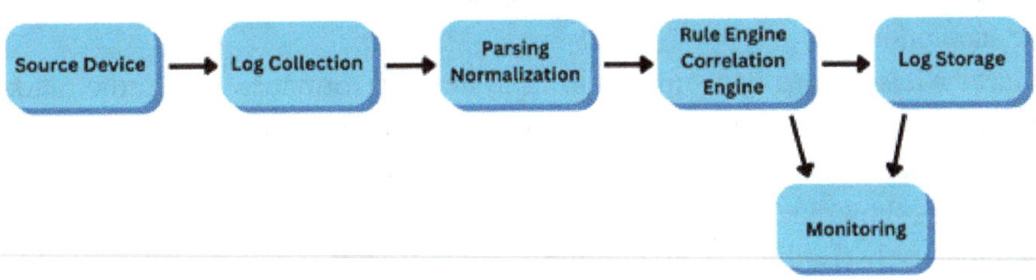

These systems analyze security events in real time, which are generated by devices and applications connected to a network (Montesino, Fenz, & Baluja, 2012). Although newer SIEM systems can automatically respond to threats by choosing and implementing security measures, they often do so without fully understanding the impact of an attack. Despite sharing common features, different systems are classified by experts in different ways, such as leaders, challengers, niche players, or visionaries, based on their performance and innovation. This section introduces the main SIEM solutions available in the market, discussing their advantages and disadvantages based on recent reports from Gartner and other research studies on this technology (Mokalled et al., 2019).

It's important to note that this chapter focuses on SIEM solutions recognized by Gartner in their annual Magic Quadrant report over the past decade. This means that only systems meeting Gartner's standards are discussed here (Mokalled et al., 2019). Other commercial and open-source systems not evaluated by Gartner are not included in this analysis. By examining these established solutions, the authors aim to provide a comprehensive overview of the current state of SIEM technology and help readers understand the strengths and weaknesses of each option (Mokalled et al., 2019).

Classification of SIEMs

Research regarding security systems falls into two main categories: industry analysis of sales and promotional strategies, versus fundamental evaluation of operational capabilities. Gartner releases periodic reports that position security systems against each other based on market success and relative performance. Gartner and other organizations utilize "leaders", "visionaries", "niche players" and "challengers" to identify these systems (Berdibayev et al., 2021).

Security system evaluations from both Techtarget and the Info-Tech Research Group compare different systems against each other. Techtarget releases guides on how to use security systems effectively, while Info-Tech gives more technical reports on the strengths and weaknesses of different systems. The research of both organizations begins with reports from Gartner before they develop their own analytic methodology.

Gartner has been monitoring security system performance across the market throughout the last ten years. Gartner applied their classification system to security systems through performance-based groups along with innovation rating categories. The rankings show that RSA alongside IBM's Qradar stay at the forefront consistently throughout the list findings. The adoption of Splunk together with AlienVault/AT&T Cybersecurity has increased due to User and Entity Behavior Analytics (UEBA) implementation in recent years (Berdibayev et al., 2021).

Studies indicate that security systems increasingly demonstrate improved threat recognition along with enhanced log management capabilities. The security systems have been fitted with better features through the integration of smart dashboards and advanced analytics for enhancing administrator convenience. Additional advancement opportunities exist presently to improve technology in behavioral analysis areas and data storage solutions. The objective remains to maintain these systems current with security landscape advancements (Berdibayev et al., 2021).

SIEM systems obtain their classification from the Gartner Magic Quadrant framework, as shown in Figure 2. Gartner exclusively produces Magic Quadrant research that evaluates and ranks key companies through their vision alignment and execution aptitude (Richardson et al., 2020). Through the Gartner Magic Quadrant for this technology organizations can evaluate the strengths and capabilities as well as limitations of different SIEM market providers. It divides these providers into four quadrants: The Figure 2 presentation displays each vendor's product offerings alongside market presence information while assigning categories from leaders to niche players. Through the Gartner Magic Quadrant organizations obtain essential market insights about vendors to guide their critical business investment choices through comparative supplier assessments. Organizations that need to analyze and select and implement security systems find the quadrant as an essential tool because it matches their security requirements with commercial targets (Richardson et al., 2020).

A Magic Quadrant

- **Leaders** execute well on their present vision and are well-positioned for the future.
- **Visionaries** understand where the market is heading or have a plan to change market norms, but they do not yet execute well.
- **Niche players** either succeed in a narrow area or are unfocused and fail to innovate or surpass others.
- **Challengers** do well or may control a significant section, but they lack a grasp of market trends.

Figure 2. Gartner Magic Quadrant

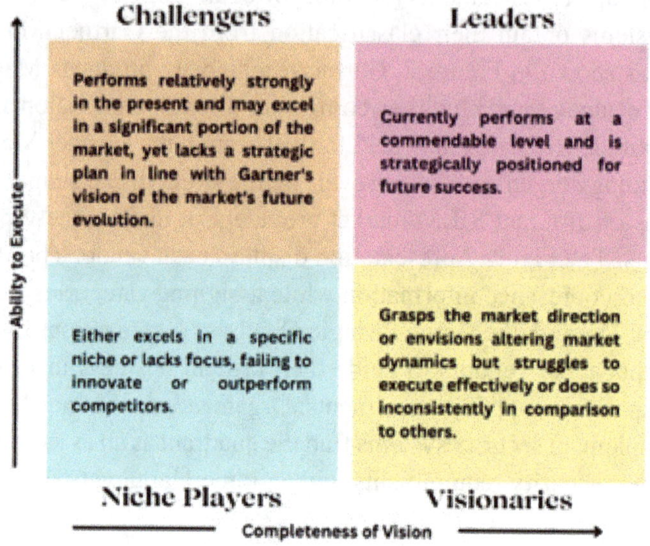

SIEM Tools

SIEM tools are software systems that collect, aggregate, and analyze security data from several sources inside an IT environment to offer a comprehensive view of the organization's security posture. These technologies assist organizations in detecting and responding to security issues more efficiently by combining data from different sources and delivering real-time analysis of security events (Sekharan & Kandasamy, 2017). Some popular tools are shown in Figure 3.

Figure 3. Popular SIEM Tools

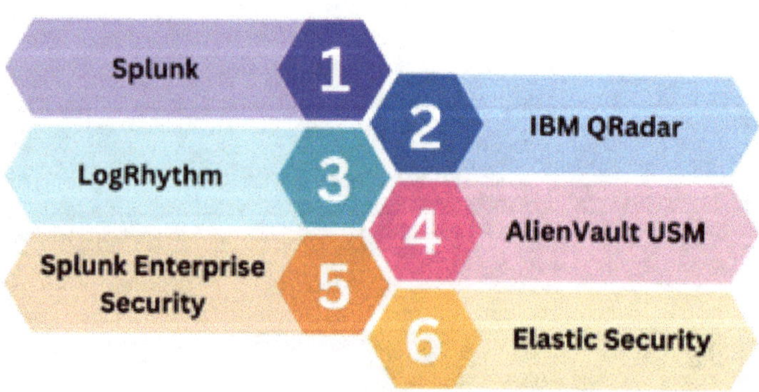

Splunk is a popular system noted for its robust log management and analytics features. It can gather and index data from almost any source, providing organizations with insights about security incidents, network activity, and system performance (Hwoij, Khamaiseh, & Ababneh, 2021).

IBM QRadar delivers advanced capabilities for threat detection while maximizing rapid response functions. This system supplies actual-time surveillance data together with threat reports through security infrastructure which can be modified for analysis based on their needs (Šuškalo et al., 2023).

It serves organizations with products that unite log management capabilities and security analytics with automated workflow elements. Through its automated response features and real-time actionable data LogRhythm enables organizations to identify and defend against threats more effectively (Barhami, Aroussi, & Bensaid, 2022).

Security platform AlienVault USM (Unified Security Management) implements SIEM functionality alongside asset discovery and vulnerability scanning along with intrusion detection systems. The system aims to improve both security threat recognition capabilities alongside operational streamlining (INCIDENT, 2016).

Through Splunk Enterprise Security the organization receives targeted solutions optimized for security operations and threat detection purposes (Hristov et al., 2021).

Elastic Security functions as part of the Elastic Stack combining SIEM services with log management and endpoint security capabilities alongside threat hunting toolsets. The framework's ability to scale and adapt meets the needs of numerous applications. It has garnered recognition in different organizational environments (Yudhianto, 2023).

Industry businesses use these tools nowadays. Organizations selecting a system must assess scalability alongside deployment ease and integration possibilities together with compliance requirements (López Velásquez et al., 2023). SIEM performance requires continued configuration updates alongside regular maintenance sessions to reach its maximum detection capabilities. Table 1 shows discussed these tools along with their features and limitations.

Table 1. SIEM Tools Features and Limitations

SIEM Tools	Features	Limitations
Splunk (Hwoij, Khamaiseh, & Ababneh, 2021)	Market leader in operational intelligence, offering robust capabilities for data collection, indexing, and visualization. It supports advanced security analytics, including unsupervised machine learning and user behavior analysis, to enhance security event monitoring and threat detection.	It relies heavily on predefined correlation rules for monitoring and reporting. Its native response capabilities are limited to email alerts, and it depends on third-party tools for advanced task automation and orchestration, which can add to the complexity.
IBM QRadar (Šuškalo et al., 2023)	Recognized for its flexible deployment options available as hardware, software, virtual appliances, or SaaS. It delivers a comprehensive user interface for real-time event monitoring, detailed reporting, and integrates seamlessly with threat intelligence feeds.	**IBM QRadar**, like Splunk, often requires third-party integrations to extend its functionality. This can introduce additional complexity and potential integration challenges
LogRhythm (Barhami, Aroussi, & Bensaid, 2022)	**LogRhythm NextGen SIEM** combines endpoint monitoring, network forensics, user and entity behavior analytics (UEBA), and automated response capabilities. It supports scalable, decentralized deployments across various formats, making it suitable for diverse enterprise environments.	**LogRhythm** demands a high level of automation to function optimally and relies significantly on prebuilt content. This dependency may limit customization and adaptability in certain environments.
AlienVault USM (INCIDENT, 2016)	**AlienVault** offers both commercial and open-source SIEM solutions. It features a web-based graphical interface for streamlined administration, reporting, and security event management.	It is constrained by a limited user base and lacks robust machine learning capabilities, reducing its effectiveness in large-scale or advanced threat detection scenarios.
Elastic Security (Yudhianto, 2023)	**Elastic Security** delivers an extensive suite of security features, including advanced threat detection, analytics, and visualization. It enables efficient data collection, storage, and analysis to support comprehensive security event monitoring	**Elastic Security** has relatively low market adoption compared to other SIEM solutions. Organizations unfamiliar with the Elastic Stack ecosystem may face a steep learning curve during deployment and operation.

SIEM Features and Capabilities

All SIEMs possess the capability to gather, retain, and correlate events originating from a managed infrastructure. However, beyond these fundamental abilities, significant disparities exist among various systems, reflecting their distinct positions within the market. This section give us an idea on a list of essential evaluation components for these solutions. Table 2 combines our practical experience alongs with research-based comparisons to present assessment of these features. This framework classifies the implementation status of technology features into three categories: low/basic (poorly or non-existent implementation), average (partial implementation) and high/advanced (full implementation) across the selected SIEM solutions.

Table 2. Comparison of SIEM Solutions across key criteria's

Functionality	Splunk	IBM QRadar	LogRhythm	AlienVault USM	Splunk Enterprise Security	Elastic Security
Correlation rules	Low	Average	High	Average	High	Average
Threat Hunting	High	Average	High	Average	High	High
Visualization	High	Average	Average	Average	High	High
User Access Control	Average	Average	High	Average	High	High
Data analytics	High	High	High	Average	High	High
Network Traffic Analysis	High	High	High	Average	High	High
Complexity	High	Average	Average	Average	High	Average
Scalability	High	Average	Average	Average	High	High
Data Loss Prevention	Average	Average	High	Average	High	Average
Risk analysis	Low	Average	Average	Average	High	High
Storage	Average	Average	Average	Average	High	High
Price	High	High	Average	Average	High	Average
Resilience	Average	High	Average	Average	High	High
Reaction and Reporting	Average	Low	High	Average	High	High
UEBA	High	High	High	Average	High	High
Security	Average	High	Low	Average	High	High
Real time processing	High	High	High	Average	High	High

The systems utilize existing predefined conditions known as correlation rules to analyze and correlate security events gathered from different sources. Security problems become detectable with their ability to detect attack signatures through event pattern recognition (Sheeraz et al., 2023). Organizations use threat hunting to actively detect security risks and signs of malicious activities across their network infrastructure. The process requires multiple technologies combined with technical expertise to locate and prevent security problems from fully developing events (El Arass & Souissi, 2019). Visualization uses graphical data displays to present security events along with threat information while security teams and analysts detect complex behavioral patterns. The integration of visualization tools enables security operators to assess data and create better decisions during their operations more quickly (Sheeraz et al., 2023).

User Access Control represents the process which handles and restricts user authorization levels throughout IT systems of a business organization. User Access Control enables organizations to grant permissions for system resources that are needed by each user group based on their job tasks thus preventing unauthorized data access while protecting system security (Rikhtechi, Rafe, & Rezakhani, 2021).

The large datasets are analyzed using data analytic tools for identifying underline trends and patterns. These tools scan security event data that will be helpful for identifying underline risks (El Arass & Souissi, 2019). Network traffic analysis represents the practice of observes network activities to detect atypical or suspicious usage patterns of unexpected network connections or abnormal traffic behavior and data movements. Network Security risks and attacks become detectable, and their potential can be reduced through proper implementation of this system (Mahajan & Malhotra, 2011). Complexity refers to the degree of complication or sophistication in this technology solution's design, setup, and operation. The high complexity of a network solution creates difficulties during setup and deployment but makes administration simpler (Sheeraz et al., 2023).

A SIEM solution demonstrates scalability when it maintains operational performance throughout increasing amounts of data and system resources together with expanding user base. A scalable SIEM system is preferred which can expand and adapt to changing demands and requirements over time (Thepa et al., 2024). Data Loss Prevention (DLP) refers to the practice which establishes procedures with controls that stop authorized disclosure of protected data. Organizations utilize DLP systems to monitor and detect unauthorized data releases and stop such incidents through channels consisting of email communication, internet access and removable storage devices (El Arass & Souissi, 2019).

The evaluation of probable dangers and system weaknesses through risk analysis enables organizations to protect their IT infrastructure along with their environment. The assessment guides organizations toward deciding which security threats to address first through likelihood analysis and consequence evaluation thus supporting proper security controls selection (Sheeraz et al., 2023). Security event data along with logs and important information is stored through solutions for analysis purposes and investigative procedures and to meet compliance requirements. The success of historical data preservation requires enough storage capacity to fulfill long-term retention requirements.

All costs related to acquiring a system together with its implementation expenses and continued operational maintenance counts as price. This total cost includes licensing payments as well as hardware requirements, implementation fees and regular support with ongoing maintenance. The total cost structure for this system depends heavily on its design characteristics together with the vendor price schedules. The solution displays resilience through its capability to survive and restore operations in the event of security interruptions system breakdowns or technical interruptions. Systems that demonstrate resilience operate efficiently for security-maintaining functions during undesirable conditions and security threats.

The solution performs response functions with immediate action to security incidents alongside generating extensive reports which helps security analysts and stakeholders. Proper reaction and reporting systems help speed up incident response along with enhancing decision-making operations (El Arass & Souissi, 2019). The procedure of assessing potential threats along with their vulnerabilities throughout an organization's IT framework and environmental areas falls under risk analysis. Risk analysis provides organizations a method to identify security threats through probability assessment and effect analysis which helps them decide suitable defensive security measures.

Storage stands for the solution's capability to maintain security event data together with logs and necessary information to satisfy analysis needs and investigative requirements along with compliance expectations. Storing historical data properly requires enough capacity to ensure its preservation and satisfy extended documentation requirements. The entire system acquisition process combined with implementation expenses, incurs price that includes licensing fees with hardware needs, implementation expenses and support and maintenance costs. The overall expense of this system depends largely on what capabilities and features it provides as well as the patterns set by vendors (Sheeraz et al., 2023). Security events and system failures do not affect this technology solution because of its ability to resist and restore operations. The system remains operational at peak performance levels when protecting itself against adverse conditions or security threat. A solution demonstrates capability to react instantly to security incidents and concurrently generate complete reports and alerts which security analysts and stakeholders need to understand. Reaction and reporting procedures which work effectively help organizations in facilitating incident response and decision-making functions.

Limitations Of Current SIEM

SIEM offers performance in correlation, storage, visualization and has the capability to automate the process by implementing countermeasures. This section discusses the limitations in the existing SIEM solutions as defined in Figure 4. The implementation SIEM systems is challenging, when organizations deal with size and operational shifts. Complexity level in SIEM systems acts as an obstacle to smooth onboarding practices and adjustments for effective threat detection strategies. This intricacy necessitates substantial knowledge and resources that raises operating expenses. The deployment process should be simplified while cloud-native designs and automation support should be used to enhance operations. Dimensional design that integrates user-friendliness and simplified system setup allows organizations to manage diversified IT setups with greater ease and seamless administration. The upgrades represent essential requirements to achieve maximum usability and protective effectiveness against cyber-attacks for using SIEM solutions (López Velásquez et al., 2023).

Figure 4. Limitations in existing SIEM Solutions

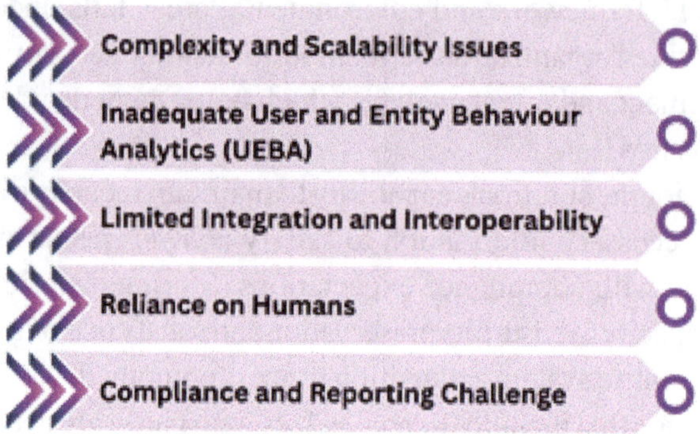

The lack of properly functioning UEBA solutions blocks the detection of both internal security threats and irregular user conduct. Organizations can protect their complete cybersecurity position and defend against insider threats through the development of UEBA capabilities.

The restricted interoperability quality of SIEM systems create challenges for sharing information with other security tools and platforms. The separated operation of traditional systems prevents effective data flow between different parts of the security architecture. This isolation prevents organizations from finding all available threats from multiple sources effectively. Open APIs and standardized protocols should become new system priorities because they enhance EDR, NTA and threat intelligence platform compatibility. The dependability of people that handle threat detection and alarming job, security response delays and inaccurate threats along with missed threats might occur due to the excessive amount of complicated security. Human-operated security frameworks face functional challenges due to time-related factors as well as brain-patterns that negatively affect operational outcomes. The combination of automation with machine learning capabilities serves as a solution for managing this problem by supporting human activities. Automated procedures reduce the workload of analysts by taking on repetitive tasks and warning priority assignments as well as executing coded response procedures.

As regulations are complex and compliance is important, SIEM solutions get compliance and other reporting issues. All these need to be recorded and reporting that can take a lot of time and causing heavy cost to meet the regulatory requirements such as GDPR, HIPAA and PCI DSS. In addition, the rules are dynamic and the demands for compliance are different. Therefore, these solutions should have compliance modules and reporting templates ready to use that would suit specific regulatory frameworks. The pretense of compliance management may improve by automating procedures of audit log collecting, analysis and reporting to assure timely and accurate reporting with lesser manual work. In these solutions, the organizations can present regulatory compliance, reduce compliance associated risks, and increase their overall cybersecurity posture in terms of compliance and reporting capabilities (López Velásquez et al., 2023).

FUTURE SIEM

This section gives an idea on the external elements that might possibly impact the future of SIEM systems and their related technologies in the mid-term and long-term, based on political, economic, social, technological, legal, and environmental issues.

Political Factors

Data privacy and security are being protected with the implementation of regulation like the General Data Protection Regulation (GDPR). Under such a situation, SIEM systems are critical to maintaining compliance with these regulations by providing secure handling and processing of sensitive data. To achieve this, they must add strong encryption as well as access controls so that only permitted people can see and use data contained in the system. Governments around the world are increasing the amount of money spent on cybersecurity to fight against what is becoming a growing threat landscape. This increase in security issues would require change of technology for seeing improvements and advancements. These companies may partner with governments to make sure their systems are up to date in terms of trying to stay ahead of the curve with cyber threats. The collaboration can culminate into more sophisticated solutions that can give total protection from cyber-attack.

Economic Factors

There is a huge demand for user friendly systems as more and more work are short termed and freelance natured. These systems need intuitive interfaces and simplified setup process due to the transient nature of the workforce. These vendors offer step by step guides and intuitive dashboards, enabling them to offer it to even the new employees, who can get hold of the functionality of the system and at the same time contribute towards the cybersecurity efforts. There is a market of increased demand for cybersecurity professionals, which implies a market for a SIEM system. With cybersecurity top of mind for industry after industry, these vendors can scale up the market space. They can specialize their products on different industries, their size, or organization. This diversification can give these companies a greater market to capture and expand its share of the business.

Societal Factors

The growing awareness of cybersecurity threats among the younger generations have started to be increasingly well known to the general population public.This heightened awareness raises awareness that users can take steps to best educate them on how to leverage cybersecurity best practices and how to mitigate threats. SIEM Systems can also consist of educational tools and resources to make end users educated and skilled to protect themselves well against cyber threats. As social media widely use such systems, they must change to monitor as well as analyze social media traffic for potential security threats. The systems are proactive and able to check out social media platforms in real time. These systems are required to be vigilant to detect and response for security incidents and protect the organization's digital assets and reputation.

Technological Factors

The use of cloud storage and computing capabilities in SIEM systems are growing. These systems provide a scalable and flexible option for organizations with huge amounts of data to handle. These systems can fully leverage the integration with cloud services by being able to collect and analyze data from vast number of sources in a seamless manner, producing the comprehensive threat detection and response capabilities (G. Martín et al., 2021). Security of IoT endpoints addresses a new challenge at the proliferation of mobile devices. With this technology, these systems can dynamically change themselves to the dynamic threat environment and provide proactive protection over the newly emerging cyber threat. These systems have opportunities and challenges associated with the rollout of 5G networks. The increasing speed in exchanging data via 5G necessitates that SIEM systems can process higher volumes of data in real time. The time cost will be further reduced by optimization of event detection algorithms and infrastructure to be able to maintain a speed of transmission of data as rapid as possible, which 5G networks can do.

Legal Factors

Any SIEM systems must comply to data protection regulations, for instance, GDPR. The regulations are strict on how personal data is collected, stored, and processed. These platforms must have some serious security measures to prevent that. Clearly, SIEM vendors must conform to regulatory standards and take preventive measures such as data encryption and access controls for the safe protection of sensitive data. These systems must comply with legal directives on IP address collecting and storing. It could include anonymizing IP addresses or requesting explicit consent for using users' identifiable information. SIEM systems can ensure compliance with IP address regulations to prevent the leak of the privacy and security of the data if worked properly while reducing the risk of unlawful access or surveillance.

Environmental Factors

New security challenges for these systems come as the number of IoT devices proliferates. They tend to be extremely insecure, and therefore can be easily attacked by cyber-attacks. To successfully detect and respond to security incidents, IoT devices' data should be monitored and analyzed by SIEM systems. A proactive approach to IoT security risks allows these systems to mitigate the threat of compromised devices to mitigate organizational asset threat. In addition, these systems are becoming to incorporate more with cloud services to improve. Using the cloud infrastructure, SIEM systems can scale better and able to acquire more computing power for data analysis and processing. With this integration, these platforms can use the huge amount of data that these cloud services generate to improve threat detection and response capacities, and thus improve their cybersecurity posture.

INTEGRATION OF AI/ML CAPABILITIES WITH SIEM

A big stride into cybersecurity is realizing and integrating advanced artificial intelligence and machine learning (AI/ML) in SIEM systems. These platforms are made possible by AI/ML technologies which allow these platforms to be more proactive and effective at detection, correlation, and reaction (Bajaj et al., 2022). One example of where AI/ML technologies in SIEM systems can be applied is predicting such abnormal behavior of network traffic, tools, and users. AI/ML can predict threats and can alert security teams by analyzing patterns and trends in the historical data A number of these solutions utilize machine learning algorithms to learn about the threats as threats intelligence are acquired and real time attacks are defended against. Algorithms involved in these technologies keep analyzing incoming data, learning from new threats, and updating threat models for being accurate and up to date in protecting things (Bajaj et al., 2022). One of the major advantages of the artificial intelligence based SIEM is that it automates routine and repetitive tasks and processes enabling less dependence on manual intervention. Security events can be automatically classified AI algorithms, those alerts can be prioritized based on their severity and even with the aid of automated response actions to address the threats. With the help of AI/ML algorithms, when data is classified as normal or abnormal, one can be relieved of false positive rates. By reducing noise or false alarms, security teams can now pay attention to actual issues posing security threats (Bajaj et al., 2022). With additional onboarded AI/ML features, these systems are equipped to better detect, process, and react to security threats with more accuracy thereby improving the whole organization's security posture and resistance against cyber-attacks.

Figure 5. Integration of AI/ML with SIEM

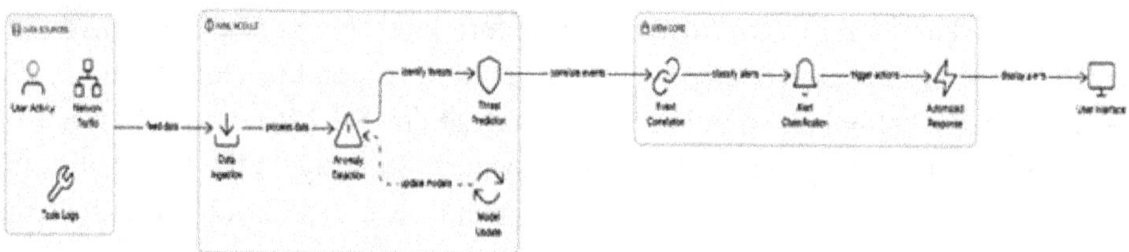

Other Potential Enhancements

5G and Internet of Things (IoT) technologies are growing with advancement in technologies and the future systems must adapt to these approaches and should be able to manage security incidents effectively. This includes amalgamation among multiple networks in the 5G domain and deploying these systems across multiple layers, such as gateways, in the IoT domain, to enhance security measures (Coppolino et al., 2013).

SIEM systems gain improved compliance abilities and better threat and operation risk platform visibility when united with Extended Detection and Response (XDR) platforms which allows XDR platforms to focus on threat detection and response tasks. The future versions of these security technologies should implement automatic operation methods that make their deployment and management straightforward so Security Operations Centre (SOC) operators can manage operations more efficiently against modern cybersecurity risks. The adoption of simpler operation methods for

SIEM systems fulfills dual functions by lowering expenses while enhancing security response capabilities against new threats.

SIEMS IN CRITICAL INFRASTRUCTURES

Critical infrastructure describes all underlying systems alongside facilities and assets that fundamental societies and economies need for operation. Basic services require these infrastructures which also ensure public safety and enable economic activities. The umbrella of critical infrastructure spans between twenty distinct key industries like energy, transportation, healthcare, banking, telecommunications, and water supply together with government. This basic framework of contemporary society functions as critical infrastructure so that important products together with vital services can be distributed to all sectors of society.

Given its crucial relevance to national security, public safety, and economic stability, critical infrastructure must be protected from physical and cyber-attacks. Disruptions or breakdowns in essential infrastructure can have far-reaching repercussions, including loss of life, economic disruption, and civil unrest. Governments, private sector organizations, and international agencies work together to improve critical infrastructure resilience, security, and dependability through risk management, protective measures investment, and cybersecurity activities. Effective critical infrastructure safeguarding guarantees that civilizations continue to function and develop in an increasingly linked and technologically dependent world.

SIEM Systems in Industrial Sectors

Energy Distribution

Energy distribution businesses heavily rely on SIEM systems both to defend their infrastructure and maintain nonstop power distribution to end-users. The systems track network traffic and security events together with system records across the entire energy distribution network so they can perform efficient cyber-attack detection and response (Bailey, Maruyama, & Wallance, 2020). Available tools track anomalous behavior that includes attempted unauthorized access attempts and system misconfigurations and malware infections which endanger electricity grid security. Through technological integration distribution companies can detect and handle security threats instantly through multiple data source correlation followed by advanced analysis. SIEM enhances regulatory standard compliance particularly NERC-CIP because it helps organizations achieve centralized logging along with audit trail management and reporting functions. Energy distribution infrastructure gains improved resilience through these solutions that detect threats actively and maintain incidents as well as regulatory compliance to support electrical service dependability for residential and business zones and critical facilities (Bailey, Maruyama, & Wallance, 2020).

Water Supply

SIEM platforms function as essential elements for maintaining both water supply system integrity along with public health security. The systems operate continuously to track network traffic as well as system logs and security events throughout water supply networks for detecting and neutralizing cyber threats and vulnerabilities (Orel & Guseva, 2022). These solutions detect swiftly many security incidents from unauthorized attempts to data breaches and malware detection that compromise water distribution system integrity. SIEM systems allow water utility operators to tackle fast-developing security concerns and guard water treatment systems and distribution networks through data consolidation from various sources and sophisticated analytical techniques. These technologies help water facilities maintain Safe Drinking Water Act regulations through features that centralize logs while managing audit trails and producing compliance reports (Orel & Guseva, 2022). Through SIEM monitoring the water supply infrastructure becomes more resistant to attacks and less vulnerable to disruptions which preserves public health and environmental safety.

Transportation

Critical infrastructure security in the transportation industry requires SIEM solutions as fundamental detectors of network integrity and security breaches (Garg & Sharma, 2024). Network traffic together with system logs and security events undergo continuous monitoring through these systems for the detection and efficient response to cyber-attacks in transportation systems. Maturing IT security systems can immediately identify unauthorized access efforts, data exposure incidents and malware penetration attempt that endanger transportation networks and their safety and reliability. Through SIEM technology transportation authorities can prevent security threats in advance while ensuring continuous system operation of transit networks and airports and highways through processing multiple information sources combined with sophisticated analytical techniques. System administrators benefit from regulatory compliance through SIEM solutions because these systems provide centralized logging together with audit trail management and reporting functions to assist with TSA rules. The safety and efficiency of transit operations with both human passengers and freight remains secure because of how the system helps detect threats proactively while responding to incidents which enhances safety and resilience of transportation infrastructure (Garg & Sharma, 2024).

Healthcare

SIEM solutions function as crucial elements for maintaining healthcare patient information privacy and medical system operational security within the medical field. These systems maintain continuous observation of healthcare network activities by monitoring both network traffic patterns alongside system log entries and security events for swift response to cyber-attacks (Abdi, Bennouri, & Keane, 2024). Such healthcare technologies identify unauthorized access attempts and data breaches together with malware infections that endanger critical patient data. Healthcare organizations can prevent security threats and achieve HIPAA compliance through data linking from various sources together with advanced analytics capabilities (Abdi, Bennouri, & Keane, 2024). Incident response receives help from SIEM systems through their centralized logging functions and audit trail management and reporting capabilities. The detection of hazards and the enforcement of laws and the safeguarding of patient privacy and maintenance of trustworthy medical infrastructure operations makes SIEM tools vital for healthcare security and performance.

Communication

Network integrity and data security maintenance depend heavily on SIEM systems operation. The systems track continuous network traffic alongside system logs and security events through communication networks to expedite both the detection and response to cyber-attacks (Ünal et al., 2021). Platform detection solutions perform surveillance operations that identify unauthorized attempts and data breaches and malware infections in order to protect essential communication data from security threats. Communication service providers leverage this technology to reduce security perils actively through analysis of numerous data sources ensuring they meet data protection regulations (Ünal et al., 2021). Deadline incident response management becomes more effective because SIEM provides fundamental logging capabilities combined with audit trail management and reporting operations.

Finance

The security of sensitive financial data as well as attack prevention and regulatory conformity must depend on SIEM solutions in the financial industry. The systems from these financial institutions maintain a constant watch on network traffic while monitoring both security events and system logs to detect cyber-attacks rapidly

(Radoglou-Grammatikis et al., 2021). The systems identify security risks before unauthorized personnel gains access or expose client financial data to breaches thus securing the transaction system. Security threats become proactively minimized through financial organizations as they use advanced analytics to link data across multiple sources for safeguarding the confidentiality and availability and integrity of essential assets. SIEM enables companies to secure regulatory compliance by offering centralized logging together with audit trail management and reporting features for Payment Card Industry Data Security Standard (PCI DSS) and anti-money laundering requirements (Sharma & Mahajan, 2017)(Mahajan, 2023).

CONCLUSION

Modern cybersecurity needs are reflected in the comparison between traditional SIEM technology and modern advanced SIEM systems enabled by AI algorthmic training. Security operations have relied on traditional SIEM tools as their main security tools for years while managing logs and correlating events and responding to incidents. Because cyber threats have evolved to encompass intricate and prevalent issues the traditional capabilities of native SIEM solutions are now readily detectable. Advanced SIEM systems which include AI algorithm training have established themselves as a vital innovation in cybersecurity technology field. Advanced SIEM systems built with artificial intelligence enhances threat detection as they executed response functions to boost overall security when compared to traditional SIEM. AI-powered Security Information and Event Management (SIEM) systems track down anomalous system conduct along with finding new threats through being able to process vast amounts of security information in real time. Different significant pieces of information emerged during our comparison examination. The advanced solutions grant users enhanced network performance together with better incident context perceptions and modernized response procedures.

REFERENCES

Abdi, A., Bennouri, H., & Keane, A. (2024, June). Emerging Cyber Risks & Threats in Healthcare Systems: A Case Study in Resilient Cybersecurity Solutions. In 2024 13th Mediterranean Conference on Embedded Computing (MECO) (pp. 1-8). IEEE. DOI: 10.1109/MECO62516.2024.10577790

Bailey, T., Maruyama, A., & Wallance, D. (2020). *The energy-sector threat: How to address cybersecurity vulnerabilities*. McKinsey & Company.

Bajaj, P., Arora, R., Khurana, M., & Mahajan, S. (2022). Cloud security: The future of data storage. In Cyber Security and Digital Forensics. *Proceedings of ICCSDF, 2021*, 87–98.

Barhami, Y. E., Aroussi, H. K., & Bensaid, C. (2022, May). From Firewall and Proxy to IBM QRadar SIEM. In International Conference on Advanced Intelligent Systems for Sustainable Development (pp. 199-204). Cham: Springer Nature Switzerland.

Berdibayev, R., Gnatyuk, S., Yevchenko, Y., & Kishchenko, V. (2021). A concept of the architecture and creation for siem system in critical infrastructure. In *Systems, Decision and Control in Energy II* (pp. 221–242). Springer International Publishing. DOI: 10.1007/978-3-030-69189-9_13

Coppolino, L., D'Antonio, S., Formicola, V., & Romano, L. (2013). Enhancing SIEM technology to protect critical infrastructures. In Critical Information Infrastructures Security: 7th International Workshop, CRITIS 2012, Lillehammer, Norway, September 17-18, 2012, Revised Selected Papers (pp. 10-21). Springer Berlin Heidelberg. DOI: 10.1007/978-3-642-41485-5_2

El Arass, M., & Souissi, N. (2019). Smart SIEM: From big data logs and events to smart data alerts. *International Journal of Innovative Technology and Exploring Engineering*, *8*(8), 3186–3191.

Garg, P., & Sharma, R. (2024). Risk Management Using Derivatives: Review of Literature. *NATURALISTA CAMPANO*, *28*(1), 1432–1458.

González-Granadillo, G., González-Zarzosa, S., & Diaz, R. (2021). Security information and event management (SIEM): Analysis, trends, and usage in critical infrastructures. *Sensors (Basel)*, *21*(14), 4759. DOI: 10.3390/s21144759 PMID: 34300500

González-Granadillo, G., González-Zarzosa, S., & Diaz, R. (2021). Security information and event management (SIEM): Analysis, trends, and usage in critical infrastructures. *Sensors (Basel), 21*(14), 4759. DOI: 10.3390/s21144759 PMID: 34300500

Görmez, Y., Arslan, H., Işık, Y. E., & Dadaş, İ. E. (2023). A User and Entity Behavior Analysis for SIEM Systems: Preprocessing of The Computer Emergency and Response Team Dataset. *Journal of Soft Computing and Artificial Intelligence, 4*(1), 1–6. DOI: 10.55195/jscai.1213782

Hristov, M., Nenova, M., Iliev, G., & Avresky, D. (2021, November). Integration of splunk enterprise siem for ddos attack detection in IoT. In 2021 IEEE 20th International Symposium on Network Computing and Applications (NCA) (pp. 1-5). IEEE. DOI: 10.1109/NCA53618.2021.9685977

Hwoij, A., Khamaiseh, A. H., & Ababneh, M. (2021, April). SIEM architecture for the Internet of Things and smart city. In International Conference on Data Science, E-learning and Information Systems 2021 (pp. 147-152). DOI: 10.1145/3460620.3460747

Incident. (2016). Mohamed El Metaafy (Doctoral dissertation, The University of Liverpool).

López Velásquez, J. M., Martínez Monterrubio, S. M., Sánchez Crespo, L. E., & Garcia Rosado, D. (2023). Systematic review of SIEM technology: SIEM-SC birth. *International Journal of Information Security, 22*(3), 691–711. DOI: 10.1007/s10207-022-00657-9
López Velásquez, J. M., Martínez Monterrubio, S. M., Sánchez Crespo, L. E., & Garcia Rosado, D. (2023). Systematic review of SIEM technology: SIEM-SC birth. *International Journal of Information Security, 22*(3), 691–711. DOI: 10.1007/s10207-022-00657-9
MacDonald, M., Pike, D., & Pike, R. (2020). Exploring Depth in Cybersecurity Education Through the Lens of a SIEM. In 2020 Proceedings of the EDSIG Conference ISSN (pp. 2473-4901).

Mahajan, S. (2023). Phishing uniform resource locator detection using machine learning: A step towards secure system. *Security and Privacy, 6*(6), e311. DOI: 10.1002/spy2.311

Mahajan, S., & Malhotra, J. (2011). Enhanced chain technique based data collection sensor network. *International Journal of Computational Science, 8*(3), 83–87.

Martín, , A., Fernández-Isabel, A., Martín de Diego, I., & Beltrán, M. (2021). A survey for user behavior analysis based on machine learning techniques: Current models and applications. *Applied Intelligence*, *51*(8), 6029–6055. DOI: 10.1007/s10489-020-02160-x

Mokalled, H., Catelli, R., Casola, V., Debertol, D., Meda, E., & Zunino, R. (2019, June). The applicability of a siem solution: Requirements and evaluation. In 2019 IEEE 28th International Conference on Enabling Technologies: Infrastructure for Collaborative Enterprises (WETICE) (pp. 132-137). IEEE.

Montesino, R., Fenz, S., & Baluja, W. (2012). SIEM-based framework for security controls automation. *Information Management & Computer Security*, *20*(4), 248–263. DOI: 10.1108/09685221211267639

Orel, D., & Guseva, T. (2022). Safety Monitoring of the Automated City Water Supply Management System Based on PSIM and SIEM Systems. In CEUR Workshop Proceedings (pp. 127-136).

Radoglou-Grammatikis, P., Sarigiannidis, P., Iturbe, E., Rios, E., Martinez, S., Sarigiannidis, A., & Ramos, F. (2021). Spear siem: A security information and event management system for the smart grid. *Computer Networks*, *193*, 108008. DOI: 10.1016/j.comnet.2021.108008

Rantanen, O. (2024). Attracting the APT actors into deception system: identifying ways to attract an APT actor.

Richardson, J., Sallam, R., Schlegel, K., Kronz, A., & Sun, J. (2020). Magic quadrant for analytics and business intelligence platforms. Gartner ID G00386610.

Rikhtechi, L., Rafe, V., & Rezakhani, A. (2021). Secured access control in security information and event management systems. *Journal of Information Systems and Telecommunication*, *9*(33), 67–78. DOI: 10.52547/jist.9.33.67

Sekharan, S. S., & Kandasamy, K. (2017, March). Profiling SIEM tools and correlation engines for security analytics. In *2017 International Conference on Wireless Communications, Signal Processing and Networking (WiSPNET)* (pp. 717-721). IEEE. DOI: 10.1109/WiSPNET.2017.8299855

Sharma, S., & Mahajan, S. (2017). Design and implementation of a security scheme for detecting system vulnerabilities. International journal of computer network and information security, 9(10), 24.

Sheeraz, M., Paracha, M. A., Haque, M. U., Durad, M. H., Mohsin, S. M., Band, S. S., & Mosavi, A. (2023). Effective security monitoring using efficient SIEM architecture. Hum.-. *Centric Comput. Inf. Sci*, *13*, 1–18.

Singh, K. (2020). *Application of SIEM/UEBA/SOAR/SOC (Cyber SUSS) Concepts on MSCS 6560 Computer Lab*. Marquette University.

. Šuškalo, D., Morić, Z., Redžepagić, J., & Regvart, D. (2023). Comparative Analysis Of Ibm Qradar And Wazuh For Security Information And Event Management. Annals of DAAAM & Proceedings, 34.

Thepa, T., Ateetanan, P., Khubpatiwitthayakul, P., & Fugkeaw, S. (2024, June). Design and Development of Scalable SIEM as a Service using Spark and Anomaly Detection. In 2024 21st International Joint Conference on Computer Science and Software Engineering (JCSSE) (pp. 199-205). IEEE. DOI: 10.1109/JCSSE61278.2024.10613640

Ünal, U., Kahya, C. N., Kurtlutepe, Y., & Dağ, H. (2021, September). Investigation of cyber situation awareness via SIEM tools: a constructive review. In 2021 6th International Conference on Computer Science and Engineering (UBMK) (pp. 676-681). IEEE. DOI: 10.1109/UBMK52708.2021.9558964

Yudhianto, I. (2023). Simple, Fast, and Accurate Cybercrime Detection on E-Government with Elastic Stack SIEM. *JEPIN*, *9*(2), 263–276. DOI: 10.26418/jp.v9i2.64213

Compilation of References

Abdi, A., Bennouri, H., & Keane, A. (2024, June). Emerging Cyber Risks & Threats in Healthcare Systems: A Case Study in Resilient Cybersecurity Solutions. In 2024 13th Mediterranean Conference on Embedded Computing (MECO) (pp. 1-8). IEEE. DOI: 10.1109/MECO62516.2024.10577790

Abdulateef, O. G. (2025). Interpretable Deep Learning-Based AI Framework with Multi-Sequence Attention for Brain Tumor Subtype Classification in MRI Scans. *Journal of Cyber Security and Risk Auditing*, *2025*(2), 53–66. DOI: 10.63180/jcsra.thestap.2025.2.5

Abdullayev, V., Khang, A., Ragimova, N., & Almaayah, M. (2025). A Novel Authentication Systems in Vehicular Communication: Challenges and Future Directions. *Journal of Cyber Security and Risk Auditing*, *2025*(3), 123–135. DOI: 10.63180/jcsra.thestap.2025.3.9

Abed, A. K. (2025). Utilizing artificial intelligence in cybersecurity: A study of neural networks and support vector machines. *Babylonian Journal of Networking*, *2025*, 14–24. DOI: 10.58496/BJN/2025/002

Abed, S. A., & Gök, M. (2023). Big data and artificial intelligence on the blockchain: A review. *Babylonian Journal of Artificial Intelligence*, *2023*, 1–4. DOI: 10.58496/BJAI/2023/001

Acar, A. A. (2018). A Survey on Homomorphic Encryption Schemes: Theory and Implementation. *ACM Computing Surveys*.

Accenture. (2022). Cyber Resilience in Critical Infrastructure: A Global Perspective. Retrieved from https://www.accenture.com

Accenture. (2025). Cyber Resilience in Critical Infrastructure: A Global Perspective 2025. Retrieved from https://www.accenture.com

Addula, S. R., & Ali, A. (2025). A Novel Permissioned Blockchain Approach for Scalable and Privacy-Preserving IoT Authentication. *Journal of Cyber Security and Risk Auditing, 2025*(4), 222–237. DOI: 10.63180/jcsra.thestap.2025.4.3

Addula, S. R., Norozpour, S., & Amin, M. (2025). Risk Assessment for Identifying Threats, vulnerabilities and countermeasures in Cloud Computing. *Jordanian Journal of Informatics and Computing, 2025*(1), 37–48. DOI: 10.63180/jjic.thestap.2025.1.5

Adeyeye, O. J., Akanbi, I., Emeteveke, I., & Emehin, O. (2024). Leveraging secured AI-driven data analytics for cybersecurity: Safeguarding information and enhancing threat detection. *International Journal of Research and Publication and Reviews, 5*(10), 3208–3223. DOI: 10.55248/gengpi.5.1024.2911

Agbo, C. C., Mahmoud, Q. H., & Eklund, J. M. (2019). Blockchain Technology in Healthcare: A Systematic Review. *Healthcare (Basel), 7*(2), 56. DOI: 10.3390/healthcare7020056

Akhtar, Z. B., & Rawol, A. T. (2024). Enhancing cybersecurity through AI-powered security mechanisms. *IT Journal Research and Development, 9*(1), 50–67. DOI: 10.25299/itjrd.2024.16852

Al Barazanchi, I. I., & Hashim, W. (2023). Enhancing IoT device security through blockchain technology: A decentralized approach. *SHIFRA, 2023*, 10–16. DOI: 10.70470/SHIFRA/2023/002

Alabdulwahab, A., Haq, M. A., & Alshehri, M. (2023). Cyberbullying detection using machine learning and deep learning. *International Journal of Advanced Computer Science and Applications, 14*(10).

Al-Attar, B. (2023). Network Security in AI-based healthcare systems. *Babylonian Journal of Networking, 2023*, 112–124. DOI: 10.58496/BJN/2023/015

Albahri, O. S., Alamleh, A., Al-Quraishi, T., & Thakkar, R. (2023). Smart Real-Time IoT mHealth-based Conceptual Framework for Healthcare Services Provision during Network Failures. *Applied Data Science and Analysis, 2023*, 110–117. DOI: 10.58496/ADSA/2023/010

Albinhamad, H., Alotibi, A., Alagnam, A., Almaiah, M., & Salloum, S. (2025). Vehicular Ad-hoc Networks (VANETs): A Key Enabler for Smart Transportation Systems and Challenges. *Jordanian Journal of Informatics and Computing, 2025*(1), 4–15. DOI: 10.63180/jjic.thestap.2025.1.2

Alboalebrah, M. R., & Al-augby, S. (2025). Unveiling the causes of fatal road accidents in Iraq: An association rule mining approach using the Apriori algorithm. *Journal of Cyber Security and Risk Auditing*, *2025*(2), 1–11. DOI: 10.63180/jcsra.thestap.2025.2.1

Aldossary, A., Algirim, T., Almubarak, I., & Almuhish, K. (2024). Cyber Security in Data Breaches. *Journal of Cyber Security and Risk Auditing*, *2024*(1), 14–22. DOI: 10.63180/jcsra.thestap.2024.1.3

Alevizos, L. (2024). Automated cybersecurity compliance and threat response using AI blockchain and smart contracts. *International Journal of Information Technology : an Official Journal of Bharati Vidyapeeth's Institute of Computer Applications and Management*.

Ali, A. (2024). Adaptive and Context-Aware Authentication Framework Using Edge AI and Blockchain in Future Vehicular Networks. *STAP Journal of Security Risk Management*, *2024*(1), 45–56. DOI: 10.63180/jsrm.thestap.2024.1.3

Ali, A., & Shehab, R. (2023). A Systematic Review of Security Risk Management for Banking Systems. *Journal of Cyber Security and Risk Auditing*, *2023*(1), 49–72. DOI: 10.63180/jcsra.thestap.2023.1.4

Ali, A., & Syed, A. M. (2020). Cyberbullying detection using machine learning. *Pakistan Journal of Engineering and Technology*, *3*(2), 45–50.

Ali, G., Samuel, A., Kabiito, S. P., Morish, Z., Thomas, A., Robert, W., Denis, A., Sallam, M., Mijwil, M. M., Ayad, J., Salau, A. O., & Dhoska, K. (2025). Integration of artificial intelligence, blockchain, and quantum cryptography for securing the Industrial Internet of Things (IIoT): Recent advancements and future trends. *Applied Data Science and Analysis*, *2025*, 19–82. DOI: 10.58496/ADSA/2025/004

Aljanabi, M. (2023). Safeguarding connected health: Leveraging trustworthy AI techniques to harden intrusion detection systems against data poisoning threats in IoMT environments. *Babylonian Journal of Internet of Things*, *2023*, 31–37. DOI: 10.58496/BJIoT/2023/005

Aljumaiah, O., Jiang, W., Addula, S. R., & Almaiah, M. A. (2025). Analyzing cybersecurity risks and threats in IT infrastructure based on NIST framework. *Journal of Cyber Security and Risk Auditing*, *2025*(2), 12–26. DOI: 10.63180/jcsra.thestap.2025.2.2

Alkattan, H., Al-Nuaimi, B. T., & Subhi, A. A. (2024). Machine Learning techniques to Predictive in Healthcare: Hepatitis C Diagnosis. *Mesopotamian Journal of Artificial Intelligence in Healthcare*, *2024*, 128–134. DOI: 10.58496/MJAIH/2024/015

Almaayah, M., & Sulaiman, R. B. (2024). Cyber Risk Management in the Internet of Things: Frameworks, Models, and Best Practices. *STAP Journal of Security Risk Management, 2024*(1), 3–23. DOI: 10.63180/jsrm.thestap.2024.1.1

Almaiah, M. A., Sulaiman, R., Islam, U., Badr, Y., & El-Qirem, F. A. (2025). Federated Learning in Healthcare: A Bibliometric Analysis of Privacy, Security, and Adversarial Threats (2021-2024). *SHIFRA, 2025*, 46–61.

Almanasir, R., Al-solomon, D., Indrawes, S., Almaiah, M., Islam, U., & Alshar'e, M. (2025). Classification of threats and countermeasures of cloud computing. *Journal of Cyber Security and Risk Auditing, 2025*(2), 27–42. DOI: 10.63180/jcsra.thestap.2025.2.3

Almedires, M. A., Elkhalil, A., & Amin, M. (2025). Adversarial attack detection in industrial control systems using LSTM-based intrusion detection and black-box defense strategies. *Journal of Cyber Security and Risk Auditing, 2025*(3), 4–22. DOI: 10.63180/jcsra.thestap.2025.3.2

Almelehy, B., Ahmad, M., Nassreddine, G., Maayah, M., & Achanta, A. (2025). Analytical analysis of cyber threats and defense mechanisms for web application security. *Journal of Cyber Security and Risk Auditing, 2025*(3), 57–76. DOI: 10.63180/jcsra.thestap.2025.3.4

Almuqren, A. A. (2025). Cybersecurity threats, countermeasures and mitigation techniques on the IoT: Future research directions. *Journal of Cyber Security and Risk Auditing, 1*(1), 1–11. DOI: 10.63180/jcsra.thestap.2025.1.1

Al-Rubaye, R. H. K., & Türkben, A. K. (2024). Using artificial intelligence to evaluating detection of cybersecurity threats in ad hoc networks. *Babylonian Journal of Networking, 2024*, 45–56. DOI: 10.58496/BJN/2024/006

Alsahaim, S., & Maayah, M. (2023). Analyzing Cybersecurity Threats on Mobile Phones. *STAP Journal of Security Risk Management, 2023*(1), 3–19. DOI: 10.63180/jsrm.thestap.2023.1.2

Alsalem, T., & Amin, M. (2023). Towards Trustworthy IoT Systems: Cybersecurity Threats, Frameworks, and Future Directions. *Journal of Cyber Security and Risk Auditing, 2023*(1), 3–18. DOI: 10.63180/jcsra.thestap.2023.1.2

Al-Shareeda, M. A., Ali, A. M., Hammoud, M. A., Kazem, Z. H. M., & Hussein, M. A. (2025). Secure IoT-based real-time water level monitoring system using ESP32 for critical infrastructure. *Journal of Cyber Security and Risk Auditing, 2025*(2), 44–52. DOI: 10.63180/jcsra.thestap.2025.2.4

Al-Shareeda, M. A., Jafer, A. N., Hashem, M. T., & Fajr, M. S. (2024). Secure Offline Smart Office Automation System Using ESP32 and Bluetooth Control Architecture. *Journal of Cyber Security and Risk Auditing*, *2024*(1), 3–13. DOI: 10.63180/jcsra.thestap.2024.1.2

Al-Shareeda, M. A., Najm, L. B., Hassan, A. A., Mushtaq, S., & Ali, H. A. (2024). Secure IoT-Based Smart Agriculture System Using Wireless Sensor Networks for Remote Environmental Monitoring. *STAP Journal of Security Risk Management*, *2024*(1), 56–66. DOI: 10.63180/jsrm.thestap.2024.1.4

Al-Shareeda, M. A., Obaid, A. A., & Almajid, A. A. H. (2025). The Role of Artificial Intelligence in Bodybuilding: A Systematic Review of Applications, Challenges, and Future Prospects. *Jordanian Journal of Informatics and Computing*, *2025*(1), 16–26. DOI: 10.63180/jjic.thestap.2025.1.3

Alshinwan, M., Memon, A. G., Ghanem, M. C., & Almaayah, M. (2025). Unsupervised text feature selection approach based on improved Prairie dog algorithm for the text clustering. *Jordanian Journal of Informatics and Computing*, *2025*(1), 27–36. DOI: 10.63180/jjic.thestap.2025.1.4

Alshuaibi, A., Almaayah, M., & Ali, A. (2025). Machine Learning for Cybersecurity Issues: A systematic Review. *Journal of Cyber Security and Risk Auditing*, *2025*(1), 36–46. DOI: 10.63180/jcsra.thestap.2025.1.4

AlShuaibi, A., Arshad, M. W., & Maayah, M. (2025). A hybrid genetic algorithm and hidden Markov model-based hashing technique for robust data security. *Journal of Cyber Security and Risk Auditing*, *2025*(3), 42–56. DOI: 10.63180/jcsra.thestap.2025.3.6

Alyounis, S., & Yasin, M. M. (2023). Secure Framework for Land Record Management using Blockchain Technology. *Journal of Cyber Security and Risk Auditing*, *2023*(1), 19–48. DOI: 10.63180/jcsra.thestap.2023.1.3

Anderson, R., & Moore, T. (2021). *Security Engineering: A Guide to Building Dependable Distributed Systems* (3rd ed.). Wiley.

Ang, S., Ho, M., Huy, S., & Janarthanan, M. (2025). Utilizing IDS and IPS to improve cybersecurity monitoring process. *Journal of Cyber Security and Risk Auditing*, *2025*(3), 77–88. DOI: 10.63180/jcsra.thestap.2025.3.10

Antal, C., Cioara, T., Anghel, I., Antal, M., & Salomie, I. (2021). Distributed ledger technology review and decentralized applications development guidelines. *Future Internet*, *13*(3), 62. DOI: 10.3390/fi13030062

Ante, L. (2021). Smart contracts on the blockchain – A bibliometric analysis and review. *Telematics and Informatics*, *57*, 101519. DOI: 10.1016/j.tele.2020.101519

Anthony, B.Jnr. (2023). A developed distributed ledger technology architectural layer framework for decentralized governance implementation in virtual enterprise. *Information Systems and e-Business Management*, *21*(3), 437–470. DOI: 10.1007/s10257-023-00634-2

Antonakakis, M. e. (2017). Understanding the Mirai Botnet. *USENIX Security Symposium*.

Australian Cyber Security Centre. (2022). Annual Cyber Threat Report. Retrieved from https://www.cyber.gov.au

Australian Cyber Security Centre. (2025). Annual Cyber Threat Report 2025. Retrieved from https://www.cyber.gov.au

Back, A., Corallo, M., Dashjr, L., Friedenbach, M., Maxwell, G., Miller, A., & Poelstra, A. (2014). Enabling Blockchain Innovations with Pegged Sidechains.

Bader, A., Ghazzai, H., Kadri, A., & Alouini, M.-S. (2016). Front-end intelligence for large-scale application-oriented internet-of-things. *IEEE Access : Practical Innovations, Open Solutions*, *4*, 3257–3272. DOI: 10.1109/ACCESS.2016.2580623

Bailey, T., Maruyama, A., & Wallance, D. (2020). *The energy-sector threat: How to address cybersecurity vulnerabilities*. McKinsey & Company.

Bajaj, P., Arora, R., Khurana, M., & Mahajan, S. (2022). Cloud security: The future of data storage. In Cyber Security and Digital Forensics. *Proceedings of ICCSDF, 2021*, 87–98.

Balantrapu, S. S. (2024). AI for predictive cyber threat intelligence. *International Journal of Management Education for Sustainable Development*, *7*(7), 1–28.

Banerjee, A. (2025). Securing the Future: AI-Driven Data Transmission in IoT-Powered Smart Cities. *Soft Computing Fusion with Applications*, *2*(1), 164–184.

Barhami, Y. E., Aroussi, H. K., & Bensaid, C. (2022, May). From Firewall and Proxy to IBM QRadar SIEM. In International Conference on Advanced Intelligent Systems for Sustainable Development (pp. 199-204). Cham: Springer Nature Switzerland.

Barron, L. (2021). The Road to a Smarter Future: The Smart City, Connected Cars and Autonomous Mobility, 2021 26th International Conference on Automation and Computing (ICAC), 1-6. DOI: 10.23919/ICAC50006.2021.9594125

Batchu, S. (2025). Cloud Infrastructure Fortification: Advanced Security Strategies in the Era of Emerging Threats. *International Journal of Scientific Research in Computer Science, Engineering and Information Technology*.

Beniiche, A. (2020). A study of blockchain oracles. arXiv preprint arXiv:2004.07140.

Berdibayev, R., Gnatyuk, S., Yevchenko, Y., & Kishchenko, V. (2021). A concept of the architecture and creation for siem system in critical infrastructure. In *Systems, Decision and Control in Energy II* (pp. 221–242). Springer International Publishing. DOI: 10.1007/978-3-030-69189-9_13

Bertucci, L. (2024). Bitcoin Ordinals: Determinants and impact on total transaction fees. Research in International Business and Finance, 70(A), 102338. DOI: 10.1016/j.ribaf.2024.102338

Bhardwaj, A. K., Dutta, P. K., & Chintale, P. (2024). AI-Powered Anomaly Detection for Kubernetes Security: A Systematic Approach to Identifying Threats. *Babylonian Journal of Machine Learning*, *2024*, 142–148. DOI: 10.58496/BJML/2024/014

Billady, R. K., & Rajlakshmi, P. V. (2024). A Novel Framework for AI-Driven, Cloud-Integrated Energy-Efficient IoT Solutions in Smart Homes. 2024 8th International Conference on Electronics, Communication and Aerospace Technology (ICECA), 327-332.

Bonneau, J., Miller, A., & Clark, J. (2015). Sok: Research Perspectives and Challenges for Bitcoin and Cryptocurrencies. *IEEE Symposium on Security and Privacy*. DOI: 10.1109/SP.2015.14

Breivold, H. P. (2017). Internet-of-Things and Cloud Computing for Smart Industry: A Systematic Mapping Study. 2017 5th International Conference on Enterprise Systems (ES), 299-304. DOI: 10.1109/ES.2017.56

Brundage, M., Avin, S., Wang, J., Belfield, H., & Krueger, G. (2018). The Malicious Use of Artificial Intelligence: Forecasting, Prevention, and Mitigation. ArXiv Preprint arXiv:1802.07228.

Buczak, A. L., & Guven, E. (2016). A Survey of Data Mining and Machine Learning Methods for Cybersecurity. *IEEE Communications Surveys and Tutorials*, *18*(2), 1153–1176. DOI: 10.1109/COMST.2015.2494502

Burhanuddin, M. A. (2023). Assessing the vulnerability of quantum cryptography systems to emerging cyber threats. *SHIFRA*, *2023*, 26–33. DOI: 10.70470/SHIFRA/2023/004

Burhanuddin, M. A. (2023). Secure and Scalable Quantum Cryptographic Algorithms for Next-Generation Computer Networks. *KHWARIZMIA*, *2023*, 95–102. DOI: 10.70470/KHWARIZMIA/2023/009

Buterin, V. (2014). Ethereum: A Next-Generation Smart Contract and Decentralized Application Platform.

Buterin, V. (2014). Ethereum: A Next-Generation Smart Contract and Decentralized Application Platform. *Ethereum White Paper*.

Camacho, N. G. (2024). The role of AI in cybersecurity: Addressing threats in the digital age. Journal of Artificial Intelligence General Science, 3(1), 143-154.

Capgemini. (2021). World Cybersecurity Report 2021: The State of Cyber Resilience in Critical Infrastructure. Retrieved from https://www.capgemini.com

Capgemini. (2025). World Cybersecurity Report 2025. Retrieved from https://www .capgemini.com

Carlo, A. (2023). The importance of cybersecurity frameworks to regulate emergent AI technologies for space applications. *The Journal of Space Safety Engineering*, *10*(4), 474–482. DOI: 10.1016/j.jsse.2023.08.002

Chandola, V. B., Banerjee, A., & Kumar, V. (2009). Anomaly Detection: A Survey. *ACM Computing Surveys*, *41*(3), 1–58. DOI: 10.1145/1541880.1541882

Chaudhary, G., Pathak, S., Choudhary, V., Chauhan, L., & Tripathi, A. N. (2024). Smart Surveillance Object Detection System. 2024 3rd International Conference on Artificial Intelligence For Internet of Things (AIIoT), 1-6. DOI: 10.1109/AIIoT58432.2024.10574574

Check Point Research. (2021). Cyber Attack Trends 2021: Ransomware and Beyond. Retrieved from https://www.checkpoint.com

Chesney, R. (2019). Deep Fakes: A Looming Challenge for Privacy, Democracy, and National Security. *California Law Review*.

Chowdhary, Y. S., & Singh, G. (2024). The Convergence of IoT and 5G: Transforming Connectivity in Smart City Applications. *2024 Second International Conference on Intelligent Cyber Physical Systems and Internet of Things (ICoICI)*, 311-318. DOI: 10.1109/ICoICI62503.2024.10696019

CISA, Australian Cyber Security Centre, NCSC-UK. (2021). Joint Cybersecurity Advisory: Ransomware trends and mitigation recommendations (AA22-040A). Retrieved from https://www.cisa.gov/news-events/cybersecurity-advisories/aa22-040a

CISA. (2025). Annual Cyber Incident Report 2025. Retrieved from https://www.cisa.gov

Cisco. (2022). Cisco 2022 Cybersecurity Report. Retrieved from https://www.cisco.com

Conti, M., Kumar, E. S., Lal, C., & Ruj, S. (2018). A survey on security and privacy issues of blockchain technology. *IEEE Communications Surveys and Tutorials, 21*(2), 1–21.

Coppolino, L., D'Antonio, S., Formicola, V., & Romano, L. (2013). Enhancing SIEM technology to protect critical infrastructures. In Critical Information Infrastructures Security: 7th International Workshop, CRITIS 2012, Lillehammer, Norway, September 17-18, 2012, Revised Selected Papers (pp. 10-21). Springer Berlin Heidelberg. DOI: 10.1007/978-3-642-41485-5_2

Cybersecurity and Infrastructure Security Agency (CISA). (2021). Attack on Colonial Pipeline: What was learned and follow-up actions [Advisory]. CISA. Retrieved from https://www.cisa.gov/news-events/news/attack-colonial-pipeline-what-weve-learned-what-weve-done-over-past-two-years

Cybersecurity and Infrastructure Security Agency. (2023). Annual Cyber Incident Report. Retrieved from https://www.cisa.gov

Dadvar, M., & Eckert, K. (2018). Cyberbullying detection in social networks using deep learning based models: A reproducibility study. *arXiv preprint arXiv:1812.08046.*

Dalvi, R. R., Chavan, S. B., & Halbe, A. (2020, May). Detecting a Twitter cyberbullying using machine learning. In *2020 4th International Conference on Intelligent Computing and Control Systems (ICICCS)* (pp. 297–301). IEEE.

Davarasan, A., Samual, J., Palansundram, K., & Ali, A. (2024). A Comprehensive Review of Machine Learning Approaches for Android Malware Detection. *Journal of Cyber Security and Risk Auditing, 2024*(1), 38–60. DOI: 10.63180/jcsra.thestap.2024.1.5

Deepa, V., & Jose, A. V. (2018). An Overview of Security in Internet of Things. *Procedia Computer Science*, 744–748.

Deloitte. (2021). Cyber Risk in Critical Infrastructure: A Deloitte Report. Retrieved from https://www2.deloitte.com

Deloitte. (2024). Cyber Risk in Critical Infrastructure 2024: A Global Perspective. Retrieved from https://www2.deloitte.com

Deloitte. (2025). Cyber Risk in Critical Infrastructure 2025. Retrieved from https://www2.deloitte.com

Desai, A., Kalaskar, S., Kumbhar, O., & Dhumal, R. (2021). Cyber bullying detection on social media using machine learning. In *ITM Web of Conferences* (Vol. 40, p. 03038). EDP Sciences.

Desai, A., & Desai, M. (2023). A review of the state of cybersecurity in the healthcare industry and propose security controls. *Mesopotamian Journal of Artificial Intelligence in Healthcare*, *2023*, 82–84. DOI: 10.58496/MJAIH/2023/016

Deshmukh, A., Mishra, A. K., Balamurugan, G., & Tyagi, A. K. (2023). Blockchain-empowered decentralized applications: Current trends and challenges. In *Privacy preservation of genomic and medical data* (Ch. 19). DOI: 10.1002/9781394213726.ch19

Dutta, P. K., Singh, B., Lal, S., Arora, M. K., Raghav, A., Mensah, G. B., & Alkattan, H. (2023). Encoding IoT for patient monitoring and smart healthcare: Connected healthcare system fostering health 6.0. *Babylonian Journal of Internet of Things*, *2023*, 48–58. DOI: 10.58496/BJIoT/2023/007

El Arass, M., & Souissi, N. (2019). Smart SIEM: From big data logs and events to smart data alerts. *International Journal of Innovative Technology and Exploring Engineering*, *8*(8), 3186–3191.

Ellis, S., Juels, A., & Nazarov, S. (2017). ChainLink: A Decentralized Oracle Network.

Elmaghraby, A. S. (2024). Cybersecurity Challenges in Smart Cities: Ethical and Legal Considerations. *Journal of Urban Technology*, 45-62.

ENISA. (2021). ENISA Threat Landscape Report 2021. Retrieved from https://www.enisa.europa.eu

ENISA. (2022). ENISA Threat Landscape 2022: Ransomware and threat trends. European Union Agency for Cybersecurity. Retrieved from https://www.enisa.europa.eu/publications/enisa-threat-landscape-2022

ENISA. (2022). Report on Ransomware Attacks in Europe. Retrieved from https://www.enisa.europa.eu

ENISA. (2023). *Threat Landscape for Smart Devices.*

ENISA. (2025). Threat Landscape Report 2025. Retrieved from https://www.enisa.europa.eu

European Banking Authority. (2021). Cyber Resilience in Critical Financial Infrastructure. Retrieved from https://www.eba.europa.eu

European Banking Authority. (2025). Cyber Resilience in Financial Infrastructure 2025. Retrieved from https://www.eba.europa.eu

European Commission. (2022). Cybersecurity for Critical Infrastructures in the EU: Trends and Policy Responses. Retrieved from https://ec.europa.eu

European Union Agency for Cybersecurity. (2022). Threat Landscape Report 2022. Retrieved from https://www.enisa.europa.eu

EUROPOL. (2025). EUROPOL. https://www.europol.europa.eu/crime-areas/cybercrime

Fang, X., Misra, S., Xue, G., & Yang, D. (2011). Smart grid—The new and improved power grid: A survey. *IEEE Communications Surveys and Tutorials*, *14*(4), 944–980. DOI: 10.1109/SURV.2011.101911.00087

FATF. (2025). The Financial Action Task Force (FATF). https://www.fatf-gafi.org/en/home.html

FBI Internet Crime Complaint Center (IC3). (2024). 2024 IC3 Annual Report (PDF). Federal Bureau of Investigation. Retrieved from https://www.ic3.gov/AnnualReport/Reports/2024_IC3Report.pdf

FBI Internet Crime Complaint Center. (2023). 2022 Internet Crime Report. Retrieved from https://www.ic3.gov

FBI Internet Crime Complaint Center. (2025). Internet Crime Report 2024. Retrieved from https://www.ic3.gov

Fielding, R. T. (2000). *Architectural Styles and the Design of Network-based Software Architectures*. University of California.

Finck, M. (2018). Blockchain and the General Data Protection Regulation: Can distributed ledgers be squared with European data protection law? *European Journal of Risk Regulation*, *9*(1), 27–46.

Floridi & Taddeo. (2016). What is data ethics? Philosophical Transactions of the Royal Society A: Mathematical, Physical and Engineering Sciences.

Forrester Research. (2021). Cybersecurity Strategies for Critical Infrastructure. Retrieved from https://www.forrester.com

Frank, J. (1994). Artificial intelligence and intrusion detection: Current and future directions. *Proceedings of the 17th national computer security conference*, 10.

Frederick, N., & Ali, A. (2024). Enhancing DDoS Attack Detection and Mitigation in SDN Using Advanced Machine Learning Techniques. *Journal of Cyber Security and Risk Auditing*, *2024*(1), 23–37. DOI: 10.63180/jcsra.thestap.2024.1.4

Frizzo-Barker, J., Chow-White, P. A., Adams, P. R., Mentanko, J., Ha, D., & Green, S. E. (2020). Blockchain as a disruptive technology for business: A systematic review. *International Journal of Information Management*, *51*, 102029. DOI: 10.1016/j.ijinfomgt.2019.10.014

Garg, P., & Sharma, R. (2024). Risk Management Using Derivatives: Review of Literature. *NATURALISTA CAMPANO*, *28*(1), 1432–1458.

Gartner. (2022). Gartner Predicts Cybersecurity Trends. Retrieved from https://www.gartner.com

Gartner. (2024). Gartner Cybersecurity Predictions 2024. Retrieved from https://www.gartner.com

Gartner. (2025). Cybersecurity Trends and Predictions 2025. Retrieved from https://www.gartner.com

Gasser, L. (2023). WEB3. In Mulder, V., Mermoud, A., Lenders, V., & Tellenbach, B. (Eds.), *Trends in Data Protection and Encryption Technologies*. Springer. DOI: 10.1007/978-3-031-33386-6_34

Gencoglu, O. (2020). Cyberbullying detection with fairness constraints. *IEEE Internet Computing*, *25*(1), 20–29.

George, A. S. (2024). Emerging Trends in AI-Driven Cybersecurity: An In-Depth Analysis. *Partners Universal Innovative Research Publication*, *2*(4), 15–28.

Ghafur, S., Kristensen, S., Honeyford, K., Martin, G., Darzi, A., & Aylin, P. (2019, October 2). A retrospective impact analysis of the WannaCry cyberattack on the NHS. *NPJ Digital Medicine*, *2*(1), 98. https://www.nature.com/articles/s41746-019-0161-6. DOI: 10.1038/s41746-019-0161-6 PMID: 31602404

González-Granadillo, G., González-Zarzosa, S., & Diaz, R. (2021). Security information and event management (SIEM): Analysis, trends, and usage in critical infrastructures. *Sensors (Basel)*, *21*(14), 4759. DOI: 10.3390/s21144759 PMID: 34300500

Gopalakrishnan, S., Ruby, E. D. K., Hemanand, D., Anitha, R., Suresh, D., & Choubey, S. B. (2024). Leveraging AI and Blockchain in MANETs to enhance Smart City Infrastructure and Autonomous Vehicular Networks. *Babylonian Journal of Machine Learning*, *2024*, 112–120. DOI: 10.58496/BJML/2024/011

Görmez, Y., Arslan, H., Işık, Y. E., & Dadaş, İ. E. (2023). A User and Entity Behavior Analysis for SIEM Systems: Preprocessing of The Computer Emergency and Response Team Dataset. *Journal of Soft Computing and Artificial Intelligence*, *4*(1), 1–6. DOI: 10.55195/jscai.1213782

Gujar, S. S., Shaikh, S. F., Shandilya, S., & Reddy, N. S. (2024). AI-Enhanced Cloud Security Framework for IoT Networks Using a Predictive Analytics Approach. 2024 3rd International Conference for Advancement in Technology (ICONAT), 1-8.

Gummadi, A. K., & Damacharla, P. (2024). An Intelligent Framework for Energy Management in IoT Networks Using Machine Learning. 2024 5th International Conference on Smart Electronics and Communication (ICOSEC), 765-771.

Hani, J., Nashaat, M., Ahmed, M., Emad, Z., Amer, E., & Mohammed, A. (2019). Social media cyberbullying detection using machine learning. *International Journal of Advanced Computer Science and Applications*, *10*(5), 703–707.

Haq, M. A., Rahim Khan, M. A., & Al-Harbi, T. (2022). Development of PCCNN-based network intrusion detection system for EDGE computing. *Computers, Materials & Continua*, *71*(1).

Hariharan, R., Tyagi, A. K., & Soni, G. (2023). A survey on blockchain–Internet of Things-based solutions. In *Privacy preservation and secured data storage in cloud computing*. IGI Global. DOI: 10.4018/979-8-3693-0593-5.ch005

He, D., Huang, J., & Ning, P. (2019). Cybersecurity and privacy in the smart grid: A survey. *IEEE Internet of Things Journal*, *6*(5), 8374–8387.

Hristov, M., Nenova, M., Iliev, G., & Avresky, D. (2021, November). Integration of splunk enterprise siem for ddos attack detection in IoT. In 2021 IEEE 20th International Symposium on Network Computing and Applications (NCA) (pp. 1-5). IEEE. DOI: 10.1109/NCA53618.2021.9685977

Hussain, L. (2024). Fortifying AI Against Cyber Threats Advancing Resilient Systems to Combat Adversarial Attacks. *EDRAAK*, *2024*, 26–31. DOI: 10.70470/EDRAAK/2024/004

Hwoij, A., Khamaiseh, A. H., & Ababneh, M. (2021, April). SIEM architecture for the Internet of Things and smart city. In International Conference on Data Science, E-learning and Information Systems 2021 (pp. 147-152). DOI: 10.1145/3460620.3460747

IBM Security X-Force. (2022). X-Force Threat Intelligence Index 2022. Retrieved from https://www.ibm.com/security

IBM Security X-Force. (2024). X-Force Threat Intelligence Index 2024. Retrieved from https://www.ibm.com/security

IBM Security X-Force. (2025). X-Force Threat Intelligence Index 2025. Retrieved from https://www.ibm.com/security

IBM. (2022). Cost of a Data Breach Report 2022. Retrieved from https://www.ibm.com/security/data-breach

Illakya, T., Keerthana, B., Murugan, K., Venkatesh, P., Manikandan, M., & Maran, K. (2024). The Role of the Internet of Things in the Telecom Sector. 2024 International Conference on Communication, Computing and Internet of Things (IC3IoT), 1-5. DOI: 10.1109/IC3IoT60841.2024.10550390

Incident. (2016). Mohamed El Metaafy (Doctoral dissertation, The University of Liverpool).

Ingole, B. S., Pandey, S., & Chandra, S. H. (2024). AI-Driven IoT Framework for Vehicle Accident Avoidance and Detection with Cloud Integrated Energy Efficient Solutions. *2024 First International Conference on Innovations in Communications, Electrical and Computer Engineering (ICICEC)*, 1-8.

International Energy Agency. (2022). Energy Security and Cyber Risk. Retrieved from https://www.iea.org

INTERPOL. (2025). INTERPOL. https://www.interpol.int/Crimes/Cybercrime

ISACA. (2022). Cybersecurity and Risk in Critical Infrastructure. Retrieved from https://www.isaca.org

Islam, M. M., Uddin, M. A., Islam, L., Akter, A., Sharmin, S., & Acharjee, U. K. (2020, December). Cyberbullying detection on social networks using machine learning approaches. In *2020 IEEE Asia-Pacific Conference on Computer Science and Data Engineering (CSDE)* (pp. 1–6). IEEE.

Jacobson, D., Brail, G., & Woods, D. (2011). *APIs: A Strategy Guide*. O'Reilly Media.

Jion, M. S. A., & Ahmad, M. (2024). A Smart and Secured Office System Using IoT. 2024 International Conference on Advances in Computing, Communication, Electrical, and Smart Systems (iCACCESS), 1-6. DOI: 10.1109/iCACCESS61735.2024.10499529

Jishkariani, M. (2024). Assessment of Cyber Security Risks in Electrical Engineering System of Georgia. *Mesopotamian Journal of Civil Engineering*, *2024*, 54–59. DOI: 10.58496/MJCE/2024/008

Justice, U. D. (2021). *U.S. Department of Justice*. CISA.

Kamuangu, P. (2024). A Review on Cybersecurity in Fintech: Threats, Solutions, and Future Trends. *Journal of Economics, Finance and Accounting Studies*.

Kareem, A. B. A. (2024). Modelling Of Blockchain Technology. *SHIFRA*, *2024*, 97–104. DOI: 10.70470/SHIFRA/2024/011

Kaspersky Lab. (2020). Kaspersky Security Bulletin 2020: Trends & Statistics. Retrieved from https://www.kaspersky.com

Kasri, W. A., Himeur, Y., Alkhazaleh, H. A., Tarapiah, S., Atalla, S., Mansoor, W., & Al-Ahmad, H. (2025). The Role of Large Language Models in Enhancing Cybersecurity. *Computation (Basel, Switzerland)*, *13*(2), 30. DOI: 10.3390/computation13020030

Kaumudhi, B. M., Sita Kumari, K., Sai, A. D., & Tejaswini, T. (2024). Smart Door Lock System using Facial Recognition with Home Automation. 2024 5th International Conference on Data Intelligence and Cognitive Informatics (ICDICI), 24-29. DOI: 10.1109/ICDICI62993.2024.10810778

Kavitha, T., Amirthayogam, G., Hephzipah, J. J., Suganthi, R., & Chelladurai, T. (2024). Healthcare analysis based on diabetes prediction using a cuckoo-based deep convolutional long-term memory algorithm. *Babylonian Journal of Artificial Intelligence*, *2024*, 64–72. DOI: 10.58496/BJAI/2024/009

Kedari, A., Singh, A., Kharche, G., & Mapari, R. (2023). Augmented Reality Enabled Internet of Things for Smart Visualisation in Applications. 2023 7th International Conference on Computing, Communication, Control and Automation (ICCUBEA), 1-7. DOI: 10.1109/ICCUBEA58933.2023.10392215

Keni, A., & Kini, M. (2020). Cyber-bullying detection using machine learning algorithms. *Computer Science. Psychology (Irvine, Calif.)*.

Khalaf, M. A., & Steiti, A. (2024). Artificial intelligence predictions in cyber security: Analysis and early detection of cyber attacks. *Babylonian Journal of Machine Learning*, *2024*, 63–68. DOI: 10.58496/BJML/2024/006

Khan, M. T., & Bibi, L. (2025). Cyberbullying in technological age: A review of legal laws. *Journal of Engineering, Science and Technological Trends*, *2*(1).

Khan, M. A. (2022). IoT security: Review, blockchain solutions, and open challenges. *Future Generation Computer Systems*, 395–411.

Khan, M. I., Arif, A., & Khan, A. R. A. (2024). AI-Driven Threat Detection: A Brief Overview of AI Techniques in Cybersecurity. BIN. *Bulletin of Informatics*, *2*(2), 248–261.

Khan, M. U., Abbas, A., Rehman, A., & Nawaz, R. (2020). Hateclassify: A service framework for hate speech identification on social media. *IEEE Internet Computing*, *25*(1), 40–49.

Khan, S., Al-Amin, M., Hossain, H., Noor, N., & Sadik, M. W. (2020). A pragmatical study on blockchain empowered decentralized application development platform. In *Proceedings of the International Conference on Computing Advancements* (pp. 1–9). ACM. DOI: 10.1145/3377049.3377136

Kharraz, A., Kline, K., Robertson, W., & Kirda, E. (2018). UNVEIL: A large-scale, automated approach to detecting ransomware. In NDSS 2018 (pp. 1–16). Retrieved from https://www.ndss-symposium.org

Khir, N. A. M., Malik, N. N. N. A., Latiff, N. M. A., Said, D. M., & Hamzah, S. A. (2019). Smart Micro-Grid Delivery Response System via Internet of Things. 2019 IEEE 14th Malaysia International Conference on Communication (MICC), 75-80. DOI: 10.1109/MICC48337.2019.9037590

Kodali, R. K., Soratkal, S., & Boppana, L. (2016). IOT based control of appliances. *2016 International Conference on Computing, Communication and Automation (ICCCA)*, 1293-1297. DOI: 10.1109/CCAA.2016.7813918

Kolias, C., Kambourakis, G., Stavrou, A., & Voas, J. (2017). DDoS in the IoT: Mirai and other botnets. Computer. *Computer*, *50*(7), 80–84. DOI: 10.1109/MC.2017.201

Kolosnjaji, B., Zarras, A., Webster, G., & Eckert, C. (2018). Deep Learning for Classification of Malware System Call Sequences. *Proceedings. IEEE Symposium on Security and Privacy. Workshops*, *2018*, 1–10.

Kshetri, N. (2021). *Blockchain and Sustainable Cybersecurity*. IEEE IT Professional.

Kumari, J. J. J., & Thangam, S. (2025). ERSA Enhanced RSA: Advanced security to overcome cyber-vulnerability. In *Advancing Cyber Security Through Quantum Cryptography* (pp. 413–440). IGI Global.

Kumari, S., & Muthulakshmi, P. (2023). Artificial intelligence—Blockchain enabled technology for Internet of Things: Research statements, open issues, and possible applications in the near future. In *Privacy preservation of genomic and medical data* (Ch. 18). DOI: 10.1002/9781394213726.ch18

Kumar, P., & Singh, P. (2019). Blockchain technology in supply chain management: Insights and implications. *International Journal of Information Management, 49*, 285–295.

Kumar, V. A., Renaldo Maximus, A., Vishnupriyan, S., Sheikdavood, K., & Gomathi, P. (2022). IoT and Artificial Intelligence-based Low-Cost Smart Modules for Smart Irrigation Systems. *2022 International Conference on Automation, Computing and Renewable Systems (ICACRS)*, 254-260. DOI: 10.1109/ICACRS55517.2022.10029299

Lin, I. C., & Liao, T. C. (2017). A survey of blockchain security issues and challenges. *International Journal of Network Security, 19*(5), 653–659.

Lippi, G., Aljawarneh, M., Al-Na'amneh, Q., Hazaymih, R., & Dhomeja, L. D. (2025). Security and privacy challenges and solutions in autonomous driving systems: A comprehensive review. *Journal of Cyber Security and Risk Auditing, 2025*(3), 23–41. DOI: 10.63180/jcsra.thestap.2025.3.3

López Velásquez, J. M., Martínez Monterrubio, S. M., Sánchez Crespo, L. E., & Garcia Rosado, D. (2023). Systematic review of SIEM technology: SIEM-SC birth. *International Journal of Information Security, 22*(3), 691–711. DOI: 10.1007/s10207-022-00657-9

Luiijf, E. (2012). *Understanding cyber threats and vulnerabilities. Critical Infrastructure Protection: Information Infrastructure Models.*

MacDonald, M., Pike, D., & Pike, R. (2020). Exploring Depth in Cybersecurity Education Through the Lens of a SIEM. In 2020 Proceedings of the EDSIG Conference ISSN (pp. 2473-4901).

Mahajan, S. (2023). Phishing uniform resource locator detection using machine learning: A step towards secure system. *Security and Privacy, 6*(6), e311. DOI: 10.1002/spy2.311

Mahajan, S., & Malhotra, J. (2011). Enhanced chain technique based data collection sensor network. *International Journal of Computational Science, 8*(3), 83–87.

Mahesh, K., Gothane, S., Toshniwal, A., Nagarale, V., & Gopu, H. (2021). Cyber bullying detection on social media using machine learning. *International Journal of Scientific Research in Computer Science. Engineering and Information Technology, 3307*, 410–416.

Malik, S. (2024). Using AI for Behavioral Analytics in Cybersecurity: Detecting Anomalies and Insider Threats. Academic Press.

Manda, J. K. (2024). AI-powered Threat Intelligence Platforms in Telecom: Leveraging AI for Real-time Threat Detection and Intelligence Gathering in Telecom Network Security Operations. DOI: 10.2139/ssrn.5003638

Mane, V. S., Pandharipande, M. M., Joshi, H. J., & Kotalwar, S. S. (2021). Manual, Internet and Bluetooth all-in-one Smart Home (MIB-AIO). *2021 International Conference on Computational Intelligence and Knowledge Economy (ICCIKE)*, 187-191. DOI: 10.1109/ICCIKE51210.2021.9410775

Martín, , A., Fernández-Isabel, A., Martín de Diego, I., & Beltrán, M. (2021). A survey for user behavior analysis based on machine learning techniques: Current models and applications. *Applied Intelligence*, *51*(8), 6029–6055. DOI: 10.1007/s10489-020-02160-x

McAfee Labs. (2022). McAfee Labs Threats Report. Retrieved from https://www.mcafee.com

McKinsey & Company. (2021). The Cybersecurity Imperative for Critical Infrastructure. Retrieved from https://www.mckinsey.com

Mensah, G. B., Mijwil, M. M., Abotaleb, M., Ali, G., Dutta, P. K., Mzili, T., & Eid, M. M. (2025). Explainable AI for Healthcare: Training Healthcare Workers to Use Artificial Intelligence Techniques to Reduce Medical Negligence in Ghana's Public Health Act, 2012 (Act 851). *EDRAAK*, *2025*, 1–6. DOI: 10.70470/EDRAAK/2025/001

Mhana, A., Jabor, F. K., Omran, G. A., Tawfeq, J. F., Radhi, A. D., Harpale, V. K., Bachute, M., Shah, P., & Sekhar, R. (2025). Strengthening cloud data protection based on a novel cyber security framework. *Applied Data Science and Analysis*, *2025*, 155–164. DOI: 10.58496/ADSA/2025/013

Miller, C. (2015). Remote Exploitation of an Unaltered Passenger Vehicle. Academic Press.

Ministry of Electronics and IT (MeitY). (2022). *Ministry of Electronics and IT (MeitY)*. Government of India.

Minoli, D., Sohraby, K., & Occhiogrosso, B. (2017, February). IoT Considerations, Requirements, and Architectures for Smart Buildings—Energy Optimization and Next-Generation Building Management Systems. *IEEE Internet of Things Journal*, *4*(1), 269–283. DOI: 10.1109/JIOT.2017.2647881

Mishra, A. (2025). Ai-Powered Cybersecurity Framework for Secure Data Transmission in Iot Network. International Journal of Advances in Engineering and Management, 7(3), 5-13.

Mohammed, S. Y., & Aljanabi, M. (2023). Human-Centric IoT for Health Monitoring in the Healthcare 5.0 FrameworkDescriptive Analysis and Directions for Future Research. *EDRAAK, 2023*, 21–26. DOI: 10.70470/EDRAAK/2023/005

Moharrer, M. M., & Nogoorani, S. D. (2020, September). A decentralized App Store using the blockchain technology. In 2020 17th International ISC Conference on Information Security and Cryptology (ISCISC) (pp. 14-21). IEEE. DOI: 10.1109/ISCISC51277.2020.9261911

Mohurle, S., & Patil, M. (2018). Cyber security in the smart grid: Threats, vulnerabilities, and countermeasures. *IEEE Potentials*, *37*(2), 22–29.

Mokalled, H., Catelli, R., Casola, V., Debertol, D., Meda, E., & Zunino, R. (2019, June). The applicability of a siem solution: Requirements and evaluation. In 2019 IEEE 28th International Conference on Enabling Technologies: Infrastructure for Collaborative Enterprises (WETICE) (pp. 132-137). IEEE.

Montesino, R., Fenz, S., & Baluja, W. (2012). SIEM-based framework for security controls automation. *Information Management & Computer Security*, *20*(4), 248–263. DOI: 10.1108/09685221211267639

Morovat, K., & Panda, B. (2020, December). A survey of artificial intelligence in cybersecurity. In *2020 International conference on computational science and computational intelligence (CSCI)* (pp. 109-115). IEEE DOI: 10.1109/CSCI51800.2020.00026

Moubarak, G., Chamoun, M., & Lahoud, S. (2020). Cybersecurity challenges in blockchain technology. *Journal of Cybersecurity Technology*, *4*(3), 157–181.

Mousa, R. S., & Shehab, R. (2025). Applying risk analysis for determining threats and countermeasures in workstation domain. *Journal of Cyber Security and Risk Auditing*, *2025*(1), 12–21. DOI: 10.63180/jcsra.thestap.2025.1.2

Nair, M. M., & Tyagi, A. K. (2023). Blockchain technology for next-generation society: Current trends and future opportunities for smart era. In *Blockchain technology for secure social media computing* (Ch. 11). DOI: 10.1049/PBSE019E_ch11

Nakamoto, S. (2008). Bitcoin: A Peer-to-Peer Electronic Cash System. Retrieved from https://bitcoin.org/bitcoin.pdf

Nakamoto, S. (2009). Bitcoin: A Peer-to-Peer Electronic Cash System.

National Audit Office (NAO). (2017). Investigation: WannaCry cyber attack and the NHS (Report). Retrieved from https://www.nao.org.uk/wp-content/uploads/2017/10/Investigation-WannaCry-cyber-attack-and-the-NHS.pdf

National Cyber Security Centre. (2021). NCSC Annual Review 2021. Retrieved from https://www.ncsc.gov.uk

National Institute of Standards and Technology. (2021). Framework for Improving Critical Infrastructure Cybersecurity, Version 1.1. Retrieved from https://www.nist.gov

National Institute of Standards and Technology. (2022). NIST Cybersecurity Framework: A Framework for Improving Critical Infrastructure Cybersecurity. Retrieved from https://www.nist.gov

Nay, T. (2024). Enhancing IoT Security with AI-Driven Hybrid Machine Learning and Neural Network-Based Intrusion Detection System. *Babylonian Journal of Artificial Intelligence*, *2024*, 158–167. DOI: 10.58496/BJAI/2024/017

NIST. (2024). *IoT Device Cybersecurity Guidance.*

NIST. (2025). Cybersecurity Framework: Next-Generation Update. Retrieved from https://www.nist.gov

Nizam, S., Matta, P., Kukreti, S., Upadhyay, R., & Dangwal, G. (2024, February). Cyberbullying: Research challenges and opportunities. In *2024 IEEE International Conference on Computing, Power and Communication Technologies (IC2PCT)* (Vol. 5, pp. 938–943). IEEE.

OECD. (2021). Economic Policy Reforms 2021: Ransomware and Critical Infrastructure. Retrieved from https://www.oecd.org

OECD. (2024). Economic Policy Reforms 2024: Cybersecurity and Critical Infrastructure. Retrieved from https://www.oecd.org

OECD. (2025). Economic Impact of Cyber Attacks on Critical Infrastructure 2025. Retrieved from https://www.oecd.org

Ohm, P. (2010). Broken Promises of Privacy: Responding to the Surprising Failure of Anonymization. *UCLA Law Review. University of California, Los Angeles. School of Law*.

Omolara Patricia Olaiya, T. (2024). Cybersecurity strategies in fintech: safeguarding financial data and assets. *GSC Advanced Research and Reviews (GSCARR)*, 1-20.

Omotunde, H., & Mouhamed, M. R. (2023). The modern impact of artificial intelligence systems in healthcare: A concise analysis. *Mesopotamian Journal of Artificial Intelligence in Healthcare*, *2023*, 66–70. DOI: 10.58496/MJAIH/2023/013

Orel, D., & Guseva, T. (2022). Safety Monitoring of the Automated City Water Supply Management System Based on PSIM and SIEM Systems. In CEUR Workshop Proceedings (pp. 127-136).

Otoom, S. (2025). Risk auditing for Digital Twins in cyber physical systems: A systematic review. *Journal of Cyber Security and Risk Auditing*, *2025*(1), 22–35. DOI: 10.63180/jcsra.thestap.2025.1.3

Oyinloye, D. P., Teh, J. S., Jamil, N., & Alawida, M. (2021). Blockchain consensus: An overview of alternative protocols. *Symmetry*, *13*(8), 1363. DOI: 10.3390/sym13081363

Papernot, N. e. (2016). The Limitations of Deep Learning in Adversarial Settings. *IEEE Symposium on Security and Privacy*. DOI: 10.1109/EuroSP.2016.36

Patel, S. (2019). Data Masking Techniques for Privacy Preservation in Big Data. *IEEE Access : Practical Innovations, Open Solutions*.

Pautasso, C., Zimmermann, O., & Leymann, F. (2008). Restful Web Services vs. "Big" Web Services: Making the Right Architectural Decision. *17th International World Wide Web Conference*. DOI: 10.1145/1367497.1367606

Perera, A., & Fernando, P. (2021). Accurate cyberbullying detection and prevention on social media. *Procedia Computer Science*, *181*, 605–611.

Petit, J. (2015). Potential Cyberattacks on Automated Vehicles. *IEEE Transactions on Intelligent Transportation Systems*.

Ponemon Institute. (2021). Cost of a Data Breach Report 2021. Retrieved from https://www.ponemon.org

Porras, E., & Daugherty, B. (2022). Bitcoin and Ethics in a Technological Society. IntechOpen. DOI: 10.5772/intechopen.96798

Praveen, R. (2023). Improved Gentry–Halevi's Fully Homomorphic Encryption-Based Privacy Scheme. *Transactions on Emerging Telecommunications Technologies*. Advance online publication. DOI: 10.1002/ett.4732

Prince, N. U., Faheem, M. A., Khan, O. U., Hossain, K., Alkhayyat, A., Hamdache, A., & Elmouki, I. (2024). AI-powered data-driven cybersecurity techniques: Boosting threat identification and reaction. *Nanotechnology Perceptions*, *20*, 332–353.

Puthal, D., Malik, N., Mohanty, S. P., Kougianos, E., & Yang, C. (2018). The blockchain as a decentralized security framework. *IEEE Consumer Electronics Magazine*, *7*(2), 18–21. DOI: 10.1109/MCE.2017.2776459

PwC. (2021). Global Economic Impact of Cyber Attacks on Critical Infrastructure. Retrieved from https://www.pwc.com

Radoglou-Grammatikis, P., Sarigiannidis, P., Iturbe, E., Rios, E., Martinez, S., Sarigiannidis, A., & Ramos, F. (2021). Spear siem: A security information and event management system for the smart grid. *Computer Networks*, *193*, 108008. DOI: 10.1016/j.comnet.2021.108008

Rahwan, I., Cebrian, M., Obradovich, N., Bongard, J., Bonnefon, J.-F., Breazeal, C., Crandall, J. W., Christakis, N. A., Couzin, I. D., Jackson, M. O., Jennings, N. R., Kamar, E., Kloumann, I. M., Larochelle, H., Lazer, D., McElreath, R., Mislove, A., Parkes, D. C., Pentland, A. S., & Wellman, M. (2019). Machine Behaviour. *Nature*, *568*(7753), 477–486. DOI: 10.1038/s41586-019-1138-y PMID: 31019318

Raji, I. D., Gebru, T., Mitchell, M., & Buolamwini, J. (2020). Saving Face: Investigating the Ethical Concerns of Automated Facial Analysis Systems. *Proceedings of the ACM Conference on Fairness, Accountability, and Transparency*, 1-12.

Raj, M., Singh, S., Solanki, K., & Selvanambi, R. (2022). An application to detect cyberbullying using machine learning and deep learning techniques. *SN Computer Science*, *3*(5), 401.

Rantanen, O. (2024). Attracting the APT actors into deception system: identifying ways to attract an APT actor.

Rauchs, M., Glidden, A., Gordon, B., Pieters, G. C., Recanatini, M., Rostand, F., Vagneur, K., & Zhang, B. Z. (2018). Distributed ledger technology systems: A conceptual framework. SSRN *Electronic Journal*. https://doi.org/DOI: 10.2139/ssrn.3230013

Raza, A., Qadeer, M. A., Tariq, Z., Ahmed, Z., Yousaf, S., & Shah, A. (2020). Smart Assistance for Disables using Bluetooth and Arduino. 2020 IEEE 7th International Conference on Engineering Technologies and Applied Sciences (ICETAS), 1-4. DOI: 10.1109/ICETAS51660.2020.9484245

Reddy, M. (2011). *API Design for C*. Elsevier.

Richardson, J., Sallam, R., Schlegel, K., Kronz, A., & Sun, J. (2020). Magic quadrant for analytics and business intelligence platforms. Gartner ID G00386610.

Rikhtechi, L., Rafe, V., & Rezakhani, A. (2021). Secured access control in security information and event management systems. *Journal of Information Systems and Telecommunication*, *9*(33), 67–78. DOI: 10.52547/jist.9.33.67

Rizal, S., & Nair, R. (2021). Legal implications of smart contracts: Decentralization and enforceability. *Journal of Legal Technology Risk*, *3*(1), 45–60.

Roy, R., Sen, H., Roy, I., Paul, R., Akthar, F., & Barman, U. (2024). Cloud-Enabled Voice Control for Home Appliances: A Secure and Accessible IoT Approach. 2024 IEEE 4th International Conference on Applied Electromagnetics, Signal Processing, & Communication (AESPC), 1-5. DOI: 10.1109/AESPC63931.2024.10872037

Russell, S., & Norvig, P. (2020). *Artificial Intelligence: A Modern Approach* (4th ed.). Pearson.

Saberi, S., Kouhizadeh, M., Sarkis, J., & Shen, L. (2018). Blockchain technology and its relationships to sustainable supply chain management. *International Journal of Production Research*, *57*(7), 2117–2135. DOI: 10.1080/00207543.2018.1533261

Safour, R. A. (2024). Electrochemical nitrogen reduction: Towards efficient ammonia production. *Khwarizmia*, *2024*, 1–3. DOI: 10.70470/KHWARIZMIA/2024/001

Saleh, H. M. (2024). A Comprehensive Review of Data Mining Techniques for Diabetes Diagnosis Using the Pima Indian Diabetes Dataset. *EDRAAK*, *2024*, 39–42. DOI: 10.70470/EDRAAK/2024/006

Saleh, H. M., Oleiwi, A. K., & Abed, A. A. H. (2023). Detecting attacks in banks by cyber security: An applied study. *Babylonian Journal of Machine Learning*, *2023*, 65–72. DOI: 10.58496/BJML/2023/011

Salem, A. H., Azzam, S. M., Emam, O. E., & Abohany, A. A. (2024). Advancing cybersecurity: A comprehensive review of AI-driven detection techniques. *Journal of Big Data*, *11*(1), 105. DOI: 10.1186/s40537-024-00957-y

Salih, H. M., & Mahmood, A. M. (2024). A electric vehicle blockchain: Problems and opportunities. *Babylonian Journal of Networking*, *2024*, 18–24. DOI: 10.58496/BJN/2024/003

Sallam, M., Al-Mahzoum, K., & Sallam, M. (2024). Generative Artificial Intelligence and Cybersecurity Risks: Implications for Healthcare Security Based on Real-life Incidents. *Mesopotamian Journal of Artificial Intelligence in Healthcare*, *2024*, 184–203. DOI: 10.58496/MJAIH/2024/019

SANS Institute. (2021). Critical Infrastructure Cybersecurity: Strategies and Challenges. Retrieved from https://www.sans.org

Sarker, I. H. (2024). Introduction to AI-Driven Cybersecurity and Threat Intelligence. In *AI-Driven Cybersecurity and Threat Intelligence: Cyber Automation, Intelligent Decision-Making and Explainability* (pp. 3–19). Springer Nature Switzerland. DOI: 10.1007/978-3-031-54497-2_1

Sarker, I. H., Furhad, M. H., & Nowrozy, R. (2021). Ai-driven cybersecurity: An overview, security intelligence modeling and research directions. *SN Computer Science*, *2*(3), 3. DOI: 10.1007/s42979-021-00557-0

Sarsam, S. M. (2023). Cybersecurity challenges in autonomous vehicles: Threats, vulnerabilities, and mitigation strategies. *SHIFRA*, *2023*, 34–42. DOI: 10.70470/SHIFRA/2023/005

Schinckus, C. (2021). Proof-of-work based blockchain technology and Anthropocene: An undermined situation? *Renewable & Sustainable Energy Reviews*, *52*, 111682. DOI: 10.1016/j.rser.2021.111682

Security, I. (2022). *The Role of AI in Cybersecurity*. IBM X-Force Threat Intelligence.

Sekharan, S. S., & Kandasamy, K. (2017, March). Profiling SIEM tools and correlation engines for security analytics. In *2017 International Conference on Wireless Communications, Signal Processing and Networking (WiSPNET)* (pp. 717-721). IEEE. DOI: 10.1109/WiSPNET.2017.8299855

Shaghaghi, A. S. (2023). A Review of Emerging Cyber Threats in Smart City Environments. *Computers & Security*.

Shahana, A., Hasan, R., Farabi, S. F., Akter, J., Mahmud, M. A. A., Johora, F. T., & Suzer, G. (2024). AI-driven cybersecurity: Balancing advancements and safeguards. *Journal of Computer Science and Technology Studies*, *6*(2), 76–85. DOI: 10.32996/jcsts.2024.6.2.9

Shankar, V. R., Suchitra, S., Pavithra, B., Rajendran, P. S., Sophia, S. G. G., & Leo, M. J. (2020). Energy Optimization for Smart Home Automation in Multi-Cloud Environment. *2020 International Conference on Inventive Computation Technologies (ICICT)*, 534-539. DOI: 10.1109/ICICT48043.2020.9112537

Sharma, J., & Sharma, S. (2024). Sustainable Solar Powered Bluetooth Enabled Smart Home Automation System Using Internet-of-Things. 2024 IEEE International Conference on Communication, Computing and Signal Processing (IICCCS), 1-6. DOI: 10.1109/IICCCS61609.2024.10763780

Sharma, S., & Mahajan, S. (2017). Design and implementation of a security scheme for detecting system vulnerabilities. International journal of computer network and information security, 9(10), 24.

Sharma, V., Vashishth, T. K., Tiwari, D., Sethi, P., & Sharma, S. (2025, April). Enhancing cybersecurity: A machine learning approach for phishing website detection. In AIP Conference Proceedings (Vol. 3278, No. 1). AIP Publishing. DOI: 10.1063/5.0261903

Sheeraz, M., Paracha, M. A., Haque, M. U., Durad, M. H., Mohsin, S. M., Band, S. S., & Mosavi, A. (2023). Effective security monitoring using efficient SIEM architecture. Hum.-. *Centric Comput. Inf. Sci*, *13*, 1–18.

Singh, N., & Kumar, S. (2025, March). AI-Driven Cybersecurity Strategies for ISPs: Balancing Threat Mitigation and Monetization. In International Conference on Cyber Warfare and Security (pp. 689-698). Academic Conferences International Limited.

Singh, A., Click, K., Parizi, R. M., Zhang, Q., Dehghantanha, A., & Choo, K. K. R. (2020). Sidechain technologies in blockchain networks: An examination and state-of-the-art review. *Journal of Network and Computer Applications*, *149*, 102471. DOI: 10.1016/j.jnca.2019.102471

Singh, K. (2020). *Application of SIEM/UEBA/SOAR/SOC (Cyber SUSS) Concepts on MSCS 6560 Computer Lab*. Marquette University.

Spasovski, J., & Eklund, P. (2017). Proof of Stake Blockchain: Performance and Scalability for Groupware Communications. In *Proceedings of the 9th International Conference on Management of Digital EcoSystems (MEDES '17)*. Association for Computing Machinery. DOI: 10.1145/3167020.3167058

Sridhar, S., Hahn, A., & Govindarasu, M. (2018). Cyber–physical system security for the electric power grid. *Proceedings of the IEEE*, *106*(5), 846–867. PMID: 30559531

Srinivasan, K. R., Mallikarjuna, B., Kavitha, M., Kavitha, R., & Naib, B. B. (2022). A Comparative Study: Wireless Technologies in Internet of Things. 2022 2nd International Conference on Advance Computing and Innovative Technologies in Engineering (ICACITE), 675-679. DOI: 10.1109/ICACITE53722.2022.9823664

Symantec Corporation. (2019). Internet Security Threat Report. Retrieved from https://www.symantec.com/security-center/threat-report

Tapscott, D., & Tapscott, A. (2016). *Blockchain Revolution: How the Technology Behind Bitcoin is Changing Money, Business, and the World*. Penguin.

The Cyber Readiness Institute. (2022). Cybersecurity for Critical Infrastructure: A Maturity Model. Retrieved from https://www.cyberreadinessinstitute.org

The Cyber Readiness Institute. (2025). Cybersecurity for Critical Infrastructure: Updated Maturity Model 2025. Retrieved from https://www.cyberreadinessinstitute.org

Thepa, T., Ateetanan, P., Khubpatiwitthayakul, P., & Fugkeaw, S. (2024, June). Design and Development of Scalable SIEM as a Service using Spark and Anomaly Detection. In 2024 21st International Joint Conference on Computer Science and Software Engineering (JCSSE) (pp. 199-205). IEEE. DOI: 10.1109/JCSSE61278.2024.10613640

Tironsakkul, T., Maarek, M., Eross, A., & Just, M. (2019). Probing the mystery of cryptocurrency theft: an investigation into methods for taint analysis. arXiv preprint arXiv:1906.05754.

Tripathi, G., Ahad, M. A., & Casalino, G. (2023). A comprehensive review of blockchain technology: Underlying principles and historical background with future challenges. *Decision Analytics Journal*, *9*, 100344. DOI: 10.1016/j.dajour.2023.100344

TRON DAO. (2018). TRON: Advanced Decentralized Blockchain Platform. Whitepaper. https://tron.network/static/doc/white_paper_v_2_0.pdf

Tsankov, V., Evstatiev, B., & Valova, I. (2024). Concept for an IoT-based Electronic System for Smart Home Automation. 2024 9th International Conference on Energy Efficiency and Agricultural Engineering (EE&AE), 1-5. DOI: 10.1109/EEAE60309.2024.10600500

Tyagi, A. K. (2022). SecVT: Securing the vehicles of tomorrow using blockchain technology. In A. A. Sk, T. Turki, T. K. Ghosh, S. Joardar, & S. Barman (Eds.), *Artificial intelligence* (Vol. 1695, pp. 122–137). Springer. DOI: 10.1007/978-3-031-22485-0_11

Tyagi, A. K., Kumari, S., Chidambaram, N., & Sharma, A. (2024). Engineering applications of blockchain in this smart era. In *Enhancing medical imaging with emerging technologies* (Ch. 11). DOI: 10.4018/979-8-3693-5261-8.ch011

Tyagi, A. K. (2023). Decentralized everything: Practical use of blockchain technology in future applications. In Pandey, R., Goundar, S., & Fatima, S. (Eds.), *Distributed computing to blockchain* (pp. 19–38). Academic Press. DOI: 10.1016/B978-0-323-96146-2.00010-3

Tyagi, A. K., Kukreja, S., Richa, , & Sivakumar, P. (2024). Role of blockchain technology in smart era: A review on possible smart applications. *Journal of Information & Knowledge Management*, *23*(1), 2450032. Advance online publication. DOI: 10.1142/S0219649224500321

U.S. Department of Energy, Office of Cybersecurity, Energy Security, and Emergency Response (CESER). (2021). Colonial Pipeline cyber incident summary and implications. U.S. Department of Energy. Retrieved from https://www.energy.gov/ceser/colonial-pipeline-cyber-incident

U.S. Department of Energy. (2021). Cybersecurity for Energy Delivery Systems. Retrieved from https://www.energy.gov

U.S. Department of Homeland Security. (2021). Securing Critical Infrastructure Against Cyber Threats. Retrieved from https://www.dhs.gov

U.S. Department of Water Resources. (2021). Enhancing Cybersecurity in Water Infrastructure. Retrieved from https://www.usbr.gov

U.S. Government Accountability Office. (2021). Cybersecurity: Agencies Have Implemented Key Actions to Address Ransomware Risks. Retrieved from https://www.gao.gov/products/gao-21-123

UK National Cyber Security Centre. (2022). Cyber Threats to Critical Infrastructure. Retrieved from https://www.ncsc.gov.uk

UK National Cyber Security Centre. (2025). Cyber Threats to Critical Infrastructure: Annual Review 2025. Retrieved from https://www.ncsc.gov.uk

Ünal, U., Kahya, C. N., Kurtlutepe, Y., & Dağ, H. (2021, September). Investigation of cyber situation awareness via SIEM tools: a constructive review. In 2021 6th International Conference on Computer Science and Engineering (UBMK) (pp. 676-681). IEEE. DOI: 10.1109/UBMK52708.2021.9558964

Upadhyay, A., Mukhuty, S., Kumar, P., & Kazançoğlu, Y. (2021). Blockchain technology and the circular economy: Implications for sustainability and social responsibility. *Journal of Cleaner Production*, *293*, 126130. DOI: 10.1016/j.jclepro.2021.126130

Vaigandla, K. K. (2025). An Extensive Examination on IOT and Industrial IOT: Attacks, Security, Detection Methods, Blockchain Solutions and Challenges. *Babylonian Journal of Internet of Things*, *2025*, 89–100. DOI: 10.58496/BJIoT/2025/004

Vashishth, T. K., Sharma, V., Kaushik, V., & Sharma, K. K. (2025). Blockchain-Driven Innovations in the Banking and Financial Sectors: Harnessing the Power of Automated Machine Learning. In Utilizing AI and Machine Learning in Financial Analysis (pp. 555-578). IGI Global Scientific Publishing.

Vashishth, T. K., Sharma, V., Kaushik, V., Singh, A., & Kaushik, S. (2025). Exploring Quantum Challenges and Opportunities of Quantum Machine Learning Adoption in Finance. Machine Learning and Modeling Techniques in Financial Data Science, 437-460.

Vashishth, T. K., Sharma, V., Kumar, B., & Sharma, K. K. (2024). Cloud-Based Data Management for Behavior Analytics in Business and Finance Sectors. In Data-Driven Modelling and Predictive Analytics in Business and Finance (pp. 133-155). Auerbach Publications. DOI: 10.1201/9781032618845-9

Vashishth, T. K., Sharma, V., Kumar, B., Sharma, K. K., Chaudhary, S., & Panwar, R. (2025). Blockchain for Securing Federated Learning Systems: Enhancing Privacy and Trust. Model Optimization Methods for Efficient and Edge AI: Federated Learning Architectures, Frameworks and Applications, 299-320.

Vashishth, T. K., Sharma, V., Samania, B., Sharma, R., Singh, S., & Jajoria, P. (2025). Ethical and Legal Implications of AI in Cybersecurity. In Machine Intelligence Applications in Cyber-Risk Management (pp. 387-414). IGI Global Scientific Publishing.

Vashishth, T. K., Sharma, V., Sharma, K. K., Kumar, B., Chaudhary, S., & Panwar, R. (2024). Enhancing Cloud Security: The Role of Artificial Intelligence and Machine Learning. In Improving Security, Privacy, and Trust in Cloud Computing (pp. 85-112). IGI Global.

Vashishth, T. K., Sharma, V., Sharma, K. K., Kumar, B., Chaudhary, S., & Panwar, R. (2024). Intelligent Resource Allocation and Optimization for Industrial Robotics Using AI and Blockchain. In AI and Blockchain Applications in Industrial Robotics (pp. 82-110). IGI Global.

Vashishth, T. K., Sharma, V., Sharma, K. K., Kumar, B., Chaudhary, S., & Panwar, R. (2024). Security and Privacy Challenges in Blockchain-Based Supply Chain Management: A Comprehensive Analysis. In Achieving Secure and Transparent Supply Chains With Blockchain Technology (pp. 70-91). IGI Global. DOI: 10.4018/979-8-3693-0482-2.ch005

Vashishth, T. K., Kumar, B., Alam, M. S., Sharma, V., & Chaudhary, S. (2024). The Impact of Artificial Intelligence on the Future of Computing: A Comparative Study. In *Applications of Block Chain technology and Artificial Intelligence: Lead-ins in Banking, Finance, and Capital Market* (pp. 1–17). Springer International Publishing. DOI: 10.1007/978-3-031-47324-1_1

Vashishth, T. K., Sharma, V., Kaushik, V., Bagar, V. K., Sharma, R., & Kumar, R. (2025). Importance of Using AI and ML in the Financial Sector for Risk Prevention and Management. In *Utilizing AI and Machine Learning in Financial Analysis* (pp. 509–530). IGI Global Scientific Publishing.

Ventures, C. (2023). *Cybercrime Report.*

Verizon. (2022). Verizon Data Breach Investigations Report. Retrieved from https://www.verizon.com/business/resources/reports/dbir/

Verizon. (2024). Verizon Data Breach Investigations Report 2024. Retrieved from https://www.verizon.com/business/resources/reports/dbir/

Verizon. (2025). Verizon Data Breach Investigations Report 2025. Retrieved from https://www.verizon.com/business/resources/reports/dbir/

Vinayakumar, R., Alazab, M., Soman, K. P., Poornachandran, P., Al-Nemrat, A., & Venkatraman, S. (2019). Deep learning approach for intelligent intrusion detection system. *IEEE Access : Practical Innovations, Open Solutions*, *7*, 41525–41550. DOI: 10.1109/ACCESS.2019.2895334

Waizel, G. (2024, July). Bridging the AI divide: The evolving arms race between AI-driven cyber-attacks and AI-powered cybersecurity defenses. In International Conference on Machine Intelligence & Security for Smart Cities (TRUST). *Proceedings*, *1*, 141–156.

Wang, Q., Li, R., Wang, Q., & Chen, S. (2021). Non-Fungible Token (NFT): Overview, Evaluation, Opportunities and Challenges. arXiv preprint.

Welukar, J. N., & Bajoria, G. P. (2021). Artificial Intelligence in Cyber Security-A Review. *International Journal of Scientific Research in Science and Technology*, *488*, 488–491. DOI: 10.32628/IJSRST218675

World Economic Forum. (2021). Global Risks Report 2021: Cybersecurity and Critical Infrastructure. Retrieved from https://www.weforum.org

World Economic Forum. (2021). Global Standards for Blockchain Technology: Enhancing trust and interoperability. Retrieved from https://www.weforum.org

Wulandari, P. D., Pramartha, C., Bakta, I. M., & Wulanyani, N. M. S. (2024, April). Utilizing technology to detect bullying in the workplace: A systematic review. In *Proceedings of the 2024 10th International Conference on Computing and Artificial Intelligence* (pp. 415–418).

Xu, X., Weber, I., & Staples, M. (2021). *Architecture for Blockchain Applications*. Springer.

Yaga, D., Mell, P., Roby, N., & Scarfone, K. (2018). *Blockchain Technology Overview*. National Institute of Standards and Technology. DOI: 10.6028/NIST.IR.8202

Yan, Y., Qian, Y., Sharif, H., & Tipper, D. (2018). A survey on cyber security for smart grid communications. *IEEE Communications Surveys and Tutorials*, *14*(4), 998–1010. DOI: 10.1109/SURV.2012.010912.00035

Yaseen, A. (2023). AI-driven threat detection and response: A paradigm shift in cybersecurity. *International Journal of Information and Cybersecurity*, *7*(12), 25–43.

Yudhianto, I. (2023). Simple, Fast, and Accurate Cybercrime Detection on E-Government with Elastic Stack SIEM. *JEPIN*, *9*(2), 263–276. DOI: 10.26418/jp.v9i2.64213

Zaman, D., & Mazinani, M. (2023). Cybersecurity in smart grids: Protecting critical infrastructure from cyber attacks. *SHIFRA*, *2023*, 86–94. DOI: 10.70470/SHIFRA/2023/010

Zhang, Y. W. (2023). A blockchain-based tamper-proof framework for secure smart grid communication. *IEEE Transactions on Dependable and Secure Computing*.

Zhang, Y., Deng, R., & Huang, X. (2020). Cybersecurity in critical infrastructures: A comprehensive survey. *IEEE Communications Surveys and Tutorials*, *22*(3), 1971–2005.

Zheng, Z., Xie, S., Dai, H., Chen, X., & Wang, H. (2017, June). An overview of blockchain technology: Architecture, consensus, and future trends. In *2017 IEEE International Congress on big data (BigData congress)* (pp. 557-564). Ieee. DOI: 10.1109/BigDataCongress.2017.85

Zhou, T. S., Shen, J., Li, X., Wang, C., & Shen, J. (2018). Quantum Cryptography for the Future Internet. *Security and Communication Networks*, *2018*, 1–7. DOI: 10.1155/2018/8214619

Zuboff, S. (2019). *The Age of Surveillance Capitalism*. PublicAffairs.

About the Contributors

Mohammed Amin is an Associate Professor in the Department of Computer Science in the Cybersecurity Program. He has published over 80 research papers in highly reputed journals such as the Engineering and Science Technology, an International Journal, Education and Information Technologies, IEEE Access and others. Most of his publications were indexed under the ISI Web of Science and Scopus.

* * *

Arudra Annepu is the Head of the Computer Science & Engineering Department at Rajiv Gandhi Institute of Technology, Bangalore, with over two decades of teaching experience.has published numerous research papers in reputed national and international journals and holds several patents in IoT and AI. She has published numerous books in the field of AI, IoT, and Blockchain.

Kaushik Chanda is an Associate Professor in the Department of Computational Sciences at Brainware University, Kolkata, and also serves as the Principal of Brainware College of Professional Studies. He holds an MCA and a PhD in Computer Science. Dr. Chanda specializes in Programming Languages, Database Management Systems (DBMS), Web Technologies, Machine Learning, and Artificial Intelligence. With extensive teaching and research experience, he is committed to fostering innovation and academic excellence in computational sciences. His work bridges theoretical knowledge with practical applications, aiming to equip students with future-ready skills in emerging technologies.

Parag Chatterjee received the B.E. degree in Computer Science & Engineering from the Karnatak University, Dharwad, India, in 1998 and received M.Tech. degree from IIEST Shibpur, Kolkata, India, in 2007. He has an academic experience of 20 years. Currently he is working as an Assistant Professor in the Department of CSE at

Global Institute of Management and Technology, Krishnanagar, West Bengal, India. His current research interests include Data ware Housing, Data mining and Wireless sensor. He has 15 publication in national and international journals and 3 Patents.

Dankan Gowda V. is currently working as an Assistant Professor in the Department of Electronics and Communication Engineering at BMS Institute of Technology and Management in Bangalore. Previously, he worked as a Research Fellow at ADA DRDO and as a Software Engineer at Robert Bosch. With a total experience of 14 years, including teaching and industry, Dr. Gowda has made significant contributions to both academia and research. He has published over 120 research papers in renowned international journals and conferences. In recognition of his innovative work, Dr. Gowda has been granted six patents, including four from Indian authorities and two international patents. His research interests primarily lie in the fields of IoT and Signal Processing, where he has conducted workshops and handled industry projects. Dr. Gowda is passionate about teaching and strives to create an engaging and effective learning environment for his students. He consistently seeks opportunities to enhance his knowledge and stay updated with the latest advancements in his field.

Shivangi Kashyap, a skillful academician, holds a Bachelor degree of Commerce with honors in Accounts and an MBA in Financial Management. Currently employed as an Assistant Professor at Brainware University Barasat, Kolkata, she passionately imparts her expertise in finance and management to aspiring minds. With a commitment to excellence, she embraces online education, leveraging technology to ensure effective learning experiences.

Mehmet Kaya has received an MSc degree in cyber security. His current research interests include crypto assets, cyber security, and software development.

Amrutha Kolhar obtained the MCA. Degree in Computer Science from the Karnatak University in 2022. she is currently working as a Research Scholar under the guidance of Dr. Sridevi, Professor, Department of Computer Science, Karnatak University, Dharwad. Received research fellowship from Other Backward Classes, (OBC), and Govt. of Karnataka. Area of research is "Network Security". At present working on the research topic: "Development and enhancing inter-operability of API and validating its authentication: X-IoT Devices". and also, IAENG student member (International Association of Engineers) (Member no: 366909).

Sheetal Vijay Kulkarni received B.E. (Instrumentation Engineering), M. Tech (Instrumentation Engineering). Her research interests include Medical Image Processing, Soft Computing, and Sensors. She has published 02 books, papers in journals, and conferences. She has Indian Granted Patent -2, Indian Design Patent-2, Indian Copyright-1, UK Design Patent-3 and Canadian Copyright-1.

Pravin Kumar is an experienced academic with over a decade of teaching Marketing Management and related subjects at reputed institutions across India. He currently serves as Assistant Professor at Brainware University, Kolkata, and has previously taught at different Management Institutions. He holds a Ph.D. in Management from T.M. Bhagalpur University, focusing on visual merchandising on consumer behavior in branded apparel. He also holds an MBA in Marketing and an M.A. in English, reflecting his interdisciplinary background. Dr. Kumar has published widely in Scopus, UGC-CARE, and peer-reviewed journals on topics including consumer behavior, brand personality, and AI in sales. He has presented at numerous national and international seminars and FDPs on subjects like cross-cultural marketing and leadership. His industry experience in the automobile and pharmaceutical sectors adds practical value to his teaching. Known for his engaging teaching style and commitment to Universal Design for Learning.

Shanmukha Sreenivas Madras is a Scientist with expertise in microbiology, molecular biology, and cell biology. Madras holds an M.S. in Biology with a concentration in Cell and Molecular Biology and a B.S. in Biology with a concentration in Microbiology, both from San Francisco State University. Madras has extensive experience in bacterial culture, DNA/RNA extraction, PCR/qPCR, molecular cloning, and biochemical analysis, working with both human cell lines and diverse microorganisms under aerobic and anaerobic conditions. Madras' background includes roles at Genista Biosciences and academic research focused on developing and characterizing bacterial exopolysaccharides for commercial applications.

Shilpa Mahajan is a distinguished Certified Ethical Hacker (CEHv11) and CISCO Certified Instructor with a notable career spanning over 16 years in research and education. Currently serving as an Associate Professor at the NorthCap University. Dr. Mahajan holds a Ph.D. in Wireless Sensor Networks from Guru Nanak Dev University, Amritsar, and graduated with distinction from Punjab Engineering College, Chandigarh. Her extensive contributions include authoring numerous papers published in prestigious international journals, books, conferences, and holding patents. In her current role, she guides doctoral scholars and successfully supervises M. Tech and B. Tech projects. Dr. Mahajan has designed courses focusing on Computer Networks, Network Security, and Cryptography. She actively participates in various academic activities, serving as a resource person for Faculty Development Programs (FDPs), workshops, guest lectures, invited talks, and panel discussions. Dr. Mahajan's expertise is underscored by her proactive involvement in chairing sessions at conferences, highlighting her standing within the academic community.

Subhadip Nandi is an Assistant Professor in the Department of Computational Sciences at Brainware University, Kolkata. He holds an M.Tech in Computer Science and Engineering, an MCA, and is currently pursuing his Ph.D. in Computer Science and Engineering at Dibrugarh University. With over 12 years of academic and industry experience, his research interests span Internet of Things (IoT), Machine Learning, Data Science, and Cloud Computing. Mr. Nandi has contributed to multiple national and international conferences and holds patents, journals and book chapter in the field of IoT, Machine Learning, cloud and smart systems. He has played a pivotal role in mentoring government-funded innovation projects, including the MSME-approved project. His career includes involvement in WHO-backed ICT-based healthcare research and various industry collaborations on digital solutions.

Soumya Roy is a dedicated assistant professor in Computational Sciences at Brainware University, with over eight years of teaching experience. He holds M.Tech (CSE), MCA, B.Ed. Proficient in Python, Pandas, JavaScript, and data analysis, he actively engages in research on AI, cybersecurity, and education technology. Soumya has published several book chapters and conference papers, and contributes to digital learning via his YouTube channel. Passionate about teaching and innovation, he integrates modern tools and interdisciplinary approaches to enhance student learning and engagement.

Thangam S., BE, ME, Ph.D., currently serves as an Associate Professor at the Amrita School of Computing, Bengaluru, Amrita Vishwa Vidyapeetham, India. Her area of interest in research includes Service Oriented Architecture, Networks, IoT, Artificial Intelligence, Data Structures and Cloud Computing. She completed her Ph. D. in Computer Science and Engineering from Anna University, Chennai. India. She has 26 years of teaching experience. She has published her research works in 50 international conferences and 15 journals and book chapters. She is a member of ISTE.

Yash Singh currently pursuing a Bachelor of Technology (B.Tech) in Computer Science and Engineering (CSE) from the Global Institute of Management & Technology, located in Krishnanagar, India. With a fervent passion for technology and problem-solving, I engaged in coding competitions, hackathons, and workshops to further hone their skills.

Puppala Naga Sravanthi is an Assistant Professor in the Department of Computer Science and Engineering at SRM University-AP, India. She holds a B.Tech and M.Tech from JNTUK and Ph.D. at Puducherry Central University. With nearly a decade of teaching and research experience, her expertise lies in blockchain technology, machine learning, and cybersecurity. She has published several papers in reputed journals, contributed book chapters, and filed patents on blockchain-based solutions. Her current research focuses on trust mechanisms in blockchain mining pools and secure data systems.

Sridevi, Professor, Department of Computer Science, Karnatak University, Dharwad. Obtained a PhD from Mangalore University, Mangalore in 2017. Research interest includes Advanced Computer Networks, Mobile and Wireless Communication, Network Security, Cloud Computing and the Internet of Things. At present guiding four research scholars and one M.Phil. awarded. And also, Reviewer for the Journal of Advances in Mathematics and Computer Science. Published more than 30 research papers in a national and international journal.

Gurkan Tuna is a Professor at the Department of Computer Technologies of Trakya University (2006–). He has authored several papers in international conference proceedings and refereed journals, and has been actively serving as a reviewer for international journals and conferences. His current research interests include cyber security and machine learning.

Amit Kumar Tyagi s working as Assistant Professor, at National Forensic Sciences University, Gandhinagar, Gujarat, India. Previously, he worked at National Institute of Fashion Technology, 110016, New Delhi, India (November 2022-September 2025). Also, he has worked as Assistant Professor (Senior Grade 2), and Senior Researcher at Vellore Institute of Technology (VIT), Chennai Campus, 600127, Chennai, Tamilandu, India for the period of 2019-2022. He received his Ph.D. Degree (Full-Time) in 2018 from Pondicherry Central University, 605014, Puducherry, India. About his academic experience, he joined the Lord Krishna College of Engineering, Ghaziabad (LKCE) for the periods of 2009-2010, and 2012-2013. He was an Assistant Professor and Head- Research, Lingaya's Vidyapeeth (formerly known as Lingaya's University), Faridabad, Haryana, India for the period of 2018-2019. His supervision experience includes more than 10 Masters' dissertations and one PhD thesis. He has contributed to several projects such as "AARIN" and "P3- Block" to address some of the open issues related to the privacy breaches in Vehicular Applications (such as Parking) and Medical Cyber Physical Systems (MCPS). He has published over 150 papers in refereed high impact journals, conferences and books.

Hemamalini Venkatesan received her B.E degree in CSE from Sri Balaji Chockalingam Engineering College, Arni, affiliated to University of Madras, Chennai in 2004, her M.E degree in CSE from S.A Engineering College, Chennai, affiliated to Anna University, Chennai in 2008 and her Ph.D degree in Wireless Security on January 2018 from Puducherry Technological University (formerly called as Pondicherry Engineering College) affiliated under Pondicherry University, Puducherry. She is currently working as Associate Professor in Department of Networking and Communications, School of Computing, SRM Institute of Science and Technology, Kattankulathur, Chengalpattu Dt., TN, India from November 2020. She is in teaching profession for more than 20 years and she had published around 35 articles in International Journals/Book Chapters/Conferences and presented papers in more than 15 regional conferences. She has also produced 4 patent publication and received 3 grant from IPR, Delhi. She has also published 2 book on Cyber Security and Networking, and is currently guiding 4 Ph.D candidates in Cyber Security using ML.

Index

A

B

C

D

E

G

H

I

L

M

N

O

P

Q

R

S

T

U

W

www.ingramcontent.com/pod-product-compliance
Lightning Source LLC
LaVergne TN
LVHW081534300926
849161LV00006B/1420